The Gateway Arch

TRACY CAMPBELL

The Gateway Arch

A BIOGRAPHY

Yale UNIVERSITY PRESS

New Haven & London

frontispiece: "Topping Out" Day, October 28, 1965. Arthur Witman Photographic Collection, State Historical Society of Missouri Research Center–St. Louis.

Yale University Press books may be purchased in quantity for educational, business, or promotional use. For information, please e-mail sales.press@yale.edu (U.S. office) or sales@yaleup.co.uk (U.K. office).

Set in Janson type by Integrated Publishing Solutions.
Printed in the United States of America.

Library of Congress Cataloging-in-Publication Data

Campbell, Tracy, 1962–
The Gateway Arch: a biography / Tracy Campbell.
pages cm. — (Icons of America)
Includes bibliographical references and index.
ISBN 978-0-300-16949-2 (cloth : alkaline paper) 1. Gateway Arch (Saint Louis, Mo.)—History. 2. Saint Louis (Mo.)—Buildings, structures, etc. 3. Arches—Missouri—Saint Louis—Design and construction. I. Title.
F474.S265G372 2013
977.8'65—dc23   2012045255

A catalogue record for this book is available from the British Library.

This paper meets the requirements of ANSI/NISO Z39.48-1992 (Permanence of Paper).

10 9 8 7 6 5 4 3 2 1

ICONS OF AMERICA

Mark Crispin Miller, *Series Editor*

Icons of America is a series of short works written by leading scholars, critics, and writers, each of whom tells a new and innovative story about American history and culture through the lens of a single iconic individual, event, object, or cultural phenomenon.

To the memory of Shearer Davis Bowman

Contents

Contents

Acknowledgments

I am grateful for the assistance provided by a host of people who work in the following libraries and archives: The State Historical Society of Missouri at the University of Missouri–Columbia; the Cranbrook Archives; the Archives of American Art at the Smithsonian; the College of Wooster; the State Historical Society of Missouri Research Center, University of Missouri–St. Louis; the Missouri History Museum; the University of Kentucky; and the Jefferson National Expansion Memorial Archives. I especially thank Sonya Rooney of Special Collections at Washington University in St. Louis and Laura Tatum, formerly of the Archives and Manuscripts Department at Yale University Library, for their help. Roger Griffin of Oxford Brookes University kindly worked on my behalf to obtain the image of the Adalberto Libera arch. Pierluigi Serraino, AIA, generously shared Saarinen interview materials conducted in 1959 by the Institute of Personality Assessment and Research.

My agent, John W. Wright, is a steadfast friend who believed in this project from the very beginning. My thanks to Jaya Aninda

Chatterjee for her help in steering the manuscript through to production. I am fortunate to have worked with Bill Frucht, a brilliant and creative editor whose critical eye was invaluable in framing the structure of this book, as well as manuscript editor Noreen O'Connor-Abel and production editor Margaret Otzel. Three anonymous readers for the Yale University Press forced me to think seriously about the larger historical meaning of the Arch.

My thanks to Deans Mark Kornbluh and Betty Lorch of the University of Kentucky for research support, as well as department chairs Francie Chassen-Lopez and Karen Petrone. Kari Burchfield, Tina Hagee, and Carol O'Reilly handled all of my last-minute requests with their customary good humor.

My friend and colleague Mark Summers read an earlier version of the manuscript and provided many helpful suggestions. I am indebted to Don Ritchie, Terry Birdwhistell, and Brooke Hicks for generously reading various drafts and their careful attention to detail. Andrew Hurley read early chapters and provided his expertise on St. Louis history. Debbie Becher of Barnard College helped me rethink some concepts concerning eminent domain and urban politics.

My sons, Alex and Drew, were wonderful companions on the ride to the top of the Arch. Throughout, they were supportive in ways I can never adequately thank. Finally, I am profoundly grateful to my wife, Robin, for her love, laughter, and keen editorial judgment and for being my best pal.

Saarinen's Cathedral

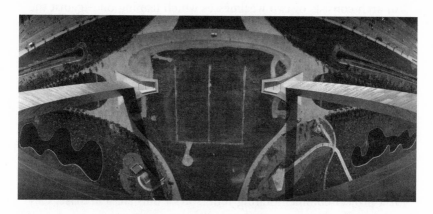

A view from the top of the Arch shortly after completion in 1965.
Arthur Witman Photographic Collection, State Historical Society of
Missouri Research Center–St. Louis.

Early each morning, the buses and cars arrive at the St. Louis river-front as they have done for nearly five decades. The tourists—some three million a year—stream out to see a gleaming stainless steel arch that towers above the Mississippi River. They explore the underground museum, watch a short film about the Arch's construction, and climb aboard claustrophobic space-age capsules for a four-minute ride to the crest. They peer out of thick, narrow windows perched more than sixty stories high, nowhere near as tall as the tops of many modern skyscrapers but somehow more magical and terrifying because they are suspended in air. The experience is a little more than some people bargained for when they realize that there is nothing under them. Perhaps they grasp for the first time the power of basic geometry, which is the only thing keeping them from falling. A few may remember Leonardo da Vinci's definition: "An arch consists of two weaknesses which leaning one against the other make a strength." After they have taken some photographs, the visitors are carried back to the underground station where they can buy souvenirs. Once they emerge from below, most crane their heads one last time at the monument towering above them and wonder about its meaning.

Throughout, tourists are presented a mythic version of history. They are told of a Depression-riddled city that struggled to rebuild a wretched wasteland of abandoned buildings and warehouses. They learn how in 1935 the citizens of St. Louis approved a bond issue for a project commemorating Jefferson's Louisiana Purchase. City leaders, responding to this expression of popular support, cleared the area of empty, "blighted" warehouses and waited patiently for the millions of promised federal funds. After postponements necessitated by World War II and the Korean War, the city embarked on an ambitious effort to rebuild the riverfront with a wonderful monument to westward expansion. Finished in 1965 the magnificent Gateway Arch (officially the Jefferson National Expansion Memorial) transformed the city and gave the nation a timeless landmark that speaks to our democratic heritage.

When we think about a great monument or skyscraper or museum or cathedral, we seldom ask: What was there before? Who benefited from its construction? Who lost? What could have been? By exploring these questions, we find that the story of the Gateway Arch is more complicated than the account given to visitors. It involves political and economic power, short-sighted city planning, and decades of disputes over the historic riverfront. It includes more than visionary architects and civic leaders: local and national politicians, landlords, renters, bankers, real estate agents, construction workers, protestors, and citizens. Their motivations and actions often had little to do with promoting modern architecture or honoring the city's role in developing the republic.

Today, the Arch is a cherished national landmark and one of the most recognized structures on earth. It is revered for the way it transforms a simple curve into an awe-inspiring experience of place. A person approaching it by car or plane cannot help but marvel at its size and elegance. For interstate highway travelers in the Midwest, the Arch is one of the most memorable sights they will encounter.

The genius of the Gateway Arch is that it is both traditional and modern. The Romans built countless arches, and they were indispensable to Gothic architecture. The vast array of bridges, aqueducts, and churches whose arches have survived for centuries testify to the form's inherent durability. Yet the one in St. Louis manages to reinvent the idea, as if it were the very first one. We are surrounded by arches, yet there is only one Gateway Arch. It is disarmingly simple and extraordinarily complex, an unadorned geometric shape on an almost inhuman scale. Reaching 630 feet high, it is the largest American monument, taller than the Washington Monument, and is exactly as wide at the base as it is tall. The Arch weighs 43,000 tons, and its exterior contains 886 tons of stainless steel. Its interior holds 5,000 tons of regular steel as well as 6,238 cubic yards of concrete. In the event of high winds, the Arch is designed to sway eighteen inches at the top. Not all of the impressive figures are so enormous. To ensure that its two legs would meet precisely at the top, its builders could not veer more than 1/64-inch in pouring the two foundations.

Although the finished Arch was a collaborative product of several architects and engineers, it is essentially the creation of Finnish-born architect Eero Saarinen. The design's monumentality matched the ego of its designer, a driven and obsessed man who was personally charming yet ruthless, supremely confident to a level somewhere well beyond arrogance, and also deeply insecure. By examining the personal and professional dynamics that inspired and haunted the architect, we can begin to understand the human element behind the stainless steel monolith. His father, Eliel, was a legendary architect who cast a looming shadow over his only son, and Eero wanted desperately to establish his own identity as a transformative designer. Winning the St. Louis architectural competition gave Eero the national recognition he craved, yet was not without frustration. Just days after the competition jury selected his entry, Saarinen was accused of stealing the design from an Italian architect who had proposed a grand arch in Rome as a memorial to Mussolini (the charge was never substantiated). His jubilation in winning the competition was tempered by more than a decade of disappointing delays. When he died, in 1961 at the age of fifty-one, he had designed some of the most imaginative buildings of his day. But his most cherished creation, an idea that started with pipe cleaners on his living room floor, remained unbuilt.

In 1935, in one of the earliest conversations about a proposed memorial on the St. Louis riverfront, former Secretary of War Newton Baker urged city and national leaders to proceed as if they were building a cathedral. Although the secular Gateway Arch carries none of the religious symbolism of Chartres or Sainte-Chapelle, it is tempting to think that their builders would have understood at least something of Saarinen's vision. The spires of the great cathedrals are visible for miles, and arches of varied and sophisticated design are necessary to their soaring interiors. In 1220, an anonymous traveler, having visited a newly built French cathedral, wrote: "The vault seems to converse with the winged birds; it spreads broad wings of its own, and like a flying creature jostles the clouds, while yet resting on its solid pillars. . . . The shafts themselves stand soaring and lofty, their finish is clear and resplendent, their order graceful and geometrical." Like the creators of the Arch, the builders of the great cathedrals spent a fortune, were required to think anew, and needed many years to realize their plans. They also had more on their minds than divine aspirations: they hoped the cathedrals would bring fame, prestige, and wealth to their towns.[1]

All great public structures tell us what a society values. Memorials are explicit statements of the events and people a society believes is important to retain in the public memory. Lenin's Tomb, the Lincoln Memorial, and the statues of soldiers in courthouse squares each convey a specific memory. The Arch is more a commemoration of a concept: westward expansion was not a single event bounded in time and space but an idea, an engine of American ambition. The structure's abstraction reflects the abstraction of what it commemorates.

Yet to see the Gateway Arch only as a symbol of westward expansion misses a larger point. Its monumentality, its sleek modernism, and its visual power are hallmarks of a different cultural marker. The Arch informs us of the wealth and audacity of the United States in the mid-twentieth century. It is the product of a supremely self-confident and rich society; conceived after the Arsenal of Democracy had won World War II, and built as the nation planned to go to the Moon. It is a symbol of affluence and influence, a bold statement of national strength.

But the Arch also represents a significant chapter in the history of American cities. Its origins and construction allow us to ask: Why do our cities look the way they do? In this vein, the Arch is more than a symbol; it is also a symptom. Tourists and the local community experience it in different ways. The Gateway Arch is an extended cautionary tale that emerged from a grand and ultimately failed experiment in urban planning. This too is part of its history and meaning—part of the less triumphant side. Just over a century ago, St. Louis considered itself the potential equal of New York City, perhaps even the site of a relocated American capital. Today it has less than half the population it had in 1950. The history of the Arch, and of the contested ground on which it stands, is deeply intertwined with the history of St. Louis, as well as East St. Louis, Illinois, directly across the river. Long before Saarinen conceived his design, city leaders debated what to do with the land adjacent to the river. It was a struggle that started with the city's birth as a modest trading post. By the early twentieth century, the area was dotted with warehouses and small businesses, some struggling and some thriving. It contained apartments and houses of various sizes, as well as a number of historic buildings, including some of the best examples of cast-iron structures in the nation. The creators of the Arch shared the belief, widely held in the mid-twentieth century, that the future of the city lay in its friendliness to automobiles. The ideology of mid-century urban planning held that downtowns would thrive to the extent that they were accessible and navigable by out-of-town visitors traveling in cars. Attractions such as sports arenas and convention centers, highways leading into and through downtowns, and vast parking towers were seen as the way to revive struggling urban cores and connect them to the more vibrant suburbs. Older modes of urban life—historic buildings, getting around on foot, dense neighborhoods where people lived, worked, and played in close proximity—were considered outdated relics that stood in the way of progress.

St. Louis, like many other American cities, embraced the mid-twentieth-century answer to urban decay. Yet unlike any other city, St. Louis turned also to what became an architectural masterpiece to lure people downtown. The Arch is a paradox: on the one hand, it has become one of the country's great tourist attractions and one of its most successful and inspiring works of art. On the other hand, just blocks away, one can walk past empty buildings and dreary lots. Though its overt function is to commemorate the city's past, the Arch's design and underlying purpose look toward the future: it was meant to renew the city that surrounds it. The steady procession of people leaving St. Louis is another marker of urban decay, and the Gateway Arch helped speed the decline.

Cities and monuments are not created overnight. They are the product of longstanding political, economic, and cultural forces. Over time, people in power made choices and implemented policies that had profound consequences. The results, reflected in our built environment, were sometimes glorious, sometimes disastrous. In uncovering the bloody history of the Basilica of Sacre-Coeur, David Harvey wrote: "The building hides its secrets in sepulchral silence. Only the living, cognizant of this history . . . can truly disinter the mysteries that lie entombed there and thereby rescue that rich experience from the deathly silence of the tomb."[2] That sentiment extends from Paris to St. Louis. Some architectural landmarks have more to tell us than meets the eye.

ONE

The New York of the West

Harland Bartholomew, a pioneering city planner who shaped modern St. Louis.
Missouri History Museum–St. Louis.

The nickname "Gateway to the West" invites one to think of early St. Louis as a remote frontier outpost, just as European explorers saw it. The term suggests a passage from the civilized world to a rugged, unexplored wilderness. One would think that before the settlers embarked on their western excursions the area was nothing but virgin forests and uninhabited lands. But considering it from an older perspective, or as the historian Daniel K. Richter terms it, "facing east," reveals a different view.

Around 1000 A.D., the continent's largest settlement north of Mexico rose in the fertile lands near modern-day East St. Louis, Illinois. The ancient Native American city of Cahokia, with more than 20,000 residents, included at its far western edge a fifty-acre rectangular riverside plaza near where the Gateway Arch now sits. This Grand Plaza was widely known for its earthen "Monks Mound," which, at 130 feet, was the third highest pyramid in the Americas. Around 1400, however, Cahokia entered a mysterious but steady decline, and by the time the Europeans arrived, many of its remnants had disappeared.[1]

The first French and Spanish explorers, coming to the region in the seventeenth century, found various native tribes, including the Osages, Missouris, Iowas, and Omahas. Modern St. Louis traces its official birth to 1764, when Pierre Laclede Liguest, a French fur trader, founded a regional trading post along a wooded limestone bluff just eighteen miles south of the confluence of the Mississippi and Missouri rivers. Laclede was drawn to the spot principally for its natural resources and geographic benefits. It offered a natural levee that kept back the Mississippi's periodic floods. A break in the bluffs allowed easy access to the river where boats could be docked and loaded. Fresh water rose from the limestone springs, and the nearby timber provided crucial building resources for the settlement. Months later another fur trader, Auguste Chouteau, arrived with nearly three dozen men and began to carve out the first vestiges of a town. Chouteau aspired to found "one of the finest cities in America," and named the new outpost "St. Louis" in honor of Louis IX, the patron saint of the reigning French King Louis XV.[2]

St. Louis was only a river's width away from territory belonging to Britain, and later to the young United States. In 1762, France ceded Louisiana to the Spanish, and the town became Upper Louisiana's borderland capital. After finding the colony too expensive to maintain, the Spanish sold the territory back to France in 1800, but a slave revolt in Haiti and a costly war with England persuaded Napoleon to unload the faraway land. In 1803, President Thomas Jefferson seized the opportunity to acquire the entire Louisiana Territory for $15 million. When Jefferson commissioned Lewis and Clark to explore the new American possession, they naturally began their journey in St. Louis. "Founded by the French, governed by the Spanish, and sold to the Americans," writes historian Adam Arenson, "St. Louis was always a borderland city on the edge of empires."[3]

The city founded by Laclede and Chouteau sat perilously close to the largest fault line in North America, which extends from modern-day northeast Arkansas into southern Illinois. In the winter and early spring of 1811–12, the most powerful earthquake in American history struck in the bootheel region of southern Missouri. Over several months, the Mississippi valley was jolted by three powerful quakes estimated at over 8.0 on the Richter scale, and more than two thousand smaller tremors. Residents as far north as Boston and as far south as Mexico felt the tremors, and one of the quakes was said to have made the ground a veritable liquid in places. Eyewitnesses reported that parts of the countryside rolled for hours and even stretches of the Mississippi River flowed backward. The quakes destroyed the small town of New Madrid, Missouri, only 150 miles south of St. Louis. Residents in St. Louis, while literally shaken, were spared from major damage because their buildings were mostly one or two stories. Yet the enormous potential energy from seismic activity far beneath the surface posed a constant threat to the city, and still does.[4]

By the 1820s, St. Louis boasted nearly 4,600 residents. When it was incorporated as a city in 1823, St. Louis was part of an extensive river traffic network that connected the Midwest territories with Philadelphia and New York. By 1840, it was home to 35,000 people and rivaled New Orleans in the volume of cargo delivered to its wharves.

Relations between the white settlers in St. Louis and the local native tribes remained relatively peaceful until 1828, when Missouri Governor John Miller announced the official eviction of Native Americans from the state, a process historian Stephen Aron has termed the "ethnic cleansing" of the region. Forced removal had been under way in the region less systematically since the Louisiana Purchase, and it accelerated after the War of 1812.[5] Governor Miller's proclamation brought the process to St. Louis's doorstep and confirmed it as an *American* city; its native culture and history, Miller hoped, would be crushed in the march of manifest destiny.

St. Louis's increasing prosperity was apparent with its architecture, as the first major commercial and religious buildings erected along the river drew wide acclaim. Visitors to antebellum St. Louis could choose among nine hotels and stroll past their choice of 1,200 new brick homes in the city. Real estate prices soared, and by 1847, lots on Front Street sold for as much as $500 per square foot. Of all the buildings near the riverfront, the most visually breathtaking was the courthouse, which slowly emerged along Third Street. In 1847, it became the site of the first Dred Scott trial, in which Scott, a slave, sued his owner to gain his freedom. The case, decided by the U.S. Supreme Court ten years later, would reverberate to the fields of Gettysburg and Appomattox.[6] The St. Louis riverfront was the center of the western fur trading business and was home to scores of burgeoning banks and businesses. Visitors encountered a town brimming with a cosmopolitan mixture of people, and poised to become one of America's great cities.

Yet St. Louis was no shining city on a hill. Since the 1820s, its robust economic growth had been fueled by cheap, local bituminous coal that enveloped the city in a sulfurous, sooty cloud. At times an eyesore and always an assault on sensitive lungs and noses, the ever-present smoke made St. Louis one of the first American cities to understand the environmental consequences of rapid industrial growth.[7] Those working on Third Street near the courthouse sometimes could not see as far as the river. Moreover, the city's streets became open sewers. Horse-drawn carriages left manure everywhere, and the blistering summer sun only added to the squalor.

During the evening of May 17, 1849, a fire erupted on a docked steamer, *White Cloud*. After the flames ate away the dock lines securing it to the wharf, the *White Cloud* became a drifting fireball. The inferno spread rapidly. Within an hour, two dozen vessels along the wharf were ablaze. Gusty winds pushed the flames over the levee, and, suddenly, entire blocks were burning. The wind threatened to drive the fire across the entire city. Desperately attempting to deprive it of fuel, volunteer firefighters destroyed buildings along the south side of Market Street, from Main to Second Street. Their actions saved the Old Cathedral (now the Basilica of St. Louis, King of France) and the fire burned itself out before reaching the courthouse under construction and a cherished limestone warehouse on the corner of Main and Chestnut that had been established by Manuel Lisa in 1818. By daybreak, residents could assess the devastation: five riverfront blocks entirely destroyed, five more heavily damaged, and three people dead. More than four hundred houses had burned to the ground, along with more than three hundred businesses. Estimates of the property damage alone ranged between $3 million and $6 million. Amid the embers, however, was the birth of a newer, and even more prosperous, St. Louis.[8]

The Great Fire came on the heels of another disaster that had besieged St. Louis in the late 1840s. The great cholera pandemic reached North America in the early 1830s and the Mississippi River system by the next decade, spreading from New Orleans north to Nashville, Memphis, and other towns. Cholera produces fever, vomiting, and intense abdominal pain, and victims can die within hours of onset if they do not consume enough water to fight the sudden dehydration. The disease does not spread from person to person, as was widely thought at the time, but from drinking infected water. As cholera ravaged St. Louis, the cure only made things worse, as those affected often drank the polluted water to counteract the dehydration. Doctors were helpless to stop the misery, and for weeks the bells of the Old Cathedral tolled relentlessly, announcing nearly three dozen funerals a day during the summer of 1849. By fall 1850, when the epidemic finally subsided, more than 4,300 people—nearly 6 percent of the total population—died of the disease in St. Louis, the highest mortality rate of any American city.[9]

Despite these calamities, the 1850 census reported more than 78,000 St. Louis residents, twice the previous count. Following the fire, the city experienced a building boom. Architect Thomas W. Walsh led this renascence and, in an attempt to avoid another catastrophic fire, began using primarily cast iron and stone in many of the new structures. The St. Louis riverfront area eventually boasted one of the greatest collections of cast-iron buildings in the nation. Many notables called the city home for a time, including Robert E. Lee and Ulysses S. Grant. It was also the proud host to such international luminaries as Charles Dickens. In 1855 a local editor enthused that "our noble city is destined to be at least the second city of the Union." Two local reporters raised the boosterism stakes by predicting that by 1900, "St. Louis will be the greatest city on either continent." At the very least it would become "the New York of the West."[10]

The second half of the nineteenth century proved more difficult. Abraham Lincoln's inauguration in 1861 sparked a secession crisis and took the nation to war. One of the first skirmishes following the battle of Fort Sumter occurred in St. Louis in May 1861, when Confederate and Union militia fought over an arsenal in the city. The brief but bloody firefight killed twenty-eight people. Among the locals who watched the fighting were future Generals Grant and William T. Sherman.

To command the western front, Lincoln chose John C. Frémont, the former Republican presidential candidate, who made St. Louis his headquarters. When violence erupted on August 14, 1861, General Frémont declared martial law in the city. Embedded within this declaration was a statement as profoundly revolutionary as Jefferson's words had been nearly a century before. Frémont ordered that the property of any Confederate would be confiscated in Missouri, and that any slaves included in this "property" would be "declared free men." Lincoln soon reversed Frémont's order, but in the interim the first American slave recorded to have been freed by federal authority was a St. Louis man named Hiram Reed.[11]

The war's economic impact was devastating to St. Louis. With Southern markets and ocean access both closed, trade along the Mississippi River evaporated, and stores and businesses along the riverfront suffered accordingly. The city's only major construction during the Civil War was William Rumbold's magnificent iron dome on the courthouse. On July 4, 1862, the dome was officially dedicated and became a permanent fixture of the St. Louis skyline. By war's end, St. Louis's "second city" ambitions were lost to Chicago. River traffic, facing new competition from railroads, never returned to prewar levels. Consequently, the drive to bridge the Mississippi took on a new urgency. In early 1867, city leaders organized the St. Louis and Illinois Bridge Company, and ordered its chief engineer, James B. Eads, to build a bridge across the waterway at a narrow point around the northern arm of Third Street. His design called for three arched spans of more than five hundred feet each. As a public works project, the scale and importance of what became known as the Eads Bridge would be outdone in the nineteenth century only by the Brooklyn Bridge.

As workers dug deep caissons to support the Eads Bridge, several experienced intense internal pains that would not subside. Unknown to local physicians, the compressed air the workers inhaled at the bottom of the caissons was potentially deadly. If one reached the surface too quickly, nitrogen bubbles formed in the blood and one could be literally doubled over in pain. The condition came to be known as "the bends." During the seven years that the Eads Bridge was under construction, 119 workers suffered from the bends, and fourteen died.

On July 4, 1874, jubilant St. Louisans paraded across their elegant new bridge to East St. Louis underneath a "great, triumphal arch" built just for the occasion. William Taussig, a member of the bridge's board of directors, noted that the bridge was "the noblest monument on the continent" and that nowhere else on the planet did something exist "so beautiful and attractive." The Eads Bridge was a sensation, and marked the beginning of a new era. By 1900, St. Louis was the second largest railroad hub in the United States.[12]

Just as the bridge expanded the city's horizons, a political development arose that would have profound consequences. In 1876, in a moment of short-sightedness, city leaders decided they did not want the responsibility for the rapidly growing rural sections of St. Louis County, and voted to separate from it in what would be called "the great divorce." The county would have to raise its own taxes to meet its needs. While this seemed a fine idea at the time for those near downtown St. Louis, it later proved disastrous as affluent citizens moved out of the city. By the middle of the twentieth century, the full effects of the division would be sorely felt.[13]

By 1880, St. Louis was the nation's sixth largest city with more than 350,000 residents. Railroad traffic facilitated by the Eads Bridge sparked yet another building boom on the riverfront. Some new buildings rose to six stories, which approached the limit that their massive stone foundations could support. One of the most famous buildings in the city was the Merchants' Exchange, completed in 1875 and located near the courthouse. Its large second-floor trading room hosted the Democratic National Convention in 1876, where Samuel Tilden accepted the nomination to run against Rutherford B. Hayes. Twelve years later, Democrats used the nearby Exposition and Music Hall to renominate President Grover Cleveland. In 1896, the Republicans nominated William McKinley in a temporary pavilion located near City Hall.

The Gilded Age political conventions signified the city's national importance. Some exuberant St. Louisans saw their hometown as the nation's true capital, and tried unsuccessfully throughout the 1870s to relocate the national government to the St. Louis riverfront. St. Louis also touted one of the nation's first "skyscrapers," the magnificent ten-story Wainwright Building on Chestnut Street, designed by the Chicago architect Louis B. Sullivan and completed in 1891.[14]

Despite its apparent prosperity, the city's growth had an unsettling effect on its riverfront. The small group of families that controlled much of the property kept rental prices too high for many businesses to bear. New businesses and families moved west to the outer parts of the city and into St. Louis County. For the riverfront, mostly composed of fur traders and dry goods businesses that relied on river traffic, the Gilded Age marked a slow decline.

All along, there were grand dreams about how the riverfront

might be restored to its earlier glory. The defeated Republican presidential candidate James G. Blaine suggested a memorial to Thomas Jefferson, honoring the Louisiana Purchase. Pierre Chouteau, a descendant of the founding families, proposed celebrating the centennial of the purchase with a riverfront replica of the original French village. He tried to organize the city's financial and political leaders to support the project, but to his disappointment, the city's elite showed little enthusiasm for his plan. They had something else in mind.[15]

Nothing on the global stage was as big in the 1890s as the World's Fair. People everywhere were fascinated by the lavish displays of the latest technological and engineering marvels. To attend a fair was to peek into the future, and to host one was a cherished prize. More than political conventions or sporting events, the World's Fair was unrivaled as a sign of a city's international stature. The attention Chicago had received from hosting the World's Fair in 1893 was on the minds of the city leaders of St. Louis, who desperately wanted to keep pace. By 1900, with more than 575,000 residents, St. Louis trailed only New York, Philadelphia, and Chicago in population, and was hopeful of better things to come. With news that St. Louis would host the 1904 exposition to commemorate the Louisiana Purchase, the city prepared for its chance to shine.

Rather than locate the fair near downtown or the riverfront, city leaders chose a site ten miles west in Forest Park, away from the smoke and grime. In the spring of 1904, President Theodore Roosevelt proudly opened the extravaganza, and although not as big a hit as the Chicago Fair, the St. Louis expo attracted more than 20 million people over the next few months. The song "Meet Me in St. Louis" was heard throughout the nation. Attendees could visit recreations of the Alps complete with snow-peaked mountains, try new creations such as the ice cream cone and Dr. Pepper, and see in person Will Rogers or an aging Geronimo. The St. Louis Fair was, by all accounts, a rousing success and proved to be the highlight of the city's history. Helen Keller remarked that the St. Louis exposition was "a great manifestation of all the forces of enlightenment and all of man's thousand torches burning together."[16]

In the summer of 1904 the city was home to yet another political nominating convention. This time, the Democrats met again at the Exposition and Music Hall to nominate Alton B. Parker for president. St. Louis also hosted the third modern Olympic Games (following Athens and Paris) throughout the late summer and autumn of 1904.[17] While the Olympics have long surpassed the World's Fair in importance, the 1904 games were a far cry from the present-day Olympiad. By current standards they were little more than a farce. The defining moment of the games, the marathon, was a complete disaster. The man initially declared the winner turned out to have hitched a ride in an automobile for much of the course.

After 1904, as more St. Louisans relocated on the western side of the city, leaders searched for ways to re-create its downtown. The city's struggle to define itself echoed a wider debate about urban life. As more people flocked to the cities from the farms, issues of livability, economics, crime, and segregation came to the fore. Architects and city planners felt that such human issues could be addressed through the landscapes themselves. The "City Beautiful" movement that emerged around 1900 sought a return to classical structures, and stressed formal plazas and expansive promenades. Bringing more order and visual appeal to the cityscape, believers felt, would encourage inhabitants to become more productive and patriotic. As Jane Jacobs noted, "the aim of the City Beautiful was the City Monumental."[18]

In 1907, the Civic League of St. Louis applied these principles to the riverfront. Their work resulted in one of the first master city plans in American history. Using Budapest and Algiers as models, the league commissioned an ambitious plan for the riverfront. A sweeping new design called for demolishing most of the thirty blocks near the wharf and replacing them with twelve "palatial" warehouses along the levee, along with a green park that connected the riverfront to the courthouse. When it came to pinpointing the reason for the city's decline, the league blamed greed. "Real estate speculators and property owners have been permitted to follow their own caprices and self interest. The results are that instead of having a city with convenient and commodious thoroughfares, plenty of open spaces and squares, and a harmonious grouping of public buildings, we have narrow streets, few breathing spaces, and a general absence, in the business portion, of those features that make a city attractive."[19]

Because of the millions of dollars required to build anything close to the 1907 suggestions, it never materialized. But that did not stop similarly audacious plans in 1913 and 1922, which met the same fate. One local architect produced a particularly noteworthy idea. In 1915, J. L. Wees envisioned a new riverfront plaza, framed by a giant arch that resembled the Arc de Triomphe in Paris, with St. Louis the Crusader King attached to the top. Whether as a reminder of the Eads Bridge or as a statement of classical design, riverfront designs kept featuring monumental arches.[20]

In 1916, the city hired a visionary engineer named Harland Bartholomew, who became a crucial fixture in shaping St. Louis, and also one of the most important city planners in the nation. He held member number 0001 in the newly formed American Planning Institute. Over his lengthy career, Bartholomew's firm wrote several reports on the problems and needs of St. Louis, and his most significant plan came in 1928. In rethinking what to do with the riverfront, Bartholomew turned to architect Hugh Ferriss, a graduate of nearby Washington University and one of the country's most gifted architectural illustrators, to sketch a dramatic vision that would make St. Louis the envy of the nation. "St. Louis has turned its back to the river," Bartholomew wrote; the new plan would create a "truly creditable front yard as well as a place where St. Louis itself might go to see the Father of Waters amid pleasing surroundings." He and Ferriss designed a grand mall along the levee that included a memorial. To Bartholomew, the overall design was not only beautiful, but would "permanently check" the growth of the business district and stabilize property values throughout the city. As one city leader saw it, developing the riverfront "will do more to anchor [land] values than anything else." The plan, however, cost an estimated $50 million, a figure that dwarfed most American public works projects at the time.[21]

In addition to suggesting a monument, Bartholomew proposed one other item that would mark every future attempt at rethinking the riverfront. Like many other planners in the 1920s, he saw the automobile as critical to the city's development. The land along the riverfront was falling in value, and the best way to correct the situation, he believed, was to redirect the automobile traffic from the northern and southern sections of the city. Bartholomew designed two levels of limited-access highways, "Third Street Elevated Highway," to intersect the mall between the memorial and the courthouse, and a north-south expressway to be submerged underneath a widened Third Street. Today, Interstate 70 does exactly that below an elevated Third Street. Bartholomew envisioned the highways along the riverfront introducing "the large volume of traffic necessary to rehabilitate and enliven the eastern end of the business district." He saw freeways as an antidote to failing businesses and declining downtown property values. Yet like so many other urban planners, Bartholomew did not understand an unintended consequence of road-building: these roads would sever the levee area from the city and ultimately contribute to the decline of downtown St. Louis.[22]

Even as the city struggled with riverfront revitalization, another, deeper problem was emerging. As in other Southern cities, African

Americans could not live in white neighborhoods. Segregated neighborhoods provided the foundation for the separate schools and other separate public accommodations that were an essential aspect of the Jim Crow system. In 1915, when a "Central Parkway" was proposed for the riverfront, opponents understood that the best way to stop the project was to appeal to the bigotry of white St. Louisans. If the zoning statute was passed for the parkway, one pamphlet warned, "15,000 Negroes who now live in that district will be forced to find other quarters. Some of them may move next door to you."[23]

That same year, neighborhood associations in St. Louis asked the city government for an ordinance banning African Americans from living in white neighborhoods under the guise of preventing "ill feeling, conflict, and collision between the white and colored races." The ordinance, which stated that no person of any race could live in a block where at least 75 percent of the residents were of another race, had the backing of the city's powerful Real Estate Exchange, but it needed to pass a city-wide referendum. Despite the objections of some of the city's leaders, such as a young attorney named Luther Ely Smith, the ordinance passed easily in 1916. But it did not last long. The U.S. Supreme Court ruled in 1918 that a similar statute in Louisville was unconstitutional. Still, segregated housing persisted. The widely supported ordinance was quietly replaced by restrictive covenants that had the same effect.[24]

The racial division in St. Louis extended across the river to East St. Louis, where the tensions grew uglier and more explosive. Although separated by just the width of the Mississippi River, the two cities had distinctly different histories. As St. Louis strove to compete with New York and Chicago, grimy, industrial East St. Louis acquired a reputation as the "Pittsburgh of the West," which was not meant as a compliment. African Americans from the South came to work in the city's railroad terminals, heavy industry, and meatpacking plants. East St. Louis became known as a place where "the law did not reach," an impression reinforced by its dangerous saloons and abundant brothels.

In the hot summer of 1917, as the United States entered the bloody European war, East St. Louis became the scene of a historic bloodbath. The East St. Louis racial riot grew out of the corrupt elections that dominated the area. For years, Democrats warned party loyalists of the practice of "colonizing" voters, or, importing Republican voters from elsewhere to swell the GOP's vote totals. In this instance, "Republican" voters meant African American voters. This wariness of black voters reflected whites' distrust and antipathy toward black workers. In response to a strike at its factory in East St. Louis, the Aluminum Ore Company imported African American workers to cross the picket line, which enraged white strikers. On July 2, 1917, white mobs began a murderous rampage, setting houses on fire before firing their guns. Black inhabitants either died inside from the smoke and the flames, or were shot down as they ran from the fire. One newspaper account described a typical scene: "A crazed negro would dash from his burning home, sometimes with a revolver in his hand. Immediately revolvers by the score would be fired. He would zig-zag through the spaces between buildings. Then a well-directed shot would strike him." The wounded victim would be thrown into the flames. "The negro would writhe, attempt to get up, more shots would be fired." After killing one young African American man, the mob could not find a strong enough rope to hang the body. When one was finally obtained, a reporter watched in disgust as "the lyncher stuck his fingers inside the gaping scalp and lifted the negro's head by it, literally bathing his hands in the man's blood."[25]

The barbarity escalated as African American women were stoned to death, while two black infants were shot in the head. Reports on the death toll vary, with the most conservative estimating that thirty-nine blacks and eight whites died. Some contemporary accounts listed the casualties at closer to two hundred. The riot destroyed three hundred homes and commercial buildings, and estimates of property damage ranged between $1.4 million and $3 million. Throughout the violence, black residents hurried across the Eads Bridge to St. Louis, hoping to escape the carnage.[26]

By the 1920s, parts of the St. Louis riverfront had become an anachronism, and the plans for segregated zones and wide highways only reinforced which areas would prosper and which would die. A 1926 referendum would have united St. Louis city and county into the country's largest city by area; its failure displayed how county and city residents viewed their futures. While voters in the city approved of the measure by a margin of seven to one, county voters defeated the measure by more than three to one. With the arrival of the Great Depression in 1929, the riverfront became more vulnerable to economic catastrophe than just about any other area of St. Louis. Businesses that had thrived after the Civil War became the first casualties. In time, the area along the levee saw the erection of cardboard shacks and other "Hoovervilles" that housed the city's unemployed, estimated in 1931 to comprise nearly a quarter of its workforce. By 1933, the city's unemployment rate was above 30 percent, and among African Americans, over 80 percent were either unemployed or working in temporary or part-time jobs.[27]

What might come of the St. Louis riverfront at that point was anyone's guess. But a remarkable glimpse into the future was there for anyone who bothered to look. In 1933, Geneva Abbott, a student at Central High School, had been asked by the yearbook to use her budding artistic skills to imagine the future of the St. Louis riverfront Abbott's "look into the future" provided an astonishing preview of the St. Louis riverfront. Standing tall and majestic, parallel to the Mississippi River, she drew a giant parabolic arch with a triangular base, tapered as it neared its apex. The *Globe-Democrat* later remarked on the uncanny resemblance: "It's the Gateway Arch as it stands today."[28]

Abbott's selection of an arch was no random whim. In the upper left corner of her drawing, she quoted Tennyson's "Ulysses":

Yet all experience is an arch wherethro'
Gleams that untravell'd world, whose margin fades
For ever and for ever when I move.
How dull it is to pause, to make an end,
To rust unburnish'd, not to shine in use!

TWO

Getting Things Done

Mayor Bernard Dickmann (center), with Senator Harry Truman (right).
Copyright unknown, courtesy Harry S. Truman Library.

25

Decay came to many cities in the 1930s. The phrase coined to denote this affliction was "urban blight," but its definition remained elusive. A Philadelphia official probably best captured the general view: "a district which is not what it should be." Despite the vagueness of the concept, it was widely agreed that the blight destroyed property values, depressed local markets, and created havens of crime and violence. The solution embraced by many city planners and civic leaders emphasized clearing out the physical structures in the affected downtowns. It would be another generation before the costs of this approach became clear: many of the areas destroyed under the guise of "slum clearance" would, if they existed today, be marked for preservation and restoration as historic neighborhoods.

Few actions expose the political and social fault lines of a city more than condemnation: when the government takes private property under its constitutional power of eminent domain. Neighborhoods and lives can be overturned in the name of the larger public good. While slum clearance often involved using eminent domain to take land from the poor, the St. Louis case is unusual. Many landowners along the riverfront, often banking and real estate companies, gladly sold their holdings to the federal government. They earned windfall profits on their properties, and the entire condemnation process necessarily raised nearby land values. Yet not everyone was anxious to sell.[1]

As the *St. Louis Post-Dispatch* noted, a typical day along St. Louis's Depression-era riverfront presented a paradoxical scene:

> Loaded trucks and executives' fine cars pass bleary, drink-soaked derelicts wandering on the streets or sleeping on the levee. Trim stenographers walk past unkempt Negroes gambling for pennies with faded cards. Factory noises drown out the calls of women beckoning in houses. Black roustabouts loaf on the waterfront

while air-cooled modern trains thunder along the elevated tracks. Homes once occupied by substantial citizens have given way to cheap lodgings for men.

Hundreds of buildings stood along the blocks just west of the river. There were more than two dozen buildings that housed fur traders, which comprised the largest business sector in the area. Buildings for printers, book binders, wholesale wine dealers, and many other small businesses were there, along with stone houses more than a century old. Many businesses worked inside cast-iron structures. Between 3,000 and 5,000 people were employed in the area in places such as Sellers-Brown Coffee, Federal Fur and Wool, Abraham Fur, Eddy and Eddy Manufacturing, A. H. Fleming Printing, and Prunty Seed and Grain. One reporter went through the district and found that half the buildings in the zone were in good shape and needed no remodeling, and estimated that while one in five buildings was vacant, "the business still carried on is greater than most St. Louisans realize."[2]

Throughout the city, thick, black smoke from coal-fired furnaces created a more or less permanent haze. These visible signs of decay were matched by declining downtown land assessments. During the 1930s, the assessed value of downtown property in St. Louis dropped 60 percent. The early years of the Depression witnessed decreased land values all over the city, but an extensive appraisal of St. Louis real estate compiled by the Home Owners Loan Corporation gave the lowest possible ratings to the properties surrounding the riverfront industrial zones. Rental prices in 1935 were barely half what they had been in 1929. The HOLC concluded that the continuing smoke hazard and the "rapidly increasing Negro population constitutes a problem in the maintenance of real estate values." People living in rented homes and working in the businesses along the riverfront took advantage of the situation to eke out a living. For many property owners, however, the economic prospects of these declining land values presented a grim future.[3]

To reverse the situation along the riverfront, two St. Louisans combined their talents. The first, Luther Ely Smith, was born in 1873 in Downer's Grove, Illinois, and studied at Amherst College, where he befriended a fellow student, Calvin Coolidge. Smith attended law school at Washington University and remained in the city after graduating to begin his practice. In 1928, President Coolidge appointed him to a commission to honor George Rogers Clark in Vincennes, Indiana. The memorial, completed in 1936 with a Congressional appropriation of $1.74 million, consisted of a classical monument with a rotunda, Doric columns, and a bronze statue of Clark. With this success, Smith became fired with the ambition of building a memorial along the St. Louis riverfront.[4]

Contrary to the mythology that later grew around the Arch's origins, Smith initially had no specific historical moment or person in mind. He originally planned to commemorate a potpourri of major historical actors and developments that had marked the "sacred soil" of the site, including Daniel Boone, Jefferson, Lewis and Clark, Robert E. Lee, Ulysses S. Grant, and John C. Frémont. He seemed focused on the pioneer image, which was not accidental. In that age of economic tumult and political uncertainty, according to historian John Bodnar, the memory of manifest destiny and the symbol of the hearty pioneer answered both "the personal needs of ordinary people and the political needs of professionals and officials." One of the strengths of the image was that it looked both backward and forward. In the Midwest, Bodnar noted, "pioneers became nation builders, conservators of tradition," while serving as "models of survival during difficult times."[5]

To achieve his ambitions, Smith needed more than a civic appeal to honor westward pioneers. He needed land and money. To get these, a second person was necessary, and no one was better suited for the task than Mayor Bernard Dickmann. Born in St. Louis in 1888, Dickmann began working for his father's real estate company in 1907. In 1923, he became the company's president, and eight years later, president of the St. Louis Real Estate Exchange, a powerful industry association. Well versed in the unspoken rules of the St. Louis real estate market, Dickmann also understood the day-to-day realities of getting and maintaining political power. He knew how to get things done.[6]

Dickmann was elected mayor in 1933 despite his vocation. Few professions were held in lower esteem than real estate, which some blamed for the economic crisis. At first, after the stock market crash of 1929, those holding commercial real estate seemed relatively safe. Yet as the Depression worsened, unemployment grew, purchasing power plummeted, stores closed, and surrounding property values plunged. In 1925, the City of St. Louis issued more than one thousand building permits. In 1932, it issued fifty. Adding to the dismal real estate market were hundreds of vacant buildings, which also decreased property values. In the 1930s, St. Louis's vacancy rate was the highest among thirty other similar metropolitan areas. The month Franklin D. Roosevelt was inaugurated, March 1933, was the worst month for real estate activity in St. Louis since 1918. Critics also blamed the real estate profession for inflated property values during the boom years. One local authority admitted in 1933 that had appraisers been "more competent" during the boom years, the Depression might have been less severe. The same expert predicted that in the 1930s, the challenge for real estate professionals was to manage land consolidation and redistribution.[7]

In this political environment, a real estate executive faced enormous challenges in winning the voters' confidence. Yet the public's hostility at real estate interests in 1933 paled next to its anger at the Republican Party. Dickmann was the first Democrat elected mayor since 1905, and he knew he needed some early accomplishments to have a chance at reelection four years later. It was here that his ambitions and Smith's coincided.

Mayor Dickmann saw the city's problems through the eyes of a real estate broker. For such a person, large-scale clearing of "blighted" property involved more than ridding the city of eyesores. Eliminating vast tracts of low-earning rentals and empty buildings would have two effects. The value of the surrounding parcels would necessarily increase as usable buildings and land diminished, and the razed areas would offer opportunities to potential speculators. For Dickmann, clearing the riverfront and building a memorial to attract tourists was an obvious path to revitalize his city. In April 1934, the business and civic leaders organized as the Jefferson National Expansion Memorial Association began lobbying local and national leaders for their support.[8]

At the time, tourism seemed an unlikely way to rebuild the riverfront. The city's climate was more likely to drive people away for much of the winter and summer. Yet Smith and Dickmann believed that a memorial could work. This approach was consistent with a national phenomenon that had been growing since the 1880s. Tourism had emerged as a way for primarily white middle- and upper-class Americans to reaffirm, in the words of Marguerite Shaffer, their "American-ness." As leisure became more prevalent and transportation improved, it became a national ritual for Americans to visit the places and events where "they could temporarily reimagine themselves as heroic."[9]

Responding to the mayor's wishes, in July 1934 city engineer W. C. Bernard presented yet another redevelopment plan for the riverfront. The riverfront district, Bernard concluded, was hurting real estate values throughout downtown. Like Harland Bartholomew, he called for a riverfront freeway to bring more traffic to the city, and he recommended that this highway "should be made the occasion for an enforced slum clearance program." Slums, and their mostly African American inhabitants, could be moved elsewhere, and in their place something beautiful could be built. His memo also included a "pedestrian sanctuary" that connected the riverfront with the courthouse and downtown. Bernard estimated the project's cost at $20 million, which he hoped could be obtained from the federal government, or perhaps through a city bond issue. A paragraph deep within Bernard's report showed how Geneva Abbott and Eero Saarinen were not alone in envisioning a giant arch. Bernard proposed that the park be graced by a "monumental arch structure marking the entrance to the city." He even suggested naming the structure the "Gateway to the West."[10]

In 1934, Dickmann led a delegation of city leaders to the White House, asking for a commission to plan a riverfront park to memorialize the Louisiana Purchase. Local architect Louis LaBeaume sketched a plan that called for a giant statue of Jefferson amid fountains and other statues along a wide plaza. The project would cost $20 million less than Bartholomew's plan for rebuilding the riverfront, but even this scaled-down version cost a whopping $30 million. While President Roosevelt supported the resolution, he carefully stipulated that the federal government "is not liable for any incidental expenses." On June 15, 1934, he signed a resolution establishing the U.S. Territorial Expansion Memorial Commission, whose purpose was "a permanent memorial on the Mississippi River at St. Louis." City leaders assumed the project might be considered a Public Works Administration development, yet the president made it clear to Dickmann that "this is scarcely the type of project that falls under the PWA." The president added, however, "I like the principle underlying the thought of a memorial to the vision of Thomas Jefferson and the pioneers in the opening of the West." By turning the memorial into a tribute to the founder of the Democratic Party, supporters of the riverfront development had finally found a strategy that could garner support from the White House.[11]

Convincing their own Congressman, John J. Cochran, proved more difficult. After listening to their initial $30 million pitch, he told Dickmann and Smith that the project "has no chance to pass." Instead, Cochran suggested, the city should build a more modest memorial, in the $2–3 million range. He refused to allow his name to be associated with the current resolution because it was so outlandish: "I do not want the people in St. Louis to feel that there is any chance for passage." A Republican congressman agreed, asking why such a memorial needed to be built "in such incongruous surroundings." Rather than admitting defeat, Smith and Dickmann forged ahead yet with little more than a seemingly benign resolution.[12]

Despite receiving only tepid expressions of support, the two men pitched a plan to St. Louis voters calling for them to initiate the "Jefferson National Expansion Memorial" project with a hefty investment. Using a three-to-one federal match, Dickmann hoped to raise $7.5 million to persuade the federal government to provide the remaining $22.5 million. Undeterred by the lack of any specific guarantee of a federal match, he proceeded as if it were ironclad. In April 1935, after the Missouri legislature passed a law allowing the city to incur a debt of one-fourth the total cost of the project, a special election was called for the following September to ask for voters to approve a $7.5 million bond issue. Dickmann needed more than a simple majority. By statute, all bond issues required approval by two-thirds of those voting. The very necessity of a bond issue was another consequence of the "great divorce" in the nineteenth century. As the city received no income from the growing county, it was increasingly dependent on borrowing to finance new ventures.[13]

Despite the much-publicized civic-mindedness of the project, Dickmann faced uncertain odds of winning voter approval. Realizing that Republicans and conservative Democrats hesitated to incur such a large debt during a time of widespread financial hardship, he claimed the project would immediately bring five thousand jobs to the city and clear away blocks of unsightly and mostly derelict warehouses. Less than a month before the election, he raised the stakes by utilizing all seven thousand city employees as campaign workers for the bond issue. "Attitude of the employees toward the issue will be an evidence of their loyalty toward the administration," the mayor said candidly. "I hate to be a dictator," Dickmann admitted, "but I don't want six or eight people to interfere and break down what we are trying to do to build up a progressive city." The workers got the message. With thousands of their neighbors on the relief rolls, a city job was not something to lose.[14]

Opposition arose to counter Dickmann's claims. One group, the Taxpayers Defense Association, argued that the bond would not deliver the jobs Dickmann promised, nor would it help raise property values or swell city coffers. Instead, the group projected that by removing the buildings and businesses currently on the site, the plan would actually decrease the city's annual revenue by $200,000. And they pointed out that the federal government had made no financial commitment, describing the project as a "37-block mud hole" that would eventually become "a "glorified parking lot."[15] For many years, this was not far from the truth.

The Taxpayers Association was not alone. The Citizens' Non-Partisan Committee, led by local Republican activist Paul O. Peters, described Dickmann's plan as a thinly veiled gift to the city's real estate interests. Predicting that the project would eventually cost over $60 million, the Non-Partisan Committee informed city voters that bankers would be the ones to ultimately benefit from the project: "The Shylocks of finance," Peters cautioned, "must get their pound of flesh before we can say 'It's paid for and it's ours.'" Peters also warned that if jobs actually came out of the project, "it would only benefit the colored people." Such a suggestion was bound to stir resentment among the city's white voters. The *Post-Dispatch*, meanwhile, endorsed the bond issue, taking the political high road and appealing to patriotism. Once the memorial was built, the paper claimed, "the world will come here to pay its reverence to this temple of the soul of democracy."[16]

Dickmann's allies published large exhortative ads promoting the bond issue. If it passed, they promised, St. Louis would "get U.S. funds; cut relief rolls; clear 37 blocks; put 5,000 men to work; build a memorial park; perpetuate our nation's history," and sweetest of all, it would all be "maintained by the federal government." Even better, work on the memorial would start just ten days after the bond was approved.[17] Forty local trade unions came out in favor, drawn by the prospect of good-paying jobs (5,111 to be exact) for skilled laborers. Yet African Americans, who were barred from many of these unions, wondered what benefits would come to them. Several of the city's African American leaders wrote to Luther Ely Smith: "Knowing that the city of St. Louis is dominated by union labor and knowing the attitude of union labor to Negro workmen," they asked, "What will be the status of the Negro workmen to the work in general?" In the end, the desperation of the Depression was sufficient to persuade the city's African American newspaper, the *Argus*, to endorse the bond issue. The *Argus*'s reasoning had little to do with a desire to memorialize Jefferson or beautify the riverfront. Passage of the bond issue, the paper reasoned, "means bread, clothing, and other sustenances of life to those who have been without work for some time."[18]

Lost within the political campaign were careful investigations of the realities along the riverfront. Although some areas showed obvious signs of economic ruin, others were not quite the wasteland of destitute and abandoned buildings ravaged by time and the Depression that the mayor portrayed. A Chamber of Commerce study revealed that within the zone, 290 active businesses employed approximately five thousand workers. An engineering survey concluded that only 2 percent of the thirty-seven blocks slated for renovation could be labeled as "vacant," while 44 percent was composed of "light industry." Businesses in the area included printing companies, fur and wool traders, seed and feed distributors, and some wholesale grocers. The Chamber noted that if the project commenced, "There will be a definite tension placed on industrial real estate available outside the riverfront area if the proposal to erect a Memorial Plaza is fulfilled. Just how much tension, it is difficult to express precisely." More than five million square feet of industrial space would have to be relocated, leading the study's authors to the heart of the issue: "The absorption of this large amount of space, together with the short period of time available for procuring new locations will temporarily, and perhaps, permanently, increase real estate values in St. Louis."[19]

The real estate community understood what was at stake. At a January 1935 meeting of the Real Estate Exchange, one of the brokers admitted, "I have been very much interested in some disposition of the properties . . . for several years. I am speaking from a selfish standpoint, as a real estate man." He continued, "Of course, this is not supposed to be a real estate venture, so far as St. Louis is concerned, but it will enter into it more or less, because in taking the historical features in connection with it, it very well happens that that section is a section that has been on the minds of the property owners, real estate men, for a good many years."

Real estate board chairman Claude Ricketts made it clear that the efforts to reconfigure the riverfront had nothing to do with either jobs or honoring Thomas Jefferson. "It has always been my idea that if we could make 4th Street valuable, it is absolutely a certainty that Sixth and Seventh streets would continue to get the rent that they contracted to get for the next 35 years." Ricketts implored the members of the real estate community to contribute all they could to help the endeavor, since passage of the bond issue would benefit them more than any other group.[20]

Closer inspection of the "blighted" thirty-seven-block area only underscores the economic and political forces at work. Although commercial buildings predominated, the proposed memorial site also held nearly two hundred houses. Only six of these properties were owned by the dwellers, and five of those were valued at more than $10,000. The rest were rented out at rates that hardly suggest "blight." Only twenty-two properties earned monthly rents under $10. Fifty-seven earned between $20 and $30 per month, equivalent to a week's wage for 75 percent of the city's workers and the most common rate charged in ten surrounding tracts. Eight properties brought in over $50 per month in rent (equivalent to more than $800 in 2011).[21] The city's real estate and financial sector owned 109 properties in the district, representing 35 percent of its assessed value. Three real estate firms were among the five largest property owners in the area, and eleven financial and realty companies ranked within the top twenty-one. Considering that the Jefferson National Expansion Memorial Association's Legal Committee was advised by "experienced real estate men" that the compensation for a condemned property would be 25 percent more than the assessed value, it was no surprise that the city's realty interests saw the riverfront project as a source of immediate income. The clearing of the site to make way for the memorial would, in turn, immediately increase neighboring property values.[22]

The goal of raising property values, of course, had to be concealed behind the cause of creating jobs and memorializing westward expansion, and having taken that public posture, supporters of the bond issue held the political high ground as the polls opened on September 10, 1935. That evening, Dickmann's forces seemed to have won, securing nearly 71 percent of the vote. With the victory, the Jefferson National Expansion Memorial project enveloped itself in the democratic will of the people. Publicity Chairman William D'Arcy proclaimed that "In a few months you won't find a man or a woman who will claim that they fought it—that they even voted NO." After selling the city on the historic value of the project and the jobs that would flock to St. Louis, D'Arcy privately offered a more sobering and accurate assessment of what the election had accomplished: "We have made every retail corner in the downtown area more valuable."[23]

Quickly capitalizing on the election victory, Smith and LaBeaume met with Senator Alben Barkley of Kentucky, a member of the Territorial Expansion Memorial Commission, to discuss the memorial's progress in light of the voters' approval of the bond issue. LaBeaume shared with the press his interest in heading a nationwide design competition for the memorial, and the Justice Department announced its readiness to begin condemnation proceedings as soon as it received notification by either Interior Secretary Harold Ickes or relief administrator Harry Hopkins that federal funds were available. The city's bankers and real estate leaders, normally opposed to governmental intervention, were more than eager for condemnation to start.[24]

But Washington balked. On November 18, Attorney General Homer Cummings ruled that the president could not approve funds for future use for the national park in St. Louis under the Emergency Relief Appropriations Act of 1935. An outraged Dickmann began a game of high stakes political poker with the president. If the federal government refused to deliver the millions he had told his voters were coming to his city, Dickmann would withhold his support for FDR in the 1936 election. Dickmann had little to lose in making such a threat. St. Louis was a Republican town, and he had staked his political future on the project. Without it, he might well lose the next mayoral election. And he was gambling that, although

FDR had carried Missouri in 1932 with 55 percent of the vote, the administration would hesitate to anger a Democratic mayor who could deliver votes.

The impasse was broken by Assistant Attorney General Harry Blair, who found a loophole that allowed the administration to change course while saving face. Blair employed the recently passed Historic Sites Act, which allowed the Interior Secretary to acquire title to the land if it was intended to be used as a historic site. After receiving a letter from Secretary Ickes that the area was of "sufficient historical importance," FDR signed the executive order shortly before Christmas 1935. The federal government would contribute $6.75 million to match the city's $2.25 million, allowing the start of the condemnation process, with the remaining amount to be considered later. An irritated Ickes noted that "since we are all committed up to our eyes on this project, I think we ought to go through with it under whatever guise."[25]

Underscoring Dickmann's clout was the apparent approval of the St. Louis electorate. Yet Paul Peters, who knew that Dickmann's City Hall cronies had conspired to manipulate the vote totals, asked President Roosevelt to nullify the results. The Non-Partisan Committee printed a pamphlet outlining the details of the election thievery, adding that "Money flowed like water amongst those political workers, judges, and clerks who not only supported the bond issue, but were vile enough to deliberately stuff ballots or make false counts." With support from the *Post-Dispatch*, the committee began investigating registration lists in St. Louis. The extent of the false registration became evident as hundreds of individuals could not be found residing at their listed addresses.

Thousands of voters were found to be supposedly living in abandoned buildings or on empty lots. One building, unoccupied for over a year, claimed 137 registered voters. Of the 160 people registered at the address of the Atlantic Hotel, the hotel owner claimed that only six had ever resided there. In other cases, some precincts voted unanimously for the bond issue, including former Congressman and current Police Commissioner William Igoe's precinct, where the bond passed 505 to 0. (In the 1950s, one of the city's most notorious public housing projects would be named for Igoe.) Thirty-four precincts recorded over 97 percent of their votes for the bond issue. At a barbershop on Franklin Street, 392 people were registered as residents. When the *Post-Dispatch* finished its exhaustive investigation, more than 46,000 false registrations had been documented.[26]

As the details of massive election fraud became known, the outcry against the bond issue election results intensified. In September 1936, the *Post-Dispatch* declared that the election "must not be allowed to rest under this doubt" of fraud hanging in the air, and that "The city cannot afford to have it said that the building of a great monument with the people's funds is being promoted by fraudulent methods." The *Washington Post* noted that considering the extent of the false registration, it was obvious that "the people of St. Louis really did not vote to spend $7.5 million, nor, in turn, the federal government's remaining $22.5 million."[27]

The means by which the bond issue passed were not the only point of contention by angry St. Louisans. In spring 1936, thirty-six property owners on the proposed site sued to halt Interior Secretary Ickes from releasing any funds to begin the project. Their attorney, Edmund Toland, called the project "a grand scheme to get rid of this property at the expense of the Government of the United States." He outlined the general zones of downtown businesses, and argued that promoters of the project "decided that if they could vacate" the riverfront district, "then the leaseholders would have to move. That's the scheme. It's not intended to memorialize Thomas Jefferson or anyone else. It's a scheme to promote real estate value." After a federal judge threw out the suit, the plaintiffs appealed, and by August 1936 the U.S. Court of Appeals issued a temporary injunction against the federal government's disbursal of funds until it could hear the case in full. The delighted property owners reported "brisk" business and noted that several new companies had actually moved into the area since the bond issue election.

A thoroughly disgusted Luther Ely Smith denied that real estate interests were behind the memorial project. All along, he insisted, there was "no scheme or successful plot to 'unload real estate at inflated prices.'" In December 1936, Peters asked Smith where the memorial's supporters would stand "when the mask has been torn aside and the fraud and corruption connected with the election made public?" Peters was growing dismayed that, after the fraud was revealed in the *Post-Dispatch*, leaders like Smith seemed to look the other way. Among the willfully ignorant was the National Park Service (NPS), whose interest in building the project, Peters wrote, rendered it "entirely indifferent to the fraud."[28]

The lawsuits and the election fraud investigation exposed the political bind in which the NPS found itself. It had been created in 1916 to maintain the vast landscapes of Yellowstone, Yosemite, and the Grand Canyon. In 1933, FDR had transferred all federally owned parks and monuments to the NPS, along with an assortment of battlefields and cemeteries, making the agency more powerful than before. The NPS became the ultimate arbiter of what sites were worthy of national remembrance. The St. Louis riverfront was one of the first examples of the agency's new role in the public presentation of American history. The leaders of the NPS were ready to get started, regardless of the outcry generated by angry St. Louisans.[29]

Peters's efforts to stop the memorial project ended in March 1937, when a federal appeals court denied the property owners' appeal. The court declared that the city of St. Louis had entered into a contract with the federal government to build the memorial. Any claim that the city's voters had actually voted against the bond issue was deemed by the court to be irrelevant. The court interpreted the election as the city's signature on a binding contract, even if that signature was forged. Considering what had transpired, the *Post-Dispatch* withdrew its endorsement of the project—something the paper did not mention years later, amid the self-congratulatory atmosphere of the Arch's construction.[30]

Yet many, including some members of Congress, believed this "contract" was a corrupt bargain. Rep. William Lambertson, a Kansas Republican, proclaimed that "The St. Louis proposal smells. It stinks." He viewed the project as nothing more than "an attempt of the St. Louis real estate promoters to unload 37 blocks of business property in downtown St. Louis onto the Federal government." As a member of the House Interior subcommittee that oversaw funds for the Park Service, Lambertson was indignant that the NPS would acquiesce to being associated with such a project. "Think of the National Park Service leaving the lofty grandeur of the Yellowstone," Lambertson said, "to dip into the cesspool of St. Louis." If Congress allowed "the public treasury to be drained of millions of dollars for this unnecessary proposal," Lambertson asked, "what right have we later to say 'No' to cities like Pittsburgh, Cincinnati, Louisville, Memphis, and New Orleans should they come forward for their chance in the national grab bag?"[31]

Lost amid the debates about exorbitant financing and stolen elections was another matter. Some of the buildings in the area were of considerable historic value. Dr. Sigfried Giedion, a Swiss architectural historian who had founded the International Congress of Modern Architecture, was outspoken in his efforts to keep many of the cast-iron buildings from being destroyed. These buildings were unlike any others in the nation, he said, and must be saved from the wrecking ball. One located at 7 North First Street was the office of the U.S. Express Company, which had doors made completely of cast iron. Another structure was a four-story warehouse at the corner of First and Washington in which graceful cast-iron pillars supported the upper floors. Many others should be kept, he said, "because they will form a real monument to early life and work of St. Louisans. It might first appear that it is not worthwhile" to save them, Giedion remarked, "but we can understand their great value when we realize they have no equivalent in other countries."[32]

Meanwhile, some desperate owners along the riverfront pleaded for help. Rev. Alva McCarver, writing to Eleanor Roosevelt in 1937 to say that he had been ordered to vacate his house, asked the First Lady if he had "squatters' rights with the Government." He struggled to "make my way without the help of relief" but saw his options diminishing if the stalemate along the riverfront continued. A. W. Albrecht asked FDR, "How would you like it if offered 10 cents on the dollar for your Hyde Park estate by some future President desirous of constructing a memorial?" Another angry landowner wrote to Mayor Dickmann that while his property taxes accumulated during the legal battles, his chances of renting his property grew dim. "The situation in fact is virtually indescribable." The *Post-Dispatch* reminded its readers that it opposed the memorial project—not only because the bond issue election had been decided by fraud, but for an additional reason: because "most of the funds would go for property."[33]

The bitter disputes that erupted between landowners and renters threw the Depression-era riverfront and its history into sharp relief. While not the gleaming jewel it had once been, the riverfront area was not a destitute wasteland. Just how "blighted" the area actually was became apparent in 1939, when the final appraisal bill for the condemned property came to nearly $7 million, 65 percent more than the 1938 assessed value. Interior Secretary Ickes found the sum "excessive" and threatened to cancel the entire project, writing that the federal government would not support "a speculative real estate boom based on how much a landowner could get through selling a holding to the government."[34]

If there was any doubt that the idea of memorializing Jefferson was simply bait to lure federal money, Dickmann himself put it to rest when, just a month after the bond issue vote, he suggested that instead of a memorial to the third president, he "heartily endorsed" the idea of building a giant football stadium on the site. The stadium could be used by Washington University's fledgling football team and, according to Dickmann, would bring economic growth to the area. Three years later, Dickmann and other city leaders repeated their call for a stadium on the supposed "memorial" site.[35]

Even if Dickmann had in mind nothing but creating jobs and Luther Ely Smith wanted only to beautify the riverfront with a dazzling architectural triumph, some essential truths remain. The people of St. Louis did not vote to support the bond issue. The Jefferson National Expansion Memorial simply did not have the democratic backing it claimed. Bankers and real estate companies profited from the condemnation of the riverfront district, while tenants and small businesses suffered. Mayor Dickmann had skillfully maneuvered the various political minefields to get his beloved riverfront reclamation project under way.

Finally, after years of suits and injunctions, on October 9, 1939, Dickmann used a crowbar to remove three bricks from an aging building on Market Street near the Mississippi River. The ceremony marked the beginning of the demolition of nearly forty square blocks. One spectator noted the irony that four years earlier, during the bond issue election, the building chosen for the event had been the home address listed for dozens of ghost voters. For some observers, the event marked the beginning of an exciting and new St. Louis. For others, it was another installment in an ongoing crime.[36]

THREE

The St. Louis Municipal Parking Lot

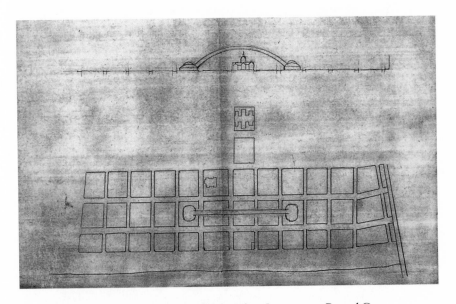

"Gateway to the West" arch drawing by Julian Spotts, 1945. Record Group 79, NPS Central Classified Files, National Archives and Records Administration, College Park, Maryland.

After the dust settled around the memorial site, three historic buildings were left standing. In the process, each became known as "old": the Old Courthouse; the Old Cathedral; and the Old Rock House built by Manuel Lisa in 1818. Eventually, the Lisa building came down to make room for a railroad tunnel, and remnants were placed in the Old Courthouse. By 1941, when the area had finally been cleared, all that remained of the rest was a huge field of gravel.

This type of destruction was not uncommon during the Depression. Most American cities experienced a sharp decline in the number of buildings during the 1930s and a sudden spike in demolitions. Large historic districts were flattened in Detroit, Bridgeport, Connecticut, and elsewhere, and homes and businesses were forced to relocate. By reducing the area available for businesses, downtown planners hoped to raise property values and rents.[1]

Many years later, in her 1961 classic *The Death and Life of Great American Cities*, Jane Jacobs would express passionate opposition to the practice of razing large sections of aging downtowns in the name of "slum clearance": "Cities need old buildings so badly it is probably impossible for vigorous streets and districts to grow without them. By old buildings I mean not museum-piece old buildings, not old buildings in an excellent and expensive state of rehabilitation, but also a good lot of plain, ordinary low-value old buildings, including some rundown old buildings."[2] Jacobs was writing about Greenwich Village, but she could easily have been describing the St. Louis riverfront circa 1935. While it would be unfair to castigate the urban planners of the 1930s and 1940s for failing to live up to the wisdom of later decades, it would also be a mistake to suppose that Jacobs's ideas arose out of nowhere. Elements of the thinking that she would assemble into a coherent manifesto in the 1960s were already apparent in the reaction against the Jefferson National Expansion Memorial Association (JNEMA) as the clearance got under way.

As the date for the demolition grew near, Sigfried Giedion made one last attempt to salvage some of the area's historic buildings. In August 1939 he implored the city to save a number of cast-iron structures. These structures, he wrote, served as "a connecting link between the humble unpretentious warehouses of the Creole merchants and the modern skyscrapers" and no other urban area contained so many examples as the St. Louis riverfront. Far more than grand palaces, they "tell of the life that was lived here. They indicate the part the city played in the expansion of the West," and as such, were precisely what the National Park Service, in sponsoring a memorial to the city's past, should seek to preserve. A friend of Luther Ely Smith's, Charles Reymershopper, regretted the destruction of so many buildings from a "traditional, historic, and even commercial standpoint," in an area that "is not a slum." The anger over the demolition extended far and wide. Waldo G. Leland, who headed the American Council of Learned Societies, protested to Interior Secretary Harold Ickes that he would be "very happy to see the project abandoned," since he felt the riverfront memorial effort had always been "much more of an effort to boom real estate in the city of St. Louis." Ickes had other suspicions that added to his doubts about the St. Louis project. In May 1939, he wrote to his staff that "word has come to me that some of the politicians of St. Louis, possibly the Mayor, have options on some of the properties that would be bought for the Jefferson Memorial."[3]

Another constituency, which Jacobs would have found instantly recognizable, also tried to save as much of the doomed area as possible. An art colony described its area around North Commercial Street as the "Greenwich Village of the West." Local restaurants proudly covered their walls with dozens of canvases of modernist art. One artist sadly noted, "It seems too bad that the one center where painters might gather and chat over their work and compare notes is about to be wiped out."[4]

More outcries were heard as one historic building after another fell. The Old Customs House at Third and Olive, a cast-iron structure built in 1859 that was once the largest federal building west of the Mississippi River, was slated for destruction in January 1941. Rather than see it demolished, a number of St. Louis leaders called for it to be moved to another site. The NPS acknowledged the building's historic importance, but noted that engineering and financial reasons made moving it "impractical." The impending loss of the Customs House gave Charles Van Raavensway, who edited the WPA Guidebook for the city, an opportunity to raise another fundamental issue: "I resent the indiscriminate clearing out of buildings without any plan having been presented as to what the memorial will be like." Raavensway believed that JNEMA leaders must "give us some idea of what they're doing with the riverfront before they tear down all of our fine old buildings." He knew, of course, that no such plan existed. To Charles Peterson, an architectural historian with the NPS, the process ran afoul of the park service's mission. "We're in the business of saving buildings, and here we are pulling them down, and *wholesale*." He described his reaction to it as "Horror."[5]

Even as the buildings fell one by one, an enduring remnant still stood—the elevated railroad track owned by the Terminal Railroad Association. The track had carried freight and passengers by the riverfront for decades and sliced through the leveled area in an unsightly way. When asked in 1935 about the fate of the tracks, proponents of the bond issue breezily left that problem to future discussion. Five years later, the Interior Department voiced frustration that the track's disposition remained unresolved. P. J. Watson of the Terminal Railroad Association proposed placing a permanent railroad line along the riverfront site, but Ickes rejected the plan outright. The proposed new path, Ickes observed, "completely separates the Memorial from the Mississippi River." Visitors wishing to stroll down to the river would need to walk over several grades of rail crossings. But while this was immediately rejected as unsatisfactory, the plan to place "National Park Drive" between the memorial and the city raised no such qualms. The *New York Times* approvingly noted that the highway would "afford a panorama of the Father of Waters as it sweeps past St. Louis."[6]

One major reason Ickes balked at the St. Louis memorial had to do with its $30 million price tag (relative to GDP, this was equivalent to $6.1 billion in 2011), of which the federal government was obliged for $22.5 million. By comparison, the federal government spent just under $1 million throughout the 1930s to carve four massive presidential heads out of Mount Rushmore in South Dakota. The world's largest dam, the Hoover Dam, cost just over $54 million during the same decade. The St. Louis project's cost was comparable to building the Pentagon, which when completed in the early 1940s cost approximately $35 million. Considering such comparisons, it is no surprise that Ickes and so many others found the St. Louis proposal excessive. Skeptical members of Congress could at least consider that the other projects generated electricity for the Southwest or housed America's war departments under one roof. The St. Louis project offered little useful value other than its benefits to local politicians and real estate stakeholders.[7]

Making matters worse, by the time workers hauled off the debris from the last riverfront building, the massive public works spending occasioned by the New Deal was essentially over. In December 1941, America's entry into World War II drew the government's attention as well as its funds, and memorial building was put on hold. Five months after Pearl Harbor, the eighty-two acres of St. Louis's riverfront were a large gravel lot with the elevated railroad tracks passing over it.

With construction halted on the riverfront, local architects could at least dream. They did so in the context of a national effort to envision the postwar city. A flood of corporate ads used modernist designs to depict a thrilling economic and built environment. World War II, writes architecture historian Andrew M. Shanken, "made the Modern Movement in America" by creating a consumer culture in which progressive architecture could thrive. In 1944, *Architectural Forum* invited St. Louis architect Harris Armstrong, along with Huson Jackson and Henry Shotwell, to create a new riverfront plan. Armstrong, a daring modernist architect, and Shotwell presented a bold vision of urban renewal with lasting consequences for St. Louis. "The embellishment of this area by monumental public buildings alone would not be successful because it fails to provide activity, a necessary component of central urban projects," Armstrong wrote. Instead, the area needed "the injection of a vital new function." He had little interest in tourist attractions and instead proposed reconstructing the riverfront as a new part of downtown containing high-density residential and commercial structures, all completely integrated with the central business district and the rest of the city.[8]

"The most important problem of the waterfront project," he wrote, "is that of circulation," specifically the postwar plans for interstate highways "paralleling the river and following the western boundary of the memorial area." Armstrong was one of the first to understand that running expressways through the heart of the city could have a negative impact: "This scheme serves only to separate the project from the central business district." Rather than reroute the highways, he suggested building them below ground through the memorial area, leaving a broad terrace that afforded "an uninterrupted visual sweep of the park and river from the city." The elevated railroad tracks would be relocated between the two lanes of sunken highways.

To achieve real renewal, Armstrong argued, the city should repurchase the riverfront from the federal government and forego plans for a garish and unnecessary memorial. Without a dramatically different and more economically productive concept for downtown and the riverfront, the central part of the city would continue to see "population loss, higher taxes, delinquencies, and foreclosures." He observed, "Memorial buildings do not create the movement of large numbers of people which is the lifeblood of an urban development." If the area was used as a memorial site, Armstrong feared the riverfront could not "avoid stagnation as a purely monumental but useless area."[9] Armstrong's plan, had it been implemented, would have avoided many of the modern-day problems of the memorial park and might have gone a long way toward saving downtown St. Louis. His mall would have allowed pedestrians to stroll from the city to the river and to have an uninterrupted view of the riverfront from the Old Courthouse.

While Chapin Newland, a member of the St. Louis Airport Commission, liked Armstrong's general plan, he believed it lacked an essential component—an airstrip. Revitalizing the area "will not be accomplished with only a park to play in," Newland said disparagingly. Other members of the Airport Commission agreed. Commissioner Oliver L. Parks imagined revolutionary possibilities that existed for private aircraft after the war. Since there would likely be a "tremendous boom" for small airplanes, Parks suggested the site be dedicated to a modest-sized airstrip to accommodate private air traffic. "The time has arrived," he wrote, "when a man can expect to walk from his house to a landing strip, get into his private airplane, and fly to work." Parks believed that with five hours training, just about anyone could learn to fly, and that there would soon be a need for airstrips across the country. Although Parks went further than most, his views were only the extreme edge of a national consensus: in postwar America, airplanes and automobiles would redefine the transportation and economic landscape. Harland Bartholomew's 1947 City Plan for St. Louis made it clear. He concluded that the city lacked the proper population density that made a subway system feasible, "any solution to downtown congestion must come from new thoroughfares."[10]

Amid these suggestions came yet another foreshadowing of Eero Saarinen. In February 1945, an NPS engineer named Julian Spotts suggested that the area needed a monumental symbol along the lines of the Washington Monument. Spotts admitted his idea might be a "stunt," but allowed that such stunts eventually "become landmarks which ripen into traditions." His plan called for a "hollow arch" rising to approximately 240 feet framing the Old Courthouse. Its base would consist of two large buildings to be used as museums. The self-supporting structure would have windows for tourists to gaze out in all directions while they viewed murals and exhibits inside the hollow core. Spotts even considered using electric cars to transport visitors inside the arch. His crude rendering revealed a rather flat, almost rainbow-like form, but one whose essential structure was eerily like what would be built on the same location years ahead. "As an inspirational and appropriate memorial," he wrote, "it might be argued that it is representative of the Gateway to the West; that it is a symbol of strength, progress, and expansion." While his Gateway Arch was "probably too bold in its conception," Spotts admitted, "I have had considerable fun delving into its possibilities. If a memorial of such proportions should be forced upon us I could take the idea seriously."[11]

Other, less attractive, plans emerged. Shortly after the war, F. F. Pearson of American Barge Lines suggested to Mayor Aloys Kaufman that the site should be turned into a giant trailer park. With returning soldiers finding no housing for their families, Pearson saw it as the best use of the land for the time being. The trailers could be obtained, he suggested, from the Oak Ridge Laboratory in Tennessee where the Manhattan Project had a surplus of the housing units. Proper supervision of the site was all that was necessary to keep the trailer park from becoming an "eyesore." The mayor's Housing Committee spokesman acknowledged there were "many advantages" to the idea.

Mayor Kaufman, meanwhile, envisioned a Veterans Administration hospital on the site. At the end of the war, the army utilized the space as a "rest camp," and Kaufman wanted to move quickly to reclaim the area. The planned construction of a Third Street "superhighway" just west of the historic site would bring in people, he argued, and a new hospital would bring even more business to the riverfront.[12]

With long-term plans for the riverfront in limbo, city leaders decided to use the graveled field to the city's advantage, at least in the short term. In May 1946, the NPS signed an agreement that allowed the city to administer it as a parking lot on a commercial basis. The city agreed to pay the federal government one dollar per month in rent. With this, the *Post-Dispatch* noted, "The JNEM became the St. Louis Municipal Parking Lot." The deal, however, did not produce a hearty revenue stream. In late June 1946, the daily parking rate was cut from 25 cents to 15 cents because not enough cars were using the lot. In its first month of operation, it raised only $1.05 in profits.[13]

Critics of the project had warned a decade earlier that razing the riverfront buildings would cost the city tax revenue. With that reality at hand and with nothing to show for their efforts except the dismal parking lot, Luther Ely Smith decided to act.

Rather than seek congressional funding before advancing, Smith and the city leadership took a different tack. In 1944, then ex-mayor Bernard Dickmann had suggested to FDR that he could jump start the memorial construction by sponsoring an architectural competition. Smith proposed that the JNEMA sponsor such a competition to produce a design that would convince doubtful federal lawmakers of the urgency of reclaiming the St. Louis riverfront. He would have to raise nearly a quarter of a million dollars to fund it. At the same time, however, the JNEMA could not guarantee that the winning entry would ever be built.[14]

The St. Louis contest became the first major American architectural competition of the postwar era and served as a window into architecture's immediate future. Architectural competitions held a special place in American history. In 1792, competitions were launched to design the U.S. Capitol building and President's house, and Thomas Jefferson himself submitted an unsuccessful entry for the latter. While such contests attracted widespread attention, they came with trade-offs. Some five hundred entries were expected in St. Louis, but long odds of winning might discourage some creative architects from devoting the necessary time to the effort, and turn away major names who would not want it known they had competed and lost. The choice of jurors would be critical, and their vision of the riverfront would necessarily inform the entrants' plans. One architect had warned Smith against such a competition in 1934, saying, "many architects of national reputation would not go into a 'free for all.'"[15]

Smith approached his wealthy friends for donations. In his solicitations, he noted the importance of selecting the right architect. "It is an opportunity to which the best talents of the New World will respond," he wrote, and the winner's design would stand for "the ages with the notable and beautiful buildings of civilization—with the Acropolis, with the Forum of Rome." Underlying the effort, he noted, was a notion expressed about the national commission by former Secretary of War Newton Baker, who had said in the mid-1930s, "Build this memorial as though you were building a cathedral."[16]

To Smith, this was a singular opportunity. "We are building here something bigger than economic interest, though business in St. Louis will profit greatly from it," he wrote. "We are building something bigger than St. Louis, though the city will be remade by it. We are building something bigger than any one of us, something even bigger than Jefferson, whose monument it is to be. We are building something worthy of that great American's idea of America."[17]

The soaring rhetoric left many of Smith's associates unconvinced. Chapin Newland, fresh off his failure to build an airstrip on the riverfront, rejected Smith's pleas. To allow architects from all over the nation to redesign the riverfront was risky because "many of them are unfamiliar with St. Louis, and might develop something not at all suited to the site." Harry B. Mathews of the Mississippi Lime Company answered that "for the last three years I have been trying to prevail upon the Jefferson Memorial Committee to forget about monuments." Instead, he wrote, "better homes on the river" would revitalize the riverfront and help stanch the constant stream of people leaving the city for the county. Mathews gave the committee $5,000, but hoped the memorial would eventually provide an area suitable for houses and apartments. I. F. Boyd, Jr., underscored the growing resentment over the leadership of the ten-year effort to build the memorial, noting that JNEMA officials "have done a rotten job of public relations on the thing and consequently, the people who might want to support it don't have sufficient confidence to make a contribution to the Competition." In Boyd's estimation, "Poor Luther" was "grasping at straws." James L. Ford of the First National Bank complained that he "had been drawn into this Jefferson Memorial very much against my will." Ford thought the riverfront project was "a moribund enterprise," but relented to Smith's pleas simply out of "my affection for Luther."[18]

Despite such grumblings, "Poor Luther" convinced enough of the corporate and retail leaders of the city to contribute to the cause so that the competition reached full funding in late 1946. The largest donations came from the Associated Retailers of St. Louis and May Department Store, which gave a combined $67,000. The largest personal donor was Edgar Queeny, the chairman of the St. Louis industrial giant Monsanto, who gave $45,000. Having realized his goal, Smith turned his attention to selecting the proper person to direct the competition. One donor suggested Bernard Dickmann, "a forceful man" who, the donor noted, had done "a great deal of good work in helping at the start." But Smith understood that the competition needed a much less provincial outlook and rejected putting Dickmann or a local architect such as Louis LaBeaume in charge. On January 28, 1947, he introduced George Howe, a prominent Philadelphia architect, as the competition director, a decision with far-reaching implications. Trained at Harvard and the Ecole des Beaux-Arts, the sixty-year-old Howe had undergone a midlife transformation to the modernist International Style and described himself as "a veteran of the Beaux Arts who has come through the conflict pretty badly cut up but not decapitated." In 1945, he had written a brief article regarding planned World War II monuments that offered glimpses into how he might approach the St. Louis project: "Are death and mourning to be immortalized in architectural forms recalling the tragedy of vanishing cultures or shall the living breath of a great nation be solidified in symbols projecting a perpetual present of hope and heroism?" For the competition, he refused to entertain the possibility of a classical monument. "If real modern competitive talent, young or old, is to be attracted to enter," he told Smith, "the jury must be selected in advance and must not represent too conservatively official a group." He told reporters he envisioned a memorial that would "not only be a monument of historic character, but an area of daily use to the city."[19]

The appointment alerted architects across the nation that this competition would not rely on the usual classical notions of monumental architecture that then dominated Washington, D.C. Howe, in turn, cast his net widely for architects and engineers who might serve on the jury. The final seven-member panel announced on April 10, 1947, included Charles Nagel, Jr., an architect who had headed the St. Louis Art Museum before becoming director of the Brooklyn Museum in 1946; Philadelphia Museum of Art director Fiske Kimball; landscape architect S. Herbert Hare of Kansas City; Roland Wank, the consulting chief engineer for the Tennessee Valley Authority; and Louis LaBeaume, who had proposed his own design for the riverfront in 1934 and had later hoped to have Howe's position. The two architects of national reputation on the jury were William W. Wurster, the dean of architecture at MIT, and Los Angeles architect Richard Neutra, who minimized his modernist credentials by calling himself a "conservative," which he said meant he wished "to save for the future, in terms of the future's healthiest growth, what was most vital to the spirit that animated the features of the past."[20] Howe also tried to enlist a third nationally renowned architect, Wallace K. Harrison, who declined because he was busy leading the international team designing the United Nations complex in New York. The final jury was a remarkable assortment of people ready to consider something new and bold.

The jury's first task was to frame the overall project in a published program. After careful inspection of the site, they worked out the major elements of the competition. The resulting twenty-four-page booklet, sent to all interested architects, provided clues into the complex nature of the site, its history, and its future. First, the contest was open "to anyone who by education or experience, was entitled to call himself an architect." Competitors were informed that the historic site was the only section that could be considered in their plans, but, "the urban area to the west, north, and south, with its pressing need for space, and the levees to the east," as well as the proposed interstate highways and the railroads, were "integral" to the overall plan. Ideas for the wider area could be offered, although the focus should remain on the riverfront site. The jury even suggested that East St. Louis, "which forms the landscape background of the River, will ultimately be incorporated in the Memorial." In all, the plan "cannot be intelligently approached without an examination of its relation to the whole area of which it is a part."[21]

With city, state, and federal governments all involved, the program advised competitors to think of themselves "as technical advisers to a Government planning agency" who would prepare a land use study that should be "tied into a city plan already projected and a regional plan in contemplation." While the jury would evaluate the entries based on "breadth of vision," competitors were not expected to "have any special knowledge of the jurisdictional and economic conditions that affect the overall planning problem." They were told to estimate the entire project to cost $30 million, of which $9 million had already been spent on acquiring and clearing the site.

A second crucial decision asked even more of the entrants. Rather than judge all the entries and declare a winner in one fell swoop, Howe devised a two-stage competition. The first round would yield five finalists, who would then be required to submit more polished versions during a second round of judging. Howe hoped for a free-wheeling first round, with the second stage offering more practical refinements. For their trouble, finalists would all be guaranteed $10,000. Fourth and fifth place would earn an additional $2,500, third place, $10,000. The runner-up would receive $20,000, and the winner would receive $40,000. The sums were impressive, yet still disappointing considering that the first place winner in the 1922 Chicago Tribune Tower competition had received $50,000.[22]

While the routes of the interstate highways and the relocation of the existing railroad tracks had not been finalized, competitors were told to think of them as "existing conditions." "Passage of the Interstate Highway without traffic crossings must be provided for somewhere in the area east of Third Street," the program said. For emphasis, designers could "offer suggestions for the approaches by road involving changes in the street and traffic systems," as long as those changes did not conflict with the general road plan sketched out in the program. They could not alter the path of the projected 140-foot-wide highway that would run along Third Street—the route established by Harland Bartholomew years before. While great attention would be paid in the coming years to the railroad relocation, relatively little was made of the roads that would cut off the site from the Old Courthouse and prevent any direct connection between the memorial and downtown.[23]

The program's design requirements were quite extensive. First and foremost, the plan called for a memorial, whose precise subject remained vague. Jefferson remained central to the plans, but the jurors, influenced by the project's scattershot history, also considered Robert Livingston and James Monroe as possible figures to be memorialized. Others would even indulge such subjects as the Louisiana Purchase, the trappers and fur traders who once made their living on the site, and "the pioneer movement in general." The memorial could be in any shape or size, but the plan had to include an accompanying area for sculpture that depicted seven different historical scenes, such as the signing of the Louisiana Purchase in Paris, the transfer of the Louisiana Territory, the outfitting of Lewis and Clark, and life and traffic on the river. The Old Courthouse must be maintained in the plan, as well as the Old Cathedral. One other historical site, the Old Rock House, "is considered desirable but not mandatory." It was not part of the memorial by the time it was constructed, having been torn down in 1959. Landscaping was central to the jury's concept, and other requested amenities included an open-air theater and a museum. The jury also sought a "living memorial" to the vision of Thomas Jefferson, broadly defined as "an activity designed to instruct and disseminate information to organized groups, or to the public at large"; in keeping with Jeffersonian ideas, this memorial "should be sponsored, administered, and manned by the civic, education, and cultural organizations and men of affairs." Last, the design was to incorporate parking structures with a capacity of six thousand vehicles. Some minor flourishes were also included, such as a heliport. The parking requirement irritated NPS Director Newton B. Drury, who told Smith the project was meant to produce a national memorial, "not the solution of local problems." Harland Bartholomew reminded Drury that parking "is about the Number One problem."[24]

The jury realized the risk it was taking by placing so many mandatory items into the competition. *Architectural Forum*, lamenting that the contest was "basically one of city planning" rather than pure design, warned that the cluttering of elements might make for mediocre entries and not push architects to concentrate on one primary aspect. Yet the jury's outline gave some leeway to architects, who must have known that not every item would be treated equally. Deciding what to highlight became a crucial part of a contestant's strategy.[25]

Each competitor could submit only one entry. An official entry consisted of two drawings, with the first being the "Presentation of the Design." This could be on white cardboard and was to be no larger than thirty-six inches high and forty-eight inches wide and was to include the plan, elevation, and cross-sections. The second drawing, "Explanation and Amplification of the Design," could be a color drawing mounted on cardboard of the same size and, the program advised, should be considered a way of "talking to the jury over the drawing board." No models or other accompanying material were permitted in the first stage. These two drawings composed the entire entry, and would be placed on easels for examination by the jury members. For this stage, applicants were asked to "give their imagination free rein," and leave the engineering and financial considerations "to a less exuberant moment." All entries would be anonymous to the jurors, and competitors were asked to keep their designs secret. The NPS thought this was important to ensure no "accusations of plagiarism." The deadline for submissions was September 1,

1947. The five finalists would have until February 3, 1948, to submit their second stage entries.[26]

Architects, it is said, are at the mercy of their clients. The stereotype of the idealistic architect stubbornly clinging to his principles against the limited vision of mediocre clients and builders achieved a certain heroic status in the 1940s, especially after the publication in 1943 of Ayn Rand's *The Fountainhead.* Howard Roark, Rand's fictional modernist architect, refused to compromise with any client or powerful figure. He even destroyed his own masterpiece rather than allow it to be changed by inferior minds. Real architects such as Frank Lloyd Wright battled endlessly with clients who were looking to cut corners, and for younger architects looking to make names for themselves, winning over clients was essential. Architectural competitions were no different. The competition in St. Louis promised an array of competing visions and agendas, from Howe and the seven-member jury to the city and the NPS. Navigating the complex requirements of the program to win over a prestigious jury was a formidable task.

In retrospect, Luther Ely Smith's decision to mount an expensive competition rather than commission one architect to produce the design represented a major and potentially disastrous gamble. Had the process yielded a mediocre result that inspired no one, the riverfront might have remained a gravel parking lot.

FOUR

A Peculiarly Happy Form

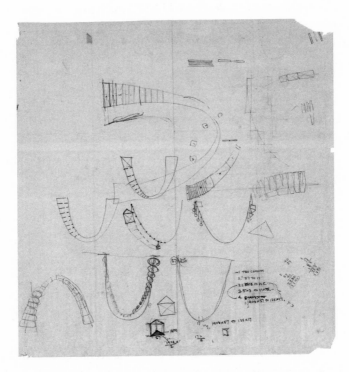

Early sketches of the Gateway Arch by Eero Saarinen. Eero Saarinen Papers, Manuscripts and Archives, Yale University Library.

News of the St. Louis competition attracted wide attention. By the end of May 1947, officials with the Jefferson National Expansion Memorial Association had received more than 1,100 application requests. Yet the decision to enter the competition carried risks. The prospect of hundreds of entries made the likelihood of winning remote. An architect or even an entire firm would have to devote hundreds of hours to planning, reviewing, and drawing a memorial design—time and energy that might be better spent on paying projects. Moreover, this process was not a simple undertaking, but a project involving several layers of design issues. Adding to the professional anxiety, entries from highly regarded architects might be tossed aside for a relatively unknown designer. Over 80 percent of those requesting applications ultimately decided not to submit an entry.[1]

Throughout the fall of 1947, 172 crates, each bearing two thirty-six-by-forty-eight-inch panels, arrived at the offices of the JNEMA. The panels, identified only by their entry numbers, were placed on easels in a large room on the second floor of the Old Courthouse. An architecture student from nearby Washington University, Harry B. Richman, helped unpack the crates. As Richman opened entry #144, he was immediately drawn to it, but wondered whether "the jurors would be up to the challenge of embracing the scale, audacity, and beauty" of the concept.[2]

Entry #144 was submitted by a thirty-seven-year-old architect named Eero Saarinen, who worked in a small firm headed by his father, Eliel, in Bloomfield Hills, Michigan. After reading of the St. Louis competition announcement the previous April, Eero had written to Howe that it "looks interesting" and requested two programs. Many within the architectural community assumed that if a Saarinen emerged as the designer of the St. Louis memorial, it would be Eliel. Robert Elkington, a St. Louis architect and the program committee chair of the American Institute of Architects, had written Eliel in April to say "you are the outstanding architect in the country, and will probably win the prize if you compete."[3]

Father and son decided to submit separate entries. Eero immediately contacted landscape architect Dan Kiley, whom he had met during the war. "You have undoubtedly heard of the Jefferson Memorial competition for St. Louis that George Howe is running," he wrote. "It looks like a fairly good competition" and it "would be fun" to work together on it.[4] Eero's early ideas for a memorial included "some kind of dome which was much more open than the ones in Washington." He added, "Maybe it could be a great pierced concrete dome that touched the ground in just three points." New forms of construction would permit "a much lighter and more transparent" design, one that might employ "three to five arched ribs meeting at the top." Early sketches proved unsatisfactory, but Eero kept returning to a fundamental element: "I felt that it had to be a simple geometric shape."

A few weeks later, Saarinen was visited by his old friend and colleague Charles Eames, who had just returned from St. Louis, his hometown. In Saarinen's living room, the two examined Eames's plan of the site and nearby properties. They quickly made a rough model of the area using matchboxes and wooden blocks. Saarinen thought an appropriate memorial should consist of "some great mass of stone pointing west." Then he returned to the concept of a "great, pierced dome." Yet that proved "too heavy" considering the long lines of the levee. Using flexible pipe cleaners, the two men constructed a flimsy model of three arches, but remained unsatisfied. Reducing the number of pipe cleaners, Saarinen envisioned a more simple approach incorporating "a huge concrete arch." He soon arrived at the conclusion Geneva Abbott, W.C. Bernard, and Julian Spotts had naively intuited years earlier, "Here, at the edge of the Mississippi River, a great arch *did* seem right."[5]

Arches, of course, had long been fundamental to architectural design. The Romans utilized them repeatedly in their aqueducts, bridges, and buildings. Arches allowed weight to be distributed down to the foundation, the two weak sides supporting each other. To prevent the legs from spreading apart, they needed to be stabilized at their base. Arched bridges, for example, were grounded in the earth or had solid concrete foundations. Domes, generated by spinning an arch on its vertical axis, had long incorporated this basic principle. Large dams and tunnels fought against enormous weights and pressures by relying on the arch concept. European cathedrals used arches to support their monumental spires and vaults. In addition to its graceful form, an arch conveyed dynamic energy, for the two sides are in constant thrust against each other. As an old Muslim proverb put it, "the arch never sleeps." While most arches since antiquity were part of larger structures, the Roman triumphal arch was among the first freestanding types. That so many Roman examples survived into the twentieth century proved their durability.[6]

Arches come in many shapes and sizes. Parabolic arches are round, almost semi-circles resembling a rainbow, while catenary (Latin, *catena*, meaning chain) arches are steeper, their structure resembling an inverted chain hanging between two points. All arches, however, share some common traits: they are familiar forms that resist gravity and differentiate space.

In considering an enormous arch, Eero drew upon examples he had seen in Europe. The dirigible hangars of reinforced concrete in Orly, France, designed by the French engineer Eugène Freyssinet were 150 feet tall and over 900 feet in length, providing a massive interior space for the airships. The Orly hangars gave Saarinen a sense of the "monumentality" the form might achieve. Modernist pioneer Le Corbusier had employed a monumental parabolic arch to support an auditorium he had submitted for a competition in the Soviet Union in 1931. "All these things came to one's mind,"

Saarinen recalled, "when we struggled to make an arch made out of pipe cleaners stand upright on the plan on the living room rug."[7]

While Freyssinet's hangars were an engineering marvel, the noted French architect Auguste Perret argued that the structure lacked critical elements: "The arch, in the form of a catenary or a parabola, has not been destroyed; you see their purpose right away.... But is this Architecture? No! Not yet! Here is the work of a great engineer, not of an architect." For the Orly hangars to become architecture, Perret insisted, required "Scale, Proportion, Harmony, and Humanity."[8]

Saarinen's challenge was to bring those qualities to a monumental arch in St. Louis. But complex questions remained. How might scale and proportion be achieved with a single, self-supporting arch? How would it harmonize with its stark surroundings? The ultimate question concerned Perret's last requirement: how could a monumental arch invoke human emotions? Before he could address those questions, Saarinen had to settle some basic issues. He considered placing one leg of an arch on the riverfront and the other across the river in East St. Louis. While that approach would symbolically tie the two cities together, Saarinen concluded that "there seemed to be enough bridges, and placing a symbolic bridge between two useful bridges didn't seem right." He considered placing both legs in the river, parallel to the levee, before finally returning to placing the entire arch on the riverfront parallel to the levee. He found the symbolism powerful: "it seemed like sort of a modern adaptation of a Roman triumphal arch." Remarkably, Saarinen assumed that at some point the arch would be replaced in his design by another form. For the time being, he "decided to just keep the arch and go on to the other problems of the competition."[9]

Had Saarinen continued with a concrete arch, it certainly would not have been as beautiful, and weathering would have soon streaked and aged the concrete before the inevitable cracks formed. He knew that the aesthetics of the arch exterior were paramount in winning over the jury. For the design to be as bold and striking as he hoped, concrete could serve as the core of the structure, but the skin would need to be some thinner, more lightweight, elegant, and permanent material.

Throughout the summer of 1947, Saarinen went through reams of paper drawing various versions of his arch, constantly redefining the curve and taper. While the act of drawing helped him conceive the entire project, drawings were not the only way he formulated ideas. He often turned to model maker James Smith to help him visualize the project in three dimensions. Initially, the living memorial ran parallel to the memorial arch, and the center of the arch did not frame the Old Courthouse. After seeing an early model, Saarinen said "the arch looked dreamy and forgotten on the levy," and he decided the location needed to be moved westward. "Here it could make a strong axial relation with the handsome, historic Old Courthouse which it frames." From this "summit," visitors "could confront the magnificent river." The arch would dominate the local buildings, a relation he considered "essential as an approach to a vertical monument." He also felt the living memorial "competed" with the Arch and moved it, for the time, to a perpendicular position. Later he would put it underground.[10]

At this early point, Saarinen was more excited about other aspects of the project than the monumental arch. He became preoccupied with designing the landscape, growing "quite enthusiastic about covering as much of the site as possible with a dense forest, because we had heard many people complain about the heat in St. Louis in the summer." For a time, he thought that a large, wooded area might serve as the memorial itself, and admitted that as his thinking evolved on the St. Louis riverfront, "we were so enthusiastic about this that we wondered whether our chances in the competition could not be greater if we forgot about the arch and just emphasized a great forest." This impulse was in keeping with other modernist concepts of memorial architecture. Frank Lloyd Wright, criticizing the "bureaucratic architecture" of Washington, D.C., had asked in 1937: "O Government, if you cannot yet learn how to say 'honor' to your bravest and best with true significance and grace as architecture, then say it with green space, noble trees, and splendid masses of verdue and bloom."[11]

In early summer, Saarinen came to St. Louis prepared to settle on his wooded area as the central motif of his entire design. It would certainly present a scene far different than the warehouses and buildings that had long stood on the site for so long, and was quite an improvement over the gravel parking lot. But after arriving at the Park Plaza Hotel in Forest Park and strolling onto a wooded area on the land of an adjacent home, Saarinen realized that "a tree-shaded park alone would be fine for the local people, but for a national memorial to Jefferson and the westward expansion, there had to be some high monument that people could see when they approached by car, could take pictures of, and could learn about in grade school." The memorial required something that commanded the eye and impressed travelers even miles away. And there was, for the time being, a more essential constituency: it had to impress the jury. The experience of seeing St. Louis and the riverfront firsthand allowed Saarinen to settle on a monumental arch. He later said that the form best represented Jefferson: "A monument to him should not be something solid and static but something open—a gateway for wider vistas—because one of his many great qualities was the ability to look toward the future."[12]

Saarinen began shaping the other components required by the program. He envisioned using a sunken area below the memorial plaza for a sculpture garden. His wife, Lily, a sculptor, conceived an area in which large sculptures would depict the westward movement.

"I haven't really had a chance to draw this up carefully," Eero wrote, "but I think it has real possibilities." The garden would "give us the chance to place sculpture in a human way so that people have the patience to look at it." Still, he was worried that the sculpture garden might utilize too much space and leave "the forest part too thin." As the project evolved, Lily's sculpture garden lost out to other ideas.[13]

By late summer, Saarinen and his collaborators—Kiley, Lily, illustrator J. Henderson Barr, and designer Alexander Girard—began work on the two murals that comprised their official entry. Saarinen spent hours determining the exact curve and shape of the arch itself. His first efforts looked like a semicircle, but Saarinen thought it resembled a rainbow and tossed it aside. He started sketching a higher pointed and tapered arch, but decided it seemed "too ecclesiastical." His first-round entry presented a sleek, parabolic curve that lacked the inspirational character of the finished form. As colleagues and friends stopped by the studio to watch as the design unfolded, they interpreted the early drawings of an arch as a "gateway," and in time called it "the Gateway to the West."[14]

Saarinen understood from the very beginning that the St. Louis memorial offered a chance to go beyond the typical heroic memorials dotting Washington, D.C., and achieve a truly inspirational design incorporating modern sculpture. Greatness seemed implicit, as the words "triumphal" and "arch" often went hand in hand. Monuments are symbolic of a time and place, and the St. Louis riverfront in the aftermath of World War II presented some remarkable opportunities for the right memorial to demonstrate America's new global dominance and sense of economic and technological self-confidence. In ways that seem obvious today, Saarinen captured the moment beautifully. His arch defined its time and would seem out of place a century earlier or even just decades later.

The design of the arch also allowed Saarinen to experiment with a concept vital to much of his architecture. A breathtaking aspect of the tapered arch is that it seems to soar, to be rising out of the ground and toward the sky. "In a way," he wrote, architecture is ultimately "man's desire to conquer gravity. All the time one works, one concerns oneself with the fight against gravity." Central to Saarinen was the understanding that "everything tends to be too heavy and downward pressing unless one really works at it."[15] In the weeks leading up to the September deadline, he labored to find the precise shape that communicated this sense of triumph over gravity.

As a professional architect familiar with the need to please his clients, Saarinen knew that to win the competition, he had to offer more than simply the best overall concept. He must understand the members of the jury and anticipate their preferences, and he knew the importance of presentation. This made J. Henderson Barr his most crucial collaborator. Saarinen was aware that George Howe had come originally from the Beaux-Arts tradition, and he wanted Barr to produce a beautiful drawing that went far beyond the usual monochromatic entries and emphasized pastels and shadows. Few other entries submitted in St. Louis incorporated such attention to the presentation drawings themselves. Growing more confident of his chances as the project neared completion, Saarinen even began considering how to distribute the prize money. He himself deserved 80 percent, he concluded, and the remainder should be divided equally among his four collaborators.[16]

By August, Barr's stunning finished drawings displayed a four-sided stainless steel arch rising nearly six hundred feet above the Mississippi River. A wide plaza walkway extended from the Old Courthouse to the memorial grounds, connecting the city to the riverfront. Rows of trees served as medians for the highways located below the plaza. After submitting his entry, Saarinen worked the architectural grapevine for any rumors regarding the competition. He enlisted Kiley to find out what he could about the other competitors, a task that irked Kiley. "Tragedy, I was his spy," he later lamented.

Yet the more Saarinen heard, the more despondent he became about his chances. Early gossip implied that his design would finish no better than nineteenth. A dejected Saarinen wrote to Kiley in early September that all was lost. "I have definitely decided that we don't have a Chinaman's chance with our dead memorial. It was loads of fun, anyway." Shortly afterward, he traveled to Harvard where he attended a party with a number of prominent architects. Discussion quickly turned to the St. Louis competition and the other entrants began sharing their design schemes. "After seeing them I felt just a little more encouraged about our chances," Saarinen confided to Kiley, adding that Walter Gropius, founder of the Architects' Collaborative, "was quite impressed by the arch."[17]

Even as the entries arrived in St. Louis, an idea was suggested that reflected a very different history from the one being celebrated by the Jefferson National Memorial. David M. Grant, president of the St. Louis NAACP, noted that the world knew of the brilliance of the blues that came from the city's taverns and street corners. Grant asked, "What trophy has the city awarded the creator" of the "St. Louis Blues," W. C. Handy? He proposed a different memorial: "On the cobble-stoned levee of the very riverfront we now seek to beautify came the inspiration. Weary, stranded and forlorn, says the composer, he slept on that levee and through that melancholy experience conceived and wrote the significant words of the tune's first line, namely, 'I hate to see that evening sun go down.'" JNEMA Chairman Edward Dail guardedly offered to "give consideration" to Grant's suggestion, but ultimately decided that the riverfront memorial was not the appropriate place to honor Handy or the blues. It would be another sixty-five years before Grant's idea was reconsidered.[18]

The jury convened on September 23, 1947, to begin reviewing the 172 submissions. On the first day, they were able to eliminate sixty-two entries. Those refusing to follow the jury's guidelines were tossed aside, as well as those that clearly did not meet its design standards. The jury deliberated on the remaining 110 entries and made notes on their initial impressions. William Wurster, taking a break from the competition to speak to the St. Louis Architectural Society, noted that "when we think of the amount of work that has gone into them, we hesitate to put any aside," but added they were progressing in paring down the entries. When the jury came to #144, they listed its "good points": "imaginative and exciting monumental arch—an abstract form peculiarly happy in its symbolism." Among its "undesirable points" was one that showed how fortunate Saarinen's decision had been to drop the wooded area as the central motif. Even so, the design was: "perhaps too heavily wooded for use or successful maintenance."

By September 25, the jurors reduced the remaining number to fifteen. On the 26th, the jurors used ballots to mark their choices for the five finalists. When the ballots were opened, #144 was listed by five of the seven jurors, putting it momentarily in first place. On successive votes, a sixth juror included #144 to his list, but it did not remain at the top of the list. On just the second vote, entry #41 leapt from four ballots to all seven. That entry came from someone with as much experience rethinking the St. Louis riverfront as anyone—Harris Armstrong. On the fifth and final ballot, Armstrong led the field with seven votes, while Saarinen and two other entries received six. When a fifth juror selected #64, the five finalists had been chosen. In addition to Saarinen and Armstrong, the other finalists were a team of graduate students at the University of Illinois, William Eng, Gordon Phillips, and George Foster; a team led by T. Marshall Rainey and John F. Kirkpatrick of Cleveland; and a team headed by Caleb Hornbostel of New York.[19]

When the JNEMA went about the task of informing the five finalists of the good news, a casual slip by a staff member created one of the more remarkable moments of the competition. A congratulatory telegram was sent to Eliel Saarinen, not Eero. Champagne corks popped at the office of Saarinen and Saarinen, and for hours the family toasted Eliel and his grand accomplishment. When Howe learned of the mistake, he immediately sent Eero a telegram advising him that he, not his father, had been selected as a finalist. Eliel graciously took the news in stride, and congratulated his son and opened a new bottle of Champagne. (Eliel, incidentally, received two votes from the jury for his scheme, an austere, four-pronged monument along the memorial plaza and a redesigned harbor on the east side.) Lily remembered Eliel being happy on two counts— "he'd come that close and his son had come first." For Eero, she knew this was a watershed moment in his life. For the ambitious young architect, the good news from St. Louis was "exactly what he needed."[20]

The list of those not making the cut included some of the most respected names in architecture, among them Louis Kahn, Edward Durell Stone, Gropius and the Architects' Collaborative, the prominent firm of Skidmore, Owings, and Merrill, a young Minoru Yamasaki, the future designer of the World Trade Center, and Saarinen's friends Harry Weese and Charles Eames.

Viewed in the aggregate, the entries must have been a considerable disappointment to the jurors, who had boldly given free rein to the applicants' imagination. Except for Saarinen's arch, none of the entries presented any central monument that struck the eye or moved the heart. *Architectural Forum* editorialized that "the conclusion seems inescapable that American architects are uncomfortable and unsteady on projects of this scale." The magazine found two reasons behind the essential "timidity" of the first-round entries. Most of the architects in the competition had never worked on "anything larger than a single house," and the jury itself had proposed a scheme that was far too complicated and involved city planning rather than strictly design. Despite the magazine's criticisms, the jury's ambitious schemes reflected a modernist concept ripe for the postwar environment. In 1946, Le Corbusier, who had described American architecture a decade earlier as reflecting "a country of timid people," made the pronouncement that "city planning and architecture are inseparable from one another, they make up a single phenomenon." No one could accuse the St. Louis jurors of timidity. The jurors expressed the hope that in the second round, "each of these preliminary offerings may be violently revamped."[21]

Harris Armstrong, whose design was the only one listed on every juror's list, became Saarinen's primary competitor. A graduate of Washington University, Armstrong had worked with Raymond Hood in New York before moving back to St. Louis, where he became known for his modernist designs. His entry called for a massive concrete inlet that reconfigured the levee as a plow would open the soil. The jury commented that Armstrong's plan was unique in its "austerity," which "would mark it as a monument amidst the natural turmoil of commerce." Armstrong incorporated some of his 1944 plans, such as the underground highways and the uninterrupted view of the river, into his first-round entry. He also thought the opposite riverbank was crucial in developing an overall plan and, perhaps remembering some of the failed early ideals for the riverfront site, had designed an airport for the riverfront in East St. Louis. The jury's comments on Armstrong's plan indicated they liked the "general distribution of the elements" and the "retention of broad open spaces adjacent to the levee." Not all of the comments were favorable. Another jury member considered "cutting into the levee" a distinct "undesirable point," and felt the axis to the courthouse was "exaggeratedly choked down." Still, one juror was completely taken with Armstrong's approach—"the use of the plow and furrow as a monument seems highly poetic." His proposal seemed most impressive from the sky, rather than the ground vantage point of pedestrians or motorists.[22]

The juror who did not list #144 on his ballot was probably S. Herbert Hare, who worried "whether the arch suggested is practical." Hare seemed more inclined toward Armstrong's plan, which "indicates a person who might, on further study, produce a very interesting result." Another juror thought Saarinen's "was easily the most facile" design in the lot, but noted that while "the great parabolic arch is impressive in conception and scale, its ultimate realization" remained doubtful. Still another juror noted that #144 "seems to be beautiful and relevant," but budget limitations "would require a reduction in size." One seemingly insignificant aspect of Saarinen's concept was noted: "The pedestrian foot-bridges across Third Street seem good and tie the area into the life of the city perhaps better than any other entry." That sense of tying the memorial grounds to the city would soon be discarded, much to the city's regret years later.[23]

At this crucial moment in the competition, the rules established by Howe and the jury played to Saarinen's advantage. In many architectural contests, the first round is the only round, and had that been the case in St. Louis, Harris Armstrong would have won and the city's riverfront would now look very different. But Howe's jury mandated a second round of the five finalists, and competitors and jurors alike were influenced by the process of the first round. While the jurors wrote the initial program based on some consensus about what they expected of the competitors, the act of scrutinizing the entries and seeing what might become a reality on the riverfront altered their thinking. Their disappointment with the overall quality of the first-round entries, though unstated at the time, affected how they would conduct the second round. They could not, of course, convey their opinions or internal discussions directly to the contestants. But Howe attached an addendum to the original program that expressed how the jury wanted to shape the final submissions. The jury hoped the addendum's not-so-subtle hints would produce a striking plan to rescue the competition from the relative mediocrity of the first round.

The addendum stressed that the jury realized how the first round's numerous requirements played a role in diminishing the architects' vision. The second stage would therefore be more limited. The architects could no longer casually place new office buildings outside the historic site but must confine their sketches to the area the JNEMA controlled. Moreover, the living memorial, the helicopter landing pad, railroad terminals, and various other first-round elements were eliminated.[24]

The memorial itself could be placed anywhere on the site, but the other buildings "should be placed near its boundaries rather than toward the centre." After seeing the strength of the memorial designs, especially Saarinen's arch, the jury wanted the finalists to direct their energies toward the memorial itself. Howe's suggestions also reflected the perspective of the NPS, which "wishes to have the site treated as a park with buildings inconspicuously distributed in it rather than as an architectural composition surrounded by a park." In clear words, the memorial was central: "The Architectural Memorial is to be conceived as a striking element, not only to be seen from a distance in the landscape but also as a notable structure to be remembered and commented on as one of the conspicuous monuments of the country. Its purpose should be to attract the interest of the multitude as well as that of the connoisseur of art."

The addendum forced Saarinen to scale back his entry. He dropped a high-rise building at the south end of the project as well as the living memorial. But in large part the addendum was an affirmation of his approach. In words that seemed directed to Saarinen, Howe's addendum concluded that the memorial "is to be essentially nonfunctional, though its interior, if any, may of course be accessible."[25] If anything convinced Saarinen he should focus on the arch in the second phase of the competition, Howe's input did it.

Saarinen paid little attention to Howe's request that the finalists' anonymity be maintained. He informed selected friends, such as Yamasaki, of the jury's decision, and tried to learn all he could about his competitors and their designs. He was not shy about inquiring of his friends how they approached the riverfront challenges, writing to Louis Kahn: "I understand that you know through the grapevine the deep secret that we are in the finals. Do you have photos of your scheme? I'd really like to see it terribly much. It sounded very good from what I heard on the telephone. Being out here in the sticks, I haven't seen anyone else's scheme and it would help in the finals to see what other solutions were." Saarinen concluded with "Sorry as hell you didn't get in. I sort of figured that you would." Kahn replied that his entry had "too many ideas" and that, unlike Saarinen, he had somehow forgotten the singular importance of "physical monumentality." He reported the rumor that the five finalists included Saarinen, "a student group" from an unknown university, and a St. Louis architect. Saarinen then embarked on a trip to New York and Philadelphia, to visit Kahn and Edward Durell Stone and study their losing entries. He found the process helpful: "I learned much."[26]

Even before the jury's final announcement, Saarinen informed his collaborators of his idea for distributing the prize money. He understood that "it might seem that we (meaning himself) are hogging most of the fee; and, in a way, we are." But, he wrote, "you have to think of a.) The greater gamble with time and money we took in the first competition; b.) The gamble we are taking in the second (it will probably cost us $5,000); c.) The other commitments to painters and sculptors (somewhat reduced), and d.) All our other work that will suffer by this mono-attention on the competition." Just a day after sending Kiley this explanation, Saarinen sent another note that displayed his enormous confidence. "It occurred to me," he wrote, "we were basing our agreement entirely on winning. Suppose we lose?" In that case, Saarinen said he should receive 90 percent of the reduced prize in order to cover expenses. As events unfolded, Kiley's and Lily Saarinen's growing irritation and resentment toward Eero's domination of the process only increased.[27]

After learning they were among the finalists, the five teams had eighteen weeks to rework their submissions. For the second round, Saarinen continued to rethink the arch, coming ever closer to the final plans:

> The great arch standing on the western bank of the Mississippi is to symbolize the gateway to the West, the natural expansion, and what not, which is all more or less to be symbolized as part of the JNEM. The arch was thought of as a stainless steel arch about 700 feet wide. For the second stage of the competition, we want to develop the arch further. This development might take the form of a somewhat more vertical arch (perhaps 20% shorter span and a little higher). It might be concrete, or it might be developed as a stainless steel box beam with an outer layer of stainless steel or whatever is the material that actually and symbolically is the most permanent.[28]

After dropping the ideas of a purely concrete structure, Saarinen had turned to a stainless steel outer skin. Since the turn of the century, steel, an alloy of carbon and iron, had become a vital material to architects and builders. Essential in the building of large skyscrapers, steel is relatively light, inexpensive, and remarkably strong, but when exposed to moisture, rusts quickly. In 1913, metallurgists found that adding a combination of chromium and nickel yields a different alloy, which does not rust easily and maintains a shimmering, silver appearance. It was called "stainless steel"—a somewhat misleading term—and would soon be used to make household items such as toasters and cooking utensils. With the notable exception of the Chrysler Building's spire in 1930, it had not been widely used in construction. Stainless steel seemed to present the perfect answer for the outer skin of the arch, but it had a major drawback: it was very expensive to mass produce. At this point in the competition Saarinen could not waste time worrying about costs. Stainless steel became indispensable to Saarinen's concept, and was sure to impress the jury.[29]

Saarinen's reading of Howe's addendum showed in his second-stage alterations. He kept the 590-foot arch standing alone on the eastern side of the plan, but moved it so that the center line of the arch framed the Old Courthouse. He also made one last significant change. In the first round, the sections of the arch were a four-sided trapezoid, which gave it a flat, uninspiring appearance. Before making his final submission, Saarinen dined with Carl Milles, a Cranbrook sculptor who had studied with Rodin. Milles convinced Saarinen that the cross-section should be an equilateral triangle. With this simple but profoundly important alteration, Saarinen's arch became more sleek and elegant. After making the final changes, he submitted his plans just before the February 3, 1948, deadline.[30]

More than the other finalists, Harris Armstrong altered his entire design concept after the first stage. Obviously, his plowed levee was neither "striking," nor visible "from a distance in the landscape" as called for in the addendum. Gone was the bold plow-like inlet. Instead, he opted for a more traditional approach utilizing a central memorial framed by wooded landscaping. For his memorial, he employed a large, concrete rectangle that had neither the monumentality nor the uniqueness of Saarinen's arch. In fact, it bore an unfortunate resemblance to a drive-in movie screen. *Architectural Forum* found it nothing more than a "slab" that "looks more like an office building than a tribute to the Pioneer Spirit." Armstrong's confident first-stage entry had morphed into a bland, almost formulaic solution, eliminating him from serious final consideration. But at least he attempted some form of "striking" memorial, which could not be said for the team headed by Rainey, which decided to address the memorial issue by omitting it entirely from their final design.[31]

To get maximum public attention for the second stage of the competition and the awarding of the top prize, some within the JNEMA leadership suggested asking Robert Moses, the country's most noted and powerful city planner, to come to St. Louis and perhaps, even to make the announcement. I. F. Boyd, Jr., underscored Moses's importance in "the selling job that needed to be done to the good citizens of St. Louis." Edward Dail asked Moses to come to the plains for the biggest day since the 1904 World's Fair. Yet the city was quickly put in its place by Moses's curt response. "I could not possibly do this because I know nothing at first hand" about the riverfront, Moses replied. "In any event, I am not an itinerant evangelist who goes about to awaken enthusiasm for City planning. . . . This sort of thing is not up my alley." Had Moses cared to study it, he might have found much to endorse in Harland Bartholomew's master plan. "Any solution to downtown congestion," Bartholomew wrote in his 1947 St. Louis City Plan, "must come from new thoroughfares." Like Moses, Bartholomew emphasized automobiles and highways over mass transit, while ignoring the negative impact of this approach on poor neighborhoods.[32]

Reconvening on Wednesday, February 18, 1948, the jury examined the five final entries and began what they assumed would be a long day of deliberation. Howe first suggested that a secret ballot be taken to see if any consensus already existed. At that point, William Wurster recalled, "something quite extraordinary happened." As the initial ballots were opened, it became clear the jury's work was already over. Entry #144 placed first on all seven ballots, whereupon the names were also opened and the jury learned who had won. Saarinen was telegraphed with word of the jury's decision; the $40,000 top prize was his.[33]

In their final report, the jury found Saarinen's second-stage entry to be "enriched and improved" from the first round, adding that the arch "is monumental in scale yet does not dwarf other structures." They called Saarinen's design "a work of genius," noting that the arch was "of that high order which will rank it among the nation's greatest monuments." Still, jurors could not mask their disappointment with Armstrong's final submission, as well as the other competitors. The memorial Armstrong proposed was little more than a "simple mass" whose only real attractive quality was that it "would stand clear of the existing structures on either river bank." In the final order, Armstrong was moved to the bottom of the list, winning a $2,500 "runner up" prize along with Rainey. Second place went to William Eng's new entry, which at least brought the memorial "from a minor to a major role." The accessibility of his scheme was also highlighted, because of its direct connection between the park and the Old Courthouse. Eng's work on the competition eventually took him from Illinois to Cranbrook, where he earned a master's in architecture working with Eliel Saarinen. In 1955, he joined Eero Saarinen's firm in Bloomfield Hills, where he stayed until 1960, when he returned to Urbana to teach. Caleb Hornbostel, who had won the 1938 Wheaton College Art Center competition over the Saarinens, received third prize.[34]

News of the jury's award catapulted Eero Saarinen to the top echelons of American architecture. The *Post-Dispatch* endorsed the design as a "distinctly original yet superbly simple landmark," adding that it represented "utility and beauty." President Truman declared himself satisfied that "Jefferson is to be so fittingly commemorated on the riverfront in St. Louis." Saarinen also received wide praise from his fellow architects. "Congratulations to a Great Architect" came from Louis Kahn. Hugh Stubbins wrote that the arch "was a brilliant solution" and noted, "when I saw your first preliminary I was quite certain you would be successful." "Ho hum again," wrote Edward Durell Stone, "congratulations on your prowess as an architect." Saarinen replied that Stone's own design "must have been close to getting in," but suggested its major drawback could have resided in its bland presentation: "it showed too much the marks of a charrette." The young architect felt justified in offering Stone some unsolicited advice: "For future reference, the rubber cement method you used to stick down the drawings seems to come through with time and discolor the paper."[35]

But many were not so taken with the idea of a large arch on the city's riverfront. A local self-described "gadget maker" grumbled that the Arch was nothing more than a "stupendous hairpin" and a "stainless steel hitching post whose beauty is unprintable." William Warren, a St. Louis real estate agent, failed to see the connection between Jefferson and "this grotesque monstrosity" paid for by the "New Deal–Fair Deal Big Spenders of Other People's Money." Proudly admitting he was not "up to date on my Modern and Futuristic Art," Warren worried about living "in the shadow of this Russian-drosky inspired" design, and asked the city to use the area for its "best and most useful purpose"—a car lot. H. J. Carroll asked now that "the experts have designed a riverfront beautiful, how about some practical designs for large groups of people to live in, not look at?" Carroll felt the proposed structure would only further anger the impoverished residents living and working along the riverfront—"it is like looking into a window, watching a chef turn pancakes, and drooling at the mouth with an empty stomach."[36]

Although the architectural community generally praised Saarinen's winning entry, many were unimpressed by the overall quality of the competition itself. *Architectural Forum* editorialized that "the generally diffident approach to monumentality apparent in these designs is too obvious to be ignored." In addition to blaming the inexperience of many of the young architects involved, the *Forum* saw a deeper problem. "The real memorials of our age have been not temples to the spirit, but monuments to utility."[37]

After *Time*, in a less than flattering story, observed that "some dissenters feared the city might come to be known as the 'Wicket City," Saarinen wrote to Mayor Kaufman that he hoped "the label 'The Wicket City' won't haunt you too much." *Newsweek*, in contrast, called the St. Louis architectural contest "remarkable." Predictably, Saarinen also received letters from strangers hoping to share in his newfound wealth. A Mrs. Stanley Swarmer noted that "it must feel great to have all the money you need" and asked for cash to buy fifty turkeys. The JNEMA office received nearly three hundred letters praising the selection of Saarinen's design, versus just fifteen that were critical. Letters to the editor of the St. Louis newspapers ranged from mildly encouraging to outright opposition. Walter Buffalo of Webster Groves put it succinctly: "a lot of slum clearance could be bought for what the stainless steel croquet wicket will cost." One thoroughly disgusted St. Louisan wrote to Mayor Kaufman that "you couldn't expect people to love that cold, naked piece of steel."[38]

A few saw the design's potential. "We are still breathless at the vision you have opened up for us by your marvelously fine design," Luther Ely Smith told Saarinen. He added, "The more we gaze upon it the more wonderful and gripping it grows." Charles E. Merriam, the vice chairman of the commission, issued one of the most ambitious appraisals of the nascent plan: "When the archeologists of 10,000 years, digging down through the deposits of the centuries when they excavate your memorial, will say 'Ah! This is America!'"[39]

Some commentators, assuming the Arch would follow a perfect catenary curve, reduced the design to a mathematical formula. Saarinen admitted to a Washington University engineer that math played but a small role in the final design: "The arch is actually not a true parabola, nor is it a catenary curve. We worked at first with the mathematical shapes, but finally adjusted it according to the eye." He added that he "suspected" a catenary arch "with links of the chain graded at the same proportion as the arch thins out would come very close to lines upon which we settled."[40]

Just days after the announcement, juror Charles Nagel, Jr., raised a problem that few others noticed. Third Street and the planned express highway were to be routed together past the memorial on its west side. In Nagel's estimation, no attention at all was given to how the routes would affect the memorial or its relation to the rest of the central city. The only concern seemed to be that local traffic not be impeded.[41] Many years would go by before anyone gave serious attention to Nagel's observations.

Despite these criticisms, the political and business leadership quickly adopted the Gateway Arch as the new identity of St. Louis, a development remarkable in its own right. It was one thing for a modernist jury to select Saarinen's entry. It was another for the city's leaders to support it. Their response was more than aesthetic: the revitalization of St. Louis as a great American city might hinge on the success or failure of the Arch to capture the civic imagination.[42]

The praise directed toward Saarinen ruffled a few feathers among his collaborators, including Dan Kiley. Saarinen wrote Kiley, "I'm getting pretty embarrassed seeing my name and picture in the papers," adding that "It must have bothered you a bit inside to see most of the publicity focused on my name and slurring over those of the associates." Kiley was not alone in feeling slighted. Lily remembered that "as long as he paid them," Eero "didn't think it was necessary to point out who did what." Saarinen's response did little to calm the tension: "All of us are a hell of a lot better off than if we had placed second or third."[43]

Worse than the critics, local and otherwise, who rejected modernist designs, a more serious attack came just days after the jury's announcement. New York landscape architect Gilmore D. Clarke noted that Saarinen's design looked eerily similar to a giant free-standing arch designed by Italian modernist Adalberto Libera (and aided by structural engineer and architect Pier Luigi Nervi) for a planned Rome Exposition in 1942. Rather than a monument to westward expansion, was Saarinen's Arch originally a Fascist shrine? One that glorified Mussolini rather than Jefferson? Immediately, a plagiarism crisis ensued that put both the Arch and Saarinen's career in jeopardy. Clarke wrote to William Wurster, the chairman of the jury, asking whether "it is appropriate to perpetuate the memory of Thomas Jefferson and to memorialize the Louisiana Purchase by constructing a monument similar in design to one originally created to glorify twenty years of fascism in Italy?" Wurster phoned Saarinen to warn him of the impending charges. Remarkably, Wurster felt it was not "pertinent" to ask Saarinen if he had seen Libera's arch. Saarinen nonetheless told Wurster he had never seen it nor was he even aware of it.[44]

In its final statement, Howe's jury noted that a monumental arch was not an original concept and explained how Saarinen's design resembled a sixth-century arch in a palace built by Chosroes the Great in modern-day Ctesiphon, Iraq. Saarinen himself dismissed Clarke's charges and thought the Italian design was nothing more than a coincidence. He acknowledged the widespread use of arches, including a 1938 proposal by Ladislav Rado for a parabolic arch to honor Tomáš Masaryk in Prague. In claiming he also had no prior knowledge of Rado's design, Saarinen said that Libera had no more claim to the form than anyone else. "Mussolini had spent most of his time portraying himself as a Roman emperor," Saarinen wrote, and many emperors built triumphal arches, and there was an American version in New York's Washington Square. When he first saw the Italian drawings, Saarinen admitted that he wondered "whose was whose?" Both designs were 590 feet tall, and Libera's arch was to be clad in shiny aluminum which looked similar to Saarinen's stainless steel. But Libera's arch was the kind of semicircular rainbow Saarinen had rejected from the start. Although Libera and Saarinen both used a four-sided arch at the beginning, Saarinen altered his version to a three-sided form after advice from sculptor Milles. Hoping to end the public discussion, Saarinen said simply, "The fact that Fascist Italy came so close to using a somewhat similar shape to the one we proposed for St. Louis does not really bother me, and I hope it won't bother anyone else."[45]

Yet the controversy would not go away, and attorneys representing Libera threatened to file suit. Libera claimed his design was known as "the gateway to the sea," and that Saarinen had violated Libera's rights by not adequately citing his design. Libera, while "not disregarding the financial aspects of the question," hoped that his claims could be settled "amicably," noting that he was "chiefly interested in an acknowledgment of his creative priority." Saarinen, realizing his early attempts to dismiss the episode had failed, fired back at his critics. "The Egyptian obelisks were built by slaves and the same form was used for the Washington Monument," he noted. "I suppose Mr. Clarke wants to tear that down?" Saarinen's lawyer responded that while Saarinen had "a great deal of respect for the work of Mr. Libera," he had not stolen any part of Libera's design. The use of the arch, he noted, "has so many precedents that any claim to protection of its use is without foundation."[46] Saarinen's acknowledgment of the form's universality should be considered when he is today given singular credit for the concept of a free-standing monumental arch.

Libera never filed the suit, and no evidence exists that suggests Saarinen stole the concept from Libera. But for some, the resemblance of the two arches was no coincidence. "A monument to extol the virtues and greatness of Jefferson ought not to be symbolized by a design originally intended to glorify Fascism," wrote one St.

Louisan to Smith. The competition jury released a statement claiming that "it is a matter for congratulation that the related example proposed in Rome was not built, and that it is left for us in this country to make the first great commemorative monument in this beautiful and inspiring form." Saarinen confided to Hugh Ferriss that the controversy may have had a beneficial effect on the project, because "St. Louis needs as much publicity as possible in order to increase the hope of getting it through Congress." Although Libera's and Saarinen's arches were different aesthetically, they shared one unmistakable similarity that could not be ignored. Both concepts were triumphant nationalist statements, a factor that had impressed many emperors and dictators.[47]

Soon after winning the competition, Saarinen returned to St. Louis, where he basked in his triumph. "St. Louis wanted a monument with national impact, a monument that would rank with those to Washington and Lincoln," he wrote. "A monument to Thomas Jefferson and the westward expansion on their strategic historical site seemed to call for a symbolic form of heroic size and great simplicity. Such a symbol should be made of a material that would last as long, or longer than, our civilization. The stainless steel arch seemed to us to carry the greatest meaning."[48]

But winning the competition, it turned out, was the easy part.

The St. Louis riverfront, looking northeast from the Old Courthouse, 1895. In this area where the Gateway Arch now stands, forty square blocks were eventually demolished, including numerous historic buildings. The area was prized by preservationists for its unique concentration of cast-iron structures. Missouri History Museum —St. Louis.

Luther Ely Smith, the St. Louis attorney who envisioned a grand memorial along the city's riverfront. Missouri History Museum —St. Louis.

Legendary architect Eliel and son Eero Saarinen at Hvittrask, Finland, 1919. Eero struggled his entire life to emerge from his father's shadow. They worked together on a number of major projects, but submitted separate entries for the St. Louis competition in 1947. When the finalists were announced, a congratulatory telegram was mistakenly sent to Eliel. Eero Saarinen Papers, Manuscripts and Archives, Yale University Library.

Shortly after graduating high school in 1929, Eero Saarinen studied in Paris, where he completed this sculpture. Saarinen had dreams of emulating his mother as a sculptor, but eventually gave way to his father's influence in becoming an architect. Sculpture remained an enduring factor in his popular furniture designs and many of his buildings, including the Gateway Arch. Eero Saarinen Papers, Manuscripts and Archives, Yale University Library.

During his European travels, Saarinen saw these dirigible hangars in Orly, France, designed by Eugène Freyssinet. They were among many examples Saarinen said were influential in his design of the Gateway Arch. Photothèque Association Eugène Freyssinet.

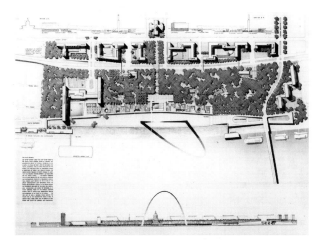

Eero Saarinen's first-round entry in the St. Louis competition, 1947. A plaza for pedestrians extends from the Old Courthouse to the Arch and covers the Third Street highways. Cluttered throughout the plan are elements Saarinen soon discarded, such as a sculpture garden and a helicopter landing pad. When he submitted his final entry in February 1948, Saarinen moved the center line of the Arch in order to frame the courthouse. Here, the arch is four-sided and parabolic. He changed the shape and curve to a three-sided and soaring catenary arch after conferring with Carl Milles, a sculptor who had studied with Rodin. Eero Saarinen Papers, Manuscripts and Archives, Yale University Library.

Had the Jefferson National Expansion Memorial competition been limited to one round, this is how the St. Louis riverfront might have looked. St. Louis modernist architect Harris Armstrong had the only entry selected by all seven jurors after the first round (Saarinen's plan received six votes). Armstrong reconfigured the levee, resembling a plow opening the soil. Realizing the plan would have little visual impact except from the air and lacking a "striking" memorial design, he scrapped this idea in the second round for a large rectangular block as a central motif. Harris Armstrong Papers, University Archives, Department of Special Collections, Washington University Libraries.

After winning the competition in February 1948, Saarinen accepts the $40,000 check from juror William Wurster, dean of architecture at MIT. His collaborators, from left, J. Henderson Barr, Alexander Girard, Dan Kiley, and wife Lilian Swann Saarinen. Eero Saarinen Papers, Manuscripts and Archives, Yale University Library.

ROMA 1942 XX
ESPOSIZIONE VNIVERSALE

Just days after winning the St. Louis competition, Saarinen was accused of stealing his design from Italian architect Adalberto Libera, who had proposed this giant arch for the 1942 Rome Exposition. Although the charge was never substantiated, the fact that such a form had been proposed as a Fascist symbol dogged Saarinen, and pointed to the differing ways such a nationalistic expression could be used. Courtesy of EUR S.p.A.

After the demolition of hundreds of buildings between 1939 and 1941, city and national leaders struggled to fund the memorial project. Alternative plans, such as a football stadium and a landing strip, were proposed. When those fell through, the area became a municipal parking lot. Eero Saarinen Papers, Manuscripts and Archives, Yale University Library.

An example of Eero Saarinen's "mirror writing," a rare trait he shared with Leonardo da Vinci. Eero Saarinen Papers, Manuscripts and Archives, Yale University Library.

With no harnesses and just a safety net under these welders, the Arch was a dangerous work site. Despite underwriters' fears of a dozen deaths on the project, there were no fatalities during construction. Arthur Witman Photographic Collection, State Historical Society of Missouri Research Center—St. Louis.

"Topping Out" Day, October 28, 1965. The north creeper derrick (right) lifts the final section into place. The strut to support the weight of the derricks is below. Arthur Witman Photographic Collection, State Historical Society of Missouri Research Center —St. Louis.

First envisioned by planners as a modern necessity, the bi-level highways sever the city from the memorial grounds (left). St. Louis officials have tried for nearly fifty years to correct what one Interior Secretary termed "the worst entry to a national park property." Author photo.

In 2011, Michael Van Valkenburgh Associates won the competition to renovate the Arch grounds. This drawing depicts the "Park Over the Highway" that will reconnect the Arch to the city. CityArchRiver 2015 Foundation/ MVVA.

FIVE

The Architect

Eero Saarinen, ca. 1948. Eero Saarinen Papers, Manuscripts and Archives,
Yale University Library.

Winning the St. Louis competition brought Eero Saarinen a level of fame that few architects achieve. In the mid-1950s, he was featured in *Vogue* and on the cover of *Time*. Describing him as emblematic of "The Maturing Modern," *Time* noted that no American architect "has a better proportioned combination of imagination, versatility, and good sense."[1] It was a heady moment to be at the forefront of American architecture, when modern technology promised to transport middle-class suburbanites into a futuristic world of streamlined cars on thousands of miles of fast-moving expressways. Modern homes boasted gleaming new appliances, and the booming post-war economy was ready and able to bankroll this prosperity. The "American Century" (a name conferred by *Time* publisher Henry Luce) unleashed stunning new expressions of power and confidence, and Eero Saarinen emerged as a leader of this brilliant new built environment.

Saarinen's public persona, however, concealed an insecure and narcissistic personality that led one sociologist who interviewed him to detect "psychopathic" tendencies. Form and function, design and structure so filtered into his personal life that he even examined women the way he might consider the pitch of a roof or the curve of a wall. Just as a building does not exist in a vacuum, neither does the architect. Saarinen had his fair share of personal and professional demons and was desperate to be more than his father's son. The Gateway Arch represented his first major opportunity to establish his own identity and reputation.

Eero Saarinen seemed destined to be a renowned architect. His father, Eliel, was one of the best known Finnish architects of his day. With his partners Herman Gesellius and Armas Lindgren, Eliel had built a thriving firm that won a national competition to design the Finnish Pavilion in the 1900 World's Fair in Paris as well as the Helsinki Central Railway station. The three partners designed a sprawling thirty-eight-room house twenty miles outside Helsinki where they lived and worked. They called the house-studio Hvittrask, meaning "White Lake." During the building of Hvittrask, Eliel divorced his first wife, Mathilda Gylden, and married Gesellius's sister, a sculptor named Loja, in March 1904. Their years in Hvittrask were filled with constant activity: Loja designed crafts while Eliel and his staff busied themselves at drafting tables in a ninety-foot-long living room that served as a studio. In 1905, the Saarinens welcomed their first child, a daughter they named Pipsan. Eero was born five years later, on August 20, 1910. For the son whose father loomed so large in his life, it was somehow fitting that he shared Eliel's birthday.

As children, Pipsan and Eero grew accustomed to the eclectic gatherings of artists, designers, intellectuals, and architects working in Hvittrask. Eero played amid blueprints and architectural models, and spent many hours drawing beneath his father's drafting table. He remembered: "I would always draw and I happened to be good at it. Therefore, I got more attention from drawing than anything else." Eliel and Loja meanwhile hosted luminaries including Maxim Gorky, Jean Sibelius, and Gustav Mahler.[2]

Eliel established his reputation in the United States through a major competition, finishing second in the international Chicago Tribune Tower contest in 1922. Some critics have suggested his design had a much greater influence on future skyscrapers than the forgettable first-place entry. Louis Sullivan, a judge on the Chicago panel, wrote that Eliel's tower was from "a voice, resonant and rich, ringing amidst the wealth and joy of life." In 1923, Eliel used the runner-up prize of $20,000 to move his family to the United States, where he taught at the University of Michigan. His reputation drew the attention of newspaper magnate George Gough Booth, one of the country's most acclaimed art patrons, who hired Eliel to convert his estate in the Detroit suburb of Bloomfield Hills into an artistic community called the Cranbrook Academy. Hoping to make Cranbrook the American equivalent of Bauhaus, where students were encouraged to think anew about all artistic concepts, he asked Eliel to run it. In 1927, Eliel moved his family to Cranbrook, where Eero, then in his teens, became part of a milieu that profoundly shaped his life and career.[3]

The modernism that pervaded Cranbrook is difficult to define beyond Ezra Pound's declaration to "Make It New!" Starting in the late nineteenth century and exploding on the scene shortly before World War I, a host of revolutionary voices and visions emerged in art, literature, and music. Picasso, van Gogh, Matisse, Mahler, Woolf, Eliot, Joyce, and so many others were united in what Peter Gay has called the "lure of heresy" and a rejection of traditional artistic and literary concepts. In architecture that impulse was especially powerful, and Le Corbusier, Mies van der Rohe, and Frank Lloyd Wright were among the leaders of the movement against the conventional neoclassical principles taught in the Ecole des Beaux-Arts. "What is 'modern'?" asked Wright in 1930. "The answer is *Power!*" and modernist design was "power applied directly to purpose in buildings." Modernist architecture had no use for ornamentation and was born, in Wright's estimation, "out of the heart of Man, permanent consort to the ground, comrade to the trees, and a true reflection of Man in the realm of his own spirit."[4]

While Eliel worked to build Cranbrook, young Eero soaked up the modernist design philosophies. Eero attended public high school in nearby Birmingham, Michigan, and struggled to overcome his poor English and social awkwardness. (He later asserted that his parents were "foolish" to enroll him in "an ordinary school" considering his precocious artistic abilities.) He described himself in these years as "pompous, awkward, and conceited," yet handicapped by "an inferiority feeling about my family" as immigrants. His high school yearbook records Eero's first-place finish in a national soap carving contest. The sculpture, titled "Sorrow," was eventually cast in bronze and featured on a national tour. His "heroes" as a teen-ager are revealing: Oscar Wilde (who said his life's mission was to make the world love beauty), Michelangelo, Leonardo da Vinci, and Machiavelli.[5]

In 1929, after graduating from high school, Eero attended art school at the Académie de la Grande Chaumière in Paris, where he spent eight months studying sculpture. He loved sculpting, but felt the heavy influence of his father. "My parents," he said later, "felt I would be an architect." Eero gravitated toward emerging modernist designers, such as Le Corbusier and Mies, yet Le Corbusier was a vocal critic of Cranbrook, sneering that the academy "is all a little farfetched, somewhat cut off from life," and questioning the school's leadership in modernist design. The Bloomfield Hills crowd, he added, was "an outpouring of self, a convent, a monkery."[6]

When Eero returned home, he worked in another area that blended his love of sculpture and architecture, designing much of the furniture for the Cranbrook Kingswood School for Girls (over the years, various boarding schools were built at Cranbrook, and alumni include Daniel Ellsberg and Mitt Romney). Eero thrived at Cranbrook, living and working with his family and a coterie of artists in a way that had greatly resembled Hvittrask. Yet the time approached for him to seek his own path.

In January 1931, Eliel wrote to Everett Victor Meeks, Dean of Fine Arts at Yale, to see if Eero could enroll as a "special student," who could take classes for two or three years without working to-ward a degree. Meeks responded that Eliel's "boy" was accepted to the architecture school, and Eero enrolled that fall. Eero remem-bered that in selecting a profession, "it never occurred to me to do anything but follow in my father's footsteps and become an archi-tect." Unlike Cranbrook, Yale in the 1930s was not the ideal place for a young modernist. *Time* described the Beaux Arts architecture school as "almost untouched by modern architecture." Eero developed the ability to please his professors with styles that matched the situation. He won first prizes from the Beaux Arts Institute of Design in New York for such projects as "A Palace for an Exiled Monarch," and "A Monumental Clock." In his first year, he won the school's Spiering Prize for a memorial tunnel that displayed some of the concepts he later used on the Gateway Arch. His drawing cut back huge blocks of a mountain, producing, in the words of the prize judges, "an approach monumental though primitive in character." He sailed through courses in architectural history and theory, mathematics, structure, and construction, and art classes in watercolor and drawing. His thesis project, a design for a technological institute, supervised by Raymond Hood (who, along with John Mead Howells, had won the Chicago Tribune competition over Eliel), received a silver medal from the Société des Architectes Diplômés par le Gouvernement Français.

Despite his status as a "special student," at the end of three years Yale awarded Eero a bachelor of fine arts degree with honors. He won numerous scholarly prizes including the prestigious Charles O. Matchum fellowship, which allowed him to travel and study in Europe. Yet he lamented he had no opportunities to study outside the professional architecture curriculum and later insisted that "I did not go to college." But his time at Yale had some redeeming features: it was the "first time I saw myself as having talent," as well as being the "first time I was independent of my father."[7]

With support from the Matchum fellowship, Eero spent the next two years traveling in Italy, France, Finland, Germany, Greece, Hungary, and Sweden. While fascinated with the modernist structures, he was also impressed by the Gothic cathedrals. "Gothic," he later wrote, "is the greatest example of all things combined into one great thing: great engineering, but at the same time great form, great knowledge, great scale, great everything."[8]

Eero returned to Cranbrook in 1936 to teach city planning.

Though tied in many ways to Eliel, he managed to find time to explore other avenues of design. In 1938, he went to New York City to work briefly for industrial designer Norman Bel Geddes. At the time, Bel Geddes was working on a project for the upcoming New York World's Fair. Known as "Futurama," the exhibit, housed in the General Motors Pavilion, displayed an automobile-centered future, complete with express highways and sprawling suburbs. Ironically, the exhibit was based on how St. Louis was projected to look in 1960.[9]

Shortly after his return to Cranbrook, Saarinen met Lilian Swann, a young ceramics student from Long Island. Lilian, or Lily, studied sculpture with Carl Milles and had been a member of the U.S. ski team that had competed at the 1936 Olympics. The two began seeing each other, and more than anything else, Lily said she was impressed by his "seriousness." "He was listening to the news constantly," she recalled. "He was so serious listening to it that I liked it, because I always liked seriousness. . . . I was sort of in awe of him." There was much in the news to be serious about in the late 1930s as war was breaking out across Europe.[10]

Years later, he admitted that what impressed him most about Lily was her "social background," especially her well-connected family. Lily's great-grandfather had been a founder of New York's Metropolitan Museum of Art. "It seemed from an opportunist point of view like an enviable setup to get into," Eero noted. By marrying a sculptor, Eero was again following in his father's footsteps. He hoped that "by guidance and education" Lily "would grow up into quite a glamorous artist." But from the beginning, it was a rocky relationship. Lily told Eero that she vacillated between marrying him and never seeing him again. "I am just so torn between thinking the worst of you and thinking the best about our being together." Her doubts were sown by Eero's erratic and clumsy efforts to assert control, "the countless times you've come to my studio and ordered everyone out and for me to come to you." She called this an "un-American intolerance and jealousy and possessiveness which frightens me terribly." Eero, in turn, was disappointed that Lily's housekeeping "did not automatically become a tasteful, sophisticated thing."

Eero's jealous streak concerned Lily. "If you loved me," she wrote at one point, "and really felt I loved you, you would let me be me and trust me to love you." Eero worried especially about Lily's relationship with Harry Weese, a young architect at Cranbrook. Weese later admitted that a furious Eero once "found me in a bronze urn curled up with his wife-to-be," at which point Eero challenged Weese to a duel. After tempers receded, Lily recalled to Eero that he "held off talking to Harry for a long time, but never for a second did you let us alone." Despite the tension, Eero and Lily married on June 10, 1939, in Syosset, Long Island.[11]

Eero worked alongside his father in their Bloomfield Hills offices. Eliel taught him a valuable lesson: "In any design problem one should seek the solution in terms of the next largest thing. If the problem is an ashtray, then the way it relates to a table will influence the design." On a grander scale, the problem remained the same—"if it is a building, the townscape will affect the solution."[12] Among the many projects designed by the Saarinens, none gained more attention than their winning entry for a Smithsonian art gallery in Washington, D.C. The entry, primarily drawn by Eero, was a sleek main building with a windowless tower that was conspicuously different from anything else on the Mall. Its nontraditional approach proved too much for the Smithsonian board, which eventually rejected the design. Interestingly, one of the competition judges was George Howe.

In 1940, Eero became an American citizen, a moment for which he had waited seven years. After Pearl Harbor, a classmate from Yale recruited him to join the Presentation Division of the Office of Strategic Services, the forerunner of the CIA. Eero spent most of the war years in Washington, where he provided illustrations for army manuals and even drafted a proposal for the White House Situation Room.[13] In 1942, Lily gave birth to their first child, Eric, and to their daughter, Susan, three years later.

One day while taking a break from his wartime duties, Saarinen and two other architects toured the presidential monuments on the Mall. In looking at the structures, Saarinen's mind leapt to conceiving how he would design a "great national monument" if given the opportunity. While his colleagues focused on monuments as utilitarian structures, Saarinen suggested they consider a "pure monument," with no function other than to convey its own beauty and historical meaning. He was also struck by how the major monuments "each had a distinct geometric shape; the Washington monument, a vertical line; the Lincoln memorial, a cube; and the Jefferson memorial, a globe." Saarinen found these shapes "simple and satisfying."[14]

After the war, Eero returned to Bloomfield Hills with his family. While his professional career flourished, his marriage slowly deteriorated. Lily confided in her diary, "I've been trying terribly to understand why I am so unhappy." She sketched a daily routine that seems straight out of *Citizen Kane:*

> Each a.m. we wake up and he makes a few pat little remarks—
> we come down and read the paper then he starts to leave. If I
> had anything to say I would have been interrupting the paper,
> then interrupting and delaying his departure, which he thor-
> oughly dislikes. At lunch we meet amid all the art club and he
> usually talks shop with the office men. We part (if we sat to-
> gether) and he goes back to work till dinnertime. When he
> comes in and turns on the radio. It is on for half or ¾ of the way
> through dinner and the rest of the time he is apt to prefer to be

silent and I am silent, too. After dinner he lies down, goes to sleep or is silent, or occasionally tells me something which means I can tell him something. He goes back to work in a hurry and stays till midnight. Then he comes back either with an architect to talk strictly shop but my presence is uninvited— or several of us go to the barbeque and talk shop. When we come back its 1:00 or 2:00 a.m. and we both hurry to bed, the main issue being to keep the window closed enough. That is my life with Eero.

Eero admitted his work was all-consuming and that "architecture is my great love and as such I propose to practice it." Lily knew this better than anyone. "I am married to someone who admits his first love is architecture. He lives, breathes, drinks, sleeps, wakes, exists architecture, of which I approve and of which he warned me before facing life." As a result, "he not only spends all his time, but his emotional life, on it."[15]

Such behavior took its toll on Lily: "Since I met him I have been nasty and ill tempered from time to time in a way that I've never been before." In 1945, she wrote that Eero was "a real wet blanket . . . a squelcher of ideas and feelings. As a result he kills the confidence of those around him." She remembered being full of confidence when she married him, but realized that sense was "based on a very romantic and unrealistic ground." Part of that diminishment occurred while the two worked on the St. Louis competition. While she stood beside her husband in 1948 as part of the winning design team, Eero had already eliminated her sculpture garden as part of the overall concept. In addition to belittling her work, Eero refused to participate in any attempts to, in Lily's words, "talk something out." The professional detachment gave way to a physical one. She grew increasingly frustrated by Eero's "inability to feed me what any female needs."[16]

Eero, seemingly oblivious to Lily's feelings, was far too busy to help care for two small children. This distance he maintained from his children replicated his experience with his own father, which he called "a curse of our civilization." Eero remained completely absorbed in architecture, and he expected those working with him to be similarly committed. His idea of fun, according to Charles Eames, consisted solely of "superadult concentration on his work." Saarinen, according to Eames, was "one genius in whom you can see the gears working because they're on the outside."[17]

Yet Eero could not escape his father's shadow, and feared he never would. In 1945, Eliel received a commission to design a $70 million research campus for General Motors outside Detroit. Winning the GM commission solidified Eliel's rarified professional stature. Two years later, Eliel received the Gold Medal from the American Institute of Architects, the AIA's highest honor "in recognition of a significant body of work of lasting influence." Since 1907, only thirteen architects had been so recognized, and Eliel won before even Frank Lloyd Wright, Mies, or Le Corbusier.[18]

Lily remembered that Eero was "very jealous" of Eliel over the GM commission, and almost desperate to establish his own identity as an architect. This did not change even after Eero won the St. Louis competition. Eero later recalled that of all the architects he admired, Eliel was the single greatest influence. Eliel's sudden death on July 1, 1950, was personally devastating, but it also liberated Eero professionally. He later recalled that after Eliel was gone "I started to create my own form," rather than work "within the form of my father."[19]

In addition to architecture, Saarinen worked in other areas of design. One produced a lasting model that garnered more praise than his early buildings. An old Cranbrook friend, Florence Knoll, asked him to create a chair in which people could do more than sit upright. She wanted one where people "could curl up." Saarinen designed one with a molded, reinforced fiberglass shell covered with rich material, with a gently curved back that flowed into an elongated seat. His "womb" chair became a sensation and was featured in the November 1948 edition of *Life*. A survey of leading designers later commissioned by the Illinois Institute of Technology ranked Saarinen's chair as one of the "best designed products of modern times." The womb chair earned the praise even of *Playboy*, which said Saarinen "possesses the poetic vision for form."[20] His later "pedestal" chairs and tables would be among the most iconic furniture designs of the postwar era.

In late 1950, Lily wrote to a friend that "things have come to such a pass that I hope I am well enough to part with Eero." He "has been most stimulating to live with but he doesn't give a damn about me," and added, "I am the wrong wife for a genius." Her growing sexual frustration was vented in her diary: "Why can't he be clever enough to entice me? All he thinks about is other people he'll sleep with." In another entry, she wrote, "poor pojo, won't you come in my bed?" Eero wrote in his diary that extramarital affairs provided him a certain "sense of security," and offered a self-fulfilling excuse: "I have had a feeling that someday I will be looking for someone else, therefore I better start practicing now."[21]

One of the first women he began "practicing" with was a Swedish weaver, Astrid Sampe. Eero saw her during his frequent European trips, and they corresponded about possibly leaving their spouses and marrying. If Astrid joined him in the United States, he said candidly, "here your place in society would be my wife but also housewife and chauffeur for children," while "many times I will be away working and you will be alone more than you wish to be."[22]

One reason Eero considered leaving Lily for Astrid was that he felt Astrid would help him build another Hvittrask in America, a "radical, beautiful home, one of the five or six best in the country." Astrid's "talents are broader and of a more cooperative nature" than

Lily's, and so she would better help him lead a life like his father's. But Astrid's background had its drawbacks: "She may be handicapped by her too-Swedish taste but I think this would change." Because, after all, she was "very mouldable." Eero also pondered giving up his professional practice for an academic appointment, such as "dean of architecture at Yale or MIT." Such musings provide glimpses into his ever-expanding ego. At forty, even a major academic appointment would not do, only a deanship at a prestigious university. His father's reach from the grave remained strong, and he evaluated his wife and his mistress not only for personal compatibility but also for how they might help him reach his professional goals.

Still, Eero was not blind to his own insecurities: "My life has been a fanatical concentration on architecture at the expense of all other phases of life—this has probably been due to the fact that I largely pattern my life upon my father's, and since competition is very keen today and my talents are not as free flowing as my father's, such a concentration has been necessary to survive."[23] A successful architect, he had learned, may contribute to the larger culture but is not necessarily "a person of culture." He blamed his own ignorance of larger cultural interests on what he considered to be his purely technical Yale education. "The life I would like to lead is largely patterned on my father's," he said, adding that he felt ready to allow other parts of family life to grow but only to a carefully measured point. "The most important factor in my life will always be architecture." He hoped, more than anything else, "to leave a place for myself in architectural history."[24]

In 1952, Saarinen began seeing a psychiatrist, and kept a written record of his conversations. Behind his professional success, he admitted, was "a scared little child" who feared whether he could "support myself in the cold, outside world." Considering his growing personal unhappiness, Eero asked, "why should I stay married to a person I will never completely love?" He recounted Lily's flaws: she took "too goddamn many sleeping pills—sleeps nine hours a night and gets nothing done during the day, and talks a blue streak I cannot stand." On the other hand, Astrid "is a fine international lady, professionally exceptionally capable and . . . a warm little girl with a sense of humor."

While visiting Astrid in Sweden in 1952, Eero told her that while he loved her more than anyone, "I was not on the market for a new wife." He took stock of her attributes: she was "a very warm and sensitive person sexually," but she had "yellow teeth," and her breasts "were too small." Arriving home undecided, he mulled over bringing Astrid to the U.S., where his friends and associates could "have her looked over." "If she passes that gauntlet, I will marry her. If she fails, I may stick with Lily until I find the right one."[25]

Ultimately, neither Lily nor Astrid held his attention. On January 29, 1953, Eero sat for an interview with *New York Times* arts critic Aline Louchheim. At the time, she was engaged to Edgar Kaufman, the wealthy heir of a Pittsburgh department store fortune, whose father had commissioned Frank Lloyd Wright to design Fallingwater. Louchheim came to Eero's office to interview him as an architect who had just recently come "into his own." She remembered during the session that she felt Eero "hadn't had a woman listen to him so intently for so long." Perhaps he remembered her from a 1948 article she had written, in which he told her the Arch was "conceived as a very simple shape—something that does not bear any imprint of the styles and fashions of our time, but will last beyond our time, both physically and in design." "In this sense," Saarinen said, "I hope it is somewhat like the Washington Monument." After the interview, in which they talked about his new projects and his larger architectural concepts, Eero drove Aline to Cranbrook, where, in a dark drawing room, they began a sexual relationship. Aline remembered the exchange as "hurried" but felt "this was only the first time." A week later, Eero met her in New York. Aline decided to end her engagement to Kaufman while Eero shared the woes of his unhappy marriage.[26]

Eero used the new relationship to influence Aline's article about his career. He made copious notes on various drafts of the manuscript, suggesting, for example, that she omit the word "surpass" and instead write that he hoped to "equal" his father. She readily accommodated every change. Sexual flirtation entered their exchanges. In response to a line saying he sent "long, provocative letters to the editors of architectural magazines," Eero noted: "You will leave out—two spanks for you!" After approving the final draft, Eero said, "you can now spank me, and that you have to do *very* hard, and I will love you for it."[27]

By early May 1953, the whirlwind courtship had evolved enough for Eero to seek a divorce from Lily. Despite her proclaimed desire to be rid of him, she refused. Although she considered the idea of a divorce "ridiculous," Lily noted that the marriage "has come to a point where he thinks I am not good enough for him and I have come to a point where I don't think that basking under reflected glory is good enough for me." She wrote to Harry Weese during the proceedings that "there is no more ugly or destructive force than the legal process of love turning into hate." In painfully candid terms, Lily ruminated on Eero and the marriage:

> I should feel lucky that I had the first good years with him, when he was more shy than arrogant, yet had the grand monumental quality I fell in love with in the old days. There was something paternal and older than his years in him then; which turned out to be the role of a little wiseacre boy, once he had to face life. Whenever Eero was mean it was in a monumental way. But I never understood what a lonely, lost soul he was till his father died and if he hadn't died I don't think we would be divorcing now.[28]

Eero and Aline corresponded daily, exchanging letters of love, eroticism, and desperate hopes that they could soon be together. Even when he made the effort to be complimentary, Eero could be judgmental in ways Lily would have found all too familiar. During the first weeks of their affair, he rose early one morning and observed Aline as she slept. He made detailed notes of her features and later shared them with her: "hair line, nothing remarkable, but OK"; "breasts do not have the naïve firmness of an 18 year old, I know, but they have many enchanting qualities"; "waist—at first I thought just a little too wide—1/4" would have been better but then I fell in love with you and I would not want that changed." In another exchange he told Aline how much he admired her "general appearance from the shoulders up—marvelous, absolutely marvelous—not glamorous in the sense of being striking, in a crowd, but glamorous when one has made contact with you."[29]

Eero's self-absorption revealed itself in an odd letter to Aline in July 1953. "In ten years," he allowed, "I could momentarily look in another direction," but he hastened to reassure her that if he did have an affair, "it will be for a small interlude." The chances that he might cheat on her might be around "five percent." He could not avoid hurting those he loved the most—"it is a phenomena that has happened every time I seriously liked someone." In the letter he drew a prostrate E with its middle digit between the legs of a capital "A."[30]

Eero and Lily's divorce was finalized in late 1953, and four months later, Eero married Aline at her New York apartment, followed by a trip to Fallingwater where the newlyweds were guests of the home's owner and Aline's former suitor, Edgar Kaufman. The next year Aline gave birth to the couple's only child, a son named Eames, after the man who had helped shape pipe cleaners on Eero's living room floor. Lily never remarried, and harbored a bittersweet memory of her time with Eero. In 1955, she wrote to a friend about seeing her ex-husband unexpectedly in public: "I saw Eero yesterday and my heart pounded, in fact, I thought I was going to faint, but fortunately a friend was near and helped me about."[31]

■

The early fifties were a busy time for Saarinen professionally. Everywhere, modernist architects worked to develop for a larger audience what previously had been seen as avant-garde. He was now in charge of the massive GM project, and Philip Johnson selected his furniture for a major show sponsored by the Museum of Modern Art to be held at the Merchandise Mart in Chicago. In 1951, his income from the firm was over $113,000 (the median income for American men that year was barely $3,000), and by 1954 his royalties from his furniture designs added $57,000. He was made a fellow of the AIA and he embarked on a variety of new commissions that taxed his forty-three-person staff that included Kevin Roche, Robert Venturi, and Cesar Pelli (by comparison, the firm of Skidmore, Owings, and Merrill topped seven hundred). Saarinen even turned down some commissions that other architects could only dream of receiving. Yale asked him to design an art gallery, but he was too busy to accept. The job went instead to Louis Kahn, whose design won wide acclaim. Saarinen designed corporate centers for IBM and John Deere, but his best-known works resulted when he combined sculpture with architecture. The elegant curves of the TWA Terminal in New York and the David S. Ingalls Rink at Yale (nicknamed the "Whale") became some of his most memorable designs. Roche remembered that during these years, the St. Louis Arch "was rarely discussed" and was widely assumed "to have been lost in the maze of Washington."[32]

His growing portfolio reveals no single Saarinen style. The critic Vincent Scully wrote that Saarinen's career could be interpreted as an attempt to "escape from the conceptual grip of style itself." Richard Neutra, a member of the St. Louis jury, was disappointed with Saarinen's work in the 1950s, calling him a "fox" who "didn't know which way he would jump next—every design was a surprise—inconsistent." Ada Louise Huxtable noted that his contemporaries were uncomfortable with many of Saarinen's buildings: "his personal take on modernism pushed its limits too fast, too far." Saarinen lamented that beyond "the form and the invention," the most difficult part of architecture was "getting people to agree with me."[33]

Saarinen's unique way of viewing the world may have had a neurological basis. Once, on an airplane, Eero took two pieces of paper and wrote a letter to a friend. With his right hand, he wrote the letter normally. With his left, and simultaneously, he wrote a mirror image of the same letter. When reversed, the mirrored letter was virtually indistinguishable from his normal writing, complete with all his usual nuances. The ability to do this, which Saarinen shared with Leonardo da Vinci and which neurosurgeons considered a genetic trait, occurs in 1 of 6,500 adults and is not only associated with certain forms of dyslexia, but can also occur with certain brain disorders.[34]

In June 1956, Saarinen appeared on the cover of *Time*. Describing him as standing out among his peers for his unmatched proportion of "imagination, versatility, and good sense," *Time* added that "Saarinen sleeps, eats, and dreams architecture." The article perceptively noted that Saarinen "reduces just about every experience in life to architectural terms, reaches for the nearest napkin or notepad to graph everything from adolescent rates of learning to the qualities that make up a beautiful woman." Eero described his overall ambition in words reminiscent of his approach to the Arch: "We must still create, but we would like to bring back some of the great awarenesses that existed in the past, expressed in our own forms and technology." Yet when he looked around him, he found modern architecture disappointing: "I think the immediate future is black. There is too much that is ugly. Architecture is not just to fulfill man's need for shelter, but also to fulfill man's belief in the nobility of his existence on earth. Our architecture is too humble. It should be prouder, more aggressive, much richer and larger." His most outrageous idea was that one day cities would be "covered in huge transparent plastic domes with air conditioning inside."[35]

Three years later, in 1959, a team of researchers at the Institute of Personality Assessment and Research at the University of California at Berkeley conducted a series of personality tests and interviews with forty architects, including Louis Kahn, Richard Neutra, Philip Johnson, and Saarinen. Pierluigi Serraino writes that the purpose of the project was to understand the socio-environmental backgrounds of leading architects in order "to devise a new pedagogical model to raise more creative designers." One of the extended interviews of Saarinen was conducted by Neil J. Smelser, who later became a distinguished sociologist. Smelser described Saarinen as having "a good deal of hostility which he handles with some difficulty," and noted that he viewed women as "non-intellectual, nurturant, and subordinate," while relating to them in a "rather contemptuous" and "rather tactless way." Smelser found in his subject "a psychopathic element" and noted Saarinen "is somewhat manipulative and devious and tries to see what he can get by with." The ambitious architect "has strong status concerns about his own greatness" that are "a function of his concern whether he is independent of his father's fame."[36]

Smelser asked Saarinen to list "those things which you have done which you consider to be innovations." Saarinen mentioned the GM Center and the MIT Chapel as "important," but foremost was a project that remained unbuilt. "In design and concepts," he said, "the St. Louis Arch is, I believe, a contribution." This was his most original work, he thought, because it was "a piece of sculpture as well as a piece of structure." This was crucial to properly understanding the Arch: "a sculptor brings to a building his special sensitivity." He hoped this quality would affect people emotionally as the great European cathedrals did. "Imagine what Chartres Cathedral would look like," Saarinen once said, "if the Gothic master builders had not placed their main effort on the inner meaning and emotional impact of this building, but instead concentrated their effort on making the plan work functionally."[37]

Much more seemed to remain in Saarinen's career, but in fact the moment served as an unintentional epitaph.

∎

Throughout these years when he attained almost everything else—much of it at great cost—the Arch remained out of reach, a cherished, unrealized ambition. It had made him famous, given him wealth and prestige. It lacked only one thing: existence.

In 1953, Saarinen visited the gravel parking lot in St. Louis. Drivers paying their fees and parking their cars likely paid little attention to the man with thick eyeglasses walking nearby. Saarinen felt at least something was happening: "they are now building the highway on its western edge—this is paid for by the state but it is in a sense part of the overall plan of the park and approved by me." Rather than seeing the highway as a barrier between his park and the rest of the city, Saarinen interpreted the construction as a sign of progress. "In a sense the project has started."[38]

Bruce Detmers, who came to the firm as a young architect in the 1950s, recalled that Saarinen wanted a "perfect form" for the Arch. Saarinen and his staff thought the form should be a square, with the base of the arch forming the two lower corners, and its upper crown centered in the exact middle of the top side. A countless number of forms could fall within this basic format and Saarinen continued to adjust the tapering by studying scale models. "I cannot understand drawings," he wrote, "and I think anyone who claims they can is a liar." Only models let him examine the work in three dimensions.

The exact curvature of the arch, he reiterated, could not be formulated by a mathematical formula. A true catenary arch, he observed, was "too pointed" (it is more accurate to call the Arch a "weighted" or "flattened" catenary). The precise curve Saarinen finally settled on was one he concluded simply "looked right."[39]

As the Arch would sit atop the bluff overlooking the river, there needed to be a series of "Grand Stairs" leading from the memorial to the wharf. Some might have considered this a casual add-on, but not Saarinen. He was obsessed with finding just the right grade for the stairs, and determining the height and length of the individual steps. To be certain he got it right, Saarinen had an elaborate scale-model built in the back parking lot of his office, where he walked the stairs every morning, making slight changes in the tread widths and the overall grade.[40]

Saarinen also knew how to balance design principles against financial necessities. Knowing that the Arch project might fail unless compromises were made, he adjusted to the needs of the city while aggressively guarding his vision of the project. One particularly revealing episode involved determining the arch's eventual height. In the late 1950s, Kansas City developer Lewis Kitchen proposed a series of three towers just a block from the memorial site. To Kitchen, this "Mansion House" development offered a modern, enclosed world of apartments, shops, restaurants, and specialty stores. To Saarinen, the forty-story towers would rival, if not overtop, his 590-foot Arch. In a 1960 meeting with Kitchen and city officials, Saarinen, in the words of his associate John Dinkeloo, was "absolutely against this extreme height." Saarinen wanted the city and Kitchen to agree to build nothing over fifteen stories, or, 150 feet. Dinkeloo related that "after much pressure" from the St. Louis contingent and Kitchen, Saarinen relented, agreeing to the maximum height of 275 feet for surrounding structures. In response, he raised the Arch's height to 630 feet.[41]

Saarinen's international fame earned him spots on significant architectural juries. Another legendary moment occurred in 1957 when he supposedly helped rescue Jørn Utzon's design for the Sydney Opera House from the reject pile. The resulting structure, with its spectacular curved roof panels resembling sails, first drew scorn from architects such as Wright and Mies but became one of the most famous buildings in the world. Reflecting on the winning design, Saarinen declared that "the only architecture which interests me is architecture as a fine art." Antonio Roman remarked that "Saarinen's influence in Sydney should be regarded as one of the decisive interventions in the architecture of the second half of the twentieth century."[42]

In 1960, Saarinen decided to move his firm closer to New York without being "swallowed up in the city." The Saarinen firm began shipping all of its belongings to a neo-Tudor castle in Hamden, Connecticut, just north of New Haven. He also became a member of the American Academy of Arts and Letters. In this moment of triumph, Saarinen reached out to a former lover. That June, he wrote to Astrid Sampe, with whom he had not spoken since ending their affair in 1952. "I just decided to-nite that I would write you a long letter to tell you what I am up to, etc." The bulk of the letter recounted his professional successes, and he reminded her of a special project: "Do you remember the Jefferson monument, the great big memorial arch (200 meters high) which I won in a competition in St. Louis? It now looks as if this will be built. At present we are building some minor parts of it and by the end of the year we will be putting in the foundations for the stairway's steel arch." He noted that he had spent the entire afternoon "trying to figure out how an elevator or similar device can be worked into the arch." Saarinen ended: "Well, I should stop now but tell us about your plans and then perhaps our paths will cross."[43] Sampe never replied.

SIX

The Laughingstock of the World

For which of you, intending to build a tower, sitteth not down
first, and counteth the cost, whether he have sufficient to finish it?
Lest haply, after he hath laid the foundation, and is not able to
finish it, all that behold it begin to mock him.

—LUKE 14: 28–29

Saarinen under an Arch model, 1957. Eero Saarinen Papers, Manuscripts and
Archives, Yale University Library/ Photograph by Richard Knight.

Nothing about the Arch was inevitable. Less than a week after Saarinen was announced as the winner of the competition, Jefferson National Expansion Memorial Superintendent Julian Spotts addressed a meeting of civil engineers in St. Louis. On the same day that Gilmore Clarke first brought attention to Adalberto Libera's arch, Spotts did not mention that he, himself, had conceived of an arch on the St. Louis riverfront two years before Saarinen. He merely endorsed Saarinen's design, calling it "a stunt" that could attain the stature of the Washington Monument or Mount Rushmore.

Spotts then turned to two major issues in the memorial site's construction. Everyone was aware, he said, of the unsightly elevated railroad tracks along the levee. But another factor also threatened the usefulness of the proposed park. Few people understood the full significance of "the interregional highway along Third Street" and how it would affect the park's relationship to the city. His concerns fell on deaf ears, however, with civic leaders who saw interstate highways as the answer to many of St. Louis's economic needs.[1]

Spotts was not alone in thinking of the Arch as a "stunt." St. Louisans had a decidedly mixed reaction to the unorthodox design they had seen splashed over the newspapers and that would quickly find its way into countless local business logos. Whether it was a "Gateway to the West" or a "Backdoor to the East," some city residents were convinced that something better and more practical should be built on the parking lot adjacent to the river. One local resident, J. Carl Blackmun, did not mince words: "Frankly speaking, I'm agin it," he said. "I'm against anything that will take badly needed acreage out of circulation just to make a place to grow grass on and to build a barrel hoop on." Like many, Blackmun hoped the Arch concept could be dropped entirely, and that the area could instead be used for decent housing. "When you get that done," he wrote in a letter to the editor of the *Post-Dispatch*, "you will have a memorial worthy of Jefferson."[2]

Other letters of opposition came to Mayor Joseph Darst's office. In 1950, a petition complete with nine signatures arrived, expressing the collective opposition of the signers to "a discarded steel corset," and demanding that the area become a "large municipal recreation area with a sports stadium." Former Congressman William L. Igoe, a longtime opponent of Bernard Dickmann, made it personal: "It looks like some people want to build a memorial to Saarinen instead of Thomas Jefferson."[3]

The mayor, who was elected in 1949 and like Dickmann had grown rich as a local real estate developer, left the door open for another outcome. In October 1949, Darst professed that he had "an open mind" about how to proceed with the riverfront. Rather than wait until all funds were available, Darst supported moving ahead with the memorial piecemeal: "The Saarinen concept easily lends itself to construction by stages, which is probably the way it will be carried out in any event." The mayor sought to hold off a St. Louis business community that was increasingly ready to drop the expensive and idealistic Arch for something more practical. The opinions expressed by the St. Louis business community are revealing. The *Post-Dispatch* noted how "downtown business already has been hurt by the removal of the old buildings in the riverfront area, because people who worked in them no longer pass through the area." One anonymous businessperson told the *Kansas City Star* that "a strong anti-arch group" had organized in St. Louis, including some civic leaders who had contributed to Luther Ely Smith's fundraising efforts in 1947 to underwrite the architectural competition. "Eight out of every nine businessmen are against the arch idea," the businessperson disclosed, "but they won't say so openly because they don't have to—the idea is a dead duck right now."[4]

John K. Branner, a highly respected San Francisco architect, congratulated Darst "for putting a stop to the so-called 'civic monument' for St. Louis." The designer of Stanford Stadium and son of

Stanford's second president, Branner reflected a contingent of older, traditional architects who had little taste for Saarinen's monumental modernism. The Arch, he wrote, "could serve no purpose except to hold your citizens up to ridicule." Branner concluded: "It is unfortunate that your competition proved a failure."[5]

Critics came from other circles. A local minister, Rev. Joseph Collins, said he "rejoiced" when he heard that Darst might cancel the Arch, force the federal government to return the deed to the city, and build a massive housing project on the site. He was later disappointed to read that the mayor vacillated. "Why waste $8 million on a monstrosity like that," Collins asked, "when the money could be used for any other purpose?" Felix Chopin, a probation officer, hated "the silver horse shoe" and said he had heard "thousands of people gripe at that damn thing and the expense." A. Carl Weber, who headed the local Chamber of Commerce, complained to Darst that Saarinen's "stainless steel hairpin" was "utterly useless," and pressed for more "usable" features on the site such as a planetarium or a recreation center. Weber found Saarinen's design deeply troubling: "Not only is the Arch a symbol of decadent thought, but it represents a colossal waste of vital material, labor, and technical ability that, in this and future time, is actually un-American." Otto Eichholf suggested a large statue of a pioneer pointing westward. While acknowledging the cliché, Eichholf defended his idea on the grounds that at least "people would not have to answer millions of questions on what the arch was for." E. A. Luchtemeyer of St. Louis offered yet another design, with a simple fountain at the river's edge, a proposal he described as "not from any 'Cranbrook School of Architectural Thought.'" Rose L. Brown worried that if the Arch were built, St. Louis would become "the laughingstock of the world."[6]

Critics generally focused on three points. The Arch was either an ugly design with no useful purpose; too expensive; or located in an area that should be used for more important civic purposes, such as housing or a sports stadium. But other concerns surfaced as well. William Plowman, editor of the *St. Louis Star-Times*, worried that the Arch might require "more labor than the pyramids" and asked William Wurster, one of the competition jurors, whether these concerns had merit. Wurster replied that the Arch "is a straightforward engineering problem" and it was "utter nonsense" to compare the construction challenges it presented to those of the Egyptian pyramids. After observing the building of the Golden Gate Bridge in San Francisco, Wurster concluded, he was convinced of "the economic and structural possibility of the Arch."[7]

Basic engineering questions had challenged Saarinen from the very beginning. For answers he turned to Fred Severud, a graduate of the Norwegian Institute of Technology who came to the United States in 1928 and formed his own engineering firm. Severud made his professional reputation through his structural work on Madison Square Garden and wrote a book on how to design buildings to withstand a nuclear blast. When Saarinen sought his advice regarding the Arch, Severud confirmed the design was "feasible," later conceding, "we just didn't know how many problems would have to be licked." A veteran builder of suspension bridges, E. B. Steinman, conducted a series of wind-tunnel tests on scale models and concluded that the Arch could withstand winds of 155 miles per hour.[8]

Severud then consulted the Otis Elevator Company to consider the possibility of building an interior elevator. No one had ever built such a device in a confined space that gradually curved from the ground to the top. Various engineers took a crack at solving the problem, but were unsuccessful. Discouraged, Severud and Saarinen put off the elevator issue for another day.

A more immediate question was how to build a self-supporting arch. Severud considered using standard erection cranes that stood outside and along the arch wall. C. Earl Webb, chief engineer of the American Bridge Company, endorsed the idea of such massive erection towers as "very practical." At this early point, Severud estimated the total project cost at $6.5 million.[9]

The Arch's exterior raised other vexing questions. Would the shiny stainless steel produce intense glare? Engineers determined that with the curved surface and matte finish, there would be no flat planes to concentrate the sun's rays, so the glare would not be dangerous. Heavy-gauge stainless steel would work far better than thinner steels and could withstand years of air pollution. Yet stainless steel was expensive, and because the Arch required more of it than any other construction project in history, the outer skin material represented a sizable portion of the total budget.[10]

Rather than construct a steel framework and attach the stainless steel to the structure, the engineers tried a different procedure in which the Arch would become an "orthotropic" structure built with an inner and outer skin. These, rather than a traditional interior framework, would actually absorb the weight of the structure. The plates would be formed into double-walled triangular sections, with an inner wall of carbon steel approximately three-eighths of an inch thick in the middle and nearly two inches thick at the corners, and the outer wall of stainless steel just a quarter-inch thick. The stainless steel was type 304, an alloy composed of approximately 18 percent chromium and 8 percent nickel. The gap between the two walls varied, from three feet at ground level to seven and three-quarters inches at the top. Both "skins" were load bearing, and would be connected with tightening bolts. For the first three hundred feet, the walls would be filled with concrete reinforced with steel rods that ran vertically through the legs and down into the foundation. Engineers first considered stabilizing the Arch with guy wires, but the "post-tensioning" rods allowed it to be free-standing. The Arch, tapering as it rose so that no two sections were identical, would be built in twelve-foot sections. At the base, the widest outer walls measured forty-eight feet, while at the very top, it narrowed to only fifteen and a half feet.[11]

Severud's work on the project was critical, but Saarinen was worried that the engineer was getting too much credit for the design. In April 1951, Saarinen learned of an article being planned for *Architectural Record* that would detail Severud's role in the project. Saarinen wrote to the editor of the magazine about his concerns: "Your men, in their enthusiasm, will write the article in such a way that it will sound as if Severud was the co-originator of the Arch." The architect wanted it known that the engineer was brought in for his analysis only "after the concept, the profile, and the material were all established."[12]

With the Arch still only a paper dream nearly two years after the competition, Luther Ely Smith warned Saarinen that they needed to mount a "re-education" effort. "We are constantly running into the lack of understanding of the Arch," Smith wrote, due to criticism started "by the enemy, and then accentuated by our friends, the headliners." In addition to their lobbying in Washington, Smith and his allies took their argument to the people of St. Louis, buying full-page ads in the major newspapers and asking local citizens whether they wanted the land to be deeded back to the city for a parking lot or a housing project. "Some would like that to happen," the ad warned, adding that if St. Louis acted in time, "the arch will be to the city what the Eiffel Tower is to Paris." The ad, paid for "by private individuals interested in St. Louis's future," asked all who favored Saarinen's plan to express their support to the Jefferson National Expansion Memorial Association offices.[13]

Former Mayor Dickmann did not hesitate to weigh in on alternative approaches, suggesting that a five-thousand-seat amphitheater would be an appropriate addition to the park. Dickmann liked the Arch design, but felt it lacked "a focal point to draw people downtown to enjoy the beauty of the memorial as a whole." Dickmann had long since proved that he could be a shrewd politician. But no one questioned his commitment to his city, and in 1949 he understood something that many others would realize too late. While the Arch would undoubtedly bring millions of tourists to the city, the riverfront offered little else to attract either visitors or locals. The proposed park looked like an afterthought to the Arch, and Dickmann hoped something else could be added to make it usable to the entire community. At this point, St. Louisans had few reasons to visit the river, and the eventual Third Street superhighway would be another barrier between city dwellers and the park.[14]

Others agreed with Dickmann that the riverfront scheme needed more than Saarinen's arch. A. Carl Weber of the Chamber of Commerce told a gathering of real estate agents in April 1950 that the site needed a massive football stadium with a seating capacity of 100,000. Chicago and Cleveland, Weber noted, had earned millions from such large stadiums. The idea of an athletic facility drew a concerned response from Saarinen himself. "As a citizen of this country, it seems to me that the memorial project would be much better than a baseball field," he wrote, adding that such a structure would change the memorial's entire focus from a national monument to one devoted to local concerns. Saarinen's objections were not shared by St. Louis Cardinals president Fred Saigh, who warned that "the futuristic arch will be of no earthly use to our people."[15]

Mayor Darst, meanwhile, tried to exploit the presence of a Missourian in the White House. "It is indeed a pleasure to be able to report to you," he had told President Truman's aide John Steelman in June 1949, "that we have made most substantial progress on plans for the ultimate development of the JNEM. The memorial, I am sure you will agree, will constitute a great achievement for President Truman's administration." Wurster reported that when he showed Truman photos of the Arch model, Truman "spoke warmly of the whole project" and Wurster added that the president "particularly stressed linking it to other projects with the great highways."[16] Rather than seeing the highway as a scar that would damage the park, Truman endorsed the vision of expressways as harbingers of urban progress. Saarinen shared this feeling, claiming that "our expressways are the finest thing done yet." He expressed a "guess and hope" that the Arch would be started by 1954.[17]

With Truman's tacit support, it seemed that Smith's momentum had turned and money for the Arch would begin flowing in early 1950. A bill appropriating funds for "certain phases" of the memorial's construction cleared a House committee, and the Senate began discussing the legislation that summer. Nothing apparently stood in the way of the bill's passage and the president's signature.

When Truman arrived in St. Louis on June 10, 1950, to dedicate the riverfront memorial, he confined his remarks to the bland celebration of the Louisiana Purchase, saying, "The park which is to be created here will bear witness to our gratitude to Jefferson and the brave men who explored and settled the area of the Louisiana Purchase." His speech focused primarily on foreign policy: he used the occasion to deliver another reminder of American plans to contain communism. Having "learned our lesson" from the previous world wars, the United States and its allies had built a "world order" where international coalitions were willing to use "collective action to prevent aggression."[18] Few who gathered under the hot St. Louis sun understood how Truman's statements related to the riverfront memorial. Just two weeks later, when North Korean troops invaded South Korea, the connection between foreign policy and domestic programs such as the Gateway Arch became readily apparent. Once Truman dispatched American troops to the Korean peninsula, as he had promised in St. Louis, hopes of obtaining quick Congressional funding for the Arch vanished.

The outlook for the Arch grew worse in April 1951, when Luther

Ely Smith suffered a fatal heart attack. The death of the seventy-seven-year-old father of the memorial initiative meant that the effort had lost its most persuasive and ardent proponent. Many St. Louis civic leaders had contributed to the ambitious architectural competition partly out of deference to Smith. With him now gone from the scene, they had little incentive to support the project further.[19]

For others, concerns about downtown St. Louis went well beyond the Arch's construction. F. A. MacKenzie, manager of the Hotel York located at Sixth and Market, asked Senator Stuart Symington to help return the riverfront to the city. "What downtown St. Louis needs is more people and better facilities for them to reach downtown," MacKenzie wrote. From his viewpoint as a downtown business owner, "we are today a disintegrating, decaying city on the Mississippi River." Saarinen's "Gateway to the West" symbolism was thus completely wrongheaded. "Our gates have been open too long for the progress and development of the west," he wrote. It was time "we closed these gates and kept a great portion of the flow of people westward here in St. Louis."[20]

In 1953, Raymond R. Tucker, chair of the Washington University mechanical engineering department, was elected mayor of St. Louis. Tucker's first item of business was the passage of a $110 million bond issue that built twenty-three city projects, mostly highways and other infrastructure items. His second priority was obtaining the Congressional authorization necessary to build the Arch.[21]

The passage of yet another bond issue demonstrated St. Louis's dependence on borrowed money to fuel urban projects. Bonds, which required voter approval, at least provided political cover and quick money, avoiding the need for tax hikes or the elimination of other services to fund priorities. As with any state or municipality, the level of St. Louis's bonded indebtedness had limits. City Hall repeatedly brought bond issues to the voters, using the same sales pitch in the 1950s as in the 1930s—that the bond issue was essential to the revitalization of St. Louis, and short-term indebtedness would be more than offset by greater commercial activity, more jobs, and an expanded tax base.[22]

Although the conflict in Korea continued to divert Washington's attention, the St. Louis memorial was not completely ignored. In May 1954, Congress authorized a $5 million appropriation for the memorial park but it specifically excluded funds for the "stainless steel Arch." Two years later, President Eisenhower requested $3 million to relocate the railroad tracks, without mentioning the Arch. Even these preliminary efforts aroused opposition from conservatives who opposed spending any more dollars on the St. Louis project. In May 1956, the White House and Congress agreed to a $2,640,000 compromise for the St. Louis project. The amount demonstrated that while the memorial project was still a possibility, whether the Arch would be undertaken was another matter entirely. The *Post-Dispatch* commented that considering the snail's pace at which the money dribbled in from Washington, the stainless steel arch "may be eliminated." When a Chicago-based consulting firm suggested that money could be saved by keeping the railroad tracks where they were, Eero Saarinen replied, "It sounds as if whoever wrote the report likes railroads very much."[23]

The question of how the tracks would be relocated, and more important, who would pay for it, was mired in an exhausting ten-year standoff. The frustrating delay convinced Saarinen that unless the railroad impasse was settled, his Arch would never be built. In 1957, his "new model" relocated the tracks one hundred feet westward and lowered them sixteen feet to an area where they would be partially hidden underground. All vehicular traffic would be prohibited from the park, and, in time, few who visited the Arch would ever know a railroad track was nearby. In all, Saarinen admitted, "We have made compromises with the problems of railroad and vehicular traffic which we believe will be of benefit to all concerned."

Mayor Tucker orchestrated a compromise in March 1958 with a solution to the costly relocation—a cut would be made into the side of the hill and concrete poured over top in order to eliminate the need for a complete tunnel. Tucker took the idea to the Terminal Association, which agreed to pay $500,000 to relocate the tracks. After a decade, the railroad track problem had been resolved.[24]

Throughout the 1950s, highways remained among the most pressing national infrastructure issues. In 1956, Eisenhower signed one of the most far-reaching domestic projects in U.S. history, an act creating the federal interstate highway system. This massive plan, packaged as a Cold War measure to ensure better evacuation and transportation routes for the military, had far-reaching economic effects. With the federal government shouldering 90 percent of the costs, road projects that states had planned for years would now become a reality. In St. Louis, the Interstate Highway act meant that millions of motorists would travel past the memorial site along the Third Street corridor. It also affected how some viewed the necessity of Saarinen's Arch. Eugene Mackey, president of the St. Louis chapter of the American Institute of Architects, said that the new highway along the waterfront "obligates us to do something fine and important, and the Saarinen plan with its huge arch would meet that obligation very well."[25]

Even though funds for the memorial project remained uncommitted, Mayor Tucker needed to silence his critics over the slow progress of the project. In a low-key ceremony on June 23, 1959, nearly twenty-four years after the original bond issue election, and nine years after President Truman dedicated the project, Tucker broke ground for the Arch using a stainless steel shovel. Alongside him stood National Park Service Director Conrad Wirth and, appropriately, former Mayor Dickmann. Even as the beaming politicians posed for photographers, the political craftsmanship used to reach this public moment had become shrouded in myth. Soaking up the optimism generated at the groundbreaking, a *Christian Science Monitor* reporter brushed away the early criticism of the project and concluded, "In time the feeling became quite general that the arch was inevitable." But any close examination of the memorial project over time makes abundantly clear that this was never true.[26]

The financing delays infuriated some St. Louisans, especially because nothing had seemed to change along the riverfront in the decades since the demolition. "I am sure that if the citizens of St. Louis had known that the government would dilly-dally for so many years," said W.W. Oberjuerge, who owned a St. Louis rubber distributing plant, "they never would have gone ahead with the project, originally wrecking about 83 acres of land." The one sign of progress, Oberjuerge noted, was that at least the Third Street highway was being built by the memorial site. Underlying the latent anger was an understanding of what had been lost. Dozens of historic buildings were gone for good, along with many local businesses. The stalled project had cost the cash-strapped city nearly $5.5 million in property taxes since Mayor Dickmann removed the first brick along the river. Far from making steady progress, the city remained, in the estimation of *Time*, "one quarter slum, and another quarter near slum."[27]

In 1959, George Hartzog was named superintendent of the Jefferson National Expansion Memorial. A native South Carolinian, Hartzog had been in the NPS Legal Office before his arrival in St. Louis, and his political and legal experience brought him into the job with the clear understanding of the congressional and bureaucratic wrangling that remained. He worked in St. Louis for three critical years before leaving for Washington, where he was eventually named director of the NPS by President Johnson. Although the memorial was intended to glorify Jefferson and westward expansion, Hartzog understood that the crucial task of securing funds called for tactics that were "less scholarly" than are popularly acknowledged.

The St. Louis example illuminated, he later recalled, "the vital role of politics—sometimes rawhide—in the establishment and preservation of America's parklands."[28]

A hopeful sign came in early 1960, when the House passed an Interior Department budget that attached an additional $4.6 million for the Arch project. By a vote of 43 to 37, mostly on party lines where Democrats supported the measure, the Senate agreed to the House version. St. Louis officials had wanted a larger appropriation, and when President Eisenhower signed the Interior bill, hopes for the Arch construction were, once again, stymied. Eisenhower's Bureau of the Budget ordered the NPS to review the schedule for constructing the Arch, with attention to two specific questions. First, what amount of federal appropriations would be needed to get the Arch built by St. Louis's two hundredth anniversary in 1964? Second, would St. Louis provide any additional funds? Many federal officials continued to suspect that St. Louis city leaders were hoarding additional funds generated as far back as the 1935 bond issue referendum. But questions about the project went well beyond money. One "highly placed official" in the Eisenhower administration considered practicality over aesthetics. If the "practical use" of the memorial was primary, the official claimed, museums should take priority over building the Arch. Disclosure of the NPS review drew protests from Missouri's Congressional delegation, which asked for an investigation into what they perceived as another delaying tactic. Rep. Thomas Curtis of St. Louis County made the delegation's position clear: "The money should flow."[29]

Of all the people who had waited patiently for construction to begin, none had more at stake than Eero Saarinen. By 1960, he was busy with exciting new commissions, including his first New York skyscraper. Yet as he worked on the CBS building and his signature terminals at Idlewild (later renamed JFK) and Dulles Airport, the Gateway Arch remained in the forefront of his mind. On August 10,

1961 (Saarinen's fifty-first birthday), Hartzog reported on a meeting he had had that day with Saarinen in St. Louis to discuss some possible change orders with the contractor. In the technical memo, Saarinen asked for a change in the concrete mixture to be used in some of the "overlook areas" that raised the initial cost from $3.50 per cubic yard to $4.00. Saarinen was always experimenting with concrete mixtures to find the right color and texture. This was the last time he ever worked on the Gateway Arch.

On Saarinen's previous trips to St. Louis, Hartzog had always provided a driver to take him to and from the airport. This time, as they left the meeting, Saarinen declined his usual ride and said he intended to make his own way to the airport. He became noticeably irritated that Hartzog continued to walk with him. Hartzog related that he had just started to wonder, "what have I done to piss this guy off?" when Saarinen's "total personality just changed" and he "totally flipped out." Saarinen ordered Hartzog not to go any further with him. On the plane back to Michigan, Saarinen became disoriented again, complaining of a severe headache and congestion.[30]

To those closest to Saarinen, it was clear something was wrong. One office worker noted that "Eero's whole personality changed in the summer of 1961." He was plagued by chronic headaches, and his staff noticed unusual behavior, such as arriving late for work, not removing his coat, and sitting for hours in his office alone. Aline told some of his close friends that Eero admitted he was having hallucinations.[31]

Part of Saarinen's personal habits had been compiling an endless series of detailed lists. On August 16, 1961, for example, he made a "to do" list of over thirty items that happened to be the day in which the first dynamite blast occurred into the foundation of the St. Louis site, marking, at long last, the actual beginning of the construction of the Arch.

On August 21, Saarinen's headaches became unbearable and he

checked into an Ann Arbor hospital for a series of neurological tests. During a two-hour emergency surgery on August 31, surgeons uncovered a stage IV tumor—the most advanced and deadliest kind—in his frontal lobe. He never recovered from the surgery and through the night his condition worsened. He died shortly before noon on September 1, 1961. After fourteen years and countless drawings, meetings, and models, Eero Saarinen would never see his beloved Arch built.[32]

At his memorial service, Saarinen's philosophy on the purpose of architecture was read. "Architecture is not just to fulfill man's need for shelter, but also to fulfill man's belief in the nobility of his existence on earth," he wrote. Saarinen felt architecture played an essential role in that existence, "almost a religious one." He explained: "Man is on earth for a very short time and he is not quite sure of what his purpose is. Religion gives him his primary purpose. The permanence and beauty and meaningfulness of his surroundings give him confidence and a sense of continuity. The question, what is the purpose of architecture? I would answer, 'To shelter and enhance man's life on earth.'"[33]

SEVEN

"*Got It Made*"

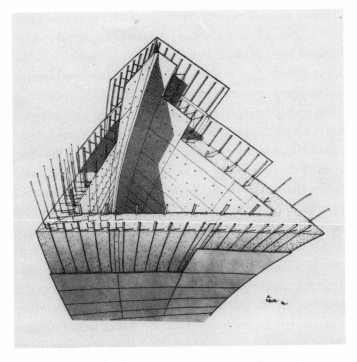

Diagram of the Arch's interior construction. Eero Saarinen Papers,
Manuscripts and Archives, Yale University Library.

After Saarinen's death, associates Kevin Roche and John Dinkeloo bore the burden of finishing the Arch project. In fact, they were responsible for finishing several of Saarinen's best-known works, such as the CBS Building in New York and the Dulles terminal, before starting their own firm. Ever since Saarinen and Charles Eames had first discussed the St. Louis competition in 1947, nearly a dozen architects, engineers, and designers played roles in developing the Arch and were indispensable to its final design and construction. But Saarinen is given exclusive credit as its architect, which is precisely how he wanted it. Saarinen guarded his creative acclaim with the Arch and his other projects, always worried that too much credit might be extended to other collaborators. Despite having to work in the shadows, many of his office colleagues were grateful to be by his side on some of the most coveted projects of the day. When he won the Pritzker Prize in 1982, Roche donated the proceeds to the Yale School of Architecture to establish the Eero Saarinen Visiting Professorship. Roche wanted to honor his old mentor in order "to remind the younger generation of his importance."[1]

When Roche first came to Saarinen's firm in 1951, the Arch "seemed to be almost forgotten." It wasn't until 1958 that Saarinen resurrected the project and threw himself into it for the next three years. After Saarinen's death, Roche and the engineers were careful to stay true to Saarinen's vision, never making any major changes. As George Hartzog recalled, "we refused to make any changes because that was the way he's designed it."[2] For Saarinen's staff, the ultimate problem, all along, was not design, but funding. In his final budget before leaving office in January 1961, President Eisenhower requested nearly $9.5 million for the St. Louis project, which was deemed enough to start construction of the Arch. Congress approved it in time for President John F. Kennedy to sign the appropriation into law in August 1961, just four days before Saarinen entered the hospital. With funding secured, the National Park Service solicited bids for the actual construction of the Arch and visitors' center. In January 1962, after receiving several preliminary bids, the NPS announced it was "disappointed" by the higher than expected budgets. The MacDonald Construction Company of St. Louis submitted the low bid of $12,139,918, which exceeded the engineers' estimate by just over $8 million.

This "sticker shock" led planners to seek other ways to lower costs, such as using another skin material or decreasing the Arch's size. Saarinen consistently opposed using aluminum rather than stainless steel, and lowering the height of the Arch to reduce the amount of metal was not seriously considered. If these issues were beyond compromise, NPS Director Conrad Wirth warned, other aspects of the overall plan might be eliminated. There perhaps could be only one interior elevator for tourists, or, maybe none. The Civil Defense Administration offered to pitch in $340,000 if the underground museum could also be used as a fallout shelter.[3]

As actual construction of the Arch approached, other details remained, including its official name. In August 1961, the U.S. Territorial Expansion Committee for the first time referred to the memorial project as the "Gateway Arch." "Gateway," according to the committee, symbolized "migration and travel as well as frontier" and underscored how the Arch looked simultaneously backward and forward. It symbolized the conquering of "Indians, vast distances, and arid lands" as well as the greater obstacles that lay ahead: "alien ideologies, population pressures, and the challenges of outer space."[4]

In order to construct the Arch according to Saarinen's plans and to keep such essential items as stainless steel and the interior elevators, the NPS needed congressional assurance of additional funds if they became necessary. In early 1962, a contingent of city and state officials, including U.S. Senator Stuart Symington and Rep. Leonor K. Sullivan, met in Washington to discuss the Arch's future. Although each wielded considerable power, by themselves they could not complete the project. They met that morning with someone who could: House Appropriations Committee Chairman Clarence Cannon. The eighty-two-year old Cannon, who represented Missouri's ninth district, had learned his craft as a young man while serving as an aide to House Speaker Champ Clark. Cannon had been elected to the House in 1922, and had become the chair of the Appropriations Committee in 1941. The St. Louis officials told Cannon that while the MacDonald bid was a good one, little money remained for contingencies. Given the Arch's singular construction challenges, unforeseen problems were assured and delays were to be expected. They needed Cannon's assurance that Congress would underwrite any additional costs and not leave the Arch standing incomplete. At a critical moment, Cannon looked at Sullivan and asked, "Lee, what do you want to do?" She replied, "I want to finish it." Cannon answered, "I do, too." Hartzog recognized immediately what had occurred. "Everybody knew when they went in there that there was only one vote, and that was Clarence Cannon." After more than a decade of haggling and negotiating, Cannon's support meant the Appropriations Committee would provide the necessary funds to complete the memorial, regardless of the inevitable cost overruns.[5]

With Cannon's imprimatur, the NPS announced on March 14, 1962, that the MacDonald Company would be the Arch contractor. The company was a St. Louis institution, owned by eighty-three-year old William MacDonald and his two sons, Robert Eugene "Gene" and Wilfred. As one of the fifty largest construction companies in United States, the MacDonald Company had considerable experience with sizable, complex projects. It had already built a $12 million campus for the McDonnell Aircraft Company in St. Louis, and was building several projects for the Air Force totaling nearly $50 million.[6]

To supply the massive amounts of stainless steel, the MacDonald Company chose the Pittsburgh–Des Moines Steel Company (PDM).

On July 4, 1962, MacDonald ordered from PDM nearly nine hundred million tons of polished stainless steel—still the single largest order for stainless steel in U.S. history. Transported by rail, the steel literally arrived at the front steps of the site starting in early 1963. The sections were welded onsite to the triangular "cans" that would then be lifted into place as the Arch progressed.[7]

Still, much about the construction process remained unresolved. PDM's engineers were skeptical that the "sandwich" method of constructing the arch would work. In fact, they concluded that once the final keystone was inserted, the Arch would fall. But Fred Severud and an associate, Hannskarl Bandel, were convinced of the orthotropic concept's structural integrity. Another crucial meeting occurred in 1963 with the representatives of PDM on one side, Severud and Bandel on the other, and NPS Director George Hartzog in between. As a former superintendent of the JNEM, Hartzog was as familiar with the Arch project as anyone. PDM asked Hartzog to approve a change order that significantly altered the entire construction process. An indignant Severud argued that the only fair way to settle the debate would be to build a scale model and submit it to stress tests. If the model failed, Severud pledged he would pay for all the expenses of the model and testing and personally approve the change order suggested by PDM. Rather than play into Severud's hands, PDM went to Interior Secretary Stewart Udall, who ordered the NPS to commission a feasibility study of the design. Hartzog was shocked to find that the study ultimately supported PDM. The NPS director understood that the basic theory of the orthotropic design was that "the strength of the structure is greater than the sum of the individual parts." Severud threatened to resign from the project if the change order was approved. Secretary Udall, meanwhile, worried over the brewing war between the builders and engineers, did not want to lose Severud. Yet if he ignored the report and the Arch later failed at some point, the Secretary would be blamed for the catastrophe. To settle the issue, Udall called Nathaniel Owings, a founder of the influential skyscraper design firm Skidmore, Owings, and Merrill. Owings's firm had submitted a design in the 1947 St. Louis competition, and a decade and a half later, they literally saved Saarinen's design. After examining the structure of the orthotropic method, Owings pronounced it fundamentally sound. With this endorsement, Udall finally agreed to proceed with construction over PDM's objections.[8]

Despite having won the contract to build the Arch, the MacDonald Company still had no specific idea for installing the Arch's sections. They considered using seven-hundred-foot crane towers, but were not certain a crane of such height could support the weight of the individual pieces. Gene MacDonald proposed another approach: "The answer may be a traveling crane suspended between the two towers." MacDonald's "traveling crane" seemed feasible, and his firm began planning how to get large cranes to rise with the Arch itself. The company arrived at an ingenious solution that used "creeper derricks," portable cranes that moved on rails up the two legs of the arch. Large construction projects in New York and Chicago had used similar derricks, but those were either vertical or horizontal construction structures. The Arch would be the first project to use creeper derricks on a curved surface. After ground-based cranes built the first few feet of each leg, workers installed three tracks of thirty-inch-wide flange steel beams twenty-four feet apart up the outer walls. The rails were anchored through the stainless steel and set in concrete. Workers then constructed two eighty-ton derricks with forty-three-by-thirty-four-foot platforms, each containing a shed, a heated room, sanitary facilities, and communication equipment. The "sled" on which the derrick rested was connected to the tracks by four high-strength pins of five-and-three-quarters inches in diameter. The derrick hoisted the various sections to the top of the leg, where workers attached the new piece. After four sections were put in place, the concrete poured, and the welds completed, workers laid more track and the derrick crept upward.[9]

On the morning of June 27, 1962, workmen began pouring concrete into a forty-four-foot-deep excavation hole that would hold the foundation of the Arch's south leg. Eight months later, they installed the first triangular section. A ground crane lifted the first six sections in place until the legs reached the height of seventy-two feet, at which point the creeper derricks took over. The sight of the two eighty-ton machines rising along with the Arch legs became a visual and engineering marvel of the construction process.

Welding was essential to the integrity of the Arch because the outside skins were weight-bearing. The three sides of the "cans" had to be welded together, and then the cans themselves had to be secured on top of each other. To ensure the structure's reliability, each weld was examined by an x-ray machine, and substandard ones were redone. As the legs rose, welders found themselves working in increasingly tilted and tight environments that tested their skills like no other project.[10]

To ensure the correct sequencing of jobs during construction, MacDonald paid nearby McDonnell Aircraft $55,000 for a two-and-a-half-minute run on its company computer. The builders wanted to use a complex algorithm created in the late 1950s called a "critical path" to keep track of the nearly two thousand individual construction tasks involved in completing the project. The printed computations exceeded five hundred pages and projected that the job would take 740 days, including bad weather and unforeseen delays. Gene MacDonald said of using a computer in the construction process, "We will feed information to the computer and push buttons and it will tell us at any time where we stand. The computer will tell us when and if we have to resort to overtime or put on more employees." The unique challenges of the Arch—no straight horizontal or vertical lines or surfaces anywhere—taxed the engineers and their equipment. The Arch was a major test case for the critical path method, which soon became the standard in aerospace, defense, and other construction projects in the 1960s.[11]

Except for that brief usage of the "critical path" algorithm, no computers were used in building the Arch. Instead, workers and engineers relied on slide rules and basic surveying equipment. Just maintaining consistency between the two legs required constant attention and many hours of exhaustive, detailed work. The stakes were high. If either leg veered off by even a fraction of an inch as the Arch rose, the sections would not join at the top; the result would have been an engineering folly of historic proportions. The pressure of avoiding that fate weighed heavily on all involved. Every night after installing a section, engineers carefully measured the day's work. The measurements had to be done at night when the heat of the sun did not distort the metal. Lights were placed atop each leg, and an engineer on the ground, using standard surveying equipment, determined the accuracy of the section within a sixteenth of an inch. To correct any problems, engineers would modify the following section, perhaps opening a wider gap than planned and filling in the difference with additional welding material. While the north and south legs were supposed to rise simultaneously, a competition naturally arose between the workers on the respective legs, and those on the "Yankee" were delighted that when they reached the 180-foot mark, "Rebel" had only made it to 132 feet.

In late 1964, an unforeseen problem emerged that slowed construction. As the sections were lifted and welded into place, the stainless steel skin started warping, or "wrinkling," especially on the north leg. When one can appeared especially wrinkled, the problematic section was removed. Some of the welds were cut to give the steel more room to expand, but that did not solve the problem. Despite their best effort, builders and engineers were unable to stop this process entirely, and certain amounts of wrinkling came to be accepted.[12]

With each new section, engineers detected slight differences in the appearance of the stainless steel itself. The hope was for the Arch to appear smooth and uniform, and fabricating all the steel in the same plant should have negated chances of irregularity. Yet variations persisted, and the answer lay at the moment of production. In the Pittsburgh mill, the stainless steel plates passed over sanded rollers that polished the steel. Each roller had a slightly different grit that could never be exactly duplicated. The architects understood that little could be done about it. From a distance, the Arch looks uniform, but closer inspection reveals the differences among sections.[13]

As the last cans were ready to be installed, another challenge arose. As the outer skin of the Arch is weight-bearing, engineers wondered, could the upper sections hold windows safely? The skin of the Arch was under heavy compression, and any windows would compromise its structural integrity. Yet without them, tourists would have no reason to go to the top of the structure. The engineers settled on sixteen narrow windows on each side, measuring seven by twenty-seven inches, with three-quarter-inch plate glass occupying minimal surface area. Anyone complaining about the small viewing spaces might feel better knowing that larger windows would weaken the entire structure.

Though structurally insignificant, the proposed elevator system for ferrying tourists to the top of the Arch had vexed the architects and engineers from the beginning. A simple elevator shaft could not work, because the passengers would be virtually on their sides when the elevator approached the top. Shortly after winning the competition, Saarinen was convinced the elevator system was "entirely feasible," but assumed they would have to stop at some point before reaching the top, and passengers would walk the remainder of the way. Even after groundbreaking ceremonies, the system's details remained sketchy, and as with so many aspects of the Arch, its actual mechanics came late in the process. Saarinen had conferred with a number of engineers, but no one knew how to configure an elevator within a steeply curved structure. The situation changed with a fortuitous meeting in 1960 between Saarinen and an engineer named Dick Bowser.

Bowser's father, Virgil, was a salesman for the Warner Elevator Company in Cincinnati, and one of his major successes coincidentally occurred in a well-placed location, the Shrine of the Little Flower in Royal Oak, Michigan. The church had drawn national attention during the 1920s for its radio priest, Father Charles Coughlin. When it was first built, the architect had placed a beam at the top of a dumbwaiter in the church's tower. When money flowed in through Father Coughlin's radio broadcasts, church leaders decided to extend the tower, but the beam seemed to prevent extending the dumbwaiter as well. A new architect needed a way for the original dumbwaiter to go up one hatchway and somehow slide over to a new tower when it encountered the beam. To solve the problem, Father Coughlin turned to Virgil Bowser.

Bowser devised an ingenious dumbwaiter system that rode up the original hatchway on a rail, and then swiveled over to a second rail when it came to the beam. For his son, who watched his father work on that elevator job, it was "a unique experience" devising an elevator system that did not ascend and descend necessarily in a straight line.[14]

Dick Bowser was working for the Montgomery Elevator Company in Moline, Illinois, in 1960 when Saarinen's office approached him about devising a method for an elevator to ascend the curved arch leg. When asked if an elevator needed to always travel vertically, Bowser replied, based on his experience with the Shrine of the Little Flower, that elevators placed on swivels could pivot around any obstacles. Saarinen's office, it turned out, was just minutes away from Coughlin's former church; Bowser told the architects to go over and see it for themselves.

After meeting with Saarinen, Bowser was given two weeks to devise a system for the Arch. He later said his task was "to get 3,500 people to the top of the Arch, which is the equivalent of a sixty-three-story building, during an eight-hour day." To complicate matters, the space within the triangular sections decreased with altitude. Conceivably, passengers could get off one standard elevator and then enter another, smaller one that rose on a more diagonal line, but waiting areas took up far too much interior space. Bowser thought about escalators, but the same problem arose—at several points along the way, passengers would have to change escalators. All of which proved too expensive and impractical. Bowser later confessed, "I thought I was pretty smart on elevators, but to try to do it in that triangularly-shaped space that was not plumb, it got to be quite a problem."

He finally envisioned the project in a radically different way. Rather than a standard car, he thought of how passengers on a Ferris wheel were transported in the same vehicle through 360 degrees. A similar concept might work for the Arch, and Bowser began thinking in terms of a series of enclosed "barrels" that swiveled on their way to the top. Instead of windowed elevators that allowed passengers to peer from their seats, Bowser devised a system whereby passengers would be offloaded near the top and walk the rest of the way. Rather than stay in a car, they could stand inside the top section and stare out windows to the city and river below. This system gave visitors the luxury of deciding when to return, and also allowed more people on and off at the same time, much like a subway system. The "Ferris wheel principle," as Bowser called it, "involved utilizing small containers of people, with their seats pivoted to swing at any angle." By using a unique combination of elevator and Ferris wheel concepts, Bowser had finally solved the problem.[15]

Bowser's invention proved a vital step in the making of the Arch. By creating a method of transport within the Arch, he gave tourists something more to do than look up from below. (The elevators are not the only way to ascend to the top of the Arch. In case of an emergency, one can use the 1,076-step stair system.) The space-age elevators and the dramatic view from the top became essential elements of the Arch experience. Visitors' primary memory concerns their claustrophobic reactions inside the capsules and the sometimes terrifying experience of gazing from above. Since their installation, Bowser's elevators have transported nearly 30 million passengers, including Dwight Eisenhower and Prince Charles.

■

As the Arch rose against the St. Louis skyline, another component of the downtown renewal effort took shape. Edward Durell Stone's new Busch Memorial Stadium, rising just blocks away, seemed an obvious way to bring more people downtown. It was designed to host both baseball and football, guaranteeing a constant stream of people to dine and shop in the area on game days. In the 1960s, such stadiums, easily accessible by interstate highways, were central to the modern notion of rebuilding downtowns. Yet their promise proved elusive, and most actually impeded the rebirth of downtowns. The vast majority of the time, these stadiums stood empty. Even on game days, they never reliably drew visitors to attractions other than the games themselves, and the tax and employment benefits offered by team owners seldom materialized.[16]

Stone included a reference to Saarinen in his stadium: a series of arches near the roof echoed the sleek taper of the Arch that towered nearby. Shortly after its completion in 1966, an exuberant Stone attended a baseball game in St. Louis, and was obviously pleased with the results. "Now I know how Nero felt when he sat in the Colisseum."[17] But his stadium was short-lived. In 2006, Stone's "modern" stadium was demolished to make way for a retro design evoking traditional ballparks that the original Busch replaced, a pattern that was repeated in Cincinnati, Atlanta, Philadelphia, and Pittsburgh.

Stone's involvement in St. Louis went beyond the stadium. In a meeting with city officials, he suggested they contact Walt Disney, who had spent part of his childhood in Missouri, for advice on rehabilitating the riverfront and downtown. In March 1963, Mayor Raymond R. Tucker traveled to Los Angeles to meet with Disney in the hope that he could serve as a consultant to a project called Riverfront Square, a tree-lined plaza just off the memorial site that would feature restaurants and theaters. At first, Disney called the project "interesting and exciting" and promised to explore the issue. But he had something else in mind. Disney went back to the planners who had studied the feasibility of Anaheim for his theme park, and asked them to examine the St. Louis project.[18]

In August 1963, Disney's advisors told him that the burgeoning St. Louis riverfront had lucrative possibilities. The cornerstone of any tourism appeal, they said, was the Gateway Arch. Disney considered something for St. Louis that he had long resisted—a counterpart to Disneyland. While the sprawling amusement park in Anaheim covered sixty-seven acres, the "new Disneyland" along the St. Louis riverfront would be far different, covering just over two acres in the area bordering the Arch site but rising five stories high. It would contain a town square, patterned after Disneyland's Main Street and centered on the history of St. Louis. A re-created historic St. Louis riverfront would contain attractions, Disney wrote, that would "make parts of Disneyland obsolete." His team also considered a venue in St. Louis for the revolutionary "Audio-Animatronics" technology, in which lifelike figures of people like Thomas Jefferson or Daniel Boone moved and spoke in remarkably human ways. As for ownership, Disney said his company needed "to be responsible for the whole thing, if it's got the Disney name connected with it."

This private-public partnership was just one of many items that Disney noted when he concluded "the fine details had not been worked out."[19]

Disney played his cards close to the vest. In November 1963, he returned to St. Louis with five company executives. At dinner, August Busch, Jr., president of Anheuser-Busch, remarked that beer should be sold at the proposed park, and anyone who thought differently "ought to have his head examined." While Busch's comment may have irritated his guests, Disney was far more concerned with the financial aspects of the negotiations. The Disney party flew the next day to central Florida, where Disney directed his private plane to circle around Orlando and a wooded area that would soon become the location of the Walt Disney World resort. Throughout 1964, he continued to meet with St. Louis leaders while secretly orchestrating an elaborate land-buying effort in Florida. It's possible that Disney remained interested in pursuing both projects simultaneously. It's equally possible that by 1964, Disney had already decided on Orlando, and St. Louis was merely a ruse while his representatives secretly bought property from unsuspecting Florida landowners.

By the summer of 1965, it became clear that no new Disneyland would be built in St. Louis. The sticking point, all along, had been finances and ownership. Disney insisted that the project would have to be financed by the city, and that after the $30 million to $50 million of capital costs were retired, the park and all its profits would be owned solely by Disney. Mayor Tucker assumed that Disney would bear the costs of investment. At one point in the discussions, Disney related the cheap prices he was "offered" on land in Florida and hoped city leaders would make him a similar proposal. The *Post-Dispatch* editorialized that "it's too bad" that "none of Walt Disney's prehistoric monsters, fairies, or resurrected river dwellers are to hold forth between the arch and the stadium." But the paper told its readers not to worry: with the Arch and the new baseball stadium, the downtown area "has 'got it made.'" Once it became clear how the area was transformed, the paper said "Mickey Mouse's boss" might well undergo a change of heart.[20]

In retrospect, the possibility of the Gateway Arch framing a second Disneyland does not seem so far-fetched. Disney's designers had envisioned a single, multileveled building that would protect tourists from the humid summers and unpredictable winters. A renovated riverfront, complete with a baseball stadium and a modernistic tourist attraction, would have had a certain appeal to Disney. He also had a city ready to make a deal, though not the one in which the city bore all the costs and Disney realized all of the profits. Mayor Alfonso Cervantes, who had just been elected in April 1965, like so many other cash-strapped city leaders, saw tourism as a "smokeless industry" that provided opportunities to levy taxes on people who could not then vote against local officials when they ran for reelection.[21]

But tourism or modernist architecture could not mask deep-seeded economic and social problems in St. Louis. In 1950, the city commissioned Saarinen's friend Minoru Yamasaki to design a high-rise public housing project just outside downtown that would be named Pruitt-Igoe. Yamasaki built thirty-three identical rectangular buildings on a fifty-seven-acre site, and when it was dedicated in 1952, Mayor Darst proclaimed that "St. Louisans can point to their city as a model of modern development." Pruitt-Igoe was conceived in the same urban planning ideology that had infused the riverfront. City leaders were worried about growing African American slums that would cause downtown property values to fall. Relocating public housing units outside the downtown business core was seen as the logical way to fix immediate housing shortages as well as stabilize downtown property values. Yet Yamasaki's bleak buildings proved a dismal failure, and within a decade, they were crime-ridden and decaying. By 1972, the first building within Pruitt-Igoe was demolished, and within four years, the entire project came down. As one scholar has noted, Pruitt-Igoe was more than a design disaster. It was "shaped by the strategies of ghetto containment and inner-city revitalization" that dominated the postwar period and cities like St. Louis.[22]

The problems that infected Pruitt-Igoe were rooted in class and race. Impoverished African Americans were systematically removed to a westward area in an attempt to remake the downtown more appealing to white citizens. In the 1960s, the Gateway Arch construction brought to the surface more of these underlying racial tensions. Local civil rights organizations saw Saarinen's design in ways far different from local whites.

When President Lyndon Johnson signed the Civil Rights Bill into law on July 2, 1964, the nation's reaction varied. In the deep South, civil rights workers quickly tested the limits of the new law. In St. Louis, civil rights activists searched for new tactics in the struggle for equality. To focus attention on the city's many remaining racial injustices, the St. Louis chapter of the Congress of Racial Equality (CORE) directed its attention on the dramatic construction project rising from the banks of the Mississippi.[23]

Despite some victories over Jim Crow in city hotels, pools, and schools, de facto segregation still cast a long shadow over St. Louis. A 1962 referendum to merge St. Louis County and the City of St. Louis failed largely because of racial fears. It marked the fourth effort in the century to correct the problems created by the "great divorce" that had limited the city's ability to grow. To CORE, meanwhile, the Arch was a gleaming reminder of broken promises. Black St. Louisans had backed the 1935 bond issue election in the hope that it would provide jobs to the city's African American workers, but the workforce on the Arch project remained all white. Contractors and building officials replied to CORE's demands by saying their hands were tied since local unions refused to admit African Americans. In the view of one local activist, St. Louis was "essentially a southern city with a lot of virulent racism."[24]

African Americans were central to the history of St. Louis and its downtown. They also provided much of the rich culture that gave life to a city otherwise increasingly known for decaying streets and parks. Pioneering blues and rock musicians Chuck Berry, Tina Turner, Fontella Bass, Albert King, and Johnnie Johnson, jazz greats Clark Terry and Miles Davis, and gospel singer Willie Mae Ford Smith came from St. Louis. So did poet Maya Angelou, singer and dancer Josephine Baker, baseball great James "Cool Papa" Bell, boxer Archie Moore, and comedians Dick Gregory and Redd Foxx. For years, many of these legends struggled for recognition behind such noted white St. Louisans as William S. Burroughs, Kate Chopin, and T. S. Eliot.

The city's racial history and the Arch were woven together with many common threads. As Alison Isenberg notes, urban renewal and improvement strategies "have gone hand in hand with policies designed to attract certain types of people downtown while ignoring or explicitly rejecting others." Population figures revealed how St. Louis had become a classic case of "white flight." From 1950 to 1970, the total population of St. Louis fell 28 percent, while that of the county more than doubled. The city's white population plummeted from over 700,000 in 1950 to 365,000 twenty years later, while its African American population grew from 153,000 in 1950 to over 250,000 in 1970.[25]

CORE was ready to fight discriminatory hiring practices on the Gateway Arch project. The local organization had already learned some tactics of direct action in its 1963 boycott of the city's Jefferson Bank and Trust Company, which had refused to hire African Americans. After continued rebuffs from builders and unions, Percy Green, the local chairman of CORE's Employment Committee, raised the stakes. He asked Senator Symington "to do everything in your power to withhold further funds" from the Arch project until "Negroes are given a fair share of the jobs on the Jefferson Memorial Gateway Arch Project." By releasing funds for the project, Green asserted, Symington would be "supporting employment discrimination against Negroes." After four months of investigation, Green claimed that no African Americans had been employed on the Arch other than a few "common laborers." Green asserted that no African Americans could be admitted to the skilled trade unions because the apprenticeship program was administered by the local public schools, which were still segregated. This gave unions an easy excuse when challenged about their policies. By any measure, St. Louis building trades systematically discriminated. Weeks later, St. Louis CORE chairman Lucian Richards upped the ante. "Since Federal Funds were not withheld from the project while an honest investigation was carried out and discriminatory conditions corrected," Richards wrote to Symington, "CORE has no other choice than to handle the situation itself."[26]

On July 6, just days after the "triumph" of the Civil Rights bill, twelve CORE protestors began picketing the Arch, carrying signs that said: "We Want Jobs." They were largely ignored by passersby. Green and other CORE workers knew they needed to make a more visible protest, and that required getting to the Arch itself. To test their ability to infiltrate the work zone, Green and a white member of the Action Committee to Improve Opportunities for Negroes (ACTION), Richard Daly, dressed like construction workers in Levi's jeans, t-shirts, and work boots. They walked to the north leg of the Arch without drawing attention.

Assured that their disguises would work, Green and CORE prepared for the next move. At a strategy session that evening, Green and Daly decided to climb to the top of the Arch ladders and stage a spectacular "sit-in" protest. Green and Daly already knew they stood a good chance of climbing up a leg of the Arch unnoticed. But ACTION took no chances. On July 14, 1964, they staged a very visible protest at the Old Courthouse, complete with pickets and homemade signs. As Green later admitted, it was "a diversionary tactic." With everyone focused on the picketers at the courthouse, Green and Daly returned to the Arch site in their construction clothes. They waited until the workers stopped for lunch, then climbed 125 feet up one leg of the Arch. They remained for several minutes, while curious workers below wondered what they were doing. It was only after the lunch break that everyone realized what had occurred. At that point, other CORE members gathered at the base of the leg, demanding that African Americans receive at least 10 percent of the jobs at the Arch site. Green and Daly stayed on their perch for four hours (the *Globe-Democrat* claimed they were actually frozen in fear), and when they descended were arrested for trespassing. Park Service officials scrambled to find a way to satisfy the protestors. After park engineer Woodrow Zenfell promised to provide "close attention" to hiring practices in letting future contracts, a CORE spokesman said the civil rights group was "satisfied" and planned no further demonstrations at the Arch. The four-hour protest received some local press attention, but little more.[27]

Superintendent LeRoy Brown saw the entire episode as a needless diversion from the task of building the Arch. When confronted with the fact that there were no jobs for African American on the project, Brown simply deferred all questions to the unions, saying there was "no evidence of any specific case of discrimination" and reiterated that "we can't tell the contractor to hire unqualified Negroes."[28] While Green and Daly's sit-in produced no immediate results, it unleashed a series of events that would have lasting significance beyond the Arch.

Zenfell recruited several African American craftsmen to work on the Arch, but when they showed up for work, white workers immediately walked off the job in protest. The U.S. Justice Department eventually filed suit against the Building Trades Council of St. Louis and five of its local unions affiliated with the AFL-CIO. Operating under language provided by the newly enacted Civil Rights Bill, it argued that the union demonstrated a "pattern or practice of discrimination"—the first time such an action had been taken since the passage of the bill. Yet courts ruled against the Justice Department, claiming no evidence indicated any discrimination after the Civil Rights Act had been passed. In August, the President's Committee on Equal Employment Opportunity found MacDonald Construction noncompliant with federal hiring regulations. Due to the legal and political uncertainties surrounding hiring discrimination, President Johnson signed an executive order to speed up the process of hiring minority businesses. The order required government contractors to take "affirmative action" toward employing minority workers. A draft order was later issued by the Labor Department directing contractors working on federal projects in excess of $1 million to institute affirmative action policies in the awarding of contracts. St. Louis was the first city to assure equality before awarding contracts, instead of the more popular, but less effective, method of trying to ensure equality after contracts were let. The NPS had to admit that because of the highly skilled specialists needed for the Arch, it could not promise that a significant number of minorities would be hired immediately, but it promised to pay "close attention" to future contracts.

CORE asked the federal government to investigate the realities of working conditions on the Arch project. In August 1964, the Equal Employment Opportunity office had summoned representatives from the major players in building the Arch to Washington to explain the obvious discrimination. According to the Office of Economic Opportunity, the MacDonald firm had not "taken the affirmative action required under his contract with the Interior Department."

MacDonald's contract with the Interior Department called for employers to ensure fair employment practices at workplaces receiving federal money. Charges of racial discrimination were met with bland denials by MacDonald and NPS Director H. Raymond Gregg.[29]

The racial division among workers on the project persisted. In 1966, white workers in the partially completed underground visitors' center walked off the job in protest against a black St. Louis plumbers' union which had successfully lobbied to have some of its members hired. Sherwood Ross, an official with the Urban League, said that "when it comes to getting Negroes into the highly skilled building crafts, labor sings the Star-Spangled Banner in the front of the union hall, and Dixie in the back." The move prompted the Labor Department to request federal action against the AFL-CIO Building Trades Council in St. Louis. Of the five thousand members in the local unions, the Justice Department noted that only three were African Americans.[30]

Still, the number of black workers on the Arch did not increase. Unions adjusted their earlier claims and implied that skilled black workers were simply too hard to recruit and train. In St. Louis's long and troubled history of race relations, the Arch represented one more example of unmet promises. While it stood for many things to many people, for the city's African Americans, the Gateway Arch symbolized the divide between those who "had it made" and those who did not.[31]

EIGHT

Expendable Culture

Workers tightening a bolt to secure the creeper derrick platform.
Arthur Witman Photographic Collection, State Historical Society of Missouri
Research Center–St. Louis.

The Gateway Arch's unique design made it a dangerous place to work. In the years before the Occupational Safety and Health Act in 1970, workers on the Arch braved extraordinarily hazardous conditions without federal oversight. Men dangled from the ends of its legs without so much as a safety harness, worked within cramped and tilted environments, and sometimes found themselves upside down. Insurance underwriters calculated there would be thirteen deaths before completion. Remarkably, not a single worker died during the Arch's construction.[1]

Official records of monumental construction projects usually designate architects, engineers, and politicians as their "builders." Those who actually assemble brick, mortar, and steel are generally lost to history. Yet without the courage and skill of hundreds of workers, Eero Saarinen's design would have remained just a model.

Native American Don White, a foreman on the Arch, was one of the few minorities among the nearly all-white crews. He had taken advantage of employers' belief that Native Americans had no fear of heights to find work on a number of bridges in New York, an experience that prepared him well for the challenges of working in St. Louis. Looking down, for example, was never a problem since the fixed structures provided a point of reference. Looking up, on the other hand, could be dangerous. "If you look up too long, watching a beam being set," White said, "you may get the impression you're leaning back too far," and there is a natural tendency to compensate by leaning forward. The constant wind, he noted, "is what you have to be careful about," and it sometimes forced workers to delay fitting a section: a section hanging from a crane might be blown into the finished leg. "You can't bang this stuff around like the way you do the steel on other jobs," White said.

The long hours in St. Louis provided little time for workers from outside St. Louis to return home. Adding to the dangers and loneliness was an aspect of working on the Arch that bridge or dam builders did not experience. In the bars where they would go at nights and weekends, the workers were inevitably subject to jokes and sneers about the "croquet wicket" they were building on the riverfront. Arch workers developed a loyalty to the project that resisted such ribbing. Gene MacDonald noted that "more than once laborers have had to be bailed out of jail on Monday mornings after Saturday night barroom brawls in which the workers defended the arch's honor against wisecrackers."[2]

There was, naturally, a hierarchy of workers. Russ Knox, who was responsible for keeping the various machines oiled and maintained, saw this first hand one day when a MacDonald engineer confronted a project superintendent, Art Pritchard. When Pritchard asked the engineer to check on something, he dismissed the suggestion, saying he had already done it. Pritchard, Knox recounted, "blew up" and "fired the man, right then and there." To Knox, it served as a warning: "If he'll do that to an engineer," he reasoned, "they'll bury me."[3]

The entire project depended on the giant creeper derricks. Operators worked in small shacks on the ground, about one hundred feet from each leg, and stayed in constant contact with signalmen atop the arch. Approximately three miles of steel cables ran from the ground to the derricks and back. One of the operators was Bill Quigley, who ran the derrick on the north leg. Quigley's job required considerable skill. While seated at the controls of the derrick, he could see very little of the actual operation. He wore earphones to listen to workers on the ground and at the top of the leg, who directed him in getting the sections, or "cans," safely into place. Quigley had four fingers missing from his right hand and would never have made it past PDM's insurance underwriters without the intervention of the local builders' union.[4]

The other principal operator was seventy-seven-year old Luther Fritts, the oldest active operator in Local 513, the International Association of Operating Engineers. Fritts had been a "derrick man" for nearly sixty years and worked on a variety of large buildings in the St. Louis area. His two signalmen were Bill Scheib and Vito Comporato. Fritts subsisted on little but coffee and cigars during the workday, and boasted that he had loaded sixty sections of the Arch in place, and never "even mashed a fingernail." When he first started working as a teenager in 1905, Fritts earned twelve cents an hour. In 1965, as the derrick operator on the Gateway Arch, he made $4.77 an hour. This was certainly higher than the $3.125 per hour for unskilled labor, yet well below the nearly $7.00 per hour rate for engineers operating air compressors.[5]

Winds near the upper level of the Arch could reach seventy-five miles per hour and sometimes made it impossible to use the elevators that carried the workers to and from the creeper derricks, forcing them to climb stairs attached to the tracks. Clifton "Red" Allison recalled that routinely "the wind whipped up the legs of my coveralls, inflating them." One terrifying moment occurred when an especially strong gust lifted his feet off the ladder rungs. "I was suspended in space, holding to the rung for dear life."[6]

Unlike a bridge or skyscraper, the Gateway Arch's unique building environment forced workers into increasingly smaller confines. Ironworker Fred Morris found himself crammed in with electrical, sheet metal, and elevator workers. In the sweltering St. Louis summer, the heat within the legs could be unbearable. At the end of the day, Morris recalled, "you'd come out and your boots would be wringing wet." Some found the angled and claustrophobic space too disorienting. Morris said he watched "some really good ironworkers come down after working on that thing for a short time and say, 'Hey, this ain't for me.'" As the legs of the arch grew increasingly tilted as they rose, "all of a sudden it looked like you could just step out and walk across, but you couldn't because it was on a slant. . . . Everything was an illusion."[7]

By the summer of 1965, the two legs had reached nearly 550 feet high, and their curvatures made the weight of the creeper derricks increasingly ominous. With each new section, the legs got thinner, and more electrical workers quit, saying they felt an "uneasy sense of tilting." The derricks could go no further without risking catastrophe. To stabilize the structure for the final construction push, engineers decided a strut had to be placed between the legs. The creepers carefully lifted a sixty-ton steel truss, which was then bolted to both sides of the Arch. It remained in place until construction was completed. NPS officials were outraged that the strut bore the giant letters "PDM." Seeing the sign as a commercial advertisement, an outraged superintendent LeRoy Brown decided to withhold $225,000 from a scheduled payment to PDM until the letters were gone. PDM workers removed the letters.[8]

Not everyone was impressed by the wonder of the Arch's construction. When architectural critic Ada Louise Huxtable visited the city in 1964, she found the setting ironic. "The visitor's first impression is that St. Louis has been bombed." She also understood a lost part of the story behind the gleaming steel fingers soaring into the sky. "The heart and history of St. Louis were in its waterfront, when the river was its life." The cast-iron façades of the buildings razed to make way for the Arch "were stored in a warehouse as a kind of backhanded gesture to the past," but then had been buried beneath a mountain of fill from the excavation of the expressway. "Call it progress and expendable culture," she later wrote. She also could not resist a dig at Walt Disney's proposal to place robots in his Riverfront Square that mimicked old St. Louis. "Add the ultimate irony," Huxtable said, "it will recreate in full, phony audio-animatronic riverboat glory just those local features that the city has destroyed."[9]

By mid-October 1965, the two legs had made their way to the point where the final section, the keystone, was ready to be set in place. Not surprisingly, another drama played out. Mayor Alfonso

Cervantes's committee of "ambassadors" mailed 1,500 invitations for the event, which they planned for Saturday, October 30. PDM, however, wanted to install the final sections on Thursday the twenty-eighth and worried about the extra days' unnecessary wait. Specifically, PDM engineers were concerned about the weight of the creeper derricks supported by the newly welded joints. Officials with PDM said they could wait the additional days if the city paid the premium on a $10 million insurance policy they had with Lloyd's of London. LeRoy Brown understood that until the keystone was in place, the arch was vulnerable to "acts of God, such as extremely high winds or an earthquake." The latter was no idle speculation. On October 21, 1965, a minor earthquake centered in Reynolds County, about a hundred miles away, shook the ground in St. Louis.

The drama escalated on the twenty-sixth, when employees with the Local 396, Iron Workers Union, walked off their jobs. The workers were angry at their local union leaders, whom they said were caving to political pressure to delay the "topping off." The result was a vulnerable arch and the workers felt their lives were at greater risk. Yet Edwynne P. Murphy, one of Cervantes's "ambassadors," was not persuaded by the workers or the engineers that topping out was that urgent. "If finishing the arch is such an emergency," Murphy asked, "why didn't they have men up there working last Sunday?" By the next day, such casual dismissals were ineffective. After the *Globe-Democrat* criticized the mayor's "ambassadors" for their obvious political posturing, Cervantes relented and the "topping out" was scheduled for Thursday. With written assurance from the NPS and PDM attesting to the Arch's safety, the union ordered the workers back on the job.[10]

Even with the strut holding them apart, the ends of the two legs were separated by only two and a half feet. For the keystone to fit, a hydraulic truss had to be inserted to widen the gap to eight and one half feet. This was not a routine operation. Under the pressure of the hydraulic truss, welds or other parts of the Arch might break, causing a section to fail and a derrick to fall to the ground. All the workers and officials at top were in jeopardy, as well as those below. Even after a successful installation, and even if all the welds held, some PDM officials were still worried that the Arch would not stand on its own.

As morning broke on October 28, dignitaries and curious onlookers gathered for the installation of the eight-foot final "can." Local television and radio stations broadcast the event. Thousands of St. Louisans prepared for either the climactic joining of the two legs or the tragic failure of the entire project. Inside the inner and outer walls of the keystone was a time capsule, containing over 762,000 signatures, newspaper articles, and other artifacts. Unlike most time capsules, no plans were made for when this one would be opened or how it might be removed from the sealed section. For all intents and purposes, the capsule can be accessed only if the Arch collapses.[11]

The 10:00 A.M. start for the "topping out" actually began at 9:30 because crews worried about thermal expansion of the steel under the morning sun. Without sunlight, the south leg was an inch and seven-eighths below the north leg, yet as the sun heated the structure, the margin expanded to nearly ten inches. To cool the steel, the fire department supplied a seven-hundred-foot hose that could reach to the upper stretches of the Arch. When the jacks had separated the legs to the necessary distance, Bill Quigley began lifting the keystone. Sue Ann Wood, a reporter for the *Globe-Democrat*, wrote, "the stainless steel sides of the triangular section glistened in the sunlight as it glided upward, steadied by two cables held on the ground by four workmen." Raising the final section into place took thirteen agonizing minutes, and when it reached its destination, workers maneuvered the section into place, tightening a series of bolts that secured both legs to each other. At 2:30 P.M., workers released the jacks that had separated the legs, and for the first time, the two sides of the Gateway Arch rested against each other. The crowd cheered while the engineers and planners all breathed a sigh of relief. LeRoy Brown noted that with the keystone in place, "the risk was over." Even though city leaders had hoped President Johnson could attend the event, the highest ranking federal official on hand was U.S. Interior Secretary John Carver, who paid tribute to the men essential for the Arch—Saarinen, Luther Ely Smith, as well as politicians Bernard Dickmann and Clarence Cannon. Aline Saarinen was there as well and called the Arch "the climax of my husband's career—the thing that meant the most to him." A relieved Gene MacDonald admitted the worries of entire construction process: "It's been like living with a time bomb and never knowing when it was going to explode."[12]

Relief was not the only thing Gene MacDonald felt. He remembered receiving a letter from a local citizen named Leonard Lipic, who recounted the story of the two arms of the Trans-Continental Railroad being joined in 1869. Lipic reminded MacDonald that the builders had driven a golden spike to mark the mammoth project's completion and suggested that the same be done to commemorate the Arch. Much to MacDonald's disappointment, there had been no real ceremony at the top of the Arch, where the workers were too consumed with the job at hand. All the fanfare had occurred among the dignitaries and crowds far below. MacDonald considered the day anticlimactic, and pondered a more appropriate measure if not for the cameras and the public, at least for himself and his crews. So he and his workers returned the next day to the top of the Arch and quietly inserted a golden bolt into the keystone. "We were remindful of your suggestion," MacDonald informed Lipic.[13] The ceremony was a quiet triumph for a company that had just built one of the most remarkable structures in the world.

Mayor Cervantes claimed that the Arch marked a transforming moment in St. Louis's history. The dream that had been realized with the topping out, he said, "calls for economic gains. It calls for social renewal." The *Globe-Democrat* acknowledged the Arch's importance, but warned that "the city must provide more on its rejuvenated riverfront to hold these guests for a longer stay than a trip to the top of the Arch." Others also heralded the completion of the Arch as a major step in the rebirth of St. Louis. The *Post-Dispatch* gushed about the city's memorial. While reminding readers that "much remains to be done" to rehabilitate downtown, the newspaper called the Arch an "undeniable triumph" that engendered "a fresh confidence" among the city's residents. The builders of the Arch had not only made a "symbol of 200 years gone, but also of a future, bright as the sky on topping out day."[14]

Over in East St. Louis, Illinois, another story unfolded. The *Globe-Democrat* noted that the opposite riverfront revealed "no signs of a national monument; no construction workers bustle about the area; only piles of trash fill weed-choked fields. . . . This is the view to the east, this is the East St. Louis riverfront." In 1947, as other architects had conceived of elaborate designs for the riverfront opposing the memorial site, Eero Saarinen had envisioned a more modest plan, emphasizing landscaping and a parkway. Instead, as the "topping out" ceremony played out, the grimy towers of the Continental Grain Company dominated the view across the river. To some officials working on the Arch, this was the way it must be. LeRoy Brown opposed any efforts to include East St. Louis in the project, concluding, "I figured it was just the east side's attempt to get in on the skirts of the Arch people." Just as rail lines had been an ongoing impediment to developing the memorial site in St. Louis, they hampered rebuilding in East St. Louis, where railroad companies owned most of the land on the riverfront. Hundreds of coal cars owned by the Peabody Coal Company awaited river barges, and railroads such as the Louisville and Nashville Company owned hundreds of acres of riverfront rights-of-way. The Terminal Railroad Association, the nemesis of Saarinen and city leaders in St. Louis throughout the 1950s, also occupied an eyesore in East St. Louis. Its elevated trestle sliced the riverfront in half as it rose slowly from the northeast corner of the site to the MacArthur Bridge. East St. Louis Mayor Alva Fields recognized the problems he faced, but used the recent history of St. Louis as a model. "We're certainly concerned about our side of the river," Fields commented, "but it took 30 years to get their side going." The *Globe-Democrat* concluded: "Meanwhile, the afternoon sun shines at once on the gleaming steel key to one city's rebirth, and on the sullen, sooty symbol of another city's challenge."[15]

When journalist Marquis Childs visited the Gateway Arch in 1967, he was captivated. "For sheer, soaring triumph of form nothing approaching it has come out of the century. . . . So many monuments are dull, spiritless, cookie-cutter nothings that the Gateway Arch must seem a miraculous accident thrust up on the levee." Another writer came away far less impressed. Lorenzo W. Milam of Seattle wrote that while the "giant, useless arch" was preferable to his town's Space Needle, "the Arch is a big put-on, a royal chuck." Walking around the site, surprised by the area's desolation, Milam concluded that "St. Louis absolutely reviles, curses, and spits on its shoreline."[16] These disparate reactions reflected the thoughts of many visitors. On one hand, the Arch was breathtaking, a modern monument standing in stark contrast to its dismal surroundings. On the other hand, it seemed absurd if viewed as an attempt to repair the St. Louis riverfront and the city surrounding it.

Following the topping out ceremony, the creeper derricks lowered the stabilizing bar to the ground and began their descent down the legs of the Arch—an operation that took five months of painstaking, precise work. The tracks above the derrick had to be removed and the holes filled so that the Arch could maintain its seamless appearance. When the holes were first made, each hole and bore was numbered, and now each of the bores had to be replaced in its exact orientation to ensure that the grain of the stainless steel matched perfectly. The workers performing this task also undertook one last chore—cleaning the Arch from top to bottom. Two crews of five workers cleaned the sections as the derricks descended, using combinations of detergent, ammonia, paint thinner, and degreasers, and washing them with water coming from five-hundred-gallon tanks.[17]

Now that it was standing on its own, city and NPS officials began worrying about what might make the Arch fall. Its designers had anticipated tornadoes and earthquakes and had built the structure accordingly. Long before 9/11, they knew that aircraft presented another possible threat. In 1965, the FAA prohibited any aircraft from flying through the Arch, but that did not stop the occasional daredevil pilot.[18]

When the Jefferson National Expansion Memorial was first presented to the voters of St. Louis in 1935, it was touted foremost as a jobs program. The promised jobs were not realized until the 1960s and the actual number created was far less than predicted. Still, the construction of the Arch employed dozens of companies throughout the area, and hundreds of contractors and subcontractors. But some of those employed on the project ended up worse off. In the months and years after the topping out ceremony, contractors and their attorneys filed several lawsuits seeking damages from the NPS over its mismanagement of the construction process. The delays in completing the interior, especially the elevator system, pushed the completion date back by years and were very costly to the companies charged with doing the work. The construction of the Arch, wrote *New York Times* reporter Richard Jacobs, "seems to be taking nearly as long as the actual winning of the West." By January 1968, the suits totaled more than $2 million. The Arch had already driven one contractor out of business, and put another on the verge of bankruptcy. The story of the contractors and the NPS, according to one contractor, "is the untold, the unpublicized story of the Gateway Arch." During construction, estimates of building costs were mere guesses, as no one had anything on which to base their projections. The final price tag for the Arch itself came to more than $13 million. The cost for the entire project was already $6,725,000 over the original $30 million estimate, and more remained to be done.[19]

The delays usually involved contractors battling each other for time to work within the tight confines of the Arch's interior. The conflicts only increased as the legs grew and narrowed. Electricians, steel workers, welders, and engineers found themselves waiting for others to finish their tasks. Many had signed contracts that carried penalties for late delivery. But their pleas to Superintendent LeRoy Brown for extensions of the deadlines fell on deaf ears. Ray Crank of the St. Louis Sheet Metal Company, which went bankrupt because of the Arch, concluded that the NPS "was not equipped to supervise a job like this. All they've ever put up are a few outhouses in the parks."

The problems did not end with angry contractors. The Mac-Donald Company itself had struggled from the beginning of construction, and that struggle extended all the way to Gene MacDonald himself. After winning the bid to build the Arch, the company found itself in a financial straitjacket. To obtain a $1 million loan from the Mercantile Trust Company in May 1965, MacDonald put up his company and his own home as collateral. In July 1967, the company lost its five-story brick building on Washington Avenue at auction. In all, MacDonald estimated 250 days were lost on the project, and the NPS withheld more than $367,000 in payments. The Mac-Donald Company did not publicize how much its final costs exceeded their accepted bid, but its cases in appeals courts totaled over $600,000. One subcontractor commented that "The Arch has come very near close to putting us out of business." Robert Hoel, owner of the Hoel-Steffen Construction Company, said "Some men live to be

80, then look back on their life to find their one big mistake," Hoel lamented. He added, "I don't have to be 80 to know mine. It was taking that contract on the Gateway Arch."[20]

Nor did the completed Arch exterior win universal acclaim. Some reacted in similar fashion to how many Parisians had first felt about the newly completed Eiffel Tower. Pennsylvanian Congressman Joseph P. Vigorito was "appalled" by the "steel monstrosity in St. Louis." Representing a district just north of Pittsburgh where the huge amounts of stainless steel were manufactured, Vigorito none-theless saw the Arch as a massive waste, and asked. "Why don't we just take an old battleship and give it to them to stand on end?" While snide comments might have been expected from frugal poli-ticians and those hostile to modern art, it is more surprising that the *New Yorker* treated the completion of the Gateway Arch as a joke. "We are not impressed by St. Louis's arch," the magazine com-mented, adding that "it's all very well for St. Louis to construct a 630-foot arch symbolizing its role as the Gateway to the West, but as it happens, Kansas City is the Gateway to the West." With tongue in cheek, the magazine suggested the Arch be transported to a more appropriate site. "We believe that any city capable of marshaling the stamina and modern knowledge to construct a 630-foot non-functional arch in the first place can figure out how to move it 235 miles to the west."[21]

By 1966, the funds to complete the museum and the memorial grounds had dried up. Once again, the city turned to bonds to raise the final $2 million. In November, the bond issue was approved by just 58 percent of the voters, well short of the necessary two-thirds majority. According to the *Globe-Democrat*, many voters were worried about higher debt and the possibility of higher taxes. The JNEMA was not ready to accept defeat just yet, and turned to an old pro in former mayor Bernard Dickmann to head the "Campaign to Com-plete the Riverfront Memorial." The effort was successful in getting a second try in a special election held in March 1967. This time, the bond issue won with nearly 69 percent of the voters supporting it. Afterward, Dickmann said, "never at any time did I think it wouldn't pass."[22]

As the Arch and Busch Memorial Stadium neared completion, Mayor Cervantes searched for other opportunities to attract visitors downtown. He raised over $2 million from local business leaders to relocate the Spanish Pavilion from the New York World's Fair of 1964–65 to a site near the Arch, yet it closed within a year. With an additional $375,000 from corporate sponsors, Cervantes bought a replica of the *Santa Maria* to the riverfront, but it soon sunk. The city's increasing investment in tourism to save downtown was already being reassessed by some city leaders. Donald Gunn, president of the Board of Aldermen, worried about tourism as a "fickle friend" and hoped the city would focus more on building good schools and improving race relations.[23]

The Arch had received several dedication ceremonies, such as President Truman's visit in 1950 and Mayor Tucker's groundbreaking in 1959. The final "official" ceremony did not occur until May 25, 1968, when Vice President Hubert Humphrey came to St. Louis for the event. The rain was so heavy that the event had to be moved inside to the visitors' center, where a minor flood ensued. Despite the water, the vice president captured the essence of what had been accomplished: "None will leave this site without a renewed sense of the elemental qualities of beauty." Humphrey understood also that "From now on, St. Louis's arch is America's magnificent monument."[24]

The civic boosterism that captivated Humphrey and so many others at the time proved too powerful to ignore. With a gleaming new baseball stadium nearby, and surrounded by expansive highways, the monumental Arch seemed almost certain to change St. Louis's fortunes. Even Eero Saarinen had been caught up in the euphoria, once boasting that the Third Street highway that cut off the memorial site from the city had "the same possibility of becoming a beautiful street as the Rue de Rivoli in Paris, often called the most beautiful street in the world." No one will ever mistake the finished area around the Arch for a Parisian boulevard. After considering the fortitude needed to cross six lanes of traffic, to stand on small slices of concrete while overlooking the underlying interstate highway, a pedestrian may understand why Interior Secretary Dirk Kempthorne remarked in 2008: "This is the worst entry to a national park property that there is."[25]

The gaping wound of the highways, and the decaying structures just blocks from the Arch, underscored how, like so many other American cities, St. Louis bet on tourism and expressways to save its downtown. It lost.

NINE

Symbol and Symptom

With the Arch serving as a symbol of the Republic, Senators Clinton and Obama
debating in 2008. *New York Times/* Damon Winter.

In a relatively short time, the Gateway Arch has become as revered as the Statue of Liberty or the Lincoln Memorial as a symbol of American democracy. The Arch is also synonymous with St. Louis, and in order to understand its legacy, must be seen as part of a larger effort to reverse the city's steady decline. As politicians and planners justified condemning forty square blocks out of a patriotic desire to honor westward expansion and provide jobs, their efforts were actually aimed at restoring real estate values by pushing businesses and people away from the city's eastern edge. In the process, they built a unique monument that retells its triumphant history to millions of tourists.

Behind every great iconic structure is the story of what was there before; the often brutal process of how the building came to be; and a clear assessment of how that building altered the lives and landscape of what remains. For decades, long before anyone living could remember, the riverfront had its own identity, a community of businesses and stores that employed thousands of people. Despite the fact that some of these buildings were unique architectural treasures, they were quickly demolished following the outcome of the 1935 bond issue fight. In the name of urban renewal, what was lost was an essential part of St. Louis, and American, history. When the last of these old buildings was gone, St. Louis was never the same.

When she visited St. Louis after the completion of the Arch, Ada Louise Huxtable noted that the "new" St. Louis might prove "a success economically and a failure urbanistically," but like so many others throughout the nation, the city found itself "in the absurd cycle of tearing down irreplaceable old structures" while promoting "expensive new projects of depressing vacuity." Huxtable was somewhat impressed by the Arch, which offered "surprising attitudes of contemporary abstract grandeur from almost every angle," but found the lone functional aspect of the structure sorely lacking. "If you must share in the great American tourist compulsion to get to the top of everything big, you can be shot up in a purple capsule, like one of five peas in a pod." Huxtable noted that the memorial park had been created out of a space where a "priceless cast-iron architectural heritage was bulldozed." St. Louis stood as a "monument to Chamber of Commerce planning and design." Huxtable then described what she saw:

> There are all of the faceless, characterless, scaleless symbols of economic regeneration—luxury apartments, hotels, a 50,000-seat stadium and multiple parking garages for 7,400 cars. Sleek, new, prosperous, stolid and dull, well-served by superhighways, the buildings are a collection of familiar profit formulas, uninspired in concept, unvarying in scale, unrelated by any standards, principles or subtleties of design. They just stand there. They come round, rectangular, singly and in pairs. Pick your standard commercial cliché.

As "a prime example of the modern landscape of urban alienation," Huxtable understood that St. Louis "gained a lot of real estate and lost a historic city."[1]

The historic city that was demolished in the 1930s is now a wooded park that comprises the bulk of the Jefferson National Expansion Memorial. A disappointed Dan Kiley, the original landscape architect for the project, had hoped for a "more spatial mystery into the whole site." He wanted to fill the site with tulip poplars, which would eventually grow to more than eighty feet and make the overall experience feel more like "a cathedral." He also envisioned places for cafes and coffee shops, to give the place a more European feeling than most American parks, which were "notorious for being so sterile." Kiley had tried to "break down the monumentality to the human scale, to the pedestrian scale," but this ambition was never realized. In the end, he lamented that the "whole land is wasted with a bunch of trees (ash trees) that are not natural in their association," making the area surrounding the arch "more like a cemetery, instead of a park of joy."[2]

This area has proven to be little more than an aesthetic afterthought, some gratuitous greenery set between the river and the highways. Jane Jacobs described this process as another casualty of urban planning: "some parks are basically unfitted, whether by location, size or shape, to serve successfully." Because of its disconnection with the city, the park is used mainly by joggers or by tourists walking back to the parking garage. St. Louisans venture to the park that surrounds the Arch sporadically, but they would never consider it a vital part of the city.[3]

Few plots of land in the United States have been as contested as these eighty acres that comprise the Jefferson National Expansion Memorial. The debate over what to do with the St. Louis riverfront has been at the center of the city's history for over two centuries. From landing pads to football stadiums to parking lots, and to even a Midwest version of Disneyland, the site's piecemeal development has left an economic, social, and visual scar on the city. Two tiers of highways sever the memorial park from the city, another remnant of the postwar ethos that culminated with Interstate highways. Robert M. Fogelson notes that these expressways "eviscerated" downtown businesses, displacing "many of the stores, offices, and other enterprises that were its lifeblood."[4]

At times, the riverfront has shown what is possible if the memorial grounds were reconnected to the city. In October 2008, when presidential candidate Barack Obama came to St. Louis, more than 100,000 people crowded onto the grounds of the memorial to hear him speak under the Arch. All traffic was shut down on Memorial Drive for the day, and for one St. Louisan, the chance to walk freely from the city to the Arch was breathtaking. "Anyone who went to hear Barack Obama speak on the Arch grounds," commented the

Post-Dispatch, "experienced how liberating it is to move seamlessly from Downtown to the Arch across Memorial Drive."[5]

Liberating the Arch grounds permanently has been on the agenda of city leaders for decades. In 2010, St. Louis conducted the first major architectural competition since 1947–48, in the hope of producing a more vibrant and accessible riverfront by the time of the Arch's fiftieth birthday in 2015. From forty-nine entries, the jury selected the design of Michael Van Valkenburgh Associates (MVVA) of Brooklyn. The MVVA plan included a tree-lined "lid" over I-70, as well as an aerial gondola ride across the river to East St. Louis. Just as the Arch faced an array of financing hurdles, so does the recent revision, yet in a very different economic environment. An initial cost estimate of $305 million left Interior Secretary Ken Salazar with little to say other than, "I don't know how we're going to get there, but I have great confidence that we will get there." In early 2011, MVVA revised the figure to $578 million, but this time there was no Bernard Dickmann or Clarence Cannon to obtain government funds. Instead, Rep. Russ Carnahan remarked that "there's certainly some sticker shock," while Missouri Senator Roy Blunt acknowledged that the funds would have to come mostly from "individuals interested in private investment." In December 2011, $57 million had been raised through local, federal, and private sources to start construction on the lid, or "Park Over the Highway," by 2014. Similar to the election of 1935 that started it all, future improvements will need the voters' approval. The Missouri legislature passed a bill allowing St. Louis residents to vote on a sales tax increase to finance part of the project, but even if that referendum passed, it would not cover all of the various portions of the project. The *Post-Dispatch* editorialized that "many of the elements of the Arch project are intended to make up for mistakes and corner-cutting that occurred over its first fifty years."[6]

The ambitious proposal to revitalize the Arch grounds was part of wider riverfront plans that included new offices, restaurants, and even a proposed National Blues Museum. In 1947, the local NAACP had suggested recognizing W. C. Handy and the city's role in blues history almost in identical fashion, yet city leaders dismissed the idea. In 2012, museum chair Rob Endicott knew a vital ingredient had long been missing from the Arch grounds. "Tourists come to the Arch," Endicott noted, "and they park and they look at the Arch and they drive away." Endicott hoped that with a blues museum, visitors would at least have "something to walk to."[7]

As planners dreamed of a new St. Louis riverfront, another vexing and expensive problem loomed. The Arch has had only one cleaning, in 1965, and is today mottled with streaks and other discolorations. Visitors to the memorial learn firsthand how the term "stainless steel" is a misnomer. In September 2012, an engineering study concluded that the exterior stains and corrosion probably originated with "rogue metals" within the welds. The report followed a corrosion investigation conducted six years earlier that found welds "have failed locally, generating points of water leakage," and acknowledged that the Arch's interior "ecosystem" sometimes produces its own moisture and even fog, causing sections of carbon steel to rust. The leakage is not new. As a deputy superintendent of the Arch noted, "condensation in the legs has been there since day one," and within the north leg workers have used mops and buckets to capture the leaking water. The 2012 report concluded that the corrosion was mostly cosmetic and did not threaten the structural integrity of the Arch.

How to inspect the welds and clean the exterior presents its own set of challenges that mirror what engineers faced when considering how to build the Arch. The 2012 study considered erecting massive scaffolds or cranes, but decided the best method would involve what St. Louis *Post-Dispatch* reporter Nicholas J. C. Pistor described as a "new extreme sport in which trained technicians would become monument mountain rappellers." Teams of workers, held by a series of "choker hitched ropes," would descend the legs of the Arch, where they would repair welds and possibly apply some sort of protective coating. The engineers did not offer a timetable or cost estimate on cleaning and repairing the structure, and stressed how a "reusable means of access should be designed as part of the cleaning procedure."[8]

The Arch's decay served as an apt metaphor for downtown St. Louis, where residents have been voting with their feet for over a half century. City leaders had hoped the 2010 census would reveal a slight population increase, but instead were shaken to learn of another 8 percent decline since the previous headcount. The total city population has plummeted from nearly 900,000 in 1950 to just 319,000 in 2010, the lowest level in over a century (table 1). In 1900, St. Louis was the nation's fourth largest city; in 1960, it was the tenth largest; by 2010, it had fallen to fifty-eighth. Those leaving

TABLE 1. ST. LOUIS CITY POPULATION,
1900–2010

1900	575,000
1910	687,000 (+19%)
1920	773,000 (+13%)
1930	821,000 (+6%)
1940	816,000 (−1%)
1950	856,000 (+5%)
1960	750,000 (−12%)
1970	622,000 (−17%)
1980	453,000 (−27%)
1990	397,000 (−12%)
2000	348,000 (−12%)
2010	319,000 (–8%)

Source: U.S. Census

TABLE 2. ST. LOUIS CITY POPULATION BY RACE, 1950–2010

	White	African American
1950	702,348 (82%)	153,766 (18%)
1960	534,004 (71%)	214,377 (29%)
1970	365,620 (59%)	254,268 (41%)
1980	242,576 (54%)	206,386 (46%)
1990	202,085 (51%)	188,408 (47%)
2000	152,666 (44%)	178,266 (51%)
2010	140,267 (44%)	157,160 (49%)

Source: U.S. Census

the city, mostly white citizens, are flocking to the western suburbs of the county (table 2). The release of the 2010 census prompted Mayor Francis Slay to comment, "This is absolutely bad news," requiring "an urgent and thorough rethinking of how we do almost everything."[9]

Those remaining residents face daunting economic prospects and a bleak urban landscape. Nearly 27 percent of the city's population in 2010 had incomes below the national poverty level (40 percent for African Americans), making it the fifth poorest city in the nation. The number of manufacturing jobs in the city fell from 142,220 in 1950 to just over 24,000 in 2000. Within St. Louis County, however, the opposite has occurred. The county's population more than doubled between 1950 and 2010 (table 3). Manufacturing jobs in the county have soared, while the retail and service jobs that once fueled the city's economy are now located in the county. "Stadiums, downtown shopping malls, tourist sites, and other postindustrial institutions," Joseph Heathcott and Maire Agnes Murphy write, "could not generate a broad and stable employment base to replace manufacturing jobs." In a 2009 *Forbes* "Most Miserable" article, which ranked cities according to such problems as corruption, taxes, violent crime, unemployment, and weather, St. Louis was the only Ameri-

TABLE 3. ST. LOUIS COUNTY POPULATION,
1900–2010

1900	50,000
1910	82,000 (+64%)
1920	101,000 (+23%)
1930	212,000 (+110%)
1940	274,000 (+29%)
1950	406,000 (+48%)
1960	703,000 (+73%)
1970	951,000 (+35%)
1980	974,000 (+2%)
1990	993,000 (+2%)
2000	1,016,000 (+2%)
2010	999,000 (−1.7%)

Source: U.S. Census

can city to score in every category. In 2012, analysis of FBI crime data revealed it to be the third most dangerous city in the United States, behind only Flint and Detroit.[10]

The Gateway Arch stands today as one of the most ironic structures in the world. As a tourist attraction, it has proven a remarkable success and occupies a singular place within American culture. Yet as a component of urban renewal, it has a different legacy. The gleaming traveler's destination is now surrounded by a decaying cityscape suffering from outdated concepts of growth. St. Louis's reliance on tourism, professional sports stadiums, and Interstate highways created a confluence of urban collateral damage that the city has spent decades trying to fix. The urban theorist Richard Florida has observed that "the physical attractions that most cities focus on building—sports stadiums, freeways, urban malls, and tourist and entertainment districts that resemble theme parks—are irrelevant" to sustained economic development. In fact, they tend to discourage the kinds of people who are vital to the high-tech sectors that drive urban economic growth in the twenty-first century.[11] St. Louis might have had a better chance at renewal if it had never torn down those historic cast-iron buildings.

Many of the same patterns that played out along the St. Louis riverfront have reappeared in other struggling cities. Some have even turned to "starchitects" to create showplace structures that hope to attract tourists and new revenue. For years, the grimy, industrial Spanish city of Bilbao was a major port, and like St. Louis, fell into decline by the mid-twentieth century. In the 1990s, the city commissioned Frank Gehry to design a new Guggenheim Museum. The result is what Philip Johnson described as "the greatest building of our time." Tourists have flocked to Bilbao to see one of the world's most celebrated "trophy buildings," yet whether the museum can do more than provide a modicum of low-paying jobs and some increased tax revenue remains to be seen. The glimmering curves of Gehry's titanium-clad museum are synonymous with Bilbao, but the city struggles to reinvent itself beyond its famous new landmark. As one commentator noted, "Bilbao is all dressed up, but hasn't figured where to go." Witold Rybczynski writes of Bilbao, "the 'wow factor' may excite the visitor and the journalist, but it is a shaky foundation on which to build lasting value," and adds that great architecture "should have more to say to us than 'Look At Me.'"[12] When cities consider building the next great iconic structure that hopes to duplicate the Bilbao effect, they would do well to remember that before there was a Bilbao, there was the St. Louis Gateway Arch.

At its essence, the Arch displays the power of art and emotion. Its sleek shape, monumentality, and clean, clear lines create far more than a mathematical formula built on a colossal scale. As George Howe's jury understood, the Arch manages to convey a "peculiarly happy" feeling. Reflecting Saarinen's first artistic inclinations, it is essentially a giant sculpture. Saarinen's first model of the Arch was a flatter, four-sided curve. When Carl Milles, a sculptor who had studied with Rodin, suggested a more elegant three-sided shape, the Arch was transformed into a work of beauty. For over a decade, Saarinen the sculptor constantly returned to "eyeballing" just the right taper and curve in making it seem to soar out of the ground, triumphing over gravity along the way. From his youth, Saarinen had been fascinated with molding curved forms, and whether it was a bar of soap, a chair, a hockey rink, or the Gateway Arch, he understood the essential sensuality and power of sculpture.[13]

The Arch is unique in other ways. It would seem out of place virtually anywhere else, and could not have been built in any other era. Today, it would be unthinkable to level forty square blocks of an American city to erect a nonutilitarian sculpture. The political, military, and economic disasters experienced by the nation since 1965 have virtually destroyed our collective desire to build audacious architectural landmarks. The nation cannot even decide how to repair its crumbling infrastructure of roads, dams, and bridges, let alone find the funds to fix the existing Arch grounds. Meanwhile, the two-hundred-story skyscraper completed in Dubai in 2010 affirms a much wider distribution of global wealth and power than existed following World War II.

We cannot know what Eero Saarinen would have thought about the finished project. He would undoubtedly be pleased that what started with pipe cleaners on his living room floor can be identified by schoolchildren around the world. Shortly before his death, he worried about his architectural legacy and whether he would ever emerge from Eliel's shadow. His reputation among architectural critics and historians has undergone a certain revival, but his eclecticism renders him hard to categorize. His furniture designs are better known today than many of his buildings. Saarinen might not be a household name, but his Gateway Arch is instantly recognizable in the popular imagination in ways that surpass modernist masterpieces such as Mies's Farnsworth House, Wright's Fallingwater, and even Gehry's Bilbao.

■

All of which presents an interesting thought experiment: a thousand years from now, what will our descendants remember about us?

One major clue will be the monuments and memorials we leave behind. They tell us what a society felt was worthy of spending public wealth to remember and reveal the creative and technical prowess of their builders. We can only imagine what observers many generations from now will think as they gaze upon the granite faces on Mount Rushmore or the obelisk along the Potomac. Some of the most impressive American structures are strictly utilitarian marvels, such as the Hoover Dam or the Golden Gate Bridge. The historical monuments in Washington, D.C., and dotted throughout the nation are usually traditional, heroic models dedicated to memories of war, but few are visually compelling. Yet the Gateway Arch is different from anything seen in this nation, or for that matter, the world. It is one of the country's greatest works of public art, and recalls a heady period in our history in which the future seemed limitless. Its real symbolism is not to the westward expansion of the nineteenth century, but to the power and dominance of the United States in the twentieth century. Through a simple yet elegant architectural vision, and sometimes ruthless political means, a timeless political monument stands tall above the Mississippi River in St. Louis. As such, archaeologists, historians, and anthropologists will be fascinated thousands of years from now by the gleaming arch that rises over the plains.

That is, if it continues to stand. If an earthquake, tornado, corrosion, or other disaster causes the Gateway Arch to fail, will its remaining stumps be considered as sacred ruins or simply bulldozed to make way for the next "modern" structure? We should not assume the permanency of either governments or buildings. The example of Cahokia reminds us that great cities and even empires can completely disappear.[14]

Let us hope that the Arch somehow survives—that it becomes, far in the future, a mysterious structure like the Great Pyramids or Stonehenge, that leads onlookers to wonder about the people who produced it and ask themselves what strange compulsions led to its creation. Let us also hope they take into account the fuller dimensions of what transpired along the St. Louis riverfront. They may discover that the actual origins and legacies of great structures are often less beautiful than the structures themselves.

Notes

The following abbreviations are used in the notes.

AAA   Archives of American Art, Smithsonian Institution, Washington, D.C.

ACP   Alfonso Cervantes Papers, University Archives, Department of Special Collections, Washington University in St. Louis

AESP   Aline and Eero Saarinen Papers, Archives of American Art, Smithsonian Institution, Washington, D.C.

AF   *Architectural Forum*

BFDP   Bernard F. Dickmann Papers, The State Historical Society of Missouri, University of Missouri–Columbia

CA   Cranbrook Archives, Cranbrook Academy, Bloomfield Hills, Michigan

CCP   Clarence Cannon Papers, The State Historical Society of Missouri, University of Missouri–Columbia

CGP   Clifford Greve Papers, Missouri Historical Society, St. Louis.

CREC   Charles and Ray Eames Collection, Manuscript Division, Library of Congress.

ES   Eero Saarinen.

ESP   Eero Saarinen Papers, Manuscripts and Archives, Yale University Library, New Haven, Connecticut.

FLWP   Frank Lloyd Wright Papers, Manuscript Division, Library of Congress.

HAP   Harris Armstrong Papers, University Archives, Department of
            Special Collections, Washington University Libraries, St. Louis.
HBAP   Harland Bartholomew and Associates Papers, University Archives,
            Department of Special Collections, Washington University Libraries,
            St. Louis.
IPSR   Institute of Personality and Social Research, University of
            California-Berkeley.
JKDP   James K. Douglas Papers, Missouri Historical Society, St. Louis.
JNEMA   Jefferson National Expansion Memorial Archives, National Park
            Service, St. Louis.
LES   Luther Ely Smith
LESP   Luther Ely Smith Papers, Missouri Historical Society, St. Louis.
LSSP   Lilian Swann Saarinen Papers, Archives of American Art, Smith-
            sonian Institution, Washington, D.C.
NPSCCF   National Park Service Central Classified Files, 1933–1949, Record
            Group 79, National Archives, College Park, Maryland.
NYT   *New York Times*
POPC   Paul O. Porter Collection, Special Collections, Andrews Library,
            College of Wooster, Wooster, Ohio.
RTPP   Raymond R. Tucker Personal Papers, University Archives, Depart-
            ment of Special Collections, Washington University Libraries,
            St. Louis.
SLGD   *St. Louis Globe-Democrat*
SLPD   *St. Louis Post-Dispatch*
SSP   Stuart Symington Papers, The State Historical Society of Missouri,
            University of Missouri–Columbia.

Introduction

1. Philip Ball, *Universe of Stone: Chartres Cathedral and the Invention of the Gothic* (New York: Harper Perennial, 2008), 279–80; William Anderson, *The Rise of the Gothic* (London: Hutchinson, 1985), 41–45.

2. David Harvey, "Monument and Myth," *Annals of the Association of American Geographers* 69 (September 1979): 381.

ONE
The New York of the West

1. Daniel K. Richter, *Facing East from Indian Country: A Native History of Early America* (Cambridge: Harvard University Press, 2001), 2–4; Timothy R. Pauketat,

Cahokia: Ancient America's Great City on the Mississippi (New York: Viking, 2009), 22–35, 101–2; Biloine Whiting Young and Melvin L. Fowler, *Cahokia: The Great Native American Metropolis* (Urbana: University of Illinois Press, 2000), 2–3, 307, 310; William R. Iseminger, "Culture and Environment in the American Bottom: The Rise and Fall of Cahokia Mounds," in Andrew Hurley, ed., *Common Fields: An Environmental History of St. Louis* (St. Louis: Missouri Historical Society Press, 1997): 38–57; Stephen Aron, *American Confluence: The Missouri Frontier from Borderland to Border State* (Bloomington: Indiana University Press, 2006), 5–9.

2. Jay Gitlin, *The Bourgeois Frontier: French Towns, French Traders, and American Expansion* (New Haven: Yale University Press, 2010), 14; James Neal Primm, *Lion of the Valley: St. Louis, Missouri, 1764–1980* (St. Louis: Missouri Historical Society Press, 1998), 2–13; William E. Foley, *A History of Missouri* vol. I, 1673–1820 (Columbia: University of Missouri Press, 1971), 23–25; Shirley Christian, *Before Lewis and Clark: The Story of the Chouteaus, the French Dynasty That Ruled America's Frontier* (New York: Farrar, Straus and Giroux, 2004), 3–17; John A. Bryan, " The Changing Scene on the St. Louis Riverfront, 1764–1954," report no. 295, box 8, JNEMA, 1; Aron, *American Confluence*, 50–54.

3. Bryan, "The Changing Scene," 9–12; Pauketat, *Cahokia*, 27; Gitlin, *Bourgeois Frontier*, 84–86; Aron, *American Confluence*, 106–8; Adam Arenson, *The Great Heart of the Republic: St. Louis and the Cultural Civil War* (Cambridge: Harvard University Press, 2011), 6–13.

4. Jay Feldman, *When the Mississippi Ran Backwards: Empire, Intrigue, Murder, and the New Madrid Earthquakes* (New York: Free Press, 2005), 15, 172–76; James A. Taylor, "Earthquake Ground Motion and Soil Amplification Effects in the St. Louis Metropolitan Area," M.S. thesis, Washington University in St. Louis, 1997, 14–16. Many seismologists consider St. Louis to be in a secondary area of potential damage from a major earthquake along the New Madrid fault.

5. Aron, *American Confluence*, 186–87.

6. *Scott v. Sandford* 60 U.S. 393 (1857); James M. McPherson, *Battle Cry of Freedom: The Civil War Era* (New York: Oxford University Press, 1988), 170–73.

7. Joel A. Tarr and Carl Zimring, "The Struggle for Smoke Control in St. Louis," in Andrew Hurley, ed., *Common Fields: An Environmental History of St. Louis* (St. Louis: Missouri Historical Society Press, 1997), 199–204.

8. Bryan, "The Changing Scene," 39–40; Arenson, *The Great Heart of the Republic*, 9–12, 21.

9. Bryan, "The Changing Scene," 39–58; Rob Wilson, "Cholera and Quarantine: St. Louis' Battle With the 1849 Epidemic," paper delivered at the annual meeting of the Western History Association, St. Louis, October 2006; Primm, *Lion of the Valley*, 154–58; *SLPD*, July 18, 2010.

10. *Daily Evening News*, March 30, 1855; *New York Journal of Commerce*,

September 14, 1856; J. A. Dacus and James W. Buel, "A Tour of St. Louis, or, the Inside Life of a Great City" (St. Louis: Western Publishing, 1878), 29.

11. Arenson, *The Great Heart of the Republic*, 120–22.

12. Bryan, "The Changing Scene," 61–68; Primm, *Lion of the Valley*, 235–53, 286–87; Maury Klein and Harvey A. Kantor, *Prisoners of Progress: American Industrial Cities, 1850–1920* (New York: Macmillan, 1976), 152–53.

13. Colin Gordon, *Mapping Decline: St. Louis and the Fate of the American City* (Philadelphia: University of Pennsylvania Press, 2008), 22–23, 35; Don Phares, "Planning for Regional Governance in the St. Louis Area: The Context, the Plans, the Outcomes," in Mark Tranel, ed., *St. Louis Plans: The Ideal, and the Real St. Louis* (St. Louis: Missouri Historical Society Press, 2007), 55–62.

14. Bryan, "The Changing Scene," 68–72; Primm, *Lion of the Valley*, 373.

15. Merrill D. Peterson, *The Jefferson Image in the American Mind* (New York: Oxford University Press, 1960), 274; Bryan, "The Changing Scene," 73–75.

16. Primm, *Lion of the Valley*, 387–93.

17. Bryan, "The Changing Scene," 75–76.

18. Jane Jacobs, *The Death and Life of Great American Cities* (New York: Modern Library, 1993; repr. of Random House ed., 1961), 33; Daniel M. Bluestone, "Detroit's City Beautiful and the Problems of Commerce," *Journal of the Society of Architectural Historians* 47 (September 1988): 245; William H. Wilson, *The City Beautiful Movement* (Baltimore: Johns Hopkins University Press, 1989), 1; Jon A. Peterson, *The Birth of City Planning in the United States, 1840–1917* (Baltimore: Johns Hopkins University Press, 2003), 176, 202–6.

19. Civic League of St. Louis, "A City Plan for St. Louis, 1907," Special Collections, Washington University in St. Louis; Mark Abbott, "The 1947 Comprehensive City Plan and Harland Bartholomew's St. Louis," in Mark Tranel, ed., *St. Louis Plans: The Ideal and the Real St. Louis (St. Louis: Missouri Historical Society Press, 2007)*, 109.

20. *SLGD*, November 21, 1915.

21. Joseph Heathcott, "Harland Bartholomew: City Engineer," in Tranel, ed., *St. Louis Plans: The Ideal and the Real St. Louis*, 83–95; Eldridge Lovelace, *Harland Bartholomew: His Contributions to American Urban Planning* (Urbana: University of Illinois Office of Printing Services, 1993), 5–10; Richard Moore to City Plan Commission, May 18, 1927, JKDP; Joseph Heathcott and Maire Agnes Murphy, "Corridors of Flight, Zones of Renewal: Industry, Planning, and Policy in the Making of Metropolitan St. Louis, 1940–1980," *Journal of Urban History* 31 (January 2005): 151–89.

22. Harland Bartholomew, Engineer, "City Plan Commission of St. Louis, 1927–28: A Plan for the Central River Front of St. Louis, 1928," 22–32; "Plans for the Northern and Southern Riverfront, St. Louis, 1929," HBAP; E. J. Russell,

"The St. Louis River Plaza," *Southern Architect and Building News*, October 1930; Abbott, "The 1947 Comprehensive City Plan," 138–39, 148.

23. Gordon, *Mapping Decline*, 204–5.

24. *St. Louis Republic*, February 17, 1916; Primm, *Lion of the Valley*, 411–14. The Louisville case is *Buchanan v. Warley* 245 U.S. 60 (1917).

25. Elliott M. Rudwick, *Race Riot at East St. Louis, July 2, 1917* (Carbondale: Southern Illinois University Press, 1964), 46–47.

26. Rudwick, *Race Riot at East St. Louis*, 4–6, 48–49, 52, 175; Primm, *Lion of the Valley*, 413–16; Harper Barnes, *Never Been a Time: The 1917 Race Riot That Sparked the Civil Rights Movement* (New York: Walker, 2008), 3. The "official" death toll in East St. Louis was forty-eight, yet the real number was undoubtedly much higher.

27. Kenneth T. Jackson, *Crabgrass Frontier: The Suburbanization of the United States* (New York: Oxford University Press, 1985), 150; Primm, *Lion of the Valley*, 447; De Anna J. Reese, "African American Women, Civic Activism, and Community Building Strategies in St. Louis, Missouri, 1900–1954," Ph.D. diss., University of Missouri–Columbia, 2004, 112–13.

28. *SLGD*, May 25, 1968. After high school, Geneva Abbott Patterson studied art and worked as a commercial artist for many years. She lived in St. Louis until 1980, when she moved to Florida. She died in 2011.

TWO
Getting Things Done

1. Jon C. Teaford, *The Rough Road to Renaissance: Urban Revitalization in America, 1940–1985* (Baltimore: Johns Hopkins University Press, 1990), 11–12; Robert M. Fogelson, *Downtown: Its Rise and Fall, 1880–1950* (New Haven: Yale University Press, 2001), 347–48; Deborah Lynn Becher, "Valuing Property: Eminent Domain for Urban Redevelopment, Philadelphia, 1992–2007," Ph.D. diss., Princeton University, 2009.

2. *SLPD*, August 15, 1935; "Downtown Riverfront Occupancy Survey," by St. Louis Chamber of Commerce, August 1935, JNEMA; "Opponents of Project, Owners and Assessment of Property," CGP.

3. Fogelson, *Downtown*, 192–93, 226; Joel A. Tarr and Carl Zimring, "The Struggle for Smoke Control in St. Louis: Achievement and Emulation," in Andrew Hurley, ed., *Common Fields: An Environmental History of St. Louis* (St. Louis: Missouri Historical Society Press, 1997), 199–220; Federal Home Loan Bank Board, Division of Research and Statistics, "Metropolitan St. Louis: Summary of an Economic, Real Estate and Mortgage Survey" (1941), 11–12; Kenneth T. Jackson, *Crabgrass Frontier: The Suburbanization of the United States* (New York: Oxford University Press, 1985), 199.

4. Biographical Sketch, LESP; John Bodnar, *Remaking America: Public Memory, Commemoration, and Patriotism in the Twentieth Century* (Princeton: Princeton University Press, 1992), 123–25.

5. LES, open letter, April 21, 1939, LESP; Bodnar, *Remaking America*, 135–36.

6. *NYT,* January 13, 1924; Lana Stein, *St. Louis Politics: The Triumph of Tradition* (St. Louis: Missouri Historical Society Press, 2002), 21–25; Colin Gordon, *Mapping Decline: St. Louis and the Fate of the American City* (Philadelphia: University of Pennsylvania Press, 2008), ch. 2.

7. *Real Estate Analyst, St. Louis Edition,* ed. Roy Wenzlick, April 1933, December 1934, July 1938; Alison Isenberg, *Downtown America: A History of the Place and the People Who Made It* (Chicago: University of Chicago Press, 2004), 128–32. The *Real Estate Analyst* was a monthly publication generated exclusively for St. Louis real estate professionals.

8. Teaford, *The Rough Road to Renaissance,* 18, 26–27.

9. Marguerite S. Shaffer, *See America First: Tourism and National Identity, 1880–1920* (Washington, D.C.: Smithsonian Institution Press, 2001), 3–7.

10. W. C. Bernard, "A Comprehensive Program for Reclamation of the St. Louis Riverfront, to be Effected By the Construction and Operation of a River-view Freeway, 1934," BFDP, Box 2.

11. FDR to Dickmann, February 19, 1934, Box 48, JNEMA; Dickson Terry, "A Monument to Thirty Years of Patience, Perseverance, and Determination," *Cherry Diamond,* September 1964; Merrill D. Peterson, *The Jefferson Image in the American Mind* (New York: Oxford University Press, 1960), 275, 423.

12. John J. Cochran to James K. Douglas, January 1, 1934, JKDP; *SLGD,* June 8, 1934; L. W. Giles, "The St. Louis Riverfront Scrapbook," Special Collections, St. Louis Public Library.

13. *SLPD,* August 16, 1935; *St. Louis Star-Times,* May 13, 16, 1935; Stein, *St. Louis Politics,* 32–34; Mark Tranel, ed., *St. Louis Plans: The Ideal and the Real St. Louis* (St. Louis: Missouri Historical Society Press, 2007), 92.

14. *SLPD,* August 9, 16, September 8, 1935; *SLGD,* August 29, 1935

15. Taxpayers Defense Association Pamphlet, CGP.

16. News Release from W. C. D'Arcy, n.d., Jefferson National Memorial Files, Special Collections, St. Louis Public Library.

17. *SLPD,* September 5, 6, 1935; SGD, September 6, 1935; Paul W. Ward, "Washington Weekly," *Nation,* March 4, 1936; Taxpayers Defense Association Pamphlet, CGP.

18. Joseph Harris et al. to JNEMA, n.d., JNEMA; *St. Louis Argus,* August 30, 1935; *St. Louis Union Labor Advocate,* September 2, 1935.

19. "Downtown Riverfront Occupancy Survey, August 1935"; John G. Marr to

Russell Murphy, April 9, 1935, Box 3, JNEMA; *Bond Issue News*, n.d., scrapbook 1, POP, box 21; *SLPD*, September 4, 9, 1935; April Lee Hamel, "The Jefferson National Expansion Memorial: A Depression Relief Project," Ph.D. diss., St. Louis University, 1983, 36–56; *St. Louis Star-Times*, September 10, 1936.

20. "Meeting of the St. Louis Real Estate Board and Jefferson National Expansion Memorial Association, January 21, 1935," JNEMA; "St. Louis Real Estate Exchange, September 5, 1935 Resolution," Box 71, JNEMA.

21. *Real Estate Analyst, Supplementary Service*, November 1932, S-1-4; Federal Home Loan Bank Board, "Metropolitan St. Louis," 6. For determining historical currency equivalencies, www.measuringworth.com.

22. Ralph W. Coale, Assessor, "Combined Assessments on Ground and Improvements on Real Estate Located Between Eads Bridge, Poplar Street, Third Street, and the Mississippi River, June 1, 1934," CGP; Legal Committee Memo, n.d., JNEMA.

23. *SLPD*, September 10, 11, 1935; SGD, September 11, 1935; Mrs. Charles Carnali to Russell Murphy, September 13, 1935, JNEMA; William D'Arcy to E. Lansing Ray, September 13, 1935, box 71, JNEMA.

24. *SLGD*, September 11, 17, 1935; Wendell E. Pritchett, "The 'Public Menace' of Blight: Urban Renewal and the Private Uses of Eminent Domain," *Yale Law and Policy Review* 21 (Winter 2003): 22.

25. *SLPD*, December 1, 21, 22, 23, 1935; Sharon A. Brown, "Making a Memorial: Developing the Jefferson National Expansion Memorial National Historic Site, 1933–1980," Ph.D. diss., St. Louis University, 1983, 24–26; Terry, "A Monument to Thirty Years of Patience, Perseverance, and Determination"; *The Secret Diary of Harold Ickes, The First Thousand Days, 1933–1936* (New York: Simon and Schuster, 1953), 489; Cary M. Schneider, "St. Louis and the Gateway Arch: A Case History of an Urban Icon," honors paper, Cornell College, 1970, 18.

26. Paul O. Peters to FDR, September 24, 1936, box 21; "Public Necessity or Just Plain Pork?" scrapbook 2, POPC; SGD, July 25, September 8, 9, 11, 1936; *SLPD*, July 23, 25, 26, 27, 28, 1936.

27. *Washington Post*, September 22, 1936; *SLPD*, September 9, 18, 1936.

28. Paul O. Peters to LES, November 26, 1936, December 9, 1936, CGP; LES to William Allen White, June 16, 1937, CGP; LES open letter, April 21, 1938, LESP; *SLPD*, January 14, 1937.

29. Bodnar, *Remaking America*, 170–71, 177; Shaffer, *See America First*, 94, 106–9.

30. *NYT*, April 10, August 18, 1936; *Balter v. Ickes 67 App. D.C. 112, 89 F.2nd 856*; *SLPD*, March 29, 1937.

31. *Congressional Record*, vol. 81, 75th Congress, 1st Session, 1937, Appendix, part 10, 2550.

32. *SLPD*, August 10, 1939.

33. *SLPD*, July 17, 28, 1937; Rev. Alva McCarver to Eleanor Roosevelt, July 17, 1937, Woodson Barnhart to Dickmann, October 22, 1937, box 2634, NPSCCF.

34. "St. Louis Real Estate Exchange, January 23, 1936, Resolution," JNEMA; *SLPD*, February 10, June 1, 19, 22, 1939; *St. Louis Star-Times*, February 14, 1939. The Interior Department eventually purchased the property for $5,970,000, 11 percent more than the assessed value. "Bulletin to Members of Special Committee," August 29, 1935, CGP; *St. Louis Star-Times*, August 24, 1935.

35. *St. Louis Star-Times*, n.d., in Giles, "The St. Louis Riverfront Scrapbook"; *SLPD*, October 3, 1935.

36. *SLPD*, October 10, 1939.

THREE
The St. Louis Municipal Parking Lot

1. Dickson Terry, "A Monument to Thirty Years of Patience, Perseverance, and Determination," *Cherry Diamond*, Missouri Athletic Club (September 1964), 38–39; *Real Estate Analyst*, ed. Roy Wenzlick, June 1941; Alison Isenberg, *Downtown America: A History of the Place and the People Who Made It* (Chicago: University of Chicago Press, 2004), 135–38.

2. Jane Jacobs, *The Death and Life of Great American Cities* (New York: Modern Library, 1993; repr. of Random House ed., 1961), 244.

3. *SLGD*, August 10, 1939; Charles Reysmershopper to LES, April 7, 1939, JNEMA; Waldo G. Leland to Ickes, February 14, 1939, box 2637, NPSCCF; Memo, Ickes to Butler, May 2, 1939, Harold Ickes Papers, Library of Congress.

4. *St. Louis Star-Times*, January 8, 1936.

5. *SLPD*, January 23, 1941; interview with Charles E. Peterson by Bob Moore, October 22, 1994, JNEMA.

6. Harold Ickes to Bernard F. Dickmann, June 14, 1940, JKDP; *NYT*, June 15, 1941.

7. Michael Hiltzik, *Colossus: Hoover Dam and the Making of the American Century* (New York: Free Press, 2010), 295–99; John Taliaferro, *Great White Fathers: The Story of the Obsessive Quest to Create Mount Rushmore* (New York: Public Affairs, 2002), 309; Steve Vogel, *The Pentagon: A History* (New York: Random House, 2007), 119; www.measuringworth.com.

8. "Riverfront Reconstruction, St. Louis, Mo.," *AF* (April 1944): 111–16; Andrew M. Shanken, *194X: Architecture, Planning, and Consumer Culture on the American Home Front* (Minneapolis: University of Minnesota Press, 2009), 10, 150–52.

9. "Riverfront Reconstruction"; newspaper clipping, original drawings, HAP; *SLGD*, May 21, 1944; *AF* (April 1944).

10. *SLGD*, April 16, 1944. In his 1947 plan for St. Louis, Harland Bartholomew proposed a total of thirty-five airfields, including thirteen "local personal fields" that would accommodate private planes. "Comprehensive City Plan, St. Louis, Missouri, 1947," HBAP; Mark Abbott, "The 1947 Comprehensive City Plan and Harland Bartholomew's St. Louis," in Mark Tranel, ed., *St. Louis Plans: The Ideal and the Real St. Louis* (St. Louis: Missouri Historical Society Press, 2007), 141–42; *The American City*, December 1944.

11. "Memo for Director," by Julian Spotts, February 9, 1945, box 2653, NPSCCF.

12. *SLGD*, December 13, February 6, 1946.

13. *SLPD*, May 7, June 26, 1946.

14. Dickmann to FDR, December 13, 1944, box 2637, NPSCCF.

15. Frederic C. Hirons to LES, December 21, 1934, LESP.

16. I. F. Boyd to James L. Ford, May 22, 1946, LESP; LES to Alex T. Primm, Jr., February 28, 1946, JKDP.

17. LES to Alex T. Primm, Jr., February 28, 1946, JKDP.

18. *SLGD*, May 21, 1944; Harry B. Mathews, Jr., to James L. Ford, Jr., July 23, 1945, U.S. Territorial Expansion Memorial Records, JNEMA; I. F. Boyd, Jr., to James L. Ford, Jr., May 22, 1946, James L. Ford, Jr., to I. F. Boyd, Jr., May 23, 1946, LESP.

19. "Minutes of the Executive Committee of the JNEMA," February 13, 1947, LESP; George Howe, "Memorials for Mankind," *AF* (May 1945): 123–24; *SLPD*, January 29, 1947; Robert A. M. Stern, *George Howe: Toward a Modern American Architecture* (New Haven: Yale University Press, 1975), 67–68, 198–99; George Howe to LES, August 29, 1946, LESP. Howe received a salary of $5,000 for the first six months of the competition, and then $1,000 per month afterward.

20. *SLPD*, September 23, 24, 1947.

21. "Architectural Competition for the Jefferson National Expansion Memorial Program, 1947," 13, HAP.

22. Of the $225,000 the JNEM raised to cover the competition expenses, $125,000 was devoted to prizes. The remaining $100,000 was set aside for the jury, administrative costs, and publicity. *SLPD*, February 28, 1947; Stern, *George Howe*, 14–18.

23. "Memorial Program," 14; *SLPD*, January 29, 1947.

24. Harland Bartholomew to Newton B. Drury, March 24, 1947, Drury to LES, March 28, 1947, NPSCCF, Box 2653; "Memorial Program," 13–24.

25. "Jefferson National Expansion Memorial Competition," *AF*.

26. "Memorial Program," 25; "Jefferson National Expansion Memorial Competition," *AF;* "Memo for Regional Director" by Julian Spotts, September 18, 1947, Box 2653, NPSCCF; Rumiko Handa, "Design Through Drawing: Eero Saarinen's Design in the Jefferson National Expansion Memorial Competition," Ph.D. diss., University of Pennsylvania, 1992, 80, 94–96.

FOUR

A Peculiarly Happy Form

1. "Report on Promotional Program for the Jefferson National Expansion Memorial Association, February 15–May 30, 1947," JNEMA. In 1981, in one of the most celebrated recent competitions, a Yale architecture student, Maya Lin, won the contest to design the Vietnam Veterans Memorial in Washington, D.C.

2. Harry B. Richman, "The Competition Commences," in Robert J. Moore, Jr., *The Gateway Arch: An Architectural Dream* (St. Louis: Jefferson National Parks Association, 2005), 30.

3. ES to George Howe, April 14, 1947, Robert Elkington to Eliel Saarinen, April 4, 1947, ESP.

4. ES to Dan Kiley, April 28, 1947, ESP.

5. "Statement by Eero Saarinen," ESP; Aline B. Saarinen, ed., *Eero Saarinen on His Work* (New Haven: Yale University Press, 1962), 18. Despite this early collaboration, Charles Eames and Eero Saarinen submitted separate entries to the St. Louis competition.

6. Philip Ball, *Universe of Stone: Chartres Cathedral and the Invention of the Gothic* (New York: Harper Perennial, 2008), 202–6; Mario Salvadori, *Why Buildings Stand Up* (New York: Norton, 1980), 144–49.

7. *SLPD,* March 7, 1948; Le Corbusier, *Towards a New Architecture* (New York: Dover, 1986, reprint of 1931 ed. published by John Rodker), 284–85; Jean-Louis Cohen, *Le Corbusier and the Mystique of the USSR: Theories and Projects for Moscow, 1928–1936* (Princeton: Princeton University Press, 1992), 179–86; Peter Blake, *The Master Builders* (New York: Knopf, 1970), 77–78.

8. Andrew Saint, *Architect and Engineer: A Study in Sibling Rivalry* (New Haven: Yale University Press, 2007), 241.

9. *SLPD,* March 7, 1948.

10. Saarinen, ed., *Eero Saarinen on His Work*, 18.

11. *SLPD,* March 7, 1948; Memo, 1937, Box 2, FLWP.

12. *SLPD,* March 7, 1948; Louis Kahn to ES, October 23, 1947, ESP; Rumiko Handa, "Design Through Drawing: Eero Saarinen's Design in the Jefferson National Expansion Memorial Competition," Ph.D. diss., University of Pennsylvania, 1992, 113.

13. ES to unknown, n.d., ESP; Jefferson National Expansion Memorial Association Records, box 3, JNEMA.

14. "Sculpture for Gateway to the West, St. Louis, 1948," in LESP; *SLPD*, March 7, 1948.

15. Saarinen, ed., *Eero Saarinen on His Work*, 5.

16. Interview with James Smith by John Gerard, April 2, 1982, Cranbrook Archives, Bloomfield Hills, Michigan; Jayne Merkel, *Eero Saarinen (New York: Phaidon, 2005)*, 199–200; interview with Ray Kaiser Eames, July 28, 1980, by Ruth Bowman, Archives of American Art, Smithsonian Institution; interview with Susan Saarinen by Bob Moore, October 12, 1995, JNEM Archives; "Competitor 'E,'" box 29, JNEMA; ES to Dan Kiley, July 30, ESP.

17. ES to Dan Kiley, September 11, 24, 1947, ESP; "Competitors Entered into the JNEM Competition, March 1948," U.S. Territorial Expansion Memorial Records, JNEMA; interview with Dan Kiley by Bob Moore, July 22, 1993, JNEMA; "Jefferson Memorial Competition" Drawing by J. Henderson Barr, Jack Goldman Collection, CA.

18. D. M. Grant to JNEMA, September 15, 1947, JNEMA; *SLGD*, Sept. 17, 1947. In 2012, the National Blues Museum was planned for the new Mercantile Exchange complex, just blocks from where Handy composed "St. Louis Blues" in 1914.

19. Louis LaBeaume, "Comments on the Jury Selection," JNEMA. The jury also selected three alternates: Percival Goodman of New York; Pilifan and Montana of Detroit; and Hugh Stubbins, Jr., and G. Holmes Patrick of Lexington, Massachusetts. "Final Report of the Jury of Award to the Professional Advisor on the First and Second Stage of the Jefferson National Expansion Memorial Competition," JKDP.

20. Interview with Lilian Swann Saarinen by Robert Brown, February 15, 1979, February 2, 1981, AAA.

21. "Jefferson National Expansion Memorial Competition," *AF* (March 1948): 14–16; "Final Report of the Jury"; Le Corbusier, *When the Cathedrals Were White: A Journey to the Country of Timid People* (New York: Reynal and Hitchcock, 1947), xix. Eliel also considered the 1940s to be architecture's "moment" in town planning and wrote that similar to a "withering body," the planner "must unearth the roots of the evil. He must amputate slums by decisive surgery." *The City: Its Growth, Its Decay, Its Future* (New York: Reinhold, 1943), 18–19, 144.

22. *AF* (April 1944); newspaper clipping, original drawings, HAP. In 1953, Saarinen stayed with Armstrong in St. Louis and found him to be "very nice and enthusiastic and very romantic in his architecture." ES to Aline Louchheim, November 15, 1953, AESP; "Final Report of Jury of Award Committee,"

"Comments on Individual Projects," JNEMA; Armstrong biography, HAP; Handa, "Design Through Drawing," 97–98.

23. "Comments of S. Herbert Hare on Designs Selected by the Jury for the Jefferson National Expansion Memorial Association Competition," JNEMA; "Notes on Five Premiated Designs," JNEMA.

24. "Jefferson National Expansion Memorial Competition," *AF; SLPD,* November 4, 1947.

25. Howe, "Addenda, November 5, 1947," JNEMA; Handa, "Design Through Drawing."

26. George Howe to ES, September 29, 1947, ES to Louis Kahn, October 15, 1947, ES to Dan Kiley, October 8, 15, November 26, 1947, ESP; *NYT,* March 30, 1947; Sarah Williams Ksiazek, "Changing Symbols of Public Life: Louis Kahn's Religious and Civic Projects, 1944–1966, and Architectural Culture at the End of the Modern Movement," Ph.D. diss., Columbia University, 1995, 64–65.

27. ES to Dan Kiley, October 25, 27, 1947; Dan Kiley to ES, October 29, 1947, ESP.

28. ES to Fred Severud, November 11, 1947, ESP; *NYT,* June 14, 1990.

29. Salvadori, *Why Buildings Stand Up,* 64–65; Saarinen, ed., *Eero Saarinen on His Work,* 6; Harold M. Cobb, *The History of Stainless Steel* (Materials Park, Ohio: ASM, 2009), 40–42, 118–22.

30. Interview with Dan Kiley, JNEM Archives; Handa, "Design Through Drawing," 160–68. Carl Milles influenced the cultural life of St. Louis in other ways. He sculpted "Wedding of the Mississippi and Missouri Rivers" for a park outside Union Station in 1940. When Saarinen failed to publicly acknowledge the role Milles played in changing the form of the Arch, an outraged Milles ended the relationship. Mark Coir, "The Cranbrook Factor," in Eeva-Liisa Pelkonen and Donald Albrecht, eds., *Eero Saarinen: Shaping the Future* (New Haven: Yale University Press, 2006), 41.

31. "Jefferson National Expansion Memorial Competition," *AF* (March 1948).

32. Robert Moses to E. D. Dail, December 10, 1947, U.S Territorial Expansion Memorial Commission Records; Robert A. Caro, *The Power Broker: Robert Moses and the Fall of New York* (New York: Knopf, 1974); I. F. Boyd, Jr., to George Howe, December 12, 1947, JKDP; "Comprehensive City Plan, St. Louis, Missouri, 1947," HBAP.

33. "Final Report of Jury of Award Committee," JNEMA; *SLPD,* February 19, 1948.

34. "Final Report of Jury of Award Committee," JNEMA; *NYT,* February 19, 1948; Lydia M. Soo, "The Work of William Eng and His Approach to Design Education," *Reflections: The Journal of the School of Architecture, University of Illinois at Urbana-Champaign* (Fall 1987), 8.

35. Louis Kahn to ES, February 19, 1948, Hugh Stubbins to ES, March 5, 1948, Edward Durell Stone to ES, February 20, 1948, ES to Stone, February 22, 1948, ESP; *SLPD*, February 19, 1948.

36. William Warren to *SLGD*, October 24, 1949, JNEMA; *SLPD*, February 20, 1948.

37. "Jefferson National Expansion Memorial Competition," *AF.*

38. Daniel A. Eberhardt interview, UP Story, February 27, 1948, ES to A. P. Kaufman, March 1, 1948, Mrs. Stanley Swarmer to ES, March 15, 1948; Mrs. Perry Forthmann to ES, November 15, 1949, ESP; *Time*, March 1, 1948; *Newsweek*, March 1, 1948; Walter Buffalo to Editor, *SLPD*, February 24, 1948; Dick Leman to Aloys P. Kaufman, March 3, 1948, JNEMA.

39. LES to ES, February 25, 1948, June 3, 1948, LES, introduction for ES, ca. 1948, JNEMA.

40. ES to H. E. Grant, March 24, 1948, ESP.

41. Wire recording of Charles Nagel, Jr., February 19, 1948, JNEMA; interview with Kevin Roche by Bob Moore, October 12, 1994, JNEMA.

42. Joseph Heathcott and Maire Agnes Murphy, "Corridors of Flight, Zones of Renewal: Industry, Planning, and Policy in the Making of Metropolitan St. Louis, 1940–1980," *Journal of Urban History* 31 (January 2005): 174–76.

43. ES to Dan Kiley, February 26, 1948, ESP; interview with Lilian Swann Saarinen, by Robert Brown, February 15, 1979, February 2, 1981, AAA; *SLPD*, February 19, 1948.

44. Gilmore D. Clarke to William Wurster, February 24, 1948, JNEMA; "Log of Week 22 Feb. to 28 Feb. Kept by William Wurster," JNEMA; *New York Herald-Tribune*, February 26, 1948; Roger Griffin, *Modernism and Fascism: The Sense of a Beginning Under Mussolini and Hitler* (New York: Palgrave, 2007), 23, 236–37; Francesco Garofalo and Luca Veresani, *Adalberto Libera* (Princeton: Princeton University Press, 1992), 107–9; Carlo Olmo and Cristiana Chiorino, *Pier Luigi Nervi: Architecture as Challenge* (Milan: Silvana Editoriale, 2010), 209. In the early 1940s, Clarke was chairman of the Commission of Fine Arts, a Washington, D.C., board established in 1910 as the "arbiter of public taste in the capital." In 1941, Clarke opposed building the Pentagon because he considered its design an "outrage." Steve Vogel, *The Pentagon: A History* (New York: Random House, 2007), 65–66. In 1952, Saarinen was a consultant for a team comprised of Nervi and two other architects for the UNESCO headquarters in Paris.

45. Statement by ES on Arch Motif, n.d., ESP; *SLPD*, February 26, 1948; Griffin, *Modernism and Fascism*, 336; Benjamin W. Jayne to ES, July 7, 1928, ESP.

46. Angelo Piero Sereni to ES, June 24, 1948, Benjamin W. Jayne to A. P. Sereni, July 7, 1948, JNEMA; ES to William Wurster, March 1, 1948, ESP; *NYT*, February 27, 1948. The Clarke charges still resonate. In 2008, architectural critic

Martin Filler noted that Robert Venturi, who had praised the Arch, "with his extensive historical knowledge, cannot have been unaware of its extraordinary resemblance to the unbuilt arch Adalberto Libera designed in 1939." "Flying High With Eero Saarinen," *New York Review of Books*, June 12, 2008.

47. ES to Hugh Ferriss, March 29, 1948, ESP; Matthew Woll to LES, March 12, 1948, JNEMA; "Statement by the Jury on the Winning Design in the Jefferson National Expansion Memorial Competition," JNEMA; William Graebner, "Gateway to Empire: An Interpretation of Eero Saarinen's 1948 Design for the St. Louis Arch," *Prospects* 18 (1993): 367–401, concludes that "the quintessential fascist arch was not the semicircle, inspired by Roman predecessors, but rather Saarinen's catenary or parabolic form" (388). This view ignores Saarinen as sculptor, but Graebner correctly highlights the relative ease with which the fascist concept could be transformed into a democratic one and how triumphal arches highlight "the lust for empire" (394).

48. ES Speech to Associated Retailers of St. Louis, April 29, 1948, ESP.

FIVE

The Architect

1. "The Maturing Modern," *Time* July 2, 1956.

2. *Time*, July 2, 1956; Aline B. Saarinen, ed., *Eero Saarinen on His Work* (New Haven: Yale University Press, 1962), 14; *Inland Architect*, January 1988, in CREC, Library of Congress.

3. *The International Competition for a New Administration Building for the Chicago Tribune, Containing All the Designs Submitted in Response to the Chicago Tribune's $100,000 Offer Commemorating Its Seventy-Fifth Anniversary, June 10, 1932*; Martin Filler, "Flying High with Eero Saarinen," *New York Review of Books*, June 12, 2008. For the influence of the Bauhaus in the larger world of modernism, see Peter Gay, *Modernism: The Lure of Heresy* (New York: Norton, 2008), 315–18.

4. Gay, *Modernism*; Frank Lloyd Wright, "To the Young Man in Architecture," speech before Chicago Art Institute, Oct. 1, 1930, in FLWP, Library of Congress.

5. *Detroit News*, October 25, 1931; *Baldwinian, 1929*; "Architects Personal History and Professional Field Interview I—Saarinen," IPSR; Gay, *Modernism*, 60.

6. Le Corbusier, *When the Cathedrals Were White: A Journey to the Country of Timid People* (New York: Reynal and Hitchcock, 1947), 143–44.

7. "Architects' Personal History," IPSR; Eero Saarinen resume, 1947, JKDP; Antonio Roman, *Eero Saarinen: An Architecture of Multiplicity* (London: Laurence King Publishing, 2002), 6–7; "Chronology," in Eeva-Liisa Pelkonen and Donald Albrecht, *Eero Saarinen: Shaping the Future* (New Haven: Yale University Press, 2006), 323–25; *Time*, July 2, 1956.

ed., *Eero Saarinen*, 325. The formula for a weighted catenary that is closely related to the Gateway Arch is y = A cosh (bx) + c. For recent mathematical definitions of the Arch, see Robert Osserman, "Mathematics of the Gateway Arch," *Notices of the American Mathematical Society* 57 (February 2010): 220–29, and Alexander J. Hahn, *Mathematical Excursions to the World's Great Buildings* (Princeton: Princeton University Press, 2012), 285–86.

40. Due to budgetary limitations, the NPS eventually discarded Saarinen's stairs. See interview with Charles Rennison by Don Haake, March 24, 1981, JNEMA.

41. John Dinkeloo to Arthur Schwarz, January 17, 1967, George Hartzog to William Crowdus, January 30, 1967, RTPP.

42. Eero Saarinen resume, AESP; James Semple Kerr, "A Revised Plan for the Conservation of the Sydney Opera House and Its Site," 3rd ed., 2003, 13–15; Roman, *Eero Saarinen*, 191. The folklore about Saarinen finding Utzon's plans in the reject bin is probably apocryphal, yet there is little argument that Saarinen was Utzon's most enthusiastic supporter on the jury. John Yeomans, *The Other Taj Mahal: What Happened to the Sydney Opera House* (London: Longman's, 1968), 34; *Sydney Morning Herald*, December 1, 2008; Anne Watson, ed., *Building a Masterpiece: The Sydney Opera House* (Sydney: Powerhouse, 2006), 47–48.

43. *Birmingham Eccentric*, November 17, 1960; ES to Astrid Sampe, June 1960, Astrid Sampe Collection, Saarinen Family Papers, CA. A highly regarded textile artist, Sampe died in 2002.

SIX
The Laughingstock of the World

1. *SLPD*, February 25, 1948.

2. *SLPD*, March 4, 1948.

3. Petition to Mayor Darst, April 19, 1950; William L. Igoe to Darst, October 27, 1949, RTPP.

4. *Kansas City Star*, October 29, 1949; *SLPD*, October 28, 1949, March 18, 1950.

5. John K. Branner to Darst, November 11, 1949, RTPP. The University of California at Berkeley awards a traveling fellowship in architecture named in Branner's honor.

6. Joseph Collins to Darst, October 26, 1949; Felix Chopin to Darst, October 21, 1949, A. Carl Weber to Darst, October 21, 1949, Rose Brown to Darst, October 23, 1949, E. A. Luchtemeyer to Darst; Anonymous to Darst, November 18, 1949, Otto Eichholf to Darst, n.d., RTPP. Even in 2008, critics referred to the Gateway Arch in terms reminiscent of those used in the 1940s. The Arch reminds

Martin Filler of "an Oldenburgian wicket awaiting its croquet ball." *New York Review of Books*, June 12, 2008.

7. William Wurster to William Plowman, November 1, 1949, JNEMA; *SLPD*, March 17, 1950.

8. Fred N. Severud, "Structural Study: Jefferson Memorial Arch," *Architectural Engineering* (July 1951): 151–53; ES memo, December 21, 1949, ESP; Mario Salvadori, *Why Buildings Stand Up (New York: Norton, 1980)*, 175. For Severud's background and obituary, see *NYT*, June 14, 1990.

9. Fred Severud to ES, April 27, 1948, December 5, 1949; Memo, n.d., ESP.

10. *SLPD*, October 18, 1961. When Frank Gehry's Walt Disney Concert Hall in Los Angeles was completed in 2003, some mirrored panels created concentrated glare that warmed adjacent sidewalks to nearly 140 degrees, and some nearby residents complained of unbearable heat. In 2005, these panels were sanded to dull the sun's reflection.

11. Clifford B. Hicks, "The Incredible Gateway Arch," *Popular Mechanics* (December 1963); Harold M. Cobb, *The History of Stainless Steel* (Materials Park, Ohio, 2009), 174; Michael J. Crosbie, "Is It a Catenary?" *AIA Journal* (June 1983); interview with Bruce Detmers by Bob Moore, October 21, 1994, JNEMA.

12. ES to Harold D. Hauf, April 23, 1951, ESP.

13. LES to ES, January 17, 1950, ESP; *SLPD*, November 8, 1949.

14. *SLPD*, February 21, 1949, November 1, 1965; Dickmann to Symington, April 15, 1957, SSP.

15. Ruth Jepson to Darst, April 19, 1950, RTPP; *SLPD*, November 2, 6, 1949.

16. Darst to John Steelman, June 14, 1949, RTPP; William Wurster to LES, May 31, 1949, JKDP.

17. *Trenton Evening Times*, October 8, 1957; ES to David Reichgott, August 10, 1949, ESP.

18. *NYT*, June 11, 1950.

19. *NYT*, April 3, 1951.

20. F. A. MacKenzie to Stuart Symington, March 5, 1953, SSP.

21. *Business Week*, September 18, 1965; Clarence Lang, *Grassroots at the Gateway: Class Politics and Black Freedom Struggle in St. Louis, 1936–75* (Ann Arbor: University of Michigan Press, 2009), 103–9.

22. Jon C. Teaford, *The Rough Road to Renaissance: Urban Revitalization in America, 1940–1985* (Baltimore: Johns Hopkins University Press, 1990), 48, 67–68, 142.

23. *SLPD*, May 18, 1954, May 16, 1956, May 8, 1957.

24. "Amendment of the Act Providing for the Construction of the Jefferson National Expansion Memorial, St. Louis, Mo.," U.S. Senate Report 2359, 85th

Congress, 2nd Session, 1958; "Chronological Outline of Major Steps in the Development of the Memorial," June 1957, SSP; *SLPD*, June 3, 1956; Dickson Terry, "A Monument to Thirty Years of Patience, Perseverance, and Determination," *Cherry Diamond*, September 1964; "Statement by Eero Saarinen, St. Louis, Missouri, October 2, 1957," JNEMA.

25. *SLPD*, June 18, 1957; Mark H. Rose, *Interstate: Express Highway Politics, 1939–1989* (Knoxville: University of Tennessee Press, 1990), 57.

26. *Christian Science Monitor*, September 17, 1959.

27. Joseph Heathcott and Maire Agnes Murphy, "Corridors of Flight, Zones of Renewal: Industry, Planning, and Policy in the Making of Metropolitan St. Louis, 1940–1980," *Journal of Urban History* 31 (January 2005): 155–57; W. W. Oberjuerge to Stuart Symington, February 16, 1953, SSP; *Time*, July 17, 1964.

28. George B. Hartzog, Jr., *Battling for the National Parks* (Mt. Kisco: Moyer Bell, 1988), 37–38; *NYT*, July 17, 2008.

29. *NYT*, March 30, May 15, 1960; *SLPD*, May 8, 11, 15, 1960.

30. Memo, George Hartzog to unknown, August 10, 1961, RTPP.

31. Interview with Joseph Lacy by Wesley Janz, January 29, 1992, CA.

32. Death certificate, Eero Saarinen, AESP; Richard Knight, *Saarinen's Quest: A Memoir* (San Francisco: William Stout, 2008), 159; interview with George Hartzog, by Bob Moore, October 25, 1994, JNEMA; interview with Joseph Lacy by Wesley Janz, January 29, 1992, CA; *Flint Journal*, September 2, 1961; *SLPD*, August 17, 1961. Just months after his death, the AIA recognized Saarinen's contributions by awarding him the Gold Medal, the organization's highest honor. Saarinen was the twenty-ninth recipient of this distinction, joining previous winners such as Frank Lloyd Wright, Louis Sullivan, Mies van der Rohe, and Eliel Saarinen.

33. Memorial Service for ES, September 9, 1961, ESP.

SEVEN
"Got It Made"

1. *NYT*, April 15, 1982.

2. Kevin Roche, "Designing the Gateway Arch," in Moore, *The Gateway Arch*, 42; interview with George Hartzog by Bob Moore, October 25, 1994, JNEMA.

3. *SLGD*, January 23, 1962; *SLPD*, November 1, 1965; Dickson Terry, "A Monument to Thirty Years of Patience, Perseverance, and Determination," *Cherry Diamond*, September 1964.

4. U.S. Territorial Expansion Memorial Committee newsletter, August 4, 1961, RTPP.

5. Clarence Cannon to Lytle S. Montrey, June 8, 1959, CCP; *Roll Call*, July 26, 1962; Conrad L. Wirth, *Parks, Politics, and People* (Norman: University of Oklahoma Press, 1980), 277–78; Hartzog interview.

6. *SLPD*, March 16, 1962.

7. *SLGD*, July 5, 1962.

8. George B. Hartzog, Jr., *Battling for the National Parks* (Mt. Kisco: Moyer Bell, 1988), 52–57; Michael J. Crosbie, "Is It a Catenary?" *AIA Journal* (June 1983): 78–79; interview with Charles E. Rennison by George Lucko, October 9, 1970, JNEMA.

9. MacDonald Construction Company, "Summary Erection Procedure for the Gateway Arch," July 19, 1962, ESP; Clifford B. Hicks, "The Incredible Gateway Arch," *Popular Mechanics* (December 1963); *Elevator World*, June, August 1964; *SLGD*, May 5, 1963; *NYT*, February 9, 1964; Severud, "Structural Study"; *SLPD*, March 16, 1962.

10. Interview with Russ Knox by Bob Moore, July 26, 1995, JNEMA.

11. *SLPD*, March 16, May 6, 1962; *SLGD*, October 28, 1965. Interview with Joe Minner by Bob Moore, August 28, 1996, JNEMA; MacDonald Company, "Summary Erection Procedures," ESP.

12. *SLPD*, October 31, 1964; Rennison interview.

13. Rennison interview.

14. Interview with Dick Bowser by Bob Moore, October 8, 1993, JNEMA; ES memo, n.d., ESP.

15. Bowser interview; Bob Moore, "About Dick Bowser," www.nps.gov/archive/jeff/dick_bowser.html.

16. Mark S. Rosentraub, *Major League Losers: The Real Cost of Sports and Who's Paying For It* (New York: Basic Books, 1997), 176–77, 286–91. In May 2012, the price tag for upgrading the seventeen-year-old Edward Jones Dome, used for the St. Louis Rams NFL franchise, was more than $700 million. How much the city and state should pay in order to keep the franchise in St. Louis was subject to intense debate about the extent to which large stadiums actually contributed to the local economy and whether taxpayers should underwrite professional sports teams and their billionaire owners. The construction of a "ballpark village" next to Busch Stadium, also underwritten by tax dollars, was labeled "a civic joke" by the Post-Dispatch. *SLPD*, May 14, 15, 24, September 21, 2012.

17. Aline Saarinen to Raymond Tucker, April 24, 1962, RTPP; *NYT*, January 6, 1964; *SLGD*, November 11, 1967; Aaron B. Cowan, "A Nice Place to Visit: Tourism, Urban Revitalization, and the Transformation of Postwar American Cities," Ph.D. diss., University of Cincinnati, 2007, 187; Bob Duffe to Dick McGee, January 13, 1969, box 56, ACP; *SLPD*, November 16, 1967.

18. *SLPD*, March 26, 29, 1963; Brian Burnes, Robert W. Butler, Dan Viets, *Walt Disney's Missouri* (Kansas City: Kansas City Star Books, 2002), 140–44.

19. O. O. McCracken to Edward Durell Stone, March 29, 1963, RTPP; *SLPD*, March 26, 29, 1963; *SLGD*, May 21, 1963; Burnes et al., *Walt Disney's Missouri*, 140–57; *NYT*, July 3, 1964.

20. *SLPD*, July 6, 13, 1965; Richard E. Foglesong, *Married to the Mouse: Walt Disney World and Orlando* (New Haven: Yale University Press, 2003), 3. Four months after the St. Louis project was declared over, Disney announced his plans to build a massive park on 27,000 acres in Florida. Neal Gabler, *Walt Disney: The Triumph of the American Imagination* (New York: Vintage, 2006), 603–5.

21. *NYT*, November 7, 1965; Cowan, "A Nice Place to Visit," 111–14; Alfonso J. Cervantes, *Mister Mayor* (Los Angeles: Nash Publishing, 1974), 121–38.

22. Katharine G. Bristol, "The Pruitt-Igoe Myth," *Journal of Architectural Education* 44 (May 1991): 163–71: *NYT*, January 25, 2012; *SLPD*, July 25, 2010.

23. *SLPD*, July 3, 1964.

24. George Lipsitz, *A Life in the Struggle: Ivory Perry and the Culture of Opposition* (Philadelphia: Temple University Press, 1988), 78; *NYT*, May 20, August 31, 1961.

25. Alison Isenberg, *Downtown America: A History of the Place and the People Who Made It* (Chicago: University of Chicago Press, 2004), 6–7; www.factfinder.census .gov.

26. Percy H. Green to Stuart Symington, May 14, 1964, Lucian Richards to Symington, July 5, 1964, SSP; Jon C. Teaford, *The Rough Road to Renaissance: Urban Revitalization in America, 1940–1985* (Baltimore: Johns Hopkins University Press, 1990), 180; Mary Kimbrough and Margaret W. Dagen, *Victory Without Violence: The First Ten Years of the St. Louis Committee of Racial Equality, 1947–1957* (Columbia: University of Missouri Press, 2000), 91; Clarence Lang, *Grassroots at the Gateway: Class Politics and Black Freedom Struggle in St. Louis, 1936–75* (Ann Arbor: University of Michigan Press, 2009), 155–85.

27. *SLPD*, July 6, 7, 1964; *St. Louis Argus*, July 17, 1964; *NYT*, August 30, 1964; Clarence Lang, "Between Civil Rights and Black Power in the Gateway City: The Action Committee to Improve Opportunities for Negroes, 1964–75," *Journal of Social History* 37 (Spring 2004): 725; Robert J. Moore, "Showdown Under the Arch: The Construction Trades and the First 'Pattern or Practice' Equal Employment Opportunity Suit, 1966," *Gateway Heritage* (1994); Lipsitz, *A Life in the Struggle*, 77–85; *SLGD*, May 25, 1968.

28. "Meeting Notes, July 23, 1964," box 19, RTPP.

29. *SLPD*, August 8, 9, 1964.

30. *Time*, January 29, 1966; *NYT*, February 5, 1966.

31. *SLPD*, August 30, 1964, May 19, 1968; Hobart Taylor, Jr., to Stuart Symington, August 10, 1964, SSP; Lang, "Between Civil Rights and Black Power," 725.

EIGHT
Expendable Culture

1. *SLGD*, October 22, 1965.

2. *SLPD*, October 27, 1963; *Wall Street Journal*, July 14, 1967.

3. Interview with Russ Knox by Bob Moore, July 26, 1995, JNEMA.

4. Interview with Bill Quigley by Bob Moore, October 28, 1995, JNEMA; *SLGD*, October 28, 1965; Robert J. Moore, Jr., *The Gateway Arch: An Architectural Dream* (St. Louis: Jefferson National Parks, 2005), 102.

5. *SLGD*, October 28, 1965; MacDonald Construction Company, "Summary Erection Procedures for the Gateway Arch," July 19, 1962, ESP.

6. *The Plainsmen*, November 1965.

7. Interview with Fred Morris by Bob Moore, October 23, 1997, JNEMA.

8. "Engineering of Saarinen's Arch," *Architectural Record*; Rennison interview; *SLPD*, June 8, 17, August 8, 25, 1965; *SLGD*, August 25, 1965; interview with LeRoy Brown by Bob Moore, October 14, 1994, JNEMA.

9. *NYT*, June 28, 1964, February 4, 1968.

10. *SLPD*, October 25, 26, 28, 1965; *SLGD*, October 22, 25, 27, 1965. Although the October 21, 1965, Missouri earthquake was a minor one, St. Louis University geophysics professor Otto Nuttle said it was "the most widely felt quake" in the area in nearly a half century. J. E. Gordon notes that arches are "extraordinarily stable and are not unduly sensitive to the movements of their foundations." *Structures: Or, Why Things Don't Fall Down* (New York: De Capo, 1978), 190.

11. *SLPD*, October 23, 2005; Moore, *The Gateway Arch*, 109.

12. *SLPD*, October 28, 29, 1965; *SLGD*, October 28, 1965; August A. Busch, Jr., to Lyndon B. Johnson, January 29, 1965, box 20, RTPP.

13. R. E. MacDonald to Leonard Lipic, November 4, 1965, ACP.

14. *SLPD*, June 29, 1965; "Mayor's Remarks, Topping Out Ceremony," ACP; *SLGD*, October 28, 1965; Joseph Heathcott and Maire Agnes Murphy, "Corridors of Flight, Zones of Renewal: Industry, Planning, and Policy in the Making of Metropolitan St. Louis, 1940–1980," *Journal of Urban History* 31 (January 2005): 178–79.

15. *SLGD*, August 30, 1965; *NYT*, November 30, 1969; Brown interview.

16. *Ann Arbor News*, September 8, 1967; *Seattle Post-Intelligencer*, August 15, 1967.

17. *SLPD*, December 29, 1965.

18. Rennison interview; *SLPD*, June 16, October 25, 1965.

19. "To Increase the Authorization for the Jefferson National Expansion Memorial," U.S. Senate Report 320, 89th Congress, 1st Session, June 1965; *SLPD*, January 14, May 19, 1968; *NYT*, November 7, 1965, July 16, 1967.

20. *SLPD*, January 14, 17, 15, 18, 1968.

21. *NYT*, June 12, 1966; *New Yorker*, November 27, 1965; Jill Jonnes, *Eiffel's Tower: The Thrilling Story Behind Paris's Beloved Monument and the Extraordinary World's Fair That Introduced It* (New York: Penguin, 2009).

22. *SLGD*, March 7, 8, 1967.

23. *NYT*, November 7, 1965; Cowan, "A Nice Place to Visit," 111–14, 126–27; Alfonso J. Cervantes, *Mister Mayor* (Los Angeles: Nash Publishing, 1974), 121–38; Lana Stein, *St. Louis Politics: The Triumph of Tradition* (St. Louis: Missouri Historical Society Press, 2002), 144–46.

24. *SLPD*, May 25, 1968.

25. Report on Redevelopment of Land Surrounding the JNM Park, St. Louis, December 14, 1948," ESP; *SLPD*, May 18, 2008; *NYT*, December 7, 2008.

NINE
Symbol and Symptom

1. *NYT*, February 4, 1968.

2. Interview with Dan Kiley by Bob Moore, July 22, 1993, JNEMA. By 2010, the emergence of the ash borer threatened the ash trees at the JNEM. NPS officials considered preemptively cutting down the trees, which account for 40 percent of the trees at the site, and possibly replacing them with tulip poplars, the type Kiley originally wanted. In March 2012, with the borers just seventy miles away, the NPS authorized cutting down the ash trees once the pests arrived. *SLPD*, Oct. 11, 2010, March 9, 2012.

3. Jane Jacobs, *The Death and Life of Great American Cities* (New York: Modern Library, 1993; repr. of Random House ed., 1961), 139–40. In his 1999 memoir, landscape architect Dan Kiley conspicuously did not write about the Gateway Arch grounds. The project is merely listed in a section on his complete works. Dan Kiley and Jane Amidon, *Dan Kiley: The Complete Works of America's Master Landscape Architect* (Boston: Little, Brown, 1999).

4. Robert M. Fogelson, *Downtown: Its Rise and Fall, 1880–1950* (New Haven: Yale University Press, 2001), 315; William E. Winter, "Development and Decision-Making in St. Louis, Missouri: Institutions, Incentives, and Urban Development," Ph.D. diss., University of Missouri–Columbia, 2006, 164.

5. *SLPD*, October 19, 2008.

6. *SLPD*, May 18, October 19, 2008, July 2, 11, 13, 2009, February 28, Sept. 22,

23, 2010, January 28, September 20, 2011, January 29, March 15, May 9, 2012; *NYT*, December 7, 2008, August 20, 2010; Aline B. Saarinen, ed., *Eero Saarinen on His Work (New Haven: Yale University Press, 1962)* 18. Details of the new riverfront plan are at cityarchriver.org.

7. Bruce Olson, "Blues Museum Planned for St. Louis Riverfront," Reuters, February 13, 2012.

8. *SLPD*, August 22, September 9, 2010, June 13, September 24, 25, 2012; NPS, Jefferson National Expansion Memorial, Gateway Arch, "Historic Structure Report—Vol. I," June 2010. In August 2010, a *Post*-Dispatch reporter was allowed to read parts of the original "Corrosion Investigation" for approximately forty minutes, but NPS officials then withdrew the report, citing reasons involving "national security."

9. STPD, February 24, 2011; www.factfinder.census.gov.

10. See www.factfinder.census.gov; *Forbes*, February 6, 2009; "City Crime Rankings, 2011–12" at cqpress.com/citycrime/2011; 247wallst.com/2012/06.11; *Business Week*, March 3, 2009; Joseph Heathcott and Maire Agnes Murphy, "Corridors of Flight, Zones of Renewal: Industry, Planning, and Policy in the Making of Metropolitan St. Louis, 1940–1980," *Journal of Urban History* 31 (January 2005): 154, 179–81.

11. Richard Florida, *Cities and the Creative Class* (New York: Routledge, 2005), 35–36. For the benefits of "walkable" neighborhoods on urban economic and cultural life, see Christopher B. Leinberger and Mariela Alfonzo, "Walk This Way: The Economic Promise of Walkable Places in Metropolitan D.C.," Brookings Institution, May 2012.

12. *The Atlantic*, September 2002; Manuel Fletcher, "The Sydney Opera House," *Guardian*, October 15, 2007; *NYT*, September 24, 2007; Keith Moxey, "Gehry's Bilbao: Visits and Visions," in Anna Maria Guasch and Joseba Zulaika, *Learning from the Bilbao Guggenheim* (Reno: University of Nevada, Reno, 2005), 174–75.

13. "Recent Works of Eero Saarinen," *Zodiac* 4 (1959): 32–33.

14. In 2012, demolition to make way for an interstate highway in East St. Louis threatened archaeological sites concerning Cahokia. Véronique LaCapra, "Ancient Suburb Near St. Louis Could Be Lost Forever," Weekend Edition Saturday, National Public Radio, June 2, 2012.

Bibliography

ARCHIVES

Archives of American Art,
Smithsonian Institution,
Washington, D.C.
Aline and Eero Saarinen Papers
Lilian Swann Saarinen Papers

Cranbrook Archives, Cranbrook
Academy, Bloomfield Hills,
Michigan
George Gouge Booth Papers
Jack Goldman Collection
Saarinen Family Papers
Astrid Sampe Collection

Institute of Personality and Social
Research, University of
California–Berkeley
"Eero Saarinen" file

Jefferson National Expansion Memorial
Archives, National Park Service,
St. Louis
Jefferson National Expansion
    Memorial Records
"Vertical Files"
U.S. Territorial Expansion Memorial
    Records

Library of Congress, Manuscript
Division, Washington, D.C.
Charles and Ray Eames Collection
Harold Ickes Papers
Frank Lloyd Wright Papers

Missouri History Museum, Library
and Research Center, St. Louis
James K. Douglas Papers

Bibliography

Clifford Greve Papers
Louis LaBeaume Papers
Luther Ely Smith Papers
St. Louis Streets and Roads
   Scrapbook

National Archives, College Park,
Maryland
National Park Service Central
   Classified Files, Record
   Group 79

Special Collections, St. Louis Public
   Library
Jefferson National Memorial Files
"St. Louis Riverfront Scrapbooks"

Special Collections, Andrews Library,
College of Wooster, Wooster, Ohio
Paul O. Peters Collection

St. Louis Mercantile Library, University
of Missouri-St. Louis
Clippings File

State Historical Society of Missouri,
University of Missouri–Columbia
Clarence Cannon Papers
Bernard F. Dickmann Papers
Stuart Symington Papers

University Archives, Special Collections,
Washington University Archives,
St. Louis
Harris Armstrong Papers
Harland Bartholomew and Associates
   Papers
Alfonso J. Cervantes Papers
Aloys P. Kaufman Papers
Raymond R. Tucker Collection

Manuscripts and Archives, Yale
University Library, New Haven,
Connecticut
Eero Saarinen Papers

NEWSPAPERS AND MAGAZINES

Ann Arbor News
Architectural Forum
Architectural Review
Bond Issue News
Business Week
Christian Science Monitor
Columbia Daily Tribune
Daily Evening News
Detroit News
Elevator World
Engineering News-Record
Flint Journal

Harper's
Life
Look
Nation
New York Herald Tribune
New York Journal of Commerce
New York Review of Books
New York Times
Plainsmen
Playboy
Real Estate Analyst
Riverfront Times

Bibliography

Southern Architect and Building News
St. Louis Argus
St. Louis Commerce
St. Louis Globe-Democrat
St. Louis Post-Dispatch
St. Louis Republic
St. Louis Star-Times

St. Louis Union Advocate
Sydney Morning Herald
Time
Vogue
Wall Street Journal
Washington Post

BOOKS

Anderson, William. *The Rise of the Gothic*. London: Hutchinson, 1985.

Arenson, Adam. *The Great Heart of the Republic: St. Louis and the Cultural Civil War*. Cambridge: Harvard University Press, 2011.

Aron, Stephen. *American Confluence: The Missouri Frontier from Borderland to Border State*. Bloomington: Indiana University Press, 2006.

Ball, Philip. *Universe of Stone: Chartres Cathedral and the Invention of the Gothic*. New York: Harper Perennial, 2008.

Barnes, Harper. *Never Been a Time: The 1917 Race Riot That Sparked the Civil Rights Movement*. New York: Walker, 2008.

Blake, Peter. *The Master Builders*. New York: Knopf, 1970.

Bodnar, John. *Remaking America: Public Memory, Commemoration, and Patriotism in the Twentieth Century*. Princeton: Princeton University Press, 1992.

Burnes, Brian, Butler, Robert W., and Dan Viets. *Walt Disney's Missouri*. Kansas City: Kansas City Star Books, 2002.

Campbell, Tracy. *Deliver the Vote: A History of Election Fraud, an American Political Tradition, 1742–2004*. New York: Basic Books, 2006.

Caro, Robert A. *The Power Broker: Robert Moses and the Fall of New York*. New York: Alfred A. Knopf, 1974.

Cervantes, Alfonso J. *Mister Mayor*. Los Angeles: Nash, 1974.

Christian, Shirley. *Before Lewis and Clark: The Story of the Choteaus, the French Dynasty That Ruled America's Frontier*. New York: Farrar, Straus and Giroux, 2004.

Cobb, Harold M. *The History of Stainless Steel*. Materials Park, Ohio: ASM, 2009.

Cohen, Jean-Louis. *Le Corbusier and the Mystique of the USSR: Theories and Projects for Moscow, 1928–1936*. Princeton: Princeton University Press, 1992.

Bibliography

Feldman, Jay. *When the Mississippi Ran Backwards: Empire, Intrigue, Murder, and the New Madrid Earthquakes.* New York: Free Press, 2005.

Florida, Richard. *Cities and the Creative Class.* New York: Routledge, 2005.

Fogelson, Robert M. *Downtown: Its Rise and Fall, 1880–1950.* New Haven: Yale University Press, 2001.

Foglesong, Richard E. *Married to the Mouse: Walt Disney World and Orlando.* New Haven: Yale University Press, 2003.

Foley, William E. *A History of Missouri, vol. I, 1673-1820.* Columbia: University of Missouri Press, 1971.

Gabler, Neal. *Walt Disney: The Triumph of the American Imagination.* New York: Vintage, 2006.

Garofolo, Francesco, and Luca Veresani. *Adalberto Libera.* Princeton: Princeton University Press, 1992.

Gay, Peter. *Modernism: The Lure of Heresy.* New York: Norton, 2008.

Gitlin, Jay. *The Bourgeois Frontier: French Towns, French Traders, and American Expansion.* New Haven: Yale University Press, 2010.

Gordon, Colin. *Mapping Decline: St. Louis and the Fate of the American City.* Philadelphia: University of Pennsylvania Press, 2008.

Gordon, J.E. *Structures: Or Why Things Don't Fall Down.* New York: De Capo, 1978.

Griffin, Roger. *Modernism and Fascism: The Sense of a Beginning Under Mussolini and Hitler.* New York: Palgrave, 2007.

Guasch, Ana Maria and Joseba Zulaika. *Learning From the Bilbao Guggenheim.* Reno: Center for Basque Studies, University of Nevada, Reno, 2005.

Haan, Hilda de, and Ids Haagsma. *Architects in Competition: International Architectural Competitions of the Last 200 Years.* London: Thamas and Hudson, 1988.

Hahn, Alexander J. *Mathematical Excursions to the World's Great Buildings.* Princeton: Princeton University Press, 2012.

Hartzog, George B., Jr. *Battling for the National Parks.* Mt. Kisco, N.Y.: Moyer Bell, 1988.

Hiltzik, Michael. *Colossus: Hoover Dam and the Making of the American Century.* New York: Free Press, 2010.

Hurley, Andrew, ed. *Common Fields: An Environmental History of St. Louis.* St. Louis: Missouri Historical Society, 1997.

Ickes, Harold. *The Secret Diary of Harold Ickes, The First Thousand Days, 1933–1936.* New York: Simon and Schuster, 1953.

The International Competition for a New Administration Building for the Chicago

Tribune, Containing All the Designs Submitted in Response to the Chicago Tribune's $100,000 Offer Commemorating Its Seventy-Fifth Anniversary, June 10, 1922.

Isenberg, Alison. *Downtown America: A History of the Place and People Who Made It.* Chicago: University of Chicago Press, 2004.

Jackson, Kenneth T. *Crabgrass Frontier: The Suburbanization of the United States.* New York: Oxford University Press, 1985.

Jacobs, Jane. *The Death and Life of Great American Cities.* New York: Modern Library, 1993.

Jonnes, Jill. *Eiffel's Tower: The Thrilling Story Behind Paris's Beloved Monument and the Extraordinary World's Fair That Introduced It.* New York: Penguin, 2009.

Kiley, Dan, and Jane Amidon. *Dan Kiley: The Complete Works of America's Master Landscape Architect.* Boston: Little, Brown, 1999.

Kimbrough, Mary and Margaret W. Dagen. *Victory Without Violence: The First Ten Years of the St. Louis Committee of Racial Equality.* Columbia: University of Missouri Press, 2000.

Klein, Maury, and Harvey A. Kantor. *Prisoners of Progress: American Industrial Cities, 1850–1920.* New York: Macmillan, 1976.

Knight, Richard. *Saarinen's Quest: A Memoir.* San Francisco: William Stout, 2008.

Lang, Clarence. *Grassroots at the Gateway: Class Politics and Black Freedom Struggle in St. Louis, 1936–75.* Ann Arbor: University of Michigan Press, 2009.

Le Corbusier. *Towards a New Architecture.* New York: Dover, 1986, reprint of 1931 ed. Published by John Rodker.

———. *When the Cathedrals Were White: A Journey to the Country of Timid People.* New York: Reynal and Hitchcock, 1947.

Lipsitz, George. *A Life in the Struggle: Ivory Perry and the Culture of Opposition.* Philadelphia: Temple University Press, 1995.

Lovelace, Eldridge. *Harland Bartholomew: His Contributions to American Urban Planning.* Urbana: University of Illinois Printing Services, 1993.

McPherson, James M. *Battle Cry of Freedom: The Civil War Era.* New York: Oxford University Press, 1988.

Merkel, Jayne. *Eero Saarinen.* New York: Phaidon, 2005.

Moore, Robert J., Jr. *The Gateway Arch: An Architectural Dream.* St. Louis: Jefferson National Parks Association, 2005.

Olmo, Carlo and Cristiana Chiorino. *Pier Luigi Nervi: Architecture as Challenge.* Milan: Silvano Editoriale, 2010.

Pauketat, Timothy R. *Cahokia: Ancient America's Great City on the Mississippi.* New York: Viking, 2009.

Pelkonen, Eeva-Liisa, and Donald Albrecht, eds. *Eero Saarinen: Shaping the Future.* New Haven: Yale University Press, 2006.

Peterson, Jon A. *The Birth of City Planning in the United States, 1840–1917.* Baltimore: Johns Hopkins University Press, 2003.

Peterson, Merrill D. *The Jefferson Image in the American Mind.* New York: Oxford University Press, 1960.

Primm, James Neal. *Lion of the Valley: St. Louis, Missouri, 1764–1980.* St. Louis: Missouri Historical Society Press, 1998.

Rand, Ayn. *The Fountainhead.* New York: Bobbs-Merrill, 1943.

Richter, Daniel K. *Facing East from Indian Country: A Native History of Early America.* Cambridge: Harvard University Press, 2001.

Roman, Antonio. *Eero Saarinen: An Architecture of Multiplicity.* London: Laurence King, 2002.

Rose, Mark H. *Interstate: Express Highway Politics, 1939–1989.* Knoxville: University of Tennessee Press, 1990.

Rosentraub, Mark S. *Major League Losers: The Real Cost of Sports and Who's Paying for It.* New York: Basic Books, 1997.

Rudwick, Elliott M. *Race Riot at East St. Louis, July 2, 1917.* Carbondale: Southern Illinois University Press, 1964.

Saarinen, Aline B., ed. *Eero Saarinen on His Work.* New Haven: Yale University Press, 1962.

Saarinen, Eliel. *The City: Its Growth, Its Decay, Its Future.* New York: Reinhold, 1943.

Saint, Andrew. *Architect and Engineer: A Study in Sibling Rivalry.* New Haven: Yale University Press, 2007.

Salvadori, Mario. *Why Buildings Stand Up.* New York: Norton, 1980.

Serraino, Pierluigi. *Eero Saarinen, 1910–1961: A Structural Expressionist.* Cologne: Taschen, 2005.

Shaffer, Marguerite S. *See America First: Tourism and National Identity, 1880–1940.* Washington, D.C.: Smithsonian Institution Press, 2001.

Shanken, Andrew M. *194X: Architecture, Planning, and Consumer Culture on the American Home Front.* Minneapolis: University of Minnesota Press, 2009.

Stein, Lana. *St. Louis Politics: The Triumph of Tradition.* St. Louis: Missouri Historical Society Press, 2002.

Stern, Robert A.M. *George Howe: Toward a Modern American Architecture.* New Haven: Yale University Press, 1975.

Swift, Earl. *The Big Roads: The Untold Story of the Engineers, Visionaries, and Trailblazers Who Created the American Superhighways.* Boston: Houghton Mifflin, 2011.

Taliaferro, John. *Great White Fathers: The Story of the Obsessive Quest to Create Mount Rushmore.* New York: Public Affairs, 2002.

Teaford, Jon C. *The Rough Road to Renaissance: Urban Revitalization in America, 1940–1985.* Baltimore: Johns Hopkins University Press, 1990.

Temko, Allan. *Eero Saarinen.* New York: George Braziller, 1962.

Tranel, Mark. ed., *St. Louis Plans: The Ideal and the Real St. Louis.* St. Louis: Missouri Historical Society Press, 2007 .

Vogel, Steve. *The Pentagon: A History.* New York: Random House, 2007.

Wenzlick, Roy. *Real Estate Analyst, St. Louis Edition.* 1933.

Wilson, William H. *The City Beautiful Movement.* Baltimore: Johns Hopkins University Press, 1989.

Wirth, Conrad L. *Parks, Politics, and the People.* Norman: University of Oklahoma Press, 1980.

Yeomans, John. *The Other Taj Mahal: What Happened to the Sydney Opera House.* London: Longmans, 1968.

Young, Biloine Whiting, and Melvin L. Fowler. *Cahokia: The Great Native American Metropolis.* Urbana: University of Illinois Press, 2000.

ARTICLES

Bluestone, Daniel M. "Detroit's City Beautiful and the Problems of Commerce." *Journal of the Society of Architectural Historians* 47 (September 1988).

Bristol, Katharine G. "The Pruitt-Igoe Myth." *Journal of Architectural Education* (May 1991): 163–71.

"Chronology." Eeva-Liisa Pelkonen and Donald Albrecht, eds. *Eero Saarinen: Shaping the Future.* New Haven: Yale University Press, 2006.

Coir, Mark. "The Cranbrook Factor." Eeva-Liisa Pelkonen and Donald Albrecht., eds. *Eero Saarinen: Shaping the Future.* New Haven: Yale University Press, 2006.

Crosbie, Michael J. "Is It a Catenary?" *AIA Journal* (June 1983).

Dacus, J. A. and James W. Buel. "A Tour of St. Louis, or, the Inside Life of a Great City." St. Louis: Western Publishing, 1878.

Filler, Martin. "Flying High With Eero Saarinen." *New York Review of Books,* June 12, 2008.

Bibliography

Graebner, William. "Gateway to Empire: An Interpretation of Eero Saarinen's 1948 Design for the St. Louis Arch." *Prospects* 18 (1993): 367–401.

Harvey, David. "Monument and Myth." *Annals of the Association of American Geographers* 69 (September 1979): 362–81.

Heathcott, Joseph. "Harland Bartholomew: City Engineer." Mark Tranel, ed., *St. Louis Plans: The Ideal and the Real St. Louis.* St. Louis: Missouri Historical Society Press, 2007.

Heathcott, Joseph, and Maire Agnes Murphy, "Corridors of Flight, Zones of Renewal: Industry, Planning, and Policy in the Making of Metropolitan St. Louis, 1940–1980." *Journal of Urban History* 31 (January 2005).

Hicks, Clifford B. "The Incredible Gateway Arch." *Popular Mechanics* (December 1963).

Iseminger, William R. "Culture and Environment in the American Bottom: The Rise and Fall of Cahokia Mounds," in Andrew Hurley, ed., *Common Fields: An Environmental History of St. Louis* (St. Louis: Missouri Historical Society Press, 1997): 38–57.

Lang, Clarence. "Between Civil Rights and Black Power in the Gateway City: The Action Committee to Improve Opportunities for Negroes, 1964–1975." *Journal of Social History* 37 (Spring 2004).

Leinberger, Christopher B. and Mariela Alfonzo, "Walk This Way: The Economic Promise of Walkable Places in Metropolitan D.C.," Brookings Institution, May 2012.

Louchheim, Aline. "Now Saarinen the Son." *New York Times Magazine,* April 26, 1953.

Mathewson, I. "Mirror Writing Ability Is Genetic and Probably Transmitted as a Sex-Linked Dominant Trait." *Medical Hypothesis* 62 (2003).

McQuade, Walter. "Eero Saarinen: A Complete Architect." *Architectural Forum* (April 1962).

Moore, Robert J. "Showdown Under the Arch: The Construction Trades and the First 'Pattern or Practice' Equal Employment Opportunity Suit, 1966." *Gateway Heritage* (1994).

Moxey, Keith. "Gehry's Bilbao: Visits and Visions." Ana Maria Guasch and Joseba Zulaika, *Learning From the Bilbao Guggenheim.* Reno: Center for Basque Studies, University of Nevada, Reno, 2005.

Osserman, Robert. "Mathematics of the Gateway Arch." *Notices of the American Mathematical Society* 57 (February 2010): 220–29.

Phares, Don. "Planning for Regional Governance in the St. Louis Area: The Context, the Plans, the Outcomes." Mark Tranel, ed., *St. Louis Plans:*

The Ideal, and the Real St. Louis. St. Louis: Missouri Historical Society Press, 2007.

Pritchett, Wendell E. "The 'Public Menace' of Blight: Urban Renewal and the Private Uses of Eminent Domain." *Yale Law and Policy Review* 21 (Winter 2003): 1–52.

"Recent Work of Eero Saarinen." *Zodiac* 4 (1959): 30–67.

Richman, Harry B. "The Competition Commences," in Robert J. Moore, Jr., *The Gateway Arch: An Architectural Dream.* St. Louis: Jefferson National Parks Association, 2005.

Roche, Kevin. "Designing the Gateway Arch." Robert J. Moore, Jr., *The Gateway Arch: An Architectural Dream.* St. Louis: Jefferson National Parks Association, 2005.

Russell, E. J. "The St. Louis River Plaza." *Southern Architect and Building News.* October 1930.

Schott, G.D. "Mirror Writing: Neurological Reflections in an Unusual Phenomenon." *Journal of Neurological Neurosurgery.* September 2006.

Scully, Vincent. "Rethinking Saarinen." Eeva-Liisa Pelkonen and Donald Albrecht, eds. *Eero Saarinen: Shaping the Future.* New Haven: Yale University Press, 2006.

Serraino, Pierluigi. "Creative Architects: An Introduction to the Archives at the Institute of Personality and Social Research." *Perspecta: The Yale Architectural Journal* 45 (September 2012): 169–77.

Severud, Fred N. "Structural Study: Jefferson Memorial Arch." *Architectural Engineering* (July 1951).

———. "Turtles and Walnuts, Morning Glories and Grass." *Architectural Forum* (September 1945).

Soo, Lydia M. "The Work of William Eng and His Approach to Design Education." *Reflections: The Journal of the School of Architecture, University of Illinois at Urbana-Champaign.* Fall 1987.

Tarr, Joel A. and Carl Zimring. "The Struggle for Smoke Control in St. Louis." Andrew Hurley, ed., *Common Fields: An Environmental History of St. Louis.* St. Louis: Missouri Historical Society Press, 1997.

Terry, Dickson. "A Monument to Thirty Years of Patience, Perseverance, and Determination." *Cherry Diamond.* September 1964.

Ward, Paul W. "Washington Weekly." *Nation.* March 4, 1936.

Bibliography

COURT CASES

Balter v. Ickes 67 App D.C. 112, 89 F, 2d 856.
Buchanan v. Warley 245 U.S. 60 (1917).

THESES AND UNPUBLISHED MATERIALS

Becher, Deborah Lynn. "Valuing Property: Eminent Domain for Urban Redevelopment, Philadelphia, 1992–2007." Ph.D. dissertation. Princeton University, 2009.

Brown, Sharon A. "Making a Memorial: Developing the Jefferson National Expansion Memorial National Historic Site, 1933–1980." Ph.D. dissertation, St. Louis University, 1983.

Bryan, John A. "The Changing Scene on the St. Louis Riverfront, 1764–1954." Report 295, Jefferson National Expansion Archives.

Cowan, Aaron B. "A Nice Place to Visit: Tourism, Urban Revitalization, and the Transformation of Postwar American Cities." Ph.D. dissertation, University of Cincinnati, 2007.

Federal Home Loan Bank Board, Division of Research and Statistics. "Metropolitan St. Louis: Summary of an Economic, Real Estate and Mortgage Finance Survey." 1941.

Hamda, Rumiko. "Design Through Drawing: Eero Saarinen's Design in the Jefferson National Expansion Memorial Competition." Ph.D. dissertation, University of Pennsylvania, 1992.

Hamel, April Lee. "The Jefferson National Expansion Memorial: A Depression Relief Project." Ph.D. dissertation, St. Louis University, 1983.

Henry, Deborah Jane. "Structures of Exclusion: Black Labor and the Building Trades in St. Louis, 1917–1966." Ph.D. dissertation, University of Minnesota, 2002.

Ksiaszek, Sarah Williams. "Changing Symbols of Public Life: Louis Kahn's Religious and Civic Projects, 1944–1966, and Architectural Culture at the End of the Modern Movement." Ph.D. dissertation, Columbia University, 1995.

National Park Service, Jefferson National Expansion Memorial, Gateway Arch. "Historic Structure Report—vol. I." June 2010.

Reese, De Anna J. "African American Women, Civic Activism, and Community Building Strategies in St. Louis, Missouri, 1900–1954." Ph.D. dissertation, University of Missouri–Columbia, 2004.

Schneider, Cary M. "St. Louis and the Gateway Arch: A Case History of an Urban Icon." Honors paper, Cornell College, 1970.

Taylor, James A. "Earthquake Ground Motion and Soil Amplification Effects in the St. Louis Metropolitan Area." M.S. Thesis, Washington University in St. Louis, 1997.

Wilson, Rob. "Cholera and Quarantine: St. Louis' Battle With the 1849 Epidemic." Paper delivered at Western Historical Association meeting, 2006.

Winter, William E. "Development and Decision-Making in St. Louis, Missouri: Institutions, Incentives, and Urban Development." Ph.D. dissertation, University of Missouri–Columbia, 2006.

ORAL HISTORIES

Archives of American Art, Smithsonian Institution
Lilian Swann Saarinen (by Robert Brown)

Jefferson National Expansion Memorial Archives, St. Louis (by Bob Moore)
Dick Bowser
LeRoy Brown
Bruce Detmers
George Hartzog
Dan Kiley
Russ Knox
Malcolm Martin
Joe Minner
Charles E. Peterson
Bill Quigley
Kevin Roche
Susan Saarinen (by Don Haake)
Charles "Ted" Rennison

Chicago Architects Oral History Project, Art Institute of Chicago
Harry Weese

Cranbrook Archives, Bloomfield Hills, Michigan
Joseph Lacy (by Wesley Janz)
James Smith (by John Gerard)

Index

Index

Index

Gateway Arch : a biography / Tracy Campbell.

F474.S265 G372 2013
Gen Stx

DATE DUE

PRINTED IN U.S.A.

The Tropical Orchid Belt

ORCHIDS YOU CAN GROW

ORCHIDS
YOU CAN
GROW

BY HARRY BRITTON LOGAN

HAWTHORN BOOKS, INC., PUBLISHERS
NEW YORK

ORCHIDS YOU CAN GROW

Acknowledgments

A thousand years ago—or so it seems, looking back at the last quarter of a century—I wrote a book with Lloyd C. Cosper about orchids. It was by no means the only book about these exotic plants, but it was one of the earliest to present them from the viewpoint of home gardeners and hobbyists.

Looked at objectively, what has happened in twenty-five years of progress in orchid culture is almost beyond belief. Nearly everything that Lloyd Cosper once predicated as possible is now common practice. Orchid knowledge is as close as the nearest library or the neighbor down the street or the commercial orchid grower nearby. Gardeners and hobbyists are the inheritors of the orchid world, once open only to specialists who often hid behind the illusion of esoteric knowledge. I am certain that Lloyd Cosper, had he lived to see this incredible revolution, would mildly shrug and say, "Why not? Understanding is everything. Why shouldn't orchids be understood?"

With this in mind I have tried to organize the knowledge and current practices of orchid hobbyists and commercial growers, from all parts of the United States, into a guide for home gardeners who will be the hobbyist-experts of tomorrow. Equally, I have tried to keep in mind the interests of the specialists and to provide both gardeners and experts with excellent illustrations.

I talked with so many orchidists, amateur and professional, and visited so many private and commercial installations that to thank each of them individually would be impossible. I hope that they will understand this and remember that I am grateful for their many courtesies. Elsewhere in this book I have credited those individuals who graciously permitted me to photograph their orchid collections and from which I selected the black and white illustrations.

More than I can say, or imply, I am indebted to John Lager, of Lager and Hurrell, who somehow always found the time to help orient my thinking and research, or to suggest sources and resources. His tremendous accumulation of experience and knowledge provided many of the answers and readily indicated exciting areas of research. Since then, John Lager has passed away, leaving a richness behind, for he was to everyone—amateur or expert, friend or stranger—a voice of reason and compassion.

And I acknowledge a debt and extend my gratitude to the following individuals and firms, whose assistance added significantly to this book:

To Mrs. L. Sherman Adams, who listened critically and whose comments served to explore the need for another book on orchids and the purpose it might usefully serve.

To Gordon Dillon and Merle Reinikka, of the American Orchid Society, who helped to plan my routes across the country and who suggested stops where challenging experiments were being made.

To Robert R. Johnson, of Rod McLellan Company, whose unfailing courtesy and continuous assistance made it possible to observe and photograph techniques and plants in all stages of production. To Mrs. Berti di Martini, who reviewed the galleys, checking them against her encyclopedic knowledge. And to the Rod McLellan Company for making their color separations available.

To Robert Scully, Sr., of Jones and Scully, for briefing me on the cultural improvements and requirements of orchids in the South. And to Jones and Scully, Inc., for the color separations of their botanical orchids.

To George Woodward, Jr., of Shaffer's Tropical Gardens, who imparted to me some of his enthusiastic knowledge and expertise about cymbidiums and Phalaenopsis. And, as well, to Shaffer's Tropical Gardens, who supplied the color separations of their Phalaenopsis.

To Ernest Hetherington, of Fred A. Stewart, Inc., who was more than courteous in furnishing color separations made by his firm, one of which is used on the book jacket.

To Don Benson, Oscar Ames and Bob Colucci, all from the Don Benson Studio in New York, who helped prepare many of the black and white photographs for publication.

To Sarah and Philip Jesup, whose Connecticut home and greenhouse are filled with magnificent mini-orchids, whose flowers are as enchantingly lovely as those of their larger relatives.

To Mr. and Mrs. William Bradley of Minneapolis, who are conducting experiments with artificial lighting which may help to establish new norms.

To Mr. and Mrs. Louis Vaughn, whose hybridizing programs at West Palm Beach reestablished the popularity of phalaenopsis and raised that beautiful orchid family to new levels of loveliness.

To Merritt Huntington, at Kensington Orchids, Inc., and to the National Capitol Orchid Society members, in and near Washington, D.C., who made their time, their experiences and their greenhouses available, particularly Kay Smith and Charles McClaskey.

To Dr. J. F. Schairer, at Bethesda, whose experiments with botanical orchids have helped to make them a mainstay of amateur collections and well known to all indoor gardeners.

To John W. Newton, of Sylvania Lighting Products, who provided the background information about orchid growth and artificial light.

To Harold Levinson and Richard Labov, of the Greater New York Orchid Society, who courteously offered their facilities for photographic studies.

To Mrs. Elliot Markell, of Ironia, New Jersey, for a review of orchid seed germination which she, as a former teacher currently engaged in orchid flasking, could make exciting.

To Janet Benes, in whose New Jersey home orchids, a challenging modification of a greenhouse, and family are integrated into an imaginative experiment in living.

To Mrs. Young C. Lott, of Miami, possibly the oldest orchidist, but whose orchid enthusiasms grow younger. And to Dorothy Schultz of the same city, whose own collection was remarkable in the manner in which Phalaenopsis was handled.

To Tom Fennell, Jr., of Homestead, whose Orchid Jungle in Florida is the country's oldest experiment in naturalizing orchids.

To John Hanes and John Wilson, of San Gabriel and San Marino, California, for their knowledgeable approach to Cypripedium culture.

To Gil Daggett, of Denver, who, after a lifetime of civil engineering, proposes to spend another lifetime investigating botanical orchids.

To Clara L. Blake, of Lord and Burnham, who offered all of the considerable knowledge and assistance of her company and, as well, photographs of appropriate greenhouses.

And, to the Horticultural Society of New York, whose excellent library and whose librarian, Miss Elizabeth Hall, were a continuous source of information and assistance.

HARRY BRITTON LOGAN

Contents

To Lyn

Equivalents

So you would like to grow orchids.

Well, why not.

Thousands and thousands of home gardeners do—casually, easily, successfully, enthusiastically and happily. They grow orchids in their gardens and on terraces, porches, patios and pavilions, in kitchens and bathrooms and near living-room windows. Some place orchids on bookshelves and wheeled carts, in cabinets and modified aquariums. Others convert garages and utilitarian basements. A few plan luxuriously small conservatories or charming shade house retreats.

Orchid hobbyists live in all the states—the coldest to the warmest, the wettest to the driest—in Alaska and Hawaii and Puerto Rico; in Canada and Mexico. They live in houses and apartments in most large cities and many small municipalities, and often on farms.

Indeed, anyplace and everywhere.

They range in age from eighty-six years young to eight years old. Every level of society is represented, and all are pleasantly divided into nearly equal groups of men and women. Some have hundreds and thousands of orchids and frivolously expensive greenhouses. Most have ten or twenty or a hundred orchids and make do with whatever simple equipment they have on hand. Few have green thumbs, but all possess more attractive qualities: patience, consideration and, above all, the capability for thoughtful effort.

Other than this there is no common denominator that explains the people who grow orchids. They could be—and are—just anyone.

Obviously, though, there is a common cause: an intense need to grow the most exotically beautiful plants in the world. No one has ever been able to explain what it is about orchids that induces this need, but it has existed for hundreds of years, even in the tropical countries where orchids are found. Adjectives such as rare or expensive or exclusive or mysterious have been suggested, but such descriptions are true only in a limited sense. More likely than not, the lure of orchids cannot be precisely explained, but is to be found in their charisma. And once it is experienced, there is no escaping, ever.

So . . . welcome!

The truth about orchids is more exciting than the myths which have been so long and so incorrectly attributed to them. There never were black orchids; there probably never will be unless they are stained with black dye. The vegetative parts of orchids contain no substance which would make an effective love

Cattleya Angel Island

White cattleyas for reasons which go beyond sentimentality have always had a strong appeal to gardeners. So more knowledge and experience have gone into developing them than most other orchid varieties. Among the white cattleya hybrids available, the gigas varieties—often called Wedding orchids —provide long-enduring, well-textured flowers and vigorous growths.

potion, although some are considered mildly diuretic by the natives of the orchid forests. Comic-page strips to the contrary, pressed or distilled essence from orchids, other than vanilla, serve no useful purpose. They cannot cure tropical anemias or produce commercial perfumes, though many orchids are exquisitely fragrant. Nevertheless, several orchid species contribute their petals to a lusty sort of aboriginal salad. Certain terrestrial orchid tubers are collected to make a salep, a mild drug for intestinal infections in children. And the leaves of a Madagascar orchid make a fragrant tea.

There are a lot of other things that orchids aren't and much they can't do. They can't live on air; they can't prey on trees and shrubs as parasites; they can't acquire carnivorous habits. They are not poisonous, although the juice of several can cause skin inflammation, or seemingly, disinfect a wound. No doubt there is always a certain delight in speculating wickedly about the unusual or the unknown. The historic period that produced Mary Shelley and Frankenstein (and introduced orchids to northern Europe) probably did not find it inconsistent to create and believe in orchid Frankensteins. The real mystery of orchids, if ever they can be considered mysterious, is how they arrived at being exactly what they are: a plant family incredibly diverse and incredibly responsive to evolutionary demands for survival. In their specialized structures and their adaptability, orchids far exceed the environmental achievements of most other plants. It is redundant, yet meaningfully necessary, to stress this unique adaptive capability of orchids. It is a clue to the whimsical, often idiotic, failures to grow them in the past. It is also an indication of the reasonableness with which they can be grown or, for that matter, accommodated to home and garden situations— if their idiosyncrasies are understood and indulged.

There is no land mass in the world where orchids are unknown, other than in regions of perpetual snow or intolerably arid desert. Where men can live— and do so continuously—orchids can also live and thrive. They can be found from the Arctic Circle southward to the edges of Antarctica. From Nome to Tierra del Fuego, from Murmansk to Cape Town. From San Francisco westward, circling the earth. From the lowest, hottest coastlands and marshes up to the highest mountains, ten thousand feet or more, where the climate can be bitterly cold.

Many orchids are burned by sunlight stronger than may be experienced in the United States; many never see the sun directly, existing in shaded seclusion. Several actually grow under the ground and are seen only when they are accidentally uncovered. Some are gently touched by moisture-laden breezes; others are buffeted from time to time by bitter winds of hurricane intensity. Some suffer from almost daily torrential rains; others are caressed only occasionally by seasonal showers.

Obviously no single orchid could long withstand all of these violently conflicting geophysical elements. But in a family of thirty thousand species many will be found whose adjustment to seemingly intolerable climates provides them with considerable vigor; often sufficient to survive reasonable captivity. And many ordinarily grow in climates not too dissimilar from those common to the United States.

As an environmental response to thick tropical forests, orchids may fasten themselves with a few roots to the trunks and branches of trees and shrubs. Then they climb upward on successive new growths until they reach the pleasantly filtered sunlight, fresh air—and cleanliness—so essential to their health. To con-

Angulocaste Apollo

Among the most beautiful orchids, the anguloas (from the Andes) crossed with lycastes (from the Cordilleros) retain the best of both families. Creamy white and citron-yellow and often fragrant, the flowers have a waxy delicacy that persists for a surprisingly long time. Terrestrials begin to grow in spring and flower in early summer under cool, somewhat shady conditions.

sider these orchids as parasites is to ignore—as early gardeners did—the only reason they are found on trees or other plants or objects: to obtain exposure to the cultural conditions they must have in order to live.

Orchids that do not find trees to their liking (some trees apparently secrete substances toxic to orchid roots), or find no trees at all, may establish themselves on conveniently located rocks or granite ledges and stone outcroppings. Some may be found in open grasslands; some even on cacti in semi-arid countries.

Those orchids that need less sun may grow lower on trees, or on the ground. Frequently these are called shade orchids, but such a description is not quite accurate. It is shade only in the sense that direct sunlight (except, perhaps, in early morning or late afternoon) does not penetrate through the covering foliage. The light, nonetheless, is ambient—luminous, soft, pervading, almost brilliant but never intense. Actually it is rather similar to indirect theatrical lighting in modern offices.

Where water or rain or atmospheric moisture is periodically unavailable, orchids have developed leathery leaves or thickened stems in which to store both water and food. Their roots, too, vary: thick, highly absorbent structures in regions where rain is inconsistent, or thin, stringlike appendages if water is abundant. Orchids that live above the ground have roots clothed in a corklike velamen; those that ordinarily remain on the ground have fleshy root systems. Both types of root are extremely brittle with an inherent reluctance to be confined, particularly in pots. And both are somewhat interchangeable. Each can—and does—function somewhat in the other's territory. Thus the distinction between tree orchids and ground orchids can occasionally become quite vague. Curiously, orchid roots have green tips that manufacture the incidental food they need, whereas the roots of other orchids are dependent on the parent plants. A few orchids consist only of roots and an annual, insignificant flower. No stems, no leaves; just a green web of roots.

Orchid plants vary immoderately in size: so small that they can be grown in thimbles, so large that a single clump could not be contained in a living room. They are equally immoderate in growth. Most orchids mature in three to seven years. Several members of the family require as much as fifteen years before they flower. But one variety, a singular orchid without green chlorophyll in its leaves, grows so fast and long that it can reach to the top of a one hundred and fifty foot tree within a few weeks.

Some orchids have mini-leaves or simply scars. Some have leaves that extend to six feet. Some leaves have the appearance of thickened bayonets, or round greenish pencils. One has the most beautifully decorated leaves in the plant kingdom and utterly insignificant flowers.

Orchid flowers are even more variable: as small as the head of a pin and delicately beautiful, as large as twelve inches across and breathlessly exotic. One orchid family has flowers whose paired sepals suddenly elongate, growing thirty inches in less than two weeks—a floral ribbon which insects are believed to climb. The flowers may be pale and wan and insignificant, or magnificently and brilliantly colored with every conceivable shade and tint or hue—except black. An astonishing number of orchid blossoms are delightfully fragrant; a few have odors no one would willingly discuss. Some flowers are borne singly on a plant; some by the dozens; often by the hundreds on sprays, resembling nothing so much as a chorus of dancing dolls. Within the many orchid families each generic

Epidendrum atropurpureum

Many orchidists regard epidendrums as weeds—which they are, so far as vigor is concerned. The thousand-plus members of the family spread from Florida to Paraguay and across the Caribbean to the West Indies. Durable, tough, although usually temperate or medium in their requirements, epidendrums are variously epiphytes or terrestrials, adjusting to the lowlands of Guatemala and the mountains of Central America. Many of them are accustomed to little humidity, and others to full sunlight. Many-flowered, from microscopic to three or four inches, often fragrant, always elegantly shaped, and multicolored beyond imagination, they are an indoor gardener's delight. The atropurpureum flowers are three inches across, curiously marked with green and brown and white and purple. They bloom in late spring.

group has flowers so strikingly different that it is difficult to believe they are all related and have a common heritage.

Even the popular names of orchids are suggestive of the bewildering diversity that exists within the family: butterfly, moth, toad, lizard, swan, nun, pansy, frog, spider, scorpion, leopard, tiger, dove, ballerina—and hundreds more.

Such names are no less significant as guides to floral orchid shapes. Or for that matter, to the remarkable similarities that exist between orchid flowers and other living things. The Spider orchid resembles nothing so much as a crouching tarantula ready to spring. Also, some of these names provide a clue to the insects that pollinate orchids. Obviously, for example, bees will select the Bee orchid; moths will search out the Moth orchid. And so on through some very exotic, even erotic, relationships.

The mechanisms by which orchids insure pollinization are as unique as the floral structures. Traps by the scores, pouches by the dozens, each carefully engineered to guide insects unerringly to the pollen masses or to the receptacle where fertilization is accomplished.

One special orchid group does not wait to capture its unwary victim. As soon as its floral lip is slightly depressed, it throws its pollen wafers accurately at the insect. Of course the startled insect flies away, carrying with it the pollen attached to its head or body by a sticky membrane. If the insect is lucky, the next orchid flower has discharged its pollen; and the insect, then guided, leaves its wafers. If unlucky, and such incidents are known, the insect may continue to collect pollen on its body until it can no longer fly.

Curiously, orchid seeds are small, so small in fact that fifty of them placed side by side would scarcely cover an inch of surface. A single seed pod will contain up to three million seeds—one and a half billion seeds to the pound. This prodigality is necessary, in view of the enormous difficulty in germinating seeds and establishing seedlings. (But once reasonably matured, orchids in their native countries are not likely to die, at least not from natural causes.)

The seed of an orchid is a simple, dry sheath enclosing a few undifferentiated dormant cells. There are no stored food reserves, nothing to provide the germinating seed with nourishment during the first critical weeks. If the seed is to live, it must have—rapidly, within days—warmth, moisture, the correct growing situation, and immediate, special assistance from a fungus which supplies it temporarily with a sort of predigested food. The chance of these favorable elements coming together is remote, particularly since the seeds are indiscriminately broadcast by the prevailing winds. In nature, millions of seeds will die before a single orchid is born. And thousands of plantlets will die in the first six months or so from storms and scavengers.

The incredible diversity of orchids, their wide geographical range, was not apparent to English gardeners two hundred years ago. Their environmental needs were completely unknown. Most of the desirable orchids were discovered in the tropics. To the first orchid gardeners, this meant an atmosphere with unbearable, depressing, suffocating heat and humidity. So they stuffed their orchids into pots of rotten wood and overripe composts, caustic with the smell of decay. Huge fires were built inside cavernous greenhouse stoves, water was dumped on the stoves to explode into steam.

Of course orchids died by the thousands. They were steamed to death, roasted to death, cooked to death by this merciless treatment. And thereby they acquired the reputation of being difficult plants. What really is amazing is that a few

Sobralia macrantha

Although most orchid flowers last for weeks even months, those of the sobralias open, wither and die in a day or two. But, for that short summer period, they are shimmering, incandescent blazes of rose, purple or yellow and usually are fragrant. Much larger (6 to 10 inches) than the flowers of cattleyas, which they closely resemble, although no familial bond of any kind exists between the two families. Sobralias are solely terrestrial, with leaves and stems not unlike bamboo, needing considerable moisture at all times, a rich compost—even liquid manure at times of rapid growth—equitable temperatures in the medium range, and considerable summer shade. They do best when garden-grown between spring and fall. Sobralias are not small plants—frequently three to six feet tall and forming clumps that can only be contained in tubs.

The many faces of orchids are engagingly different, though some orchid families (such as cattleyas) have a consistent, quickly recognizable floral characteristic. This is part of the lure and the lore of orchids, a delightful inconsistency within a fundamental consistency. From left to right, top to bottom, beginning on the opposite page (top): Cattleya Dorothy Mackail (a commercial hybrid), Cattleya schileriana (Brazil), Schomburgkia superbiens (Mexico, related to cattleyas); (center): Angraecum eichlerianum (Madagascar), Miltonia Funny Face (a commercial hybrid with parents from Brazil and Colombia), the Odontioda hybrid (Peru and Colombia); (bottom): Cychnoches ventricosum (Guatemala), Lycaste deppei (Mexico), Epidendrum pseudo-wallisii (Central America). This page (top): Epidendrum Coral Miss (southern Mexico), Vanda hybrid (Himalayas), Paphiopedilum Maudiae (Thailand); (bottom): Restrepa guttata (Venezuela), Phalaenopsis sumatrana (Sumatra), Bulbophyllum meduseae (Malaya).

orchids survived. At least they lived long enough to bloom, setting into motion by the sheer loveliness of their flowers the incredible and dismaying orgy that followed.

Huge sums of money were willingly offered for small pieces of transit-damaged plants. Gardeners fought to outbid one another at plant auctions. Plant hunters enthusiastically stripped tropical countries of their orchid crops on the off-chance of providing a moneyed Englishman or a titled Frenchman with a few hours or days of exquisite beauty and an opportunity to indulge in horticultural snobbery. Happily, this foolishness did not persist, although its impact lingers as a popular fiction that orchids are prohibitively expensive and exceedingly rare.

Sensible people began to ask sensible questions, to observe their orchids and make experiments. The factual reports of botanists and the diaries of plant hunters (those not afraid to release the geographical locations of their plant discoveries) filtered slowly back to England and the continent of Europe. Soon tropical orchids no longer necessarily meant "tropical" climates. Gardeners quickly learned that within the tropics, the loveliest orchids—especially cattleyas—came from the mountains of South America, where the climate was cool, the air sweet and softly moist. So common sense began to replace preconceptions and certain common gardening practices were formalized as acceptable cultural methods. Orchids quickly responded by becoming manageable—not always easily so, but reasonably predictable and capable of further management and understanding.

But somehow orchids became a cult, permissible for the aristocratic, the wealthy or the elect; directed by specialists who were as likely to promote myth as to share reality. For all too long a time, orchids seemed by consensus to be reserved for those in the know. Inevitably this mildly conspiratorial monopoly was broken. Yet the reform was a long and tedious and nearly thankless task which, more often than not, was initiated by amateur gardeners and persistent hobbyists.

Perhaps the first continuously sound approach to orchid culture—at least the first recorded one—was made in 1830 when Joseph Cooper, an English grower, lowered the killing temperature around his orchids, gave them plenty of fresh air and more light. His results were good enough to be published—and imitated.

John Lindley, the dean of orchid botanists, credits Sir Joseph Paxton with similar successes, writing: "The success with which (orchids) are cultivated by Mr. Paxton is wonderful. The climate in which this is effected, instead of being so hot and damp that the plants can only be seen with as much discomfort as if one had to visit them in an Indian jungle, is as mild and delightful as that of Madeira."

Years later another grower, Benjamin Williams, predicted "orchids for the millions"—and wrote a book with that title. James Veitch, one of the great orchidists of all time, issued his *Manual of Orchidaceous Plants*—as sound a book now as it was when originally published. The English *Orchid Review* and the *Gardeners' Chronicle* began printing generous factual articles about orchids. Contained in these nineteenth-century books and magazines—stated and re-stated—is enough practical orchid experience and knowledge to have made orchids a readily available garden hobby for everyone.

But that eventuality did not occur. It could not, because in those times there was no great community of shared knowledge or the techniques with which to disperse it, as there is in the electronic age. So the culture of orchids grew or

Restrepa guttata

An elegant miniature in spite of its shape—or because of it. Found, so far, only in Venezuelan rain forests up to 8,000 feet, it withstands a variety of treatments in cultivation, taking most kindly to medium temperatures and consistent moisture. The flowers, appearing in early spring, are barely an inch long, orangish and spotted with deeper red. The petals are attenuated, hairlike; the dorsal sepal elongated like a wand. And the two lateral sepals are joined to make one long unit, the entire flower resembling some strange insect. Suitable for aquarium-terrarium arrangements.

lapsed in small periodic jumps largely dependent on accident and the slow progress of an educated few.

One of the first great achievements in orchid education within the United States began in the early 1920's, when the American Orchid Society was organized. Its magazines and brochures made widely available the knowledge of professionals and the experiences of hobbyists. It put amateurs across the country in touch with each other for the first time and quickly developed an association of men and women remarkably dedicated and ingenious.

There is no question that the research of Dr. Lewis Knudsen at Cornell University had an unimaginable impact on the spread of orchids as a hobby. In 1922 he succeeded in germinating orchid seeds in sterile flasks of nutrient agar gel—without the orchid fungus. The result was explosive. Orchids, previously difficult to grow from seeds, now could be obtained by the thousands.

And, of course, they were.

Crosses were made by the thousands; seedlings were grown by the hundreds of thousands. Some orchid crosses were spectacular, most were not; the science of hybridizing orchids had to be learned. But the basically important fact was that orchid plants, for the first time, were available at prices which gardeners could afford to pay.

In 1934, Dr. H. O. Eversole at LaCanada, California, pioneered orchids in gravel culture, growing and flowering Phalaenopsis in half the time previously required. Orchids could be fed chemical fertilizers and, in fact, needed them. And Lloyd Cosper, in nearby Pasadena, showed that consistent chemical feeding produced plants that were larger, healthier, more prolific; and this was the first indication that orchids did not necessarily need restrictive rest periods. Other experiments by investigators since then have shown that many orchids, under rigidly controlled temperatures and atmospheric conditions and artificial light, may grow and flower continuously.

The most dramatic advance in orchidology occurred a few years ago in France. A physiologist, Dr. Georges Morel, cut out minute sections of plant tissues from the rapidly growing tips of a Cymbidium, one of the most beautiful orchids grown today. These slivers of tissue he placed in scrupulously clean flasks of nutrient agar, where they increased in size and developed leaves and roots.

A refinement of his technique now makes it possible to produce hundreds of orchid plantlets, each exactly like the parent stock, in months, whereas formerly only a few orchids could be propagated vegetatively over many years. This is a fantastic development that already has created new markets for commercial florists, new demands by gardeners and hobbyists. Prize orchids, previously limited in number, can now be secured in quantity and at significantly lower prices.

It would almost seem that orchids have come of age, that nothing more can be expected of them, that Benjamin Williams' prophecy of "orchids for the millions" has been realized.

On the contrary. Simple as routine orchid culture has become, there is still much to be learned. Few other plants have been less studied, though few have proved more receptive to a little study and more productive thereafter. Nevertheless, amateur gardeners, hobbyists and professionals are learning to grow orchids in new ways and with new equipment never before considered remotely possible. Each forward step brings other steps into view. And each advance brings orchids more and more into an intimate and pleasing association with gardens and homes.

Macodes petola

Often described as jewels, the leaves of the macodes are glittering spectaculars, emerald green veined with shimmering gold. The natives of Java believe them to be the clothing of an Indian goddess who visited them and, unrecognized, was driven into the forests. Thorns tore her clothing, and where the fragments of gold-threaded cloth fell to the ground, plants appeared with gold-veined leaves. It is not an easy plant to grow (although extraordinarily popular in Europe at the turn of the century), since it requires continuous warmth, humidity and subdued shade. Some kitchen and bathroom windows might again, as they once did, provide a suitable growing atmosphere. However, the macodes do unusually well in aquariums lighted with plant fluorescent tubes. Their excessive atmospheric moisture requirement is more easily satisfied in such small cases. The ludisias, whose leaves can be nearly midnight black and marked with ribbons of silver, and anoectochilus—related families—also grow well in a terrarium, where the three- to four-inch leaves are beautifully displayed under supplemental lighting.

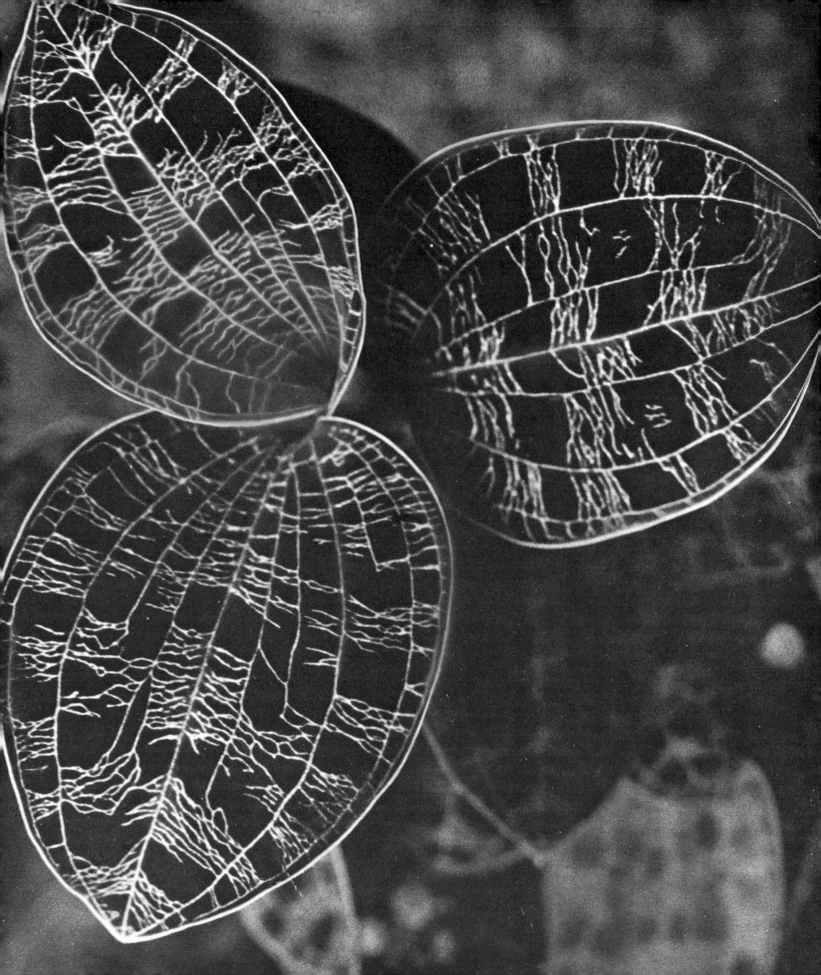

Beginnings

What are orchids?

If they can take so many shapes and sizes, grow so large or so small, look so different from each other (as well as from other plants)—how can they ultimately be recognized? Actually, these extreme visual differences are part of the physical adaptations orchids have made to their environments over hundreds of thousands and millions of years, and need not be considered for the moment. Orchid flowers, no matter how dissimilar in appearance, always have three characteristics in common: THREE SEPALS—usually narrow, always greenish as buds, but which, after opening, change color quickly. THREE PETALS—two of which look alike; wider than the sepals, balancing the shape of the flower; white, brilliantly colored, or mottled with unusual color combinations and patterns. The bottom petal, modified into a useful and beautiful lip, is used by insects as a sort of aerial landing strip. Sometimes gaudy in shape and color, the lip is a distinctive mark of the orchid flower.

Though it seems unlikely, the lip is often upside down. As the bud opens, it rotates clockwise through an arc of 180° (two flowers on the same plant will rotate differentially) and the lip thus achieves a suitable position for insects to use. Marks of the spiraling movement can be seen on the ovary which, incidentally, always serves as a floral stem. The group of Cypripediums have further modified the lip; combining two petals into a pouch fancifully resembling a lady's heel-less slipper.

THE COLUMN is the most distinctive characteristic of an orchid flower, a fleshy projection which combines the reproductive organs (the stamens and pistils) into one cohesive unit. This unusual structural modification exists only in the orchid family; it is what makes an orchid different from all other flowering plants. At the front of the column is the pollen; hard, waxy, yellow wafers lightly hinged, but easily removed by insects brushing against them. Behind the pollen is a sticky receptacle to receive and hold pollen from a related orchid. It is safe-guarded from its own pollen by an obstructing membrane, nature's device to prevent self-pollenization—a hazard against which orchids are scrupulously protected. At the base of the column the ovary begins: long, slim and serving as the stem of the flower, unexpectedly large when swollen with ripening seeds.

Of such parts and pieces are orchid flowers made. No matter how large or small they may be, or how unusual their shapes, these floral elements always will be present.

The vegetative forms of plants have a definite correlation to their environments, and orchids are no exception: terrestrials, epiphytes, monopodials and sympodials. Unwieldy words, perhaps, but concentrating a lot of useful information.

TERRESTRIALS are ground plants, growing in loose soils or rich humus, their fleshy roots remaining underground. They may be found everywhere—from the tropics to the polar circles, in sun or shade and where the soil moisture is consistent.

Phalaenopsis hybrid

The current preoccupation with phalaenopsis, those predominantly complex hybrids of beautiful forms and colors, frequently overlooks the strength of seedling phalenopsis species, which can be used in the subtropical United States for naturalization. The flopping deep green leaves, the startling purity of the white flowers, look well against old oak bark and foliage. Protected by overhanging tree leaves from the sun and the heavier rain storms, it is a very satisfactory ornamental—bowing to no Florida hurricane and, seemingly, considerably more impervious to leaf rots than when grown in greenhouses.

EPIPHYTES—the orchids most frequently commercially grown—as their name implies, use trees and shrubs for support, obtaining their water and food from the moisture in the air, from rain and from decomposing litter that may be washed against their exposed roots. Spectacular as their growing habit seems to be, it serves only to secure for them the quality of sunlight and air they need in order to survive, and to protect them from destructive animals. A telephone pole, a rock, a dead shrub—all other conditions being suitable—can, and do, substitute for live trees. The root systems of epiphytes—glossy white when dry, slightly greenish when wet—are difficult to confine in pots. Special composts that dry quickly or cannot become waterlogged help.

MONOPODIAL orchids grow in one direction, continuously. Their single stem lengthens season after season. Some grow an inch or less each year; others several feet; leaves develop regularly and symmetrically. Monopodials that are accustomed to sunlight have thick, narrow leaves and tough stems; those found in shade have wider, more succulent leaves and, often, no apparent stems. Such orchids have no storage organs, a characteristic that is consistent with the climate where they are found; rain is frequent, soil or air moisture is constant. There is little need for them to store food.

SYMPODIAL orchids grow horizontally although it seems otherwise. Their stems, actually comparable to rhizomes, rest lightly against the bark of trees or on the surface of soils. From the rhizomes, year after year, grow lateral shoots (orchidists call them leads) which turn quickly upward as new branches. Some of the branches are long, thin and covered with leaves and closely resemble the stems of monopodials. They, too, are natives of regions where water is always available. The branches of other sympodial orchids are thickened into elongated or oval pseudobulbs, food storage organs. At the tip of the pseudobulbs, one or several leaves may develop. Pseudobulbs may be so tiny as to escape notice; or they may resemble onions in shape, or cigars or bamboo stems. Actually, they are not seasonal growth responses—as known in North America—to warmth and moisture. Rather, they are orchid reactions to alternating periods of wetness (rapid maturity) and dryness (dormancy or rest); and flowering usually occurs just before or just after resting. Once the pseudobulbs have matured and ripened, their stored vigor is such that it is almost impossible to prevent flowering—a fact that once gave rise to "unbelievable" anecdotes of wild orchids, stripped of their roots, flowering on shipboard and in cabins while en route to Europe.

For the most part, sympodial orchids are compact in growth, vigorous because of their food storage capabilities, and contain many of the lovely flowers for which orchids are famous. They are, and rightly so, the basis for most amateur and garden collections.

Curiously, the physical difference among orchids themselves is not always an exact indication of cultural requirements. Some epiphytes can thrive on the ground; some terrestrials may frequently lodge happily on tree trunks. Leaves may serve as storage organs, successfully replacing pseudobulbs. A few delightful species have corms or tubers, much as many garden perennials do, and easily survive northern winters.

All green plants, and orchids as well, require five conditions: warmth, light, water, air, food. Deny them any one of these necessities and they will die. Vary their proportions in an unsuitable manner and they will die, perhaps not so soon but just as inevitably. The correct strategy, of course, is to learn exactly what proportions of these elements orchids require, and to stay reasonably

Maxillaria chlorastha

From Mexico to Brazil and in the West Indies, maxillarias are found high up on the sides of mountains; this indicates a cool to medium temperature treatment. And they usually require more sunlight than one might expect, since they are likely to grow on the edges of rain forests where the sunlight is intense. Maxillarias are related to the lycastes, with which they may be cultivated as semiterrestrials. They are mostly yellowish in color, sometimes white, frequently small in size (½-inch) (M. picta is the major exception), largely summer-flowering although a few come into bloom around December. One of the maxillarias (bicolor) is used as a fever cure in South America.

within the boundaries of that pattern. There has never been any secrecy about this. Neither has there been any doubt, at least for more than a hundred years, about the basic orchid requirements.

Once so little was known about orchids that each small success was built upon a previous one. Each new item of information was slowly added to the last until a system developed, a system so rigid that deviation was frowned on and flexibility discouraged. Orchidists were rote-trained, especially in early English establishments. Plants under their supervision flourished or waned as the climate, in the city of their employment, was similar or dissimilar to the place where they were trained. This was system gardening, and the plants had to fit into it or suffer. All too frequently they suffered.

Today it is readily accepted that the difference of one mile, or one block, can change environmental conditions enough to require wholly different manual responses to basic orchid needs. In New York overcoming winter chill is a decidedly different problem from in California. Light does not have the same intensity in Minnesota that it does in Florida. Humidity is almost unknown in New Mexico and outrageous in Kansas. But orchids are grown in all of these states—successfully. And though these are extreme conditions and involve long distances, hazardous climatic variations are no less true of nearby cities or adjacent neighborhoods.

Orchidists now take the local climate as they find it and add or subtract the various orchid requirements until a balanced climate is achieved, one suitable to the range of the orchids chosen. Herein lies the art of orchid growing, the skills that must be learned and developed, the knowledge gained, the challenge that ultimately yields to conquest: climate control—outdoors, indoors, glass cases or greenhouses.

The extreme diversity among orchids would seem to indicate that they have little in common other than the inevitability of confusion. But just as all the members of the family have floral elements in common, they also have essentially similar cultural requirements, which differ not so much in kind as in quantity. This kinship can be stated in broad generalizations—precepts, if they may be called that, which apply to all orchids regardless of their origins.

PROVIDE ORCHIDS WITH THE MAXIMUM AMOUNT OF SUNLIGHT THEY CAN STAND WITHOUT INJURY. All too frequently, orchids are heavily shaded—a persistent holdover from the days when a depressingly gloomy atmosphere was incorrectly associated with the tropics. Within reason, the more light orchids receive, the more food they manufacture, the faster they grow and the better they flower. Too much shade inhibits growth, reduces or prevents flowering. It must always be remembered—and remembered—that orchids living in trees do so to secure the optimum amount of sunlight; those that live in shade do so most often in an ambient, luminous light.

Yet the curious anomaly in this country, where the sunlight can be both more and less intense than at the equator, is that some sort of gentle shade is needed for most orchids. This is particularly true during the hot summer midday hours. However, shade is urgent more as a method of cooling orchid leaves than to prevent injury from sunburn. Indeed, very little shade is required in greenhouses where moist air is continuously circulated and orchids are fed soluble chemical fertilizers. In North America, shade also serves to balance the light intensity from summer to winter, to even out the high-low extremes to whatever constant light value an orchid group may require.

Calanthe harrissii

Among terrestrial orchids, calanthes are consistent favorites—when their culture is understood. The pseudobulbs are rooted, like cuttings, in semi-moist peat moss and gravel (or vermiculite) during the early days of spring when new growths appear. They are taken outdoors as soon as the frosts have gone, and potted in very rich, very aged composts well mixed with old manures. The young plants are accustomed gradually to as much light as they can stand, a ripening process that helps to insure flowering. In the fall, usually after the foliage withers (and before frosts return), calanthes can be placed in well-lighted windows—among ferns and maidenhair—where they will bloom almost until Christmas. Then, dried out, the pseudobulbs are stored on open shelves in a dark, cool basement. The one-to-two-inch flowers are predominantly white, pink or yellow although many other colors are known.

Opposite page: When the flower of an orchid (top left) is cut apart, it separates into a diagrammatic scheme of threes: Three sepals (originally enclosing the flower as a bud), which on the face of an imaginary clock would occupy the 12, 5, 7 positions; three petals in the 2, 6, 10 positions, the bottom petal being the distinctive lip. Rising from the center of the flower, the column bears on its tip the pollen wafers (behind a hinged cap); below the wafers is the stigmatic surface. This column, more than other floral characteristics, is the significantly recognizable feature of all orchids. At the base of the column the ovary (not shown) acts as a floral stem. The shapes of the plants, too, have basic similarities. Dendrobium senile (top right) has short, bristle-covered pseudobulbs. Epidendrum mariae's pseudobulbs (bottom left) are squat, rounded. Some orchids, Cychnoches chlorochilon (bottom right), may have long thickened stems (from one to ten feet) as pseudobulbs. All of these growths are called sympodial, because as each old growth ripens, a new shoot develops from its base. This page: Epidendrum criniferum is also sympodial, but its straggly, weedy growth is without pseudobulbs. Also without pseudobulbs is the miniature Oncidium varigatum, a sympodial with sharp-edge, pointed leaves somewhat like iris. The mini-Dendrobium loddesii, however, has only the vaguest suggestion of a stem swelling, indicating that it is really a pseudobulb. The monopodials, the Vanda hybrid and Phalaenopsis violaceae, grow only in one direction, upward; and without pseudobulbs or annual side growths. All orchids have a root system similar to Schomburgkia humboltdii, with roots cased in velamen, from very thin to very coarse and thick.

Orchids react rather quickly to light changes, and their leaves show it plainly. Healthy growth is robust; the leaves are clear green or yellow-green with a shiny, crisp look. Deep blue-green and a slightly soft texture are the result of too much shade. Too much sunlight induces a yellowish white or yellow-green and a strong tendency for the leaves to wither. They look bleached, and they are, for the green chlorophyll has been destroyed. Orchids with thick, leathery leaves or deciduous orchids—those with hard, roundish pseudobulbs—are likely to need considerable sunlight; those with thin or succulent leaves, much less.

In recent years attempts have been made to measure the light in well-managed greenhouses and to arrive at standard light values for orchids. The minimum for shade orchids (low-light-energy) has been set at 200 footcandles. The maximum for those in nearly full sunlight (high-light-energy) is over 8,000 footcandles. Orchidists generally consider values between 600 and 3,000 as practical light levels. Footcandle measurements can be made easily with a photographic light meter—the type sold for incident light, and which possess a fixed light-gathering sphere. Readings are taken from many places within a greenhouse (or window) just above the plant foliage, the sphere always facing the sun or other light source. All of the readings are added, then averaged. Frequently the meters are calibrated in footcandles. At other times the meter readings must be multiplied by a simple conversion factor provided by the manufacturer in order to arrive at footcandles.

Shade can be supplied in many ways, although it is ordinarily indicated by the method of culture. Outdoors, trees and tall shrubs—even laths and screens—are most frequently used. Indoors, at least in homes, curtains and draperies and skillfully applied plastic sheets are readily available. Greenhouses, and similar structures, utilize many systems of shading from white paint to cheesecloth, from roller blinds to plastic screens. Automation, unlike most other orchid routines, is not easily or inexpensively accomplished. Applying shade materials, or removing them, is still very much a manual job in spring and fall. Happily, that occurs each six months.

MOST ORCHIDS REQUIRE PROTECTION ONLY FROM HEAVY FROSTS, SNOW AND CONSISTENTLY HIGH TEMPERATURES. This does not mean that orchids cannot live through extreme climatic changes. Some do. Others may not be injured by short periods of excessive temperatures, either high or low. For the most part, the best temperature range for orchids is a median one, neither unduly hot nor cold; and a ten to twenty degree differential between day and night, winter and summer—in other words, about the same temperature range that keeps the average home comfortable.

Man-made heat can never supplant or even equal nature's balanced warmth. Whatever its source—steam, hot water, warmed forced air, radiant coils, soil cables—the dryness of artificial heat is deadly to orchids until softened with moisture in the air. Heat must be used with discretion, handled with great care and resorted to as infrequently as possible.

A hundred years of experience has determined that MOST ORCHIDS MUST BE GROWN WITHIN A DAILY TEMPERATURE VARIATION FROM 55° TO 90° F; NIGHTLY, FROM 50° TO 70° F. Somewhere within these minimums and maximums, each orchid will have a preferential range. Further experience and study separate nearly all orchids into three minimum temperature categories, depending on their homelands: COOL ORCHIDS, from the higher mountains, 50°; MEDIUM ORCHIDS, from the plateaus, 55°; WARM ORCHIDS, from the lowlands, 65°.

Epidendrum Bumble Bee

By 1920, when the first list of orchid hybrids was published, hardly more than a hundred epidendrum crosses had been made; there have not been a great many more since then. Most professional breeders did try at one time or another to introduce the strength of epidendrums into the cattleyas; but because the flowers were not significantly improved, such programs were not pursued. But years later, when epidendrums, because of their trouble-free habits, became a slight vogue, such hybrids as Bumble Bee were introduced. It has, really, no apparent resemblance to that flying insect, except at a distance when the many inch-and-a-half brown-yellow-white flowers are gently tossed about by late spring breezes.

These temperatures are called the minimum-winter-night indexes. They can go lower, but they normally should not. They will go 10° to 20° higher in the daytime. During summer nights, the basic indexes are 5° to 10° higher than in winter, and during summer days, about 20° more.

High night temperatures will harm all orchids, irreparably damage many of the cool ones and often prevent flowering. In Florida and southern California this is a problem; many cool orchids cannot be grown there. In the Midwest, where day and night summer temperatures are almost the same, there is a similar difficulty. Without a 10° or 20° drop at night, many orchids will not bloom. Such a temperature fluctuation seems to harden new growth, to stimulate chemical changes essential to flowering. The simplest solution in these and similar regions is some form of air conditioning or evaporative cooling.

Consistently high temperature develops rapid, weak, immature growth. The pseudobulb cannot hold itself erect. Leaves become soft and flabby. Cold slows growth and makes leaves brittle. Frost ruptures plant tissues, producing watery brownish black spots. And, as would be expected, sudden extremes of heat and cold are also inadvisable; temperature changes must be gradual or growth is temporarily checked.

Gardeners who come to orchids without preparation are often perplexed by the problem of warmth. Climatic conditions vary widely from coast to coast, from north to south. So does equipment. The answer is to select orchids—in the beginning—whose temperature requirements are casually in keeping with the local climate. Then modify the climate with a minimum investment. Warm orchids, for example, are easily grown in Florida; cool orchids are impossible there, but they are beautifully grown in the Northeast. Medium-temperature orchids are adaptable nearly everywhere, with some precautions. And their normal range is much greater than is generally suspected.

PROVIDE ORCHIDS WITH A MOIST ATMOSPHERE (HUMIDITY) USUALLY NOT LESS THAN 40 PERCENT, NOR MORE THAN 80 PERCENT. The eccentricity of many orchids, if it may be called that, is their requirement for atmospheric moisture far beyond the needs of other garden plants. In fact, humidity is essential to their life. In a totally dry atmosphere they lose water fast, shrivel and die. Humidity controls the loss of water from orchids and prevents them from drying out. It cools the leaves, wards off scorching and makes very high temperatures bearable for a short time.

Humidity also has some bad features when incorrectly applied. At night or during cold, cloudy, rainy days—when humidity is least desirable—it condenses on orchid foliage, creating wet conditions in which bacterial and fungus diseases thrive. And at any time it may be damaging to flowers, causing bud drop and spotting. Blooming plants should be kept in a drier, cooler place.

Actually, humidity is not a difficult factor in orchid growth. Important, yes; but responsive to simple controls. It has a daily pattern, a proportionate increase-decrease, closely related to temperature and light—little or no humidity in the morning, building to 30 or 40 percent by midday, as both temperature and light increase; perhaps more by mid-afternoon. It is a curious fact that as the temperature rises, humidity tends to decrease unless replenished. In effect, warm air doesn't lose humidity; it is merely capable of holding more, and should be helped to do so. Then, as the sunlight becomes less intense, as the warmth of day diminishes—so does the humidity. Little humidity is needed at night except to alleviate the harshness of artificial heat.

Bulbophyllum gigantea

In spite of its name—gigantea—this bulbophyllum is not large; its size is relative, since most of the family is actually rather small. One of them, a native of Australia (B. minutissimum), has pseudobulbs barely one-fifth of an inch in diameter. Another bulbophyllum curiosity in Borneo (B. beccarii), also small, has flowers that smell like rotting meat. Yet it is a delightful family of more than a thousand species, spreading from Japan to New Zealand and jumping across the Indian Ocean to West Africa. There is a welcome variety of shapes and sizes and colors (grayed shades of red and yellow), enough to delight a collector's heart; very few are known in commercial cultivation, though not unavailable. Warm to medium temperature epiphytes, they are often small enough to fit into an aquarium or terrarium, to the enchantment of all who see them.

Humidity is added to the atmosphere by syringing or misting orchid foliage indoors or outdoors, by dampening benches and walks and floors in greenhouses and lathhouses, by mist sprays or humidifiers—in nearly any installation—that may be automatically correlated to temperature and humidity variations, by pans of water or water and pebbles in homes. Toward the end of each day, humidity may be lowered by opening air vents or by small exhaust fans in closed installations. Humidity, incidentally, is rarely damaging if the air is circulating gently and continuously.

How much humidity should orchids be given? It varies according to the group in which an orchid is classified. Terrestrials need little as a rule; epiphytes more. Thin-leaved orchids require more than those with thickened leaves. Monopodial orchids may have a high requirement, as do orchids in the warm category; sympodials, less. Most cool orchids do best when the humidity level is reasonably consistent, day and night. Orchids in the medium-temperature group—primarily from Mexico and Central America—as well as deciduous species, have an astonishing capacity for enduring low humidity, provided that other conditions are favorable.

ORCHIDS MUST HAVE ABUNDANT ACCESS TO FRESH AIR. After the comments about humidity, the urgent necessity of supplying orchids with fresh air may seem contradictory. In a way, it is. Unrestricted air reduces humidity dangerously in closed areas. Plants are desiccated, temperatures may drop—or rise—with shocking rapidity. Sudden drafts shock orchids, their growth is impaired; continuous drafts dehydrate them. On the other hand, if fresh air is not available, a stuffy atmosphere is created, and stagnant air breeds diseases. Orchids are robbed of carbon dioxide, an essential component of their food. Temperatures, also, may shoot upward dangerously.

Air movement is, in many ways, as important as the air itself. Gently circulating air maintains an even temperature, preventing hot or cold spots. It reduces the hazard of moisture condensing on the plants, evaporates moisture left on the foliage and forces an exchange of air around orchids—thereby maintaining fresh supplies of carbon dioxide.

Within their homelands, orchids—epiphytes particularly—are never bothered by stagnant air; it is always in motion, day and night. In homes and greenhouses, gardeners now duplicate that condition with small electric fans or air turbulators operating constantly. They are placed beneath tables and benches or near ceilings, and baffled so that directional air currents are avoided.

Another modern technique for improving orchid culture—still somewhat controversial—is to add carbon dioxide to the atmosphere around the plants. Growers release a minute stream of bottled carbon dioxide into greenhouses during the brilliant, clear days of winter when fresh air may be limited by the cold. A current trend is to use carbon dioxide also when spring and summer temperatures are high. It does work surprisingly well with seedlings during the first few years of growth. Gardeners duplicate this procedure simply by burning a candle or an alcohol lamp in some protected or secluded corner.

Ventilation—air—outdoors is never a problem so long as natural air pockets are avoided. In greenhouses, coupling air movement automatically to both temperature and humidity removes much of the guesswork. Indoors, orchids and human beings require essentially the same balanced atmosphere. The gaseous exchange in most homes, either by diffusion or from slightly opened windows, is usually sufficient.

Renanthera monachica

The explosive growth of orchid culture as a hobby during the past twenty years helped to make renantheras deservedly popular, far beyond the excitement their floral shapes, red or orange, scarlet spotted two-inch flowers normally cause. Sturdy, upright monopodials growing sometimes to fourteen feet (modern hybrids tend toward miniforms), they are cared for—like their cousins the vandas—in medium to warm conditions. Discovered in Indochina and the Philippines, a renanthera was one of the first orchids to be grown with some success. In 1813 George Fairbairn, an English gardener, planted his renantheras in wooden baskets, dipping them several times a day into a barrel of rain water. Tedious but essentially correct; and his successes were greatly admired.

The fascination of orchids does not necessarily begin and end with the flowers. There are other opportunities such as collecting paintings, the still life of blue orchids by Mai Thu, for example. Or orchid stamps and coins (although the Guatemalan fifty centavo piece may be the only coin). And botanical prints from the old floral registers whose value, incidentally, has tripled in the last twenty years.

In homes, though, as well as elsewhere, it is not so much what the atmospheric conditions may be, as it is the balance between the elements that make up the atmosphere. It is very easy to separate them, treat them individually—as has been done so far. The art is to combine these elements in the proportions that orchids require, and, at the same time, to prevent orchids from being exposed to sudden atmospheric changes and unfavorable extremes. The indispensable prerequisite is moderation: gradually rising-falling temperatures, gradually increasing-decreasing humidity, slow and mild air exchange.

ORCHIDS MUST BE GIVEN WATER IN A ROUTINE CONSISTENT WITH THEIR NATIVE REQUIREMENTS. The cultural imitation of nature, by which orchids so long have been grown, is nowhere so evident as in the simple matter of watering them. The amount of water and its frequency are determined by their botanical and physical classification, their root systems and their composts.

Terrestrial and monopodial orchid composts are kept moist, never permitted to dry out. Epiphytes—almost invariably—must have their composts dried out between each watering. Watering increases in frequency and quantity as new growths and roots develop, and may decrease just before or just after flowering.

Add to these three practices a major commandment: Don't overwater! More orchids—of all kinds—die from overwatering than from any other single reason, or from any combination of other orchid errors. If there is any doubt about the need to water orchids—don't! None have ever been injured by a few days of dryness.

The root systems of terrestrials, with little protective covering, cannot adjust to extended dryness; they will shrivel. Neither can they adapt themselves to continuously saturated composts in which soil air is excluded; the roots will rot.

On the other hand, the roots of epiphytes—exposed to air, rain and sun—are protected by a thick velamen, a corklike layer of highly absorbent plant tissues. The velamen is capable of extracting moisture from the air and from damp refuse. And it has an incredible capacity for almost instantaneously accepting several times its weight in rain water. Necessarily, by virtue of their aerial habit, epiphyte roots are hardier than those of terrestrials. Dryness may not injure them, even for a week or two. But continuous saturation will, quickly. Again, it is the lack of air that permits these roots to rot.

It is desirable to distinguish two variations among epiphytes. Those without pseudobulbs have somewhat similar moisture requirements to the terrestrials; so do some epiphytes with pseudobulbs, if their roots are slender and thin. But the ordinary epiphyte, with pseudobulbs and heavy roots, adheres strictly to the wet-dry system of watering. A convenient clue to the health of epiphyte roots is their visual appearance. When dry, the roots usually are white and glossy; when surcharged with water, greenish and dull. If they do not return to their original gleaming white condition, trouble develops rapidly.

Just as rain—with the arrival of favorable weather—supports new orchid growth, so its withdrawal or cessation induces a resting period; particularly if there is an accompanying temperature drop, drier air and less light. Depending on the type of orchid, the rest period may be very short or nonexistent; or it may be several weeks, and even several months. During this resting period, watering may be light and infrequent, but never nonexistent.

The physical character of orchid roots and their water requirements practically dictate the materials used in the two major orchid composts. Although aeration and rapid drainage are common to both, composts for epiphytes are

Peristeria pendula

Within the peristerias (Central America) is the Flor de Espiritu Santo (the Flower of the Holy Ghost), Peristeria elata. There is an extraordinary resemblance, within the flower, to a white dove (the front of the column) hovering over a white altar (formed by the orchid's lip). As beautiful as Peristeria elata is, it is an uncomfortably large plant. P. pendula is more manageable with its four-inch pseudobulbs and pendant floral scapes that, while short, produce about 20 two-inch fragrant flowers. They are greenish white on the outside, flushed with rose on the inside and spotted all over with purple. Peristeria pendula is inclined to need warmth while growing and plenty of moisture; a decided cooler period while resting and barely enough water to keep the bulbs plump. It is an easy orchid to mature and can be grown in most rich humus composts.

coarse, easily dried; terrestrial composts are finer, hold moisture longer and may contain considerable amounts of humus and organic foods. For all too long a time orchid composts largely consisted of the dried roots of osmunda ferns, shredded for terrestrials and sometimes mixed with humus and sand; or chopped and wedged tightly in pots for epiphytes. Osmunda was, and is, difficult to use and often untrustworthy except when expertly handled. That it was used for so long is more an acknowledgment of the skill that growers attained, than a sign of any merit it may have as a medium for growing orchids. Osmunda is now almost completely replaced by chopped and graded fir bark specifically manufactured for orchids, which is much easier to manage and much safer to use in relation to watering.

It is not difficult to determine when any compost needs further water. Thrust a finger into the compost by the edge of the pot. If it is cool and moist, no water is needed. If warm and dry, add water. Very often, watering becomes a routine, every few days, or weekly, or longer. Sometimes it may be determined by the size of the pot. Pots up to four inches in diameter probably will need water every day or so. Over that size, every third or fourth day. The frequency will depend on the weather and the humidity. High humidity tends to delay watering by preventing evaporation; high temperature, to increase the need for water. In summer it can be somewhat less; in winter it may stretch to two weeks. On cold, dreary, cloudy days orchids preferably should not be watered.

More often than not, the garden water used for orchids is suspected of being dangerous to them. An excessive concentration of mineral salts in water, or a strongly alkaline reaction, can injure orchid roots, of course; but that is a very rare condition. Normally, water in contact with soil—or orchid composts—becomes buffered, its mineral content made harmless. At other times, or as an occasional practice, a drop or two of phosphoric acid in each gallon of water makes it more suitable. In the few extreme cases that do exist, only an analysis made by Department of Agriculture Experiment Stations is helpful. Actually the temperature of water is a greater danger than its chemical content. It should always be used at greenhouse or garden or room temperature; never higher, never much lower. Warm water has a tendency to soften or cook orchid roots, cold water temporarily stuns them.

ORCHIDS MUST BE FED A SUFFICIENT AMOUNT OF MINERAL AND ORGANIC NUTRIENTS. Regardless of the apparently unorthodox habits of epiphytes—attaching themselves to trees—their roots search out food, as well as water. In this, they are no different from all other green plants. Within the limited spaces in which they live, epiphytes are merely more efficient at finding food, merely more effective in utilizing it. Decomposing leaves caught in the crotches of trees, the refuse from birds, particles of soil embedded in bark or mosses or lichens, the run-off of rain water gathering chemical solutes—never very much in the way of a food supply, but consistent. A fact to keep in mind when applying fertilizers to orchids in cultivation: very little food, regularly, goes a long, long way.

There never was any question about feeding terrestrial orchids. Because their roots roam freely through the forest litter and humus soils, orchidists provided them with similar conditions. Failures, and there were plenty at first, resulted from using either excessively rich composts or excessively poor ones. An overabundance of any fertilizer materials—mineral or organic—is always injurious. Terrestrial orchids are often described as vigorous feeders, which they are. But they do not like their food in sudden, heavy concentrations.

Gongora galatea var. *luteola*

Among the twenty or so members of the gongoras, the species G. galatea is one of the most gracious. The pendulous racemes, about twelve inches long, carry from six to twelve inverted yellow flowers, appearing in the summer. The incurving floral stems (actually the ovaries) place the two-inch fragrant orchid flowers upside down. It is a Mexican native, responding easily to indoor culture when grown as a semiterrestrial in medium temperatures, and given a cool period, little water, while resting. The other species, some white and densely red-spotted, are found in Central America and in parts of South America. The name Gongora bears no relationship to the plant's appearance; it was a courteous gesture to the mid-nineteenth-century bishop of Córdoba, Spain.

Currently, the practice is to feed all orchids a little at a time—during warm, bright days (either summer or winter)—carefully using dilute fertilizer solution, then to alternate each feeding with a normal watering in order to leach out chemical salts that could accumulate in harmful quantities. The selection of a fertilizer usually is determined by the composts. A balanced formula, written numerically as 10–10–10 or 20–20–20, is recommended for terrestrial orchids grown in a combination of rich soil, humus and sand, and also for some cool orchids with thin roots, as well as for most orchids grown in osmunda. Orchids of all families—when grown in bark, or bark and gravel—require a formula rich in nitrogen (30–10–10) as new growth begins. Later, a fertilizer with a high phosphorous content (10–20–10) is substituted to support flowering. There is little natural or available food in bark and it is surprisingly low in nitrogen; therefore supplemental food is a necessity. And this practice pays remarkable dividends in healthier growth, more rapid maturity and better flowers. Orchids, for all too long in the past, were incredibly starved.

There are many kinds of orchid fertilizers: concentrated chemical mixtures or bulky powders, tablets soluble in streams of water, fish emulsions and many ingenious local preparations. All are excellent when used, for orchids, exactly according to the manufacturer's instructions.

There are other important aspects of orchid culture. Composts and potting and propagation, for example; or orchid equipment, heaters, humidifiers and, if it is desirable, the substitution of automation for personal involvement. But these considerations, explained elsewhere in this book, may vary from one family of orchids to another, from one gardener to the next. How they are resolved is a personal matter; gardeners should make these decisions for themselves. Equally important—at times even more so—is observation. No book or lecture can replace actual seeing. Visit commercial nurseries and, as well, hobbyists. Watch and ask questions. They will always be answered, instructively and pleasantly.

For all practical purposes, however, light, temperature, humidity, air, water and food are the essential basics of orchid culture. As they are understood and applied correctly and imaginatively—orchids will thrive in gardens, in greenhouses, in homes. They are manageable fundamentals, easily learned and easily practiced since most orchids are extraordinarily tolerant. Even a few failures make success a heady triumph.

The First Collection

Some gardeners describe the hobby of orchids as a benign disease infinitely contagious; others, as a mania. Others make no comment, convinced that words alone will never explain the beauty inherent in a single orchid flower. This is probably true. No gardener or botanist, plant hunter or traveler has succeeded in using words. Invariably, they end with the comment: "This doesn't do the

Epidendrum radiatum

Very few orchid gardeners are without this species, for several reasons. They have compact foliage and a short floral stem with a half-dozen yellowish-brown, strongly fragrant flowers opening in slow succession, each two or three inches across and beautifully formed. And they are topsy-turvey! The lip is carried in the normal position for most flowers, not upside down as is more usual with orchids. Several attempts were made early in this century to breed E. radiatum with cattleyas, notably Cattleya bowringiana, and then abandoned. It was once believed that the hardiness of epidendrums, the ease with which their seeds germinated and their habit of maturing quickly could be imparted to related, commercially important families.

orchid justice. You should have seen the flower!" And that is exactly what this chapter is about—the flower, the reason for, and the end of, all orchid culture; and the plant qualities, as well, that support flowering.

What is a desirable flower? A color, a size, a shape? How does a gardener arrive at a choice among the twenty or thirty thousand orchids known, or the hundreds that are commonly grown. Ordinarily the corsage orchids—cattleyas, Cymbidiums or Phalaenopsis—set the floral style. It is sustained by seeing them flowering in a friend's living room, or growing in a garden or a plant house. But there is much, much more to look for. There is the strange, the unique, the multicolor, the fragrant. It can be temporarily resolved by looking at orchid catalogs.

All commercial growers publish yearly lists of orchids by name, description, size, price, date of flowering and the temperature classification. These are the facts that must be considered in any selection. Growers also invite correspondence and suggest the importance of personal visits, usually on weekends. The loveliest catalog can never replace the excitement of seeing hundreds of orchids in bloom, deciding on a floral type and—with a grower's personal assistance—arriving at an expertly advised decision.

After a floral choice is made, select only those orchid plants that can withstand some error and neglect—vigorous plants that can manage by themselves when overlooked for several days. Vigorous plants are not necessarily large ones. Windows and Wardian cases are not ideal places for orchids with two-foot-high foliage and three-foot flower spikes. Compact miniatures are as easily grown, and more of them can be handled in less space.

If the question of expense is bothersome, don't worry. Excellent orchids cost no more than other garden plants sold in pots, and much less than foliage greenery. They can be bought for as little as fifty cents, as much as $3,000. The low price is not uncommon for jungle orchids or unrooted back bulbs (pseudobulbs no longer useful to the parent plant). Nearly always both are poor bargains, requiring special care for several years before they are sufficiently established, if ever, to flower. There are firms, however, that specialize in jungle orchids, importing, grading, and establishing them before releasing them for sale at very reasonable prices.

High prices are for rare breeder orchids, those so consistent as parents that growers cheerfully pay the exorbitant prices asked. Or more often, for one-of-a-kind hybrids, so beautiful they become a collector's dream. A gardener, though, will rarely pay less than $5.00 or more than $25.00. Within that price range there are enough magnificent and spectacular orchids to fill a dozen small greenhouses, to say nothing of smaller windowsills. These prices, also, are competitive and will be always about the same in any city or state. Such budget prices are remarkable, considering the years of labor and time and the materials needed to mature orchids.

The value of orchids is determined by rarity, size, vigor, the type of flower and its color and shape. Ideally, a commercial flower is round, forming a perfect circle, somewhat flat in depth (no curling of the sepals and petals) and with a large lip that is ruffled. The bigger the flower is the better, although this is not always good reasoning. At present, a more realistic goal is more flowers per stem. Colors are expected to be rich, deep, full of contrast: for example, velvet-red petals and sepals, an orange-yellow lip. The substance—texture—of the flower must be heavy in order to withstand abuse and to last for weeks or several

Top row, left: Brassolaeliocattleya Fortune 'Spellbound', HCC/AOS *(left); and Brassolaeliocattleya* Fortune 'Golden Land' HCC/AOS *(right). Cattleya intermedia* 'Aquinii'. *Center row: Cattleya* Bob Betts 'Williamsons'; *Brassolaeliocattleya* Fortune 'Golden Fantasy', HCC/AOS. *Bottom row: Laeliocattleya* Lee Langford 'Copper Queen', HCC/ODC; *Brassolaeliocattleya* Norman's Bay 'Gothic', AM/RHS—AOS. *Courtesy of Fred A. Stewart, Inc.*

Opposite page, top row: Laeliocattleya Grand Gate; *Brassolaeliocattleya* Mount Hood. *Center: Laeliocattleya* Louella Parsons 'Hattie' x *Laeliocattleya* Matilija 'Venus'; *Laeliocattleya* Pink Fairy. *Bottom: Laeliocattleya* Western Sunset; *Laeliocattleya* True Depth. *This page, center: Cattleya* Highlight; *Cattleya* Roman Silver. *Bottom: Laeliocattleya* Winland; *Cattleya* Terry Rinaman. *Courtesy of Rod McLellan Company.*

months. The stem should be strong and erect, thrusting well above the leaves.

Of course nearly all commercial orchids will fail in one or more of these ideals, for seedling variation is enormous. But within these variations will be found hundreds—sometimes thousands—of charmingly flowered orchids, most of them reasonably priced.

The most economical buys are unflowered seedlings, either from flasks, from community pots ready for transplanting, or in small, individual containers. Priced from $1.50 to $3.50 each, seedlings will bloom in two to four years, and may become prize plants. At least, it is hoped that they will. This gamble is called orchid roulette, for obvious reasons. The quality of the flower cannot be accurately predicted, although seedlings so offered are from parents of known and exceptional productivity. Actually the average of excellence is so high that seedlings should always be a major portion of every orchid purchase.

Whatever the ultimate reason for growing orchids, the flowers must originally have instigated it. So begin with them. Visit nurseries, see orchids in bloom and then make a selection. The first plants in any beginning collection should be mature and either in flower or in bud. Choose the less expensive, since some may die before their culture is understood. There is nothing dismaying about this. Not everyone who has grown orchids succeeded completely at first. It is in the nature of the game.

It is fun to have orchids that will bloom close to specific dates: Christmas, Easter, special birthdays and anniversaries. Fill in the missing months with flowering plants for year-round bloom. Twenty-four or more plants are needed to insure flowers each month. But eight mature plants well chosen for seasonal bloom will provide about twenty-four weeks of flowers.

In Florida and other subtropical regions, start with warm orchids. The cool types are difficult to grow there, usually requiring extensive cooling equipment; but in the Northeast and Northwest there is no better initial choice. Within reason, orchids in the medium-temperature group will be suitable in most places.

Match orchids to the major light conditions in specific locations for shade, sun or whatever may be the prevailing circumstances. If it is not possible to provide normal humidity, single out orchids that are not too demanding in that respect: terrestrials, or hardy epiphytes with thick, leathery leaves, and nearly any of the deciduous species. In other words, integrate the idiosyncrasies of orchids with those of a region or a garden or a home.

There are other considerations in putting together the first collection of orchids—none so important, though, as beginning with reasonably priced, vigorous, mature plants in flower or bud, plants which can easily exist in the conditions created for them and do so without taking much space. Color and size and whimsical shapes have made up famous collections. Sir Jeremiah Colman had a collection of blue orchids; the Sultan of Mahore possessed a huge plant really transportable only with elephants. The amateur can have a wonderful time collecting botanical orchids, most of which are simple to grow, vigorous, regular in their flowering habits and usually not expensive. They have variety and scandalous colors, mimicry, quaint habits, and fragrance. They are endlessly interesting, endlessly exciting and an endless quest, since many thousands of them have never been introduced to cultivation. Central America is particularly rich in orchids, and licensed collectors often list rare species.

Top row: Laeliocattleya Marysville; *Sophrolaeliocattleya* Allgold; *Center: Sophrolaelia* Psyche, *Sophrolaeliocattleya* Yellow Doll, *and Sophrolaeliocattleya* Yum-Yum. *Center right: Brassolaeliocattleya* Goldfield; *Bottom: Brassolaeliocattleya* Golden Spires; *Brassolaeliocattleya* Challenge. *Courtesy of Rod McLellan Company.*

Indoor Gardens

Many home gardeners grow orchids on their windowsills, on kitchen shelving and open cabinets. They can do this because they observed the plant hazards present in their homes: dry air, hot air, drafts, steam heat, too little sunlight, no humidity. They went to work modifying these hazards, selecting small spaces in their homes in which a microclimate suitable to orchids could be built. Such modifications, in their simplest forms, are: maintaining a moderate room temperature (60° to 80°); providing humidity immediately adjacent to the orchids by setting them over pans of moist gravel; mist-spraying orchid foliage on hot, bright days; making the most of too little sunlight by installing supplementary light; giving orchids summer outings on a terrace or balcony from June through September. And by choosing orchids wisely—securing only the toughest within the medium-temperature group, those ordinarily found on the Central American plateaus—terrestrials with low humidity requirements, epiphytes that delight in shade, compact miniatures with not-so-mini flowers.

Out of such careful practices come the sensational success stories printed in newspapers and magazines. Yet these achievements are neither sensational nor magical, but just common sense applied to orchid garden routines which were developed with patience, understanding and skill. As a matter of history, gardeners have been growing orchids without greenhouses for nearly a hundred and fifty years. Hardy orchids were not uncommon from spring to fall in old German and English gardens. In both countries kitchen windows were frequently satisfying homes for semihardy varieties. Of course, in those days kitchens were more suitable for plant life, as well as for human comfort.

The simplest approach to home orchid culture is windowsill gardening. A bright window is needed, bright in the sense of brilliant or luminous, not burning-bright, direct sunlight (although the latter can be modified). If the sunlight from morning to night, with normal midday increases, averages 300 footcandles—good. If more, excellent; best of all is 1,500 to 2,000 footcandles. Such a high light incidence can be desirable since light in the home only comes from one side, not all sides as it does outdoors.

A southern-oriented window is preferable; then, an eastern; lastly, a western exposure. North windows are often lacking in light intensity unless they extend out some distance from the building. The exception is a skylight or a northern wall of glass, the sort of construction that artists and photographers once demanded for their studios. Extraordinarily beautiful shade orchids grow well in such an exposure.

Mesh curtains, fine cloth draperies, plastic films or metal screens will moderate the heat and light of a summer midday sun, the gravest danger. Storm sashes prevent injuries from winter chill (newspapers, wrapping paper, tissues, heavier draperies and plastics can be substituted). Whatever materials are used and whatever the manner of combining them, make them decorative as well as utilitarian. Raw wood, dirty pots, clutter of any kind are not ideal home com-

Pleurothalis quadriema

A dozen of the white or pale rose flowers of P. quadriema could cover a fifty-cent coin. Yet, carried as they are on eight-inch arching stems, the flowers seem to be larger than the minute lilies which they slightly resemble. As with other members of the pleurothalis family, its requirements are temperate and consistent: humidity, moisture, bright reflected light, and a temperature range between 60° and 80°. All pleurothalis may be conveniently established on small plaques of tree-fern fiber which has some humus netted against its surfaces.

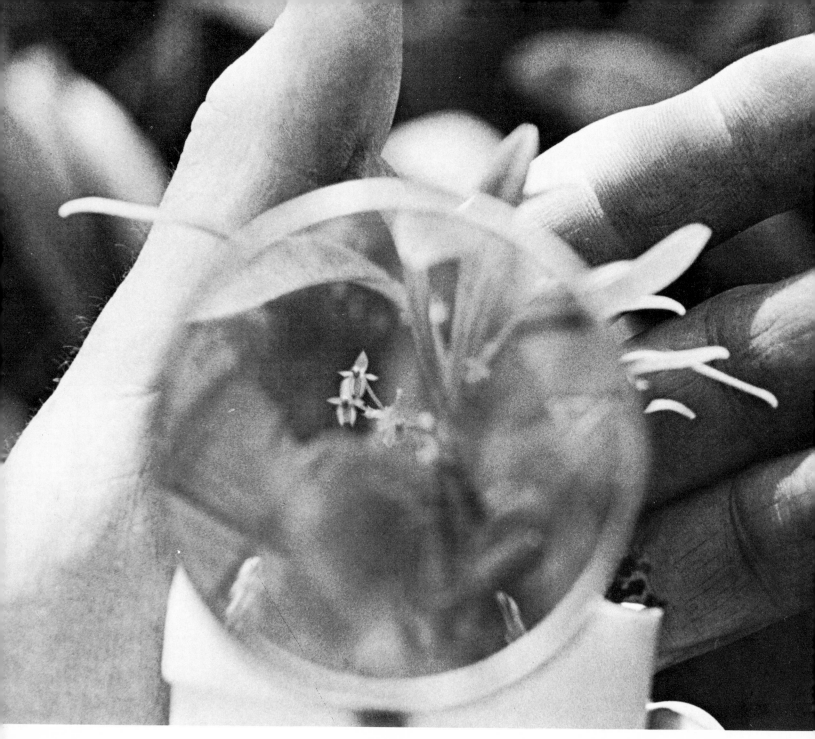

Pleurothalis oratilabra

The tiny pleurothalis (above) are a collector's delight. There are more than a thousand different kinds, and dozens of them may be grown in a small aquarium. Not all of the flowers are as minuscule as those of P. oratilabra. Many are a half-inch long, brash in color—yellows and whites and purples often streaked with carmine—the flowers usually carried just above the foliage in masses, like a giddily decorated dark green carpet. They are temperate in their requirements: medium temperatures, consistent soil moisture (they are semiterrsetrials without pseudobulbs), and a bright window—but one without direct sunlight.

Cattleya Sandra Mary *(right)*

This is one of the cattleya hybrids that has fulfilled a long and urgent need for short foliage and numerous large flowers, beauty in the most compact form. It was not an easy task for hybridizers to accomplish, although several delightful dwarf cattleya species are known.

46

panions; neither do they add the look of elegance that orchids should have as a background.

It is nice to have a tall window and a wide window ledge—as many older houses do—on which to place an orchid collection. Nevertheless, small extensions can be handsomely installed, such as low book cases or cabinets pushed against the window wall and level with the sill. Very wide ledges are unnecessary as the light falloff from most windows is rapid. A foot from the window, light intensities are halved; at two feet they are quartered. So it becomes a discretionary battle, in a way, between burning or chilling orchid foliage next to a window pane, or pushing them away from the glass and losing light.

Sometimes fluorescent lights may be installed on sectional chains, raised by day and lowered at night to provide supplemental light—a mildly dismaying project since such lighting systems are awkward and can be unattractive. It is much better, when additional light is needed, to remove the orchids to a separate and fixed installation where that phase of culture is automatic and conveniently out of the way.

The sill or ledge can be covered with glass or plastic sheets for protection. Printed toweling adds cheerful colors and absorbs accidentally spilled water. On the windowsill place shallow pans—two or three inches deep—wide and long enough to cover most of the flat area. Fill the pans with small pebbles (a quarter-inch to a half-inch in diameter), marbles or similar inert material. Add water to within a half-inch, or a little less, of the pebble surface. From time to time as the water becomes discolored with algae, dump it. Clear the pebbles and the pans in a chlorine bleach solution, wash and refill with water. The algae will hurt nothing but a sense of cleanliness.

Set orchid pots on the pebbles, never letting them touch the water or adding so much water that it reaches the orchid pots and saturates the compost. Water in the pans only modestly satisfies the humidity requirements of the orchids. Curiously enough, it does that rather well, particularly if the edges of the pans extend well beyond the outer edges of the foliage. Don't let the pots touch each other. Air space around both pots and orchid foliage is always necessary to help maintain a uniform humidity and temperature. Any more pleasing arrangement of the orchids than this is a matter of aesthetics and personal pleasure.

Oiled wood ribs, an inch or so apart, or extruded metal grills may be placed over the pans, supported by their edges. Shallow pots inverted and plunged into the pebbles, or bricks, are interesting supports for orchids. Glazed tile trays, painted or etched glass dishes, waterproof earthenware—anything that retains water easily—can replace aluminum baking pans or plastic trays. Basket orchids, or orchids grown on tree fern slabs, may be suspended within the framework of the window, and as close as possible to the trays. Glass shelves may be added at intervals above the sill for truly miniature plants.

On very bright, very warm or hot days, orchid foliage should be mist-sprayed with room-temperature water (drugstores have satisfactory atomizers for that purpose). The spraying should never be done later than early afternoon. Between the occasional mist-spraying and the pans of water and pebbles, more than just the minimum humidity requirements of many orchids will be satisfied. Yet no window or room will be adversely affected by the atmospheric moisture. Humidity can be increased by other expedients. Packaged humidifiers and evaporative coolers, relatively low in cost, are beneficial to the health of both orchids and people. It is not important to saturate a room. People like a

Brassavola Paulae

The brassavolas have the curious disadvantage of being country cousins of the cattleyas—not quite as beautiful, perhaps, but definitely more interesting and culturally as hardy under similar growing conditions. They have several floral forms which set them apart from their commercially more acceptable cousins. A trumpet-shaped lip which varies from the simple one of B. Paulae to the utterly whimsical and magnificent cornucopia of B. nodosa. Or, as another example, the fringed lip and rather stiletto-like sepals of B. digbyana. The pseudobulbs of some of these tropical American orchids are stemlike leaves thickened and rounded, somewhat in the shape of pencils —an indication of their strong demands for high light intensities.

humidity around 40 percent; they feel better and so do orchids.

Ventilation in windowsill culture is naturally automatic. Temperature differentials, inside and outside of the house, tend to push fresh air in and stale air out. The process can be increased by slightly opening a nearby window or door, never the orchid window itself. Small electric fans or air turbulators, placed well away from the orchids and not directed toward them, create gentle and healthy air currents.

Heating an orchid window is rarely a difficulty, except in overheated homes. The problem is to keep orchids near 60°, or slightly less at night, or flowering is inhibited. The alternative, if higher temperatures must be maintained, is to begin with warm orchids. When severe cold is anticipated, one of the best windowsill heating devices is the sealed-tube aquarium unit placed in the bottom of the pans of water and pebbles. Set the temperature of the unit at 70° as an educated guess. Check the air temperature around the orchids and change the aquarium heater thermostat accordingly. The mildly increased water evaporation gently bathes and warms the orchids. Electric heaters, either radiant or blower types, are satisfactory when placed some distance away and baffled. Brooder heaters with wafer thermostats, soil cables, masked tungsten lamps (25 to 150 watts) and shielded infrared lamps, if carefully installed and controlled, can make window temperature adjustments easier.

By and large, the less windows and homes look like greenhouses and need greenhouse care, the more handsome they will appear. Windows are decorative features, and homes must be lived in. There is a point, all too easily reached in indoor orchid gardening, beyond which no gardener should go. When orchids crowd a window, other arrangements should be made for growing them.

Watering is routine in indoor gardening, although the time interval between watering will vary from home to home, from window to window. Only close observation of the composts will determine the need. Plants may look dry and the compost still be quite wet. A spouted can keeps water from dripping on orchid foliage and directs it carefully within the pots. Plants may be moved to the kitchen, soaked thoroughly and then replaced in the window.

Orchid feeding is expected indoors, but at half the quantity and half the frequency that is acceptable elsewhere. Osmunda or terrestrial composts ordinarily will furnish considerable food. Dilute balanced fertilizers may be watered in during the growing seasons. Bark—a recommended compost for all house orchids—either alone or with some fibrous additions, will require routine applications of fertilizers. Only experience and local recommendations can determine the routine that will be most successful. Until then, move cautiously, carefully and considerately.

Window orchids will indicate their likes and dislikes as quickly and as clearly as those in greenhouses. The symptoms are identical, and window orchid troubles tend more toward light deficiencies than anything else. Pests and diseases are almost unknown indoors, other than household pests which are quickly eradicated. Window gardens are always close enough at hand to be effortlessly watched, and pests can be stopped before they become a hazard.

Not often, but persistently enough to cause some dismay, orchids take their time adapting themselves to windowsill and home gardens. Those previously grown in nearby greenhouses may take a few months or a year. Those from longer distances have been known to wait three years before flowering again. This is one of the important reasons for buying orchids in bud or flower, and

Dendrobium minax

More garden collectors grow this dendrobium for its unusual appearance than for its beauty, of which it has more than a fair share. For very obvious reasons, the upright, twisted, yellow-tipped petals are reminiscent of antelope horns; and the white "bodies" of the flowers, in some silhouettes, are not unlike animal skulls—hence the common name for this dendrobium: the Antelope orchid. It is an evergreen Tom Thumb sort of orchid, the leaves and pseudobulbs about ten inches—the flowers, top to bottom, about 3 inches—flowering in summer and continuing to do so for several months. Although a native of the Pacific islands, its night temperature minimum is about 60°; it needs midday shade and, often, can do without a rest period during the winter months.

for buying several of a kind. Window culture is not so much at fault as the slightly changed growing conditions to which they must accustom themselves.

GLASS CASES ATTACHED TO WINDOWS, regardless of their sizes, and bay windows with glass doors are essentially small greenhouses. They can be managed, as can windowsill gardens, simply and without much fuss, or luxuriously and indulgently. In these miniature structures all the difficulties, the importunities and the pleasures of greenhouses come into being. They are part of the living quarters, hence accessible and intimate. They can be automated, less care is required, and also there is a slightly wider choice of orchids available to grow in them. These home installations, however, are not easily tolerated. Bay windows, as well as picture windows, are reluctantly changed to other purposes than attractive views. Glass cases, unless well planned, are not architecturally appealing. Gardeners ready for more than a windowsill unhesitantly make the jump to small greenhouses. Gardeners who want less space, and those who cannot in justice close off large windows, drift naturally toward Wardian cases.

A WARDIAN CASE, as an ornamental and a practical way to grow orchids, is not a new idea. Ever since Dr. Nathaniel Ward invented it a hundred years ago to protect rare plants shipped to London, it has been invaluable: for studying tropical plant habits, making propagations of delicate plants, and pampering seedlings—especially orchid seedlings. As with similar gardening improvements, Wardian cases were an accidental development. Dr. Ward, studying Sphinx moths, placed a cocoon on damp earth in a small bottle lightly stoppered. In a few weeks, to his mild astonishment, a blade of grass and a fern appeared. Later, realizing that the virtue of the bottle was in holding moisture and warmth, he built a glass cabinet and turned it over to the Royal Horticultural Society. It was an immediate success. Many valuable plant cargoes, including Chinese tea and quinine seedlings from Peru, made the long sea journey to England comfortably installed in a Wardian case.

Reduced to absolute essentials, a Wardian case for orchids consists of three square glazed sashes (perhaps thirty inches square) bolted together to make three rigid sides of a box. The bottom is solid plywood or bolted planking, lined with metal or plastic to prevent water from seeping through. Several small holes in the bottom act as air vents. The front of the case is a hinged sash, substituting as a door, which can be closed and locked. Primarily for ventilation, the top of the case, also a sash, is hinged at the back. The wood or metal of the sash is brushed well with aluminum paint as a preservative, then with a weatherproof enamel. The color of the enamel is optional. Of course the size of the Wardian case is not limited to thirty inches in any dimension. It can be rectangular, and it can be any convenient depth, height or length.

Without any heating elements, other than warmth normally contained in a room, the case can safely handle most medium-temperature orchids. Thermostatically controlled with a heating unit as simple as a small incandescent lamp, it is suitable for both medium and warm orchids. Other heating systems may be as complex as soil cables, aquarium heaters, brooder systems or infrared lamps.

Humidity is supplied by pans of gravel and water, and it can be rapidly increased and even intense when the case is closed. Good judgment is required to open and close the top sash or the door just enough to maintain the correct percentage of air moisture. If the condensation on the glass panes is heavy, fresh air is needed. If the panes look misty but show no condensation, the humidity is about right. When they are clear and dry, there is no atmospheric

Masdevallia echnia

This miniature—and it truly is—is better known as the Horrid Masdevallia. Yet it is not unattractive, if its slightly Martian aspect is quickly overlooked. If that is not possible, it still is one of the best conversation pieces among orchids, since its half-inch flowers grotesquely suggest an insect-catching ability—which it doesn't have. Like its better-known relatives (M. veitchiana and M. chimaera), it is a cool-growing orchid from the highest Latin American mountains. Planted in chopped osmunda or tree-fern fiber in two-inch pots, it can be grown along with odontoglossums; or placed within a cool terrarium.

No room in a home is impossible for orchid growing once it is correctly and attractively prepared. The process may be as simple as placing orchids on their own saucers in a southeast sun room window where the massed foliage of other plants helps to keep the air moist (top left). Or a breakfast room can be used, with its own tray of water and marble chips (top right). The Wardian case is hospitable to the phalaenopsis and also displays them well in a foyer adjacent to a living room. As an indoor method of pampering orchids, a Wardian case is easily one of the most efficient. Even alone (opposite page), on its own ornamental tray of moist marble chips, a flowering cattleya in a window surpasses all other ornamentation.

moisture and the case must temporarily be closed and later reopened slightly to prevent the air from becoming stuffy. Plants stay moist longer and foliage may remain uncomfortably damp unless ventilation is carefully balanced. The temperature response is also rapid, either up or down. Because of the possibility of these sudden extremes, everything that is done for orchids in Wardian cases must be accomplished slowly, gently.

Light is not a problem. The case either fits closely into a window area or is wheeled to a sun porch, balcony, terrace or even outdoors in good weather. Supplementary lighting is provided by placing lamps or tubes in their reflectors directly over the case and as close to the top sash as possible. On dull, overcast days daylight is extended with the lamps until ten or eleven o'clock in the evening. In winter, with little or no daylight—or away from a window entirely—the lamps may be turned on all day and up to eleven o'clock.

A Wardian case is large compared to a window but small in relation to the number of orchids it can hold. Compact orchids are a desirable limitation. Yet one or two large specimen plants are not to be overlooked if that is a specific and a deliberate intention. Neither is a Wardian case a grow-all, be-all for orchids. It is impossible to cool a case below the room temperature; at least, it is not easy. Orchids selected for the case will fall conveniently within the medium and warm temperature ranges. The low light intensities, although supported by artificial light, further limit selections to orchids more likely to be accustomed to shade.

Nonetheless the knowledge and techniques applicable to Wardian cases are sound introductions to larger orchid installations. There are few better ways of learning efficiently, and with little cost, the total management of an orchid greenhouse.

Aquariums and terrariums are a delightfully simple form of indoor gardening. Both are easily managed, especially aquariums that come equipped with automatic heating and lighting systems—even with ventilation slots. By adding gravel over the heating unit, some water and a small plant platform, an aquarium is immediately converted into a miniature greenhouse. The very, very mini-orchids from warm climates do well in such an environment. Some of the most beautiful ornamental-leaf orchids are best grown only in such enclosures, making them a decorative addition to any room.

Ordinarily, leave the aquarium top off—or slightly raised—during daylight hours; or vent the aquarium to insure air circulation; small containers generate excessive humidity. Lighting is conveniently easy, either daily or as it may be required. Later, as orchid collections grow out of bounds, as they inevitably will, it is a simple procedure to use the aquariums for growing seedlings, making propagations, or regenerating rootless back bulbs.

Sun porches, as well as balconies, can be adapted to orchid culture, and within their limitations they are as satisfactory as greenhouses. They are also more satisfying, since they are intimately associated with homes, can be attractive and serve as useful areas for pleasure and entertainment. In this sense, sun porches are just below conservatories and atriums in the scheme of orchid houses and are, as well, less expensive. Some orchidists have considered sun porches solely as working areas subject to disorderly messes. But orchids in or adjacent to a home are grown for a different reason—unqualified beauty. As such they become a reflection of the desires and the personalities of their owner.

Sun porches do have roofs, which really is no handicap. Roofs keep the

Oncidiums

Another way of displaying orchids in a home is to naturalize them; growing them—especially the miniatures—on small oak logs, two or three inches in diameter. The oncidiums in the illustration (from the Dominican Republic) could each rest securely on a tablespoon. The trick in establishing orchids is to bind them firmly to the bark without injuring such growths or roots as they may already possess. Watering is managed by dipping the log (it must not be too heavy) into a pail of water in which dilute nutrient chemicals have been dissolved. During summer this may be as frequent as three or four times a week; in winter, once or twice weekly.

porches warmer in winter, cooler in summer, and they can be replaced in part or fully with glass or plastic constructions. If any aspect of a porch presents a problem, it will only be that of insufficient light. Limited in the amount of light to begin with, porches can be further obstructed by nearby buildings or trees or a poor exposure. The alternative to these difficulties is artificial light as a permanent installation to supplement sunlight or replace it entirely.

Porches not already enclosed should be glassed in. Floor-to-ceiling glass is effective and dramatic, adding immeasurably to the health and the appearance of orchids. But glass from table height up is better than none at all. Plastics and fiber glass are replacing the classic sheets and panes of glass. They are as efficient and as rigid, but they do not shatter in a hailstorm. They can be cut, sawed, nailed, bolted or screwed to wood and metal supports. They can be ordered in sheets and panes, with corrugated and frosted surfaces, or delicately tinted. The light from fiber glass is soft and diffuse, luminous and almost shadowless. Plants are not easily burned. Somehow frosted and tinted fiber glass seems to maintain a comparatively even light from day to day, winter through summer. Except in a brilliantly hot region, shading is limited, being used more as a cooling device.

How fiber glass is incorporated into a sun porch or balcony is a matter of individual taste and inventiveness. Yet nothing is achieved in such an installation unless it is both durable and aesthetically desirable. A sun porch should be in keeping with the architectural structure of the house and be arranged for comfortable living as well as being comfortable for orchids. The interior can be waterproofed handsomely, with synthetic tile laid over tarred felt. Drains are needed to prevent water from running into homes rather than outward. Walls are aluminized with paint, then coated with a long-lasting flat enamel. None of these improvements is, perhaps, absolutely essential, but all of them contribute to functional safety and attractive appearance.

Orchids are arranged on the tile floor or set on trays of gravel and water, hung from ceiling rafters or from inset ring bolts. Table groupings are pleasant and convenient and are as useful as benches. Comfortable chairs and a settee of rattan or metal are usefully diversionary. So are strategically placed reading lamps. It is important that all members of a family may still use the porch for relaxing, for tea or coffee and cake, and that at all times the orchids become attractions which may be seen, touched, smelled and admired.

As a consequence of being so well integrated into a home, the cultural maintenance of a sun porch should be as automatic as possible, and always tempered toward human comfort as well as toward orchid requirements. The two are not incompatible. Automation shortens many seemingly endless routines, and practical heating-cooling-humidifying equipment is available everywhere. The simplest method of heating, of course, is with small electric radiant units, adequately baffled from the orchids and thermostatically controlled. An inconspicuous electric fan (four- or five-inch-diameter blades) near the ceiling will insure gentle air circulation. Ventilation is only a matter of a slightly opened pane of glass. Humidity is supplied by large pans of gravel and water.

When automated heat and humidity are impracticable, particularly in temperate areas, keep the sun porch slightly cooler than the rest of the house. Each morning let the sun's warmth raise the temperature of the porch slowly, retaining the heat as long as possible after nightfall. Offset low humidity by mist-spraying orchid foliage during the bright warmer days. Air exchange is likely to

Platyclinis glumaceae

The delicately fragrant and pendant sprays of P. glumaceae are white or ivory. Other platyclinis (perhaps a half-dozen species) tend more toward yellow and pale green flowers. Each tiny flower on the ten-inch stems is not easily seen, but, densely arranged, they make a pleasing display. This warm species takes to household situations with remarkable ease and can be beautifully grown in baskets, where the short leaves fill a decorative need. Most platyclinis bloom in or near March, and all are epiphytes though grown as semiterrestrials. Water is liberally supplied while growing, not so much when resting. The pseudobulbs have an agreeable habit of sending up three or more side shoots, which makes propagation rather rapid.

be sufficient from the interstices of frames and connecting forms. In good weather a door opened into the house is often enough to freshen the air and to permit some warmth to reach the porch.

Install, if necessary, supplementary lighting and dramatize it. Don't light all of the plant area, only a small part. Isolate it with curtains at night and move into it those orchids that may need additional stimulation. A more adroit practice is to fill a porch only with flowering plants. Orchids not in bloom are kept in basements or garages under continuous light and more ideal conditions. As flower buds begin to open, orchids are moved to the porch. Such an arrangement is not a tedious operation, and it does achieve rather spectacular results. It is, indeed, one of the best ways to keep a constant display of orchids in the home.

The Cattleyas

The best-known orchid flower, beloved of hobbyists and cherished by elegant women for nearly a hundred years, is the cattleya, popularly called the corsage orchid. Its delicate formality, texture, shape and color are incomparably suitable for all ceremonial occasions, either as a dress accessory or as a table accent. Yet within the cattleya family of species and hybrids are other, often lovelier, floral variations than those commonly seen in florist shops. In size they may be as large as a formal service plate, exquisitely small, or anywhere in between these extremes. They may be multicolored or pleasantly monochromatic, even fragrant. And all of them will possess an elegance almost beyond belief. Somewhere within this tremendous range there will be a flower to please each individual. Fortunately, because of their popularity, cattleyas are among the easiest orchids to grow—not too demanding in their cultural requirements, and comfortably adapting themselves to most home and garden situations. Reasonable attention to their needs is almost an assurance of success.

Within this orchid family, some cattleya hybrid or an improved species will always be in bloom. It is the only orchid family—or plant family of any kind—in which some member blooms every month of the year. Homeowners who have neither the equipment, the place, nor the desire to keep many orchids exploit this floral calendar. They buy a mature cattleya in bud, enjoy the developing flowers for a month to six weeks, then pass it along to friends who salvage it. This is like having cake and eating it as well. As far as it goes, such cultural expediency is not unsound. It is not usually more expensive than buying good cut flowers. And it can easily be made more permanent at any time. Homes are nearly always comfortable for cattleyas.

The first of the great cattleyas, a labiate—so named for its magnificent lip—was bought by William Cattley long ago at a London auction. It was a poor specimen, badly damaged, so the story goes, and there was little expectancy that it would live, let alone bloom. But it did, flowering in 1823 or soon thereafter and perpetuating the name of the hobbyist. The fragile and inexpressibly

Laeliocattleya Goliath

When two orchid families are crossed, the product of the union bears the names of both parents in some euphonious arrangement. So a Laelia crossed with a Cattleya becomes a Laeliocattleya, or Lc. as an abbreviation. Add a Brassavola to the mixture and the legend reads Brassolaeliocattleya, or Blc. If a fourth relative (Sophronitis) is brought into the complex, a new botanical name is created: Potinara. It is a sort of orchid shorthand which saves a lot of effort. Lc. Goliath is the latest and one of the greatest of the laeliocattleya hybrids, the end product of a long line of intense selective breeding for orange and yellow shades which John Dominy began in 1863 at the English nursery of Veitch—a cross that his predecessors considered impossible since orchids, they then believed, could not be cross-bred.

exotic qualities of the bloom and its rose-lilac color explosively set off one of the greatest plant hunts in the history of gardening and a long-lasting speculative frenzy over orchids. Sheer chance had permitted one of the loveliest of the cattleya species to be found early in the history of plant exploration, and it became the standard by which all orchids were to be judged for many years. Indeed, it still persists as the popular standard—dismayingly so.

Countries in South America's tropical belt were searched and stripped to locate other and better cattleyas. Many were found, some as delightful as the original, which was not rediscovered until seventy years later—a curious oversight since Mr. Cattley's orchid thrives in the Organ Mountains, sixty miles from Rio de Janeiro. Most modern hybrids are descendants of these early importations. Generally they are lovelier than the species, more colorful or blazingly pure white, better-shaped and longer-lasting flowers. The current trend toward miniaturization has shortened the foliage and provided a wide variety of floral sizes.

Also the intermingling of the species and hybrids with many of the orchids related to the cattleyas has produced multigeneric orchids with no definitive seasonal and flowering growth. These not infrequently may grow continuously (without a normal rest period) and flower twice, occasionally three times a year—an excellent habit which tends to negate the singularly unattractive leaves, not unlike certain kinds of cacti.

Watering, a critical routine with cattleyas, as it is with other epiphytes, therefore follows each orchid's growth pattern. As new leads appear from the base of the plant, water is added to the compost in limited quantities. More water is needed as the leads curve upward and grow vertically, and also as the roots break out. Low humidity during this period helps to initiate strong roots. The compost is saturated as the leads reach their vertical height and thicken into pseudobulbs. Then water less as the pseudobulbs ripen. No matter how much or how little water is used, there must be an extensive drying-out period afterward, one long enough to leave the compost completely dry. At least several days in summer, perhaps a week in winter. The amount of humidity, the nature of the compost, the size of the pot—all can delay or speed up the time it takes for the compost to dry. The factor is strictly a local one and must be learned through observation and experience.

The trouble lies in the cattleya's root system, which is not extensive—at least in culture. But once initiated, they are easily damaged by poorly aerated composts, by frequent handling, by concentrated fertilizers which burn them, and most of all by injudicious watering which rots them. Such careless injuries occur so regularly at first that a warning about them must be both insistent and emphatic.

Composts of any kind should be renewed every two or three years, at which time large plants may be divided into clumps of three or four pseudobulbs. Don't repot or divide cattleyas more often than is necessary. Feed cattleyas a high-nitrogen fertilizer, if chopped bark is used, and do so lightly during the growing season. Follow with a high-phosphorus food to strengthen flowering. Alternate feeding and watering so that the chemicals will not build up damaging concentrations.

Light can be critical. A lot of it is needed to ripen the pseudobulbs and produce flowers—so much light, in fact, that gardeners new to orchid culture consistently make the mistake of thinking that a little light is too much. Well-grown

Cattleya Brabantiae

During the early days of orchid hybridizing, indiscriminate crosses were made as fast as new species were introduced. There was little excuse for most crosses, except the desire to be the first to introduce a new creation. So Cattleya Brabantiae was made and lost—a combination of Cattleya loddigesii (a tall orchid) and C. aclandiae (small and excitingly different). The result was a dwarf orchid with a large flower resembling the C. aclandiae parent. Only in recent years, after the cross was remade, was C. Brabantiae recognized as an intriguing floral pattern in and for itself, fragrant, extremely well textured and lasting, and certainly one of the easiest cattleyas to grow.

Different from each other as these five flowers are, they are related, all with similar medium cultural requirements. Cattleya Tango (top left) is a color carrier, passing along its deep red shades to its progeny. The multi-fringed lip of Brassavola digbyana (bottom left)—a happy discovery in the Mexican-Honduran highlands—is a characteristic of many hybrids. Opposite page: Broughtonia sanguinea (top left), a dwarf from the Caribbean islands, is grown more for its own diminutive loveliness than for any hybrid contribution. Schomburgkia thompsonianum (top right), despite its robust and attractive appearance, has not been used much either, except for some early combinations with laelias. On the other hand, Diacattleya Colmanae (bottom), basically an epidendrum-cattleya combination, is producing cattleya-like flowers on miniature plants.

cattleyas, gradually hardened to sunlight, can stand 8,000 footcandles. That is about as bright as any day in the northern states is likely to get. The best cattleya range is within 2,000 to 3,000 footcandles. Inside a home, that amount of light is almost the equivalent of a fully exposed eastern or western window, or a mildly protected southern exposure.

Another indication of a cattleya's adaptability is its acceptance of rather wide temperature variations: a winter night minimum of 50° to a summer day maximum of 90°. The temperature can go higher or lower for a short time, even several days, but it is the better part of orchid wisdom to try and remain within acceptable lmits. Changes in temperature must be gradual, even the important day/night variation of 15° to 20°. Ventilation is continuous, mild, gentle, indirect and never suddenly hot or chillingly cold.

Flowering in cattleyas is commonly initiated by lower night temperatures followed with little water or, sometimes, a slightly longer drying-out period than is usual. Since they are all within the medium-temperature group, the customary temperature differential between day and night is normally sufficient. Flower sheaths, envelopes of tissue projecting from the top of pseudobulbs, normally continue growing along with the leaves. Sometimes, though, buds do not immediately develop within them; buds may wait several months or longer before appearing and then grow rapidly. More often the buds are part of the orchid's progressive development, and the flowers emerge as part of a continuing sequence.

Humidity follows the daily pattern: little in the morning, increasing with the temperature, and falling off toward nightfall. Some orchidists believe that 50 percent is a good average for humidity; others maintain more or less humidity as their local conditions may indicate.

Characteristically, the less artificial heat is used, the healthier cattleyas seem to be. In Florida and the Southwest, where little or no winter heat is applied, the flowering response of cattleyas is incredible. Some of this vigor can be duplicated elsewhere by moving cattleyas outdoors late in spring, leaving them under trees or lath or saran shade until early fall. As they harden themselves to these more natural conditions, they seem to store enough food to carry them through difficult winters.

As sympodial epiphytes, cattleyas have been divided into two botanical groups: the labiates, with one leaf, large, showy flowers and quixotic lips; and the bifoliates, which have two leaves carried on tall, spindly, unattractive pseudobulbs. The many-clustered flowers of bifoliates are smaller, of better substance and longer lasting. In recent years the hybrids between these groups have reduced the spindly pseudobulbs to better proportions, and increased the floral sizes.

The leaves of labiates and bifoliates are similar—hard, waxy, leathery and stiff when healthy. They are direct clues to cultural errors; blue-green in too much shade, yellow-green when correctly grown in sufficient light, wrinkled when desiccated by dry air or heat or lack of water and even destroyed root systems, spotted brown from sunburn, or dotted with watery black spots from cold and damp atmospheres.

Labiates will generally flower during the winter and spring; bifoliates, from summer to fall. Their hybrids bloom somewhere between the extremes of the parents. This is also true of the multigeneric crosses between cattleyas and laelias, epidendrums, sophronitis, brassavolas, schomburgkias, and broughtonias, all of whose culture, for the most part, is remarkably similar to that for cattleyas.

Diacrium bicornutum

Almost unknown for years, Diacrium bicornutum (now known as Caularthron bicornutum) has all the advantages of a vigorous heritage (it is closely related to the epidendrums, with which it is often confused) and surprisingly lovely white, three-inch flowers gently touched with crimson spots. A native of Trinidad and Guiana, it flowers in late spring. When actively growing, it can use more warmth and moisture than would be expected of its medium temperature classification. It has been grown as a semiterrestrial, but bark or chopped tree-fern fiber is a more suitable compost base.

They can be grown as companion plants in any collection. The extraordinary diversity among cattleyas, their relatives and their incredibly mixed progeny is so great that the most exacting gardener or hobbyist can find exciting choices of appealing flowers, useful sizes, textures strong enough to last for weeks or longer, colors that are brighter than a rainbow and softer than velvet—almost without limit in shades and tints and hues, even to the palest of crystal blues.

The following tabulation is merely a condensation of the cultural requirements of cattleyas: TEMPERATURE: medium, 55° to 90°. HUMIDITY: 40 to 80 percent. LIGHT: 2,000 to 3,000 footcandles. AIR: mild circulation. WATER: alternately wet-dry. FEEDING: 30–10–10 while growing, 10–20–10 before flowering. PROPAGATION: division. REPOT: 2 to 3 years. COMPOST: bark; optional: tree-fern or osmunda. HABIT: sympodial epiphyte. REST: short to several weeks.

The Cymbidiums

Easy to grow. How nice that sounds about any plant, and most of all about an orchid. Yet it is quite true. Of all orchids, cymbidiums are the least troublesome and yield fabulous amounts of flowers.

The major impetus to cymbidium culture came from the huge, hybrid-cymbidium ranches of southern California. Outdoor culture under lath, the filtered light of oak trees, in sheltered gardens and terraces was—and remains—so effortless that it astounded experts. Californians suddenly and enthusiastically became orchid-conscious. Since then, cymbidiums have become the second most important orchid flower crop, equalling or replacing cattleyas in home gardens.

It is so simple to grow a large clump of cymbidiums with ten or twenty flower stems and upward of four hundred flowers. Every spring garden show will have one or two such exhibition plants. The record may have been set by an Englishman whose cymbidium had 270 stems, 6,750 flowers. Of course such a plant is too large for the average garden or home, but the relative ease with which cymbidiums can be grown makes a hundred flowers a distinct possibility.

There is, however, a small catch. Cymbidiums will not flower unless summer nights are cool: 45° to 55°, never higher. And the day/night temperature difference should be 10° to 20°. If those temperatures can be provided—or induced artificially—cymbidiums will flower prodigiously. The absence of a low night temperature in summer is the major reason cymbidiums will not grow well in Florida, many of the other southern states and Hawaii. It is also why they don't flower easily. The Hawaiians get around this limiting factor by moving their cymbidiums to the lower mountains near Honolulu, and, most successfully, by shifting them to the higher elevations on Maui and Hilo. Such a custom, when not inconveniently ridiculous, would be acceptable in this country where low mountains are accessible.

Another method of insuring low night temperatures is to install evaporative coolers, sometimes described as desert coolers, or air conditioning. On August 1—give or take a few weeks—as new cymbidium growths start to swell and form

Cymbidium hybrid

Nothing can be said about cymbidiums that they cannot better show for themselves. Hardy nearly everywhere in the subtropical United States where the night temperature is low, equally hardy and better-flowered in the more equitable temperate regions, cymbidiums are essentially garden plants. They repay considerate attention to their requirements with sturdy flowers, colorful and profuse. If any orchid can be described as the common man's orchid, it is the cymbidium.

pseudobulbs, turn on the cooler in the late afternoon. Turn it off at eleven o'clock in the evening. How many days or weeks the cooler operates depends on the night temperature. When it is stabilized at 55°, cooling is no longer mandatory. It is not too much of a hardship to carry a few plants indoors, place them under artificial lights and cool them with the home's air conditioning. It may be troublesome, but it is rewarding. Elsewhere in the United States it is helpful to move cymbidiums outdoors after the last spring frost. Leave them under laths or trees or screens until the first frost of fall. Their health is incomparably improved. Sunlight, too, is important to cymbidiums. Some orchidists suggest giving cymbidiums full morning and late afternoon sunlight and 50 percent of the midday light, more than that in winter. Others variously estimate the intensity of the sunlight as 2,000 to 8,000 footcandles. Cymbidiums have been grown at both extremes, but the optimum is somewhere in between—probably around 3,000 footcandles.

Cymbidiums, since they are terrestrials, must be fertilized. But doing so may involve many different practices and as many different opinions. All of them are likely to be correct for the particular locality in which they were conceived. It is always desirable, as well as a sound garden practice, to observe and to apply local disciplines, particularly when soil-based composts are used. Then cymbidiums are nourished with a balanced formula at least biweekly, and more often in summer. During August or September, change to a low nitrogen, high-phosphorous formula to insure vigorous flowering.

Unless grown in coarse fir bark, cymbidium composts are as varied as the locality in which they are found. Most orchidists accept local materials and mix them with commercial products. Composts in the South, for example, are likely to be softer and more porous than those used in northern states. But all will consist of some selective and limited combinations of old osmunda, bark, redwood fiber, gravel, sand, vermiculite, leaf mold, aged manures, poultry peat, bone meal, powdered horn meal, perhaps superphosphate or potash and—always—rich humus soil. Although lime is occasionally added to composts as a buffering influence, cymbidiums prefer an acid reaction. Whatever the materials, the indispensable element in any Cymbidium compost is porosity—the capability of draining quickly and yet retaining considerable moisture for good root development. One of the simplest formulas was suggested by a California grower: fir bark, 50 percent; horticultural peat, 30 percent; clean, washed sand, 5 percent. The bark and the peat are dampened before mixing; otherwise it is difficult to wet them later. To each small sackful of the compost, add a large handful of crushed limestone and a very small handful of superphosphate.

When cymbidiums are grown outdoors in garden borders, almost any soil will do if it is thoroughly laced with sand or gravel and rich humus and raised above the surrounding ground for better drainage. A simpler plan is to grow the cymbidiums in large pots, sink them into the ground and remove them to sheltered places as the weather dictates.

Watering is consistent—considerable moisture during the growing season, slightly less at other times. Outdoors this may be daily; indoors, once a week. The composts and the cymbidium leaf tips can indicate the frequency. Too little water shows up in the blackened tips of the leaves. While not aesthetic, it isn't dangerous, and the leaf tips are better left uncut since a contagious virus disease is so easily spread by infected garden tools. Too much water is indicated by yellowing leaves, shriveling pseudobulbs—the result of rotted, useless roots. The

The most successful of new orchid creations are the mini-cymbidiums, hybrids between the standards and the dwarfs from warmer regions (China, Japan and Australia). They possess the same outstanding cultural characteristics of the larger varieties, the same ease of growth, vigor, and many beautiful flowers. A plant in a five-inch pot may have seventy to a hundred flowers. They are less dependent (frequently not at all) on low night temperatures to induce flowering, or maintain healthy growth. The flowers can be as small as a quarter but are more likely to be two or three inches wide. In homes the mini-cymbidiums occupy no more window space than the smaller-leaf begonias—and do so to better advantage. Top row: Cymbidium Pipeta; *Cym.* Minneken 'Pink Glow', AM/ODC; *Bottom row: Cym.* Flirtation; *Cym.* Impish.

only remedy is to clean the cymbidiums, repot them, proceed more carefully.

Humidity is needful but not objectionably so; perhaps from 20 to 40 percent. Never avoid it, although its absence from time to time will not be injurious. Merely syringing the foliage takes care of much of the requirement indoors and outside. In very dry regions a mist spray, controlled automatically, can drift moisture over the foliage.

The first cymbidiums, parents of the modern hybrids, came from an extremely limited plant belt in northern India, Burma, Thailand and Vietnam. Although this belt is part of the tropics, cymbidiums live so far up on the mountains that they cannot be considered tropical (at least in relation to heat) by any stretch of the imagination. Their homeland temperature stretches from 70° to 100° in the daytime. Nights are always cooler, occasionally down to freezing and lower. Rain is heavy, 120 inches, during the cymbidiums' growing season. The rich soil is never without moisture in the dry season. These are the factors which must be translated into garden practices. Mentioning them at this point is only to reemphasize cool nights, indifferently high day temperature if accompanied by cooling mists, indirect but strong sunlight, moderately heavy fertilizer requirements, copious amounts of water and a well-drained loam or compost.

The exceptions to these conditions are the small flowering species—dwarf cymbidiums from the warmer, lower mountain levels; miniatures from China, Japan and Australia. Their value, an inestimable one, is as parents (bred with the larger cymbidiums) capable of producing medium-sized plants that are compact in foliage and retain almost normal flower sizes. Their virtue is that they do not insist on cool nights and a temperature differential in order to flower. They will be as much at home in Florida as they would be in Maine or Texas. A five-inch pot holding a miniature cymbidium with a hundred flowers is not uncommon. Cymbidium flowers, averaging four inches for the standards and two or three inches for the dwarfs, open in winter and spring and last for several months uncut. There is a fascinating spread of pastel colors and of deep, rich hues. The lime-green and emerald shades are justly famous in the plant world. For this reason, as well as for ease of culture, it is probably impossible to surpass cymbidiums as garden plants. As one gardener exclaimed with delight, after growing cymbidiums for several years, "If you can't grow any other plant, you can grow cymbidiums!"

TEMPERATURE: cool to medium, 45° to 90°. HUMIDITY: 40 to 60 percent. LIGHT: 2,000 to 4,000 footcandles. WATER: consistent moisture. AIR: vigorous. FOOD: balanced, biweekly. HABIT: sympodial terrestrial. PROPAGATION: division. REPOT: 2 to 4 years. COMPOST: terrestrial, porous. REST: little or none.

The Dendrobiums

The tremendous spread of the great dendrobium genus over East Asia, across the Pacific islands and into northern Australia is an explicit indication of their garden requirements. Many dendrobiums will need continuous warmth and moisture; others will expect some cooler seasons and a longish dry period. By

Cymbidium finlaysonianum

Not all the botanical cymbidiums are attractive in a commercially acceptable way, but many of them more than make up for that in unusual and interesting appearance. The sort of tigerish look of Cymbidium finlaysonianum from Malaysia is handsome by any standard. Its two- to three-inch flowers, opening in early summer and carried on pendant stems, are brownish yellow and the white lip is striped with red. It is a warmer-growing orchid than the larger cymbidiums and at ease, culturally, in the subtropics of the United States.

Dendrobium Hawaii *(opposite);* Dendrobium nobile *(below)*

When dendrobiums come into flower, their appearance is so eminently satisfying that hobby growers try from time to time to commercialize them. But this has never really succeeded. For some reason, dendrobiums have only had a kind of fringe attraction for the flower-buying public. Nonetheless, they will always be a continuous source of pleasure to gardeners. Dendrobium nobile will often look overloaded with rosy-purple, three-inch flowers. And it, as well as a companion species, D. superbiens, summer-ripen outdoors so well that both will succeed in flowering even when occasionally neglected later indoors. Dendrobium Hawaii is no less attractive; its gorgeous scarlet combinations make up for its relative shortage of flowers.

and large, that is exactly how it works out. Botanists separate the family of dendrobiums into five subsections—nice to know as a fact of orchid life or as a detailed index of their floral and vegetative structures. But a simpler division is the cultural one: evergreen and deciduous. The evergreen dendrobiums are grown as warm orchids. The deciduous species, which lose their leaves before or during flowering, require warmth while actively growing. Then they demand a cooler temperature, at least 10° lower to initiate flower buds, little or no humidity and almost no water around their roots while resting.

Not all deciduous dendrobiums survive so easily. For some, the months following a monsoon can be hazardously dry. Others struggle constantly against a hostile climate—baked, broiled, shriveled for three months by the Australian sun. Then, as more temperate conditions return, they suddenly break into bloom. Over the hundreds of thousands of years that they have existed, their floral response is triggered by this unsympathetic condition. Without it they will not flower.

Of course it would be ridiculous to duplicate such perils in home gardens. They can, however, easily be simulated by lowering the night temperature, by increasing the light and air that reach the plants and by withholding water to the extent that the pseudobulbs tend to shrivel. One of the best ways of accomplishing this, no matter where or how dendrobiums ordinarily are grown (even the warm species), is to take them outdoors as early in spring as possible. Leave them there until the night temperature drops back to 55°. Protection from summer midday sun is desirable, although deciduous dendrobiums can be acclimated to full sunlight.

Among their thousand members (dendrobiums are the largest orchid family) are species that scarcely reach an inch in length; others stretch upward to ten feet. A few are pendulous and must be hung downward from baskets or tree-fern slabs. One species looks like small clusters of fuzzy, greenish caterpillars—although most dendrobium pseudobulbs resemble nothing so much as bamboo stems.

Some dendrobiums have sprays of ten to twenty flowers. Some bear flowers in clusters of two or three from nodes on the stems. Some may have hundreds and hundreds of flowers, falling in a curtain of gold. In Asiatic gardens well-grown dendrobiums may carry four thousand flowers, and nine thousand have been counted on a single plant. All in all, this is an exciting group of orchids whose red, magenta, purple, gold, white, and yellow flowers are magnificent— a family full of surprises and joys, not the least of which is the extraordinary fact that so few of them have been introduced to culture.

In garden collections dendrobiums may be grown with cattleyas, except that the evergreens will occupy the warmer situations; the deciduous, the cooler sections. And both should be exposed to as much light as they can stand. Indoors this means, almost mandatorily, a large southerly window with protection from radiant burns and chills and probably, even then, supplementary lighting in the northern states during the winter. Shading is minimal with both groups: only sufficient to prevent burning or dehydration.

Should the temperature remain high while the deciduous dendrobiums are resting, the chances are better than good that only vegetative offshoots will be produced, not flowers. This is pleasantly advantageous if more plants are wanted. It is also the primary reason these deciduous orchids do not flower well in subtropical areas of the country, whereas the evergreens are more tolerant.

To recapitulate briefly: dendrobiums grow in the summer, flower in winter

Dendrobium **Purple Crown**

and spring. The evergreens are best grown warm, with lots of water most of the year, considerable humidity and plenty of light and air. Conditions should be mildly cooler and drier as they get ready to flower. The deciduous varieties are carried as warm orchids during their active growth, with copious water, light and air, and relatively good humidity. Once the thin, bamboo-like pseudobulbs are fully developed, a temperature drop into the cold group is necessary. Then very little water about their roots, barely enough to prevent the pseudobulbs from shriveling.

Feeding is essential since the growth of both dendrobium groups is rapid. The type of fertilizer will depend upon the compost: in bark a 30–10–10 followed by a 10–20–10 before flowering. A balanced fertilizer for other composts, usually at weekly intervals or biweekly; none after flowering until new growth commences again.

EVERGREEN DENDROBIUMS. TEMPERATURE: warm, a minimum of 60°. HUMIDITY: 50 to 70 percent. LIGHT: 1,500 to 2,500 footcandles. AIR: brisk, no drafts. WATER: moist at all times. FEEDING: 30–10–10 biweekly while growing. PROPAGATION: division. REPOT: 2 years, as new growth starts. COMPOST: bark or tree-fern. REST: slight. HABIT: sympodial epiphyte.

DECIDUOUS DENDROBIUMS. TEMPERATURE: warm, 60° while growing; medium 50° while resting. HUMIDITY: 40 percent. LIGHT: 1,500 to 3,000 footcandles. AIR: brisk. WATER: moist while growing. FEEDING: 30–10–10 during active growth. PROPAGATION: division, offshoots, cuttings. REPOT: 2 years, as new growth starts. COMPOST: bark or tree-fern. REST: 2 weeks to a month. HABIT: sympodial epiphyte.

Outdoor Gardens

An orchidist once described orchid gardens as "a precious gift of benevolent nature." Nature's benevolence may vary widely, but orchids in the garden are a pleasure that everyone should indulge—all the time where it is possible to do so, and part of the time in those regions where the climate is less permissive.

Orchids grown outdoors the year round in Florida, Hawaii and Puerto Rico possess a subtle richness of color not easily duplicated in artificial surroundings. Indeed, there is something about the outdoor life, if only for a month or two, that imparts vigor to orchids, ripens their pseudobulbs, and prepares them for voluminous flowering through the dull days of winter.

European gardeners have long known and understood this fact of orchid life. Many of the early orchid imports did not flower until weathered outdoors. Indeed, most terrestrials and semi-epiphytes will not perform well until summer-hardened. Mexican and South American gardeners, with climates remarkably similar to the temperate zones, flower the hardier orchids in patios. But other than in parts of Florida and southern California, American gardeners have been

Oncidium altissimum

A graceful native of the West Indies, Oncidium altissimum naturalizes quickly in southern Florida and, when left intact for years, can regain all of the charm it possesses in the orchid forests of the Caribbean islands. In fact, it is best grown in such outdoor situations, since its flowering spikes may be six feet long and covered with hundreds of nodding, dancing yellow and brown one-inch flowers.

indifferent to naturalized planting and have avoided summer vacations for their orchids. The weather is most frequently cited as the offender: too hot, too dry, too humid, too cold, too windy or too short a season. Nevertheless, many of these natural limitations can be altered, the excesses modified, the missing elements included so that normal orchid growth may be unimpeded, or at least extended, outdoors.

In the San Fernando Valley, where frosts may last intermittently for several months, infrared lamps or strong air currents tend to prevent accumulations of ice crystals in orchid tissues. Heavier shading and mist sprays, the morning after a frost, slow down the progress of melting crystals so that liquid pressures within leaf tissues are not suddenly injurious. Gardeners in Arizona, where the dry climate is a virtue for people, construct low cloth or lath or plastic houses to conserve humidity built up with sprinklers. Gusty winds that dehydrate plant tissues are tempered by preventive fencing or shields of plastic; shrubs and small trees also offer considerable protection. Certainly there are many problems in different climates and locations across the country, but nothing that is impossible to modify for the two or three months that orchids may be outdoors.

It is difficult to offer rules for the selection of garden locations for orchids. They have succeeded in many places. The best starting point may be a cool, semi-shaded porch or terrace, or the cool ground beneath a large tree. Plants can easily be tended and carefully watched for danger signs until they are well established. Later, more natural garden spots may be chosen and tried and, where necessary, made temporarily suitable. But whether terrace or garden, tree or border, the area will need good air circulation and filtered light at midday. Not heavy or dense shade, only the sort of semi-light that is found beneath old oaks. The ground should be cool and moist, not so much for the orchid roots (keep the plants in pots) as for providing coolness near the roots and the gradual release of moisture into the surrounding air. Regardless of dry air anywhere else in the garden, moist soil—its saturation moderately increased by sprinkling or hosing—provides adequate humidity close to the orchids, where it is most needed.

Only in the mild areas of the country should orchids be naturalized permanently. When that is possible the fun and enjoyment are tremendous, the labor brief and inconsequential. A border of vandas growing in the sun must be seen to be believed. A few sobralias, although their flowers only last a day, flower successively with delightful ease. Phalaenopsis placed in the crotches of oak and mango trees spill their flowers from sprays like dancing butterflies. Many oncidiums and most epidendrums will grow on nearly anything—and do. Bletias used as ground covers can overwinter in the ground as far north as Washington, D.C. Many of the warm orchids are potentially good for naturalization, and most of the medium-temperature group are excellent. However, common sense and the climate will limit any selection to the hardiest varieties.

Orchids in pots and on tree-fern slabs are probably the most convenient, as well as being inherently ornamental. They can be hung from the branches of trees in the most favored positions, protected thus from the ravages of occasional squirrels and rodents who consider young orchids so delicious, or easily shifted to new or better locations. Whereas establishing orchids on trees is something of a job and, unless it is correctly done, the orchids may suffer. Their roots must be held firmly against the rough bark until they rigidly and inescapably anchor themselves. Select the strongest orchids and clean their roots thoroughly of all previous composts. Spread the roots along the bark of a branch or tree trunk.

In most of the United States it is possible to grow orchids outdoors at least for several months, and often longer, without too much involvement. Protective structures can be as simple as the northern lathhouse, a formal extension of the residence. Or they can be informally located in a garden, as illustrated by the extruded metal-lattice house in southern Florida. And there are all sorts of constructions between these extremes, both larger and smaller, in which orchids may usefully and healthfully be indulged outdoors during the warmer days between early spring and late fall.

Cover the roots with an inch of osmunda, holding it tightly in place with nailed hardware cloth or nylon fish netting. Water well, and repeat the watering every few days. Success thereafter is merely a matter of time.

The Miltonias

Except for a moderate difference in light requirements and a slight temperature differential, both cool and warm miltonias have the same culture. Yet the failure to realize the importance of these two distinctions—or just not being aware of them—caused many of the early failures with miltonias. Growers and hobbyists once considered them difficult horticultural subjects. Also, the urgent need of both miltonia groups for cool nights in order to initiate their flower buds was overlooked, and their floral habits were considered to be temperamentally indifferent.

Difficult, temperamental, indifferently responsive—miltonias are not. After the climatic key to their culture unlocked their beauty, they became for a while popular kitchen and parlor plants in European homes. That they were ever replaced in the affection of gardeners was due only to the increasing numbers of plants available, introduced during a period when novelty was the fashion. Within their modest limitations, miltonias are still excellent house guests and are superbly at home in basements and garages totally under artificial light and air conditioning. In all of the northern states, from east to west, and in some of the mountainous regions, miltonias are simple to grow, since the highest temperature these so-called Pansy orchids will accept is 80°; the lowest, 55°.

Miltonias are lovely beyond the obvious charms of giant garden pansies, which they do resemble remarkably in size and round, flat showy flower faces. There, however, the similarities end and the miltonias dramatically go further. Their flower faces, four or six to a gently arched stem, are not pinche. Neither do they wither early; they last for weeks in spite of their fragile appearance. Conceivably, even the most beautiful of garden pansies would be envious of the miltonias' color range: white, pink, red, yellow, peach and purple, and simple, striking combination of these colors. Miltonia foliage is neat, and the thin, light green leaves fan out over the edges of the pots in an attractive manner. When not flowering, the handsome miltonia foliage has many ornamental uses.

The most important single fact to remember about miltonias is that there are two kinds: warm and cool. Visually, it is impossible to determine the difference between them. Only a botanical reference book or grower's catalog will indicate their classification. Sometimes the temperature may be indicated as medium, which will probably indicate a hybrid that has split its parents' preferences. It is also a good starting point for miltonias whose temperature status is unknown. In a very short time miltonias will indicate by their growth a decided partiality for either a cooler or a warmer position.

Occasionally a geographical or national name may be used to describe mil-

Miltonia Eros var. Kensington

The dark, dark three-inch faces of this Miltonia—*so deeply velvety purple as to appear almost black— are simple by comparison with the ornate, complex structures of other orchids. Yet within this simplicity is, possibly, the purest form of beauty. Such at least is the opinion of gardeners who specialize in the modern hybrids of this orchid group, whose original members total fewer than twenty-five.*

Following two pages:

Miltonia Dearest *(left)*

Miltonia Funny Face *(right)*

tonias: Brazilian or Colombian—a designation often utilized to describe differences in coffee, and for much the same reason. The warm miltonias come from an area near Rio de Janeiro; these are the ones referred to as Brazilian. Usually they, and their hybrids, are amenable to indoor culture and windowsill gardening. The cool group is found in the cordillera highlands of South America and are called Colombians. Success with cool miltonias depends in great part on avoiding excessive warmth and stabilizing the temperature around 70°.

In actual practice, the terms warm and cool, as applied to miltonias, are relative. They do not mean exactly what they would with other orchid groups—only that within the optimum 20° range, from 60° to 80°, the Colombian miltonias will prefer the cooler end by day; the Brazilians, the upper limits. Both are adamant about night temperatures as close to 60° as possible. When the temperature does go to 80° or beyond, the best remedy is to increase the shading.

Another fact to bear in mind is the light intensity. Brazilian miltonias can use 3,500 footcandles; the Colombians rarely more than 1,500, except in winter—seemingly a contradiction since both groups come from mountainous regions. The Colombians, however, are used to morning mists which dilute the sunlight. The light for both groups is luminous rather than intense, brilliant yet soft. In terms of familiar conditions, such light is quite similar to the bounced or reflected illumination found in the most advanced electrically equipped homes.

It can be easily and correctly inferred from these slight temperature and light differentials that miltonias do not like abrupt changes. Everything done for them should be done in moderation.

Water carefully and consistently to insure a moist (though not saturated) compost at all times. Miltonia roots are very thin, not very extensive, and seem to have a sort of semiterrestrial attitude toward their composts. Leaves that are wrinkled indicate too little water or none at all. And avoid spilling water on the thin leaves; at low temperature levels, damp rot is almost inevitable, particularly if there is little air movement. One of the sounder practices today is to have a small fan operating day and night where miltonias are grown.

Humidity is moderate, 50 to 70 percent, and can be drastically increased for a little while should temperatures go above 80°. Under such circumstances, humidity is only a temporary aid at best; shade and evaporative coolers are more practicable and effective.

Soft osmunda composts, loose and porous, mixed with gravel, have long been standard for miltonias. Recently, small fir bark particles mixed with various local products (shredded redwood and tree-fern fiber) have come into favor. This mixture seems to give better water control. A monthly or biweekly feeding of a very dilute, balanced liquid fertilizer is beneficial when miltonias are grown in osmunda, and a 30–10–10 is mandatory for bark mixtures.

Underpot rather than overpot, and use clay containers rather than plastic pots. Divide miltonias cautiously after flowering, and as indicated by decayed compost rather than the size of the plants. Repotting is a definite shock to their systems. Also, large clumps, retaining their vigor, flower more heavily. Specimen plants are very showy, as each newly matured pseudobulb tends to send up two flowering stems.

There is no real resting period for miltonias. As a result, they continue growing at a remarkable pace. Although they generally flower from late spring to early summer, many of the hybrids will bloom at other times of the year, and frequently twice. So it is entirely possible to extend the flowering season, by

Brassia gireoudeana

Some people purport to see in the shape of Brassia gireoudeana's yellow-green flowers the head, horns and tongue of a dragon. It is possible; but even more curious is the fact that brassias are related to odontoglossums and miltonias. Brassias are indulgent plants indoors, since their Mexican origin is definitely a hardy one. Medium warmth while growing, but cooler than would be expected. Moderate shade and good moisture, but a definite rest period (since they are epiphytes with pseudobulbs), and a semiterrestrial compost for the roots, which are thin, will produce an abundance of the twelve-inch (overall) flowers.

wise choices, as well as to include a tremendous floral color spectrum.

TEMPERATURE: moderately cool to warm, 60° to 80°. HUMIDITY: 40 to 70 percent. LIGHT: Colombian, 1,000 to 1,500 footcandles; Brazilian, 2,000 to 3,500 footcandles. AIR: mild. WATER: consistent moisture. FOOD: dilute 30–10–10 or a balanced fertilizer, biweekly. REPOT: 2 to 4 years, or as required. COMPOST: bark, shredded redwood and tree-fern, osmunda. PROPAGATION: division. REST: none. HABIT: sympodial epiphyte.

The Odontoglossums

The culture of few orchids has been so thoroughly investigated as that of Andean odontoglossums. Yet were it not for their classical beauty, probably no attempt would have been made to grow them. Early orchidists found it difficult to reconcile themselves to the fact that these singularly attractive exotics could not live without an alpine environment. They cannot be well grown much above or below 70°, prefer a longish day with soft, even lighting and need a consistent level of humidity. This very narrow limitation of the temperature-humidity-light relationship does not permit much leeway. Nonetheless, acceptance of these exacting terms, and compliance with them, results in the most stunning floral shapes and color spectrums within the orchid world—many four-inch, star-shaped, frilled-edge flowers carried on elegantly arched stems and bewitchingly mottled with red or yellow or mahogany on a background of pure white. No two flowers on separate plants are ever exactly alike.

As might be expected from these color variations, there is an extraordinary abundance of natural hybrids among the Andeans, and botanical nomenclature is a nightmare. Just naming them—and there are at least several hundred known hybrids for each known parent—is utterly bewildering, not to mention attempting to identify parents of the hybrids with any accuracy. Sometimes the reasons for selecting botanical names surpass credulity. The word odontoglossum, for example, means tooth-tongue—a reference to an insignificant protuberance on the floral lip. Among the orchid groups to which odontoglossums are closely related—and very easily crossed—are miltonias, named for an English viscount and garden patron, and oncidiums, whose name freely translates to "waxy excrescence"! Two more relatives, brassias (named for William Brass, a nineteenth-century collector) and cochliodas (meaning a spiral), intercross with themselves and with all of the others in a complex botanical patchwork of bi-, tri- and quadrigeneric hybrids, each with its own new name. The simpler names are recognizable combinations of two families, Odontioda and Brassidium, for instance. Vuylstekeara, Wilsonara, Colmanara, Sanderara and Burrageara—in honor of long-dead plantsmen who merited recognition—are composites of three of the families. And there are other major multigeneric crosses among these orchid families (about twenty of them) to be made!

If this is not enough potential confusion, consider the vegetative characteristics. A description of one is remarkably like any other—short pseudobulbs with two or three thin leaves about a foot long—which, incidentally, makes all of them great

Odontoglossum hallii

In spite of being overshadowed by the popular crispum varieties, Odontoglossum hallii is a grogeous botanical orchid. A well-known Ecuadorian, its white, three-inch flowers are vividly splashed with red, and it is not so unreasonable to grow as the crispums sometimes can be. For that matter, most of the botanical odontoglossums, especially the dwarf species from Costa Rica, Guatemala and Mexico, are often recommended as houseplants in the cooler sections of the United States. O. pulchellum flowers in spring and is said to be fragrant, although most botanists and plant collectors insist that odontoglossums are not scented. O. Rossii has cream, green, brown and white flowers which are a welcome winter touch. And O. citrosum has variably colored flowers—though most frequently white and yellow—that appear in spring.

space savers in any collection. Fortunately, however, for gardeners, the immediate family of odontoglossums can be reduced to five cultural divisions, of which only three are important horticulturally.

THE ANDEAN GROUP, known commonly as Colombians and familiarly as cris-pums, are the most popular and beautiful of the odontoglossums. Found in the Colombian Andes near Bogotá, they spread southward to Ecuador. Few wild plants remain of this absorbingly interesting family now almost extinct from excessive collecting.

As a cool group, the Andeans have little tolerance for temperatures much above 70°, but they won't die if the temperature occasionally rises to 90° or drops to 30°. Although plant explorers often mention seeing frost and icicles on Andeans, their growth is impeded at the low point, and their resistance to disease is drastically reduced at the high. A prolonged exposure to a hot spell is completely disastrous. A daytime spread between 70° and 75° with a nightly drop to 60° is an ideal arrangement. This extremely narrow temperature range is an almost adamant requirement for their cultural health. In fact, when grown completely with artificial light, exactly temperature-controlled air conditioning at 70° day and night, humidity constant at 70 percent all of the time—then the Andeans' response is incredible. They grow and flower continuously, or so nearly so as to make no essential difference. And this in spite of the fact that in their homeland they do have a sort of resting period, flowering primarily in spring and early summer.

Happily for all orchidists, the breeding program among the odontoglossums—including their close relatives—is improving their cultural habits. The low temperature standard is being raised to a medium level with a better light-humidity relationship. It should not be long as such programs go before the Andeans have little scruples, if any, about their culture. In the meantime, it is the better part of orchid wisdom to grow Andeans within regions where a suitable climate prevails: the northwestern and northeastern coastal areas, some of the mountain states, and those along the Canadian border. Elsewhere the only solution is some form of air conditioning or evaporative coolers. No one has priced the cost per flower of these cooling and humidifying systems. It may be high in terms of monetary values, when applied to Andean odontoglossums, but certainly not prohibitive in terms of gardening, where productivity and profit are related only to pleasure and beauty.

Where the temperature-light-humidity-air-food bàlance is correct, many Andeans can stand nearly full summer sunlight, although flowering is consistently better beneath partial shade. An average intensity of 1,500 footcandles is about right and, if possible during the winter, a day extended to twelve hours with supplementary lights. Humidity should be maintained close to 70 percent during the day and not much less at night. Its bad features are checked by constantly circulating the air with small fans so that foliage remains dry. Watering is frequent, sufficient to prevent the compost from drying out. Andeans placed in shallow trays of water—about an inch deep and changed weekly—have thrived for years. The only hazard is the concentration of chemical salts that may accumulate in the compost, and this is easily remedied by leaching the compost once a month by top watering.

Feeding is very important, as much in osmunda and conventional composts as it is in fir bark. Little fertilizer is needed (perhaps a fifth or less of the usual recommendations) each time the plants are watered, and a balanced formula is

Top row: Cymbidium Show Boat 'Southern Lace', BM/5WOC; *Cymbidium* San Miguel 'Limelight', HCC/ODC. *Bottom: Cymbidium* Bethlehem 'Christmas Day', HCC/AOS; *Cymbidium* Suva 'Lucifer'. HCC/AOS. *Courtesy of Fred A. Stewart, Inc.*

Paphiopedilum San Francisco
(opposite).

This page: the nine paphiopedi-lums in the group illustration are, top row left to right: Paphiopedilum Claire de Lune; *Paph.* Tendresse. *Center: Paph.* Cinderella; *Paph. sukhakulii; Paph.* Mildred Hunter; *Paph.* John Hanes. *Bottom: Paph.* Mooreheart; *Paph.* Leyburnense; *Paph.* Wallur. *The other illustrations (center): Paphliopedilum* Sunol; *and Paph.* Golden Acres. *(Bottom): Paph.* Sandra Mary 'Orchid Acres', AM/ODC; *Paph.* Halo 'Spring Shower'. *Courtesy of Rod McLellan Company.*

preferred, except in bark. Once a month, neutralize excess acidity in the compost by watering with a solution of agricultural lime, a tablespoonful dissolved in four gallons of water.

Repotting is infrequent, largely on a demand basis: when the pots are too small for the plants; when, or just before, the compost has deteriorated. The shock of dividing the pseudobulbs and the disruption of root activity is debilitating. Customarily, repotting is performed only as new roots appear on new growths—which can be any time of the year; Andean growth is not strictly seasonal.

Heat, dry or hot air or too little humidity may wrinkle pseudobulbs and shrivel roots and leaves. Equally dangerous, dry air encourages heavy infestations of red spiders. Concentrated fertilizer salts in the compost cause root rot. Leaves and pseudobulbs may turn reddish for the same reason, but prior to the loss of roots. Leaf burn and chlorosis are indicative of too much light.

The Andean odontoglossums are perhaps the best examples of why orchids should be grown within their temperature classifications. Although few other orchids are so restrictive, they do have certain limitations beyond which it is not safe to go. However, modern hybridizers are reconstructing the horticultural characteristics of the Andean odontoglossums to more comfortable standards. Meanwhile, Andeans—which must be seen to be believed, and once seen are never forgotten—will continue to be grown regardless of inconvenience, and justifiably so.

THE CENTRAL AMERICAN ODONTOGLOSSUMS easily adapt themselves to cool, even medium, temperatures and more opportune culture. Although they are found at nearly the same altitudes as the Andeans, and the temperature range is comparable, their vigorous growth sustains them over fairly wide variations. Most of them will accept 80° as normal during the day; a few will not balk at 85°, or at 50° for a nightly low in winter. They are raised from time to time in the South, in Texas and the Midwest, not summered or flowered well unless kept indoors where air conditioning is commonly operated. Otherwise, their cultural necessities are the same as the Andeans.

Unlike the Andeans, there are few hybrids among the Central Americans—a curious oversight since their flowers are correspondingly large and, in their own way, as excitingly marked. The two- and three-inch flowers are bewilderingly striped and spotted with combinations of brown, green, pink, rose-lilac, crimson, yellow and white. Of the five or six species available from nurseries, all but one flower only in the spring.

THE GRANDE GROUP, also from Central America, but from the lower highlands, is the darling of careless collections. Indoors, outdoors, windows or greenhouses, north or south, the grandes play no favorites. Minimum care and maximum pleasure is the rule, and in practice it nearly always works out that way.

The grandes, of which the orchid bearing that specific name is typical, are generally regarded as a medium-temperature group with an inborn complacency toward moderately cool and extremely warm conditions, and preferring a definite wet-dry compost. Given considerable indifference (though some care is wise), their progress in home garden installations is remarkable. And indifference, here, is not used casually. The grandes are actually killed by indulgent kindness.

Humidity is not a critical or compulsive requirement as it is with other odontoglossums. Any moderate amount is suitable, and sometimes none at all. Plenty of fresh air without abrupt changes is required. Light is strong, from 2,000 to

Top row: Cymbidium Peach Bloom; *Cymbidium* Green Wings. *Center: Cymbidium* Lagoon; *Cymbidium* Red Orange *(a miniature cymbidium). Bottom: Cymbidium* Rosemary Upton; *Cymbidium* Trade Winds 'Picture', HCC/ODS. *Courtesy of Rod McLellan Company.*

3,500 footcandles. Water is freely provided, and then the compost—most likely a terrestrial one—is allowed to dry out. Feeding is heavier and less often than with other odontoglossums.

The flowers of the grande section have a varnished look that correctly suggests their extremely long-lasting qualities. Most of them begin opening in spring and carry on through fall when grande itself comes into bloom with its five-inch flowers looking like a sort of Halloween accessory. As a matter of fact, its flowers are very much in keeping with that holiday; with its yellow and white and cinnamon brown stripes, it has been referred to as the Halloween orchid. In Mexico, though, its colorful stripes suggest its common name, the Tiger orchid. The other flowers from this group, two or three inches in size, are not so sportive in color. The browns and yellows are more subdued; white through rose pink is not uncommon, and one of the species is deliciously fragrant.

All in all, a delightful assembly of orchids for novices—if the grandes alone are grown. A challenging group, among the Central Americans, for those more experienced or learned. And a defiantly beautiful family of orchids—the Andeans—for the truly experienced. What more could be asked—or wanted—of any orchids?

ANDEAN GROUP. TEMPERATURE: cool, 45° to 70°. HUMIDITY: 70 percent. LIGHT: 1,200 to 1,500 footcandles. AIR: mild and constant. WATER: abundant. COMPOST: bark, osmunda, tree-fern. FEEDING: 30–10–10 or 20–20–20, dilute; biweekly in bark, monthly in osmunda. REPOT: as required. PROPAGATION: division. HABIT: sympodial epiphyte. REST: none, or short.

CENTRAL AMERICAN GROUP. TEMPERATURE: cool to medium, 50° to 80°. HUMIDITY: 50 to 70 percent. LIGHT: 1,500 to 2,000 footcandles. AIR: constant, mild. WATER: partially dry between waterings. COMPOST: bark, osmunda, tree-fern. FEEDING: 30–10–10 and 20–20–20, dilute; monthly in osmunda, biweekly in bark. REPOT: as required. PROPAGATION: division. HABIT: sympodial epiphyte. REST: very slight.

GRANDE GROUP. TEMPERATURE: medium, 45° to 80°. HUMIDITY: 40 to 60 percent. LIGHT: 2,000 to 3,500 footcandles. AIR: vigorous. WATER: dry out between waterings. COMPOST: terrestrial or bark. FEEDING: 20–20–20, as required. REPOT: 2 to 3 years. PROPAGATION: division. HABIT: sympodial epiphyte. REST: few weeks.

The Oncidiums

The group of oncidiums is a happy one, giddy with brilliant colors and at home nearly everywhere in the orchid world. Gay with strong swirls of yellow-barred-with-cinnamon-brown flowers and oversized frilled lips in white and golden yellows. Spinning ballerinas with lilac skirts, dancing dolls and dancing ladies sheathed in amethyst gowns brocaded with crimson. Such are the names and terms that often have been used to describe them. Yellow, of course, is the

Oncidium ampliatum var. *majus*

Oncidiums are the flower factories —there is no better description—of the orchid world. And their lives seem to be devoted entirely to the single-minded purpose of producing more flowers per stem per plant. Oncidium ampliatum var. majus, is no exception. It is not a large plant and the stems are rather short by oncidium standards. Yet it can easily carry hundreds of inch-and-a-half yellow flowers resembling a cluster of brightly colored butterflies or fat golden bumblebees. There is something about the tropical sunlight at middle altitudes which seems to produce these gentle hues of yellow, as well as rose and brown. At low elevations the orchid colors are likely to be strong and glaring, and high in the mountains the colors become crystal-clear, cold rather than radiant.

Oncidium boissense (above)

For sheer, absolute fun it may be impossible to improve on the oncidiums. From midget to giant, from giddy to gaudy flowers, from challenging cultural needs almost to cultural indifference—there are oncidiums for everyone. Oncidium boissiense is—as it appears to be—small in relation to its four-inch pot. But it is a giant in the quantity and the size of its pale yellow and chocolate-brown flowers, each a potential boutonniere of charm and distinction. Its culture is casually temperate and medium and is suitable to indoor locations. It was first developed, as a primary hybrid, in France in 1924, and it reflects the stamina of Oncidium varicosum (a veritable giant among oncidiums) and Oncidium forbesii, a true dwarf.

Oncidium Summit Gold *(opposite)*

Oncidium Summit Gold's *two-inch flowers come close to being a perfect example of the ballerina form, for which the oncidiums are famous. Complete with flaring skirt of pale gold, a chaste bodice of rust brown trimmed with white, and a more sumptuous bonnet than couturiers have designed in a hundred years.*

preponderant oncidium color; but it is randomly diffuse from gold through chartreuse and amber, including the palest mauve and deepest purple that are somehow warmed with the softest tinge of yellow.

The shapes of the flowers are singularly ornate—enameled jewelry with lips either almost nonexistent or fringed spectacularly. The flowers are not prohibitively large, making ideal corsages for sportswear and cocktail dresses, for hairdos and wristlets and as boutonnieres; as tall sprays they make stunning floral arrangements. Cheerful, bright, adaptable—there is really no other orchid quite like them. They produce more flowers per inch of stem, often in the hundreds; and more flowers per plant, sometimes several thousand—and not very large plants at that. The foliage is uniformly low; perhaps twelve inches on the average. Yet some mature oncidium plants from the Caribbean islands could hide behind a silver dollar, thrusting ethereally delicate half-inch flowers six or eight inches above the diminutive iris-like leaves.

The ornamental pseudobulbs and leaves have much in common with their relatives, the odontoglossums and miltonias, but with two interesting variations. One species without pseudobulbs has purplish-brownish-greenish leaves that look so much like donkey's ears that it has earned the sobriquet though not the implied characteristics. Another resembles nothing so much as a stack of varnished green pencils with blunted points.

Two other species, both popularly known as Butterfly orchids, have a devoted following among all plant hobbyists, orchidists or not. From their mottled leaves—blackish green or reddish brown and rather decorative in themselves—the flower stems arch upward twenty or thirty inches. Each stem produces a single flower in nearly perpetual succession, a new flower appearing as the old one dies. For this reason the flower stems are never cut. The top sepals and petals have been extraordinarily modified to resemble the antennae of butterflies, with the lower floral elements becoming vividly believable wings and bodies. Predominantly golden yellow, lined and spotted with rich brown, the effect is completely and overwhelmingly enchanting. It is not surprising that these floral butterflies from Central and South America helped start the fad for growing orchids so long ago. Neither is it unexpected that they should have been successfully grown from the beginning. They are warm orchids, requiring consistent moisture and humidity and shade—conditions not really too far from the later and more moderate assumptions and practices of the early orchidists.

There is no limited or well-defined geographical section in which oncidiums may be isolated. Nor is there a single, common climate. They grow far and wide in Latin America, from Mexico well into the southern continent. They are found along the seacoast, high in the Andes and at every level in between. So, by and large, each species grown can be placed in one of the three temperature categories. Most nurserymen and orchid growers list the oncidium preference in their catalogs or readily supply the information. Their catalogs, incidentally, often contain a concise world of orchid knowledge and are good to have on hand as references. The illustrations are a constant record of the finest flowers.

In many cases oncidiums have a wider temperature-climate tolerance than is indicated by their classification. Oncidiums in Florida have withstood surprisingly consistent warmth. In California their resistance to wide alterations of hot-cold-dry-hot-moist conditions has endeared them to casual gardeners. Elsewhere in the country, considerable indifference toward their usual requirements has not seemed to set them back, particularly in indoor gardens. Although care-

Oncidium kramerianum

The Butterfly orchid from Ecuador —Oncidium kramerianum—is an absolutely delightful example of floral mimicry. The flowering stems, almost invisible among the dense jungle foliage, hold the yellow and brown spotted flowers like hovering butterflies. The topmost sepal and two petals stick up like antennae. The other two sepals enclose the body—which is the orchid lip—like wings. It closely resembles another species, Oncidium papilio, except that its sepals are spotted—not banded—with brown.

The thin stem, rising to thirty inches, should not be cut. It bears summer flowers (five inches from tip to tip) in single succession, year after year, on the same stem.

less violations in their culture is never advisable, many oncidiums apparently have a built-in safety factor. Perhaps it is a reserve of food which can carry them through a disconcerting period, rather than a catholicity of temperament. It would be nice to know, since most oncidiums, infrequently cultivated, have always been grown by the book, as it were.

Other than being separated by a temperature classification, most oncidiums have similar cultural requirements. Their roots are thin and numerous, sometimes in heavy masses. Hence they need continuous moisture, thorough watering when watered, less water while flowering, very little while resting—which they all do, more or less. The inevitable exceptions are those without pseudobulbs, the miniatures and some of the warm oncidiums—notably the Butterfly orchids— that prefer a more stable temperature-moisture relationship and wetter composts. But no oncidium kept saturated with water will flower; its roots will eventually deteriorate. There is a nice balance of wet-to-almost-dry that should be maintained in composts. Watering oncidiums requires an attitude of moderation, not of extremes; but if an error must be made, make it on the dry side.

Oncidiums tend to be heavy feeders, but heavy in relation to orchids always means more dilute fertilizers than is normal with ordinary garden perennials. In the case of oncidiums, fertilizers may vary from half strength to, perhaps, nearly the normal recommendations made by fertilizer companies for their products. A 30–10–10 in liquid form is preferable in order to prevent chemical damage to the roots. This should be followed late in the growing season with a 10–20–10 to harden pseudobulbs and initiate buds. Thoroughly leach the composts before applying fertilizers again.

Composts are as variable as the habits of the oncidiums. Those that climb do better on tree-fern slabs. Although they do not actually climb in the sense that vines do, there is a distinct gap between old and new pseudobulbs and the latter are carried somewhat higher—a trait conveniently acquired for moving up sloping branches. Other oncidiums may be grown in loose osmunda, fir bark (particularly for coarse-rooted oncidiums), chopped tree-fern, coconut husks, or even on thick slabs of coarse wood. Very light mixtures in which humus has been included are not unusual. If the oncidiums have hanging flower sprays, the cultural preference is toward osmunda, loosely packed in baskets.

All oncidiums love as much light as they can tolerate, which is always a good deal more than is expected. Except for the few species requiring shade, the best approach is to hang oncidiums outdoors under filtered light for as long as possible, weather permitting. Gradually harden them to increasing intensities, almost to the extent of leaf burn. The medium-temperature group is certain to want full sunlight, with the exception of midday in areas of intense radiation. The food-water ration can be increased carefully as the light and temperature increase. When well accomplished, the result is unbelievable vigor and flowering.

For most of the oncidiums, humidity is nice to have around but not unduly missed if the foliage is gently syringed indoors, not so gently outdoors. The minimum humidity requirement is 20 percent, and their average is 40 percent— a fairly normal countrywide condition. The few oncidiums in the warm group are best maintained in a humidity between 40 and 70 percent.

If these cultural suggestions seem to be surprisingly casual—they are. Oncidiums themselves are, in a way, the most casual plants in the orchid world. And the most surprising fact about oncidiums—all seven hundred of them (and more)—is not their ease of culture indoors, outdoors in shade houses, or in

Odontioda hybrid

At the turn of the century in Belgium, Charles Vuylsteke's success with odontoglossums was the envy of the Continent and the despair of English competitors. To make such matters worse (or better), he introduced in 1904, at London's Temple Show, Odontioda vuylstekeae. The achievement was sensational because botanists implicitly believed odontoglossums and cochliodas to be incompatible. And, equally dramatic, the hybrid flowers were completely red, another impossibility if only the odontoglossums were considered. Since then, Vulysteke's breeding program has been carried on by others who have produced larger flowers—some to three and four inches—and better plants.

greenhouses. It is only that oncidiums have been, and continue to be, unknown. Only recently have hybridists taken a long look at this orchid family and started to work with it. As a result, there are increasing numbers of oncidium hybrids becoming available, many with larger flowers. Intergeneric crosses show many indications of superior vegetative habits, and exciting flower shapes and colors. Where it will end, or whether it will, no hybridist seems to know. But a word of warning: old hat or new creations, oncidiums are for happy people. They are like having all of the ice cream one wants—and then being offered more.

TEMPERATURE: cool, medium, warm, 45° to 90°. HUMIDITY: moderate to 60 percent. LIGHT: 2,000 to 4,000 footcandles. AIR: good to vigorous. WATER: abundant while growing. FEEDING: 30–10–10 or balanced, biweekly. PROPAGATION: division. COMPOST: bark, tree-fern, osmunda. HABIT: sympodial epiphyte. REPOT: as required, after flowering (2 to 4 years). REST: mild.

Orchid Houses

There is much to be said in favor of greenhouses, and much to be considered against them, although—even from such a seemingly contradictory viewpoint—greenhouses do have one element in common. They work. They are certainly the most effective way—if not the simplest—to modify a hostile climate by artificially adjusting it to specific orchid needs. But greenhouses are not a beginning, even for orchids; they are an end, to be tried only after most other gardening approaches have been experienced and learned and the need for more space is both a practical and an esthetic necessity.

Though not particularly exigent in the subtropics, greenhouses can be fun—sometimes. Important in the temperate zone and imperative in the chill of northern winters, greenhouses do provide a satisfyingly creative interest—sometimes. The implied reservations have little to do with the reasons for having them in the first place. Time and labor aside—and greenhouses often may have too much of both for the concerned hobbyists—for a hundred years gardeners have abjectly submitted to designs for greenhouses based on commercial blueprints. Most greenhouses were built in expanding lengths of drab iron or rough wood and bland glass, or, more recently and better, aluminum and steel multiples.

Such uninspired structures are effective only for stocking, growing and selling plants, not displaying them—especially orchids—or adding gardening zest to living. Few buildings are so terrifyingly destructive to the pride of ownership than prefab glass boxes dropped squarely into the centers of lawns, stuffed into previously lovely corners, or indiscriminately bolted to the edges of houses and left barren of architectural influences. There is nothing in horticultural or architectural literature which forbids northern locations for greenhouses; nothing which stipulates that greenhouses cannot be sheltered by deciduous trees; nothing which refuses to consider low or small **constructions** as essentially sound,

Epidendrum Pinar del Rio

The tall, arching spray of this epidendrum hybrid carries a cluster of fragrant flowers that need no excuse for being a member of a so-called secondary orchid family. It has all of the virtues of epidendrums (vigor and ease of growth at medium temperatures), and the miniature—in a sense—delicacy of cattleyas. Its many ornamental possibilities and its decorative uses are inherent in its appearance. Primarily grayed browns and purples, the two-inch flowers have a quiet look, frequently blooming two or three times a year; and maturing rapidly (three years) from seedling to flowering adult.

and even imperative in several cases. Many gardening hobbyists have consistently violated the so-called rules of greenhouse gardening—accidentally and successfully—either by supplying the obvious lacks or by restricting themselves to suitable plants.

Indeed, such seemingly apparent violations may be necessary in order to grow some of the most beautiful orchids. Northern-oriented greenhouses produce many of the best shade orchids. The midday shelter of deciduous foliage trees may save trouble and effort in balancing shade and sunlight at otherwise critical periods of the year. Low greenhouses with walks below the ground level are quickly, efficiently and inexpensively air-conditioned, humidified and warmed since so little air space is involved.

Equally important, there is no regulation, other than preconception, which prohibits greenhouses from being a structurally significant, attractive and ornamental part of homes. Neither is there any book that insists greenhouses be squared, peaked, even-spanned; or that glass is the only functionally sound translucent material, either plain, whitewashed, muslin-covered or equipped with roller blinds. In private homes and gardens there are other materials as suitable and infinitely more decorative.

The only inference possible is that home greenhouse misconceptions—even errors, and there have been those indeed—were unintentionally and unfortunately inspired by commercial practices. As such, garden greenhouses were smaller editions of commercial houses and were considered to be inviolate and unchangeable. It should never have been forgotten that commercial growers must make a profit. They do so by minimizing expenses, maximizing efficiency, doing without luxuries. But a gardener's involvement with orchids is anything but commercial. Orchid gardening is economical of labor only in terms of automation; meaningful only in terms of sharing an extraordinary experience; profitable only in terms of recreation; justifiable only in terms of beauty and of love.

Accordingly, many of the earlier concepts of strictly utilitarian hobby greenhouses are changing. Orchid houses are again becoming beautiful as well as fashionable—and practicable. The hobby of growing orchids—interesting as it may be as a sort of challenge—needs the further satisfaction that is achieved only when orchids and their flowers are appropriately displayed in comfortable quarters. This is by no means a new idea, only the rediscovery of a charming way of life that goes back to the earliest days of hobby gardening. In old English and Continental homes, all favored plants were given well-designed houses of their own, with ample room in which to display them, to admire them, to sit down and relax and talk about them.

In recent years the departure from standardized greenhouses has included such radical substitutes as enclosed cabinets, basements, garages, and sun porches, whose necessary modifications have made orchid culture both automated and autonomous. Simple double-hung windows have broadened in scope, becoming larger, deeper and brighter as the quest for the sun has become a fashionable convenience. Great walls of glass and plastic and special screens have made sun-rooms and breezeways a delight. Solariums and atriums (the best of all the revivals) are modestly redesigned to be also comfortable sitting rooms, especially in winter. Conservatories are losing their botanical garden image as huge piles of curved glass for housing palms, and have become small, attractive fiber-glass enclosures, living-dining room extensions, and kitchen-breakfast room annexes. If this is a gardening rebellion, it is a healthy one, since it emphasizes both

Acineta alba

The ten or so members of the acinetas have waxy, yellowish globular flowers spotted or splashed with red, although A. alba, as its name indicates, is white. And one, A. superba, has chocolate-colored flowers dashed with crimson. All acinetas are fragrant. Allied to the peristerias (the Dove orchids of Central America), it is grown under similar conditions. It needs more warmth while growing, but is later carried in the medium temperature range with a definite dry period, but not a prolonged one, to induce flowering. The decorative three-inch flowers have a single misfortune: the floral stems are thrust directly downward through the compost; if there is not a wide bottom opening, the flowers cannot appear. It is best grown as a semi-terrestrial from hanging baskets of wood, wire or wicker.

The gardening pleasure derived from orchid houses comes from what is accomplished within them after they are built. The personally designed fiber glass house on the opposite page was planned for living with orchids. The commercial orchid house shown on this page (top) permits dining with an intimate background of flowering orchids, and contains plant-working areas that are concealed when not in use. The orchid house (right) made from surplus metal skylight sashes will last as long as the home itself. All of these orchid houses possess an important feature: they are intimately accessible.

beauty and health, bringing the pleasures of gardening indoors the year round, where it is integrated with family living—a pleasure for all and a problem for none.

Reason suggests that these garden rooms should not be overcrowded. In a limited sense, the fewer the orchids, the more stunning the display and, naturally, the less work—for some needful, occasional care is usually apparent. A wise, limited selection of orchids will insure ample flowers, and some of them should be fragrant. Fragrance is common among botanical orchids, spicy or sweet, and an eloquent reminder of faraway places and strange people and customs, as well as being pleasant for itself.

Inevitably, even the most commodious garden rooms may become overcrowded. The Victorians loved such an atmosphere, and combined exotic plants and wicker furniture in attractive confusion. It can be fun, but most hobbyists simply convert some out-of-the-way spot into a growing area, perhaps masking a small section of a basement with plastic sheeting over rigid supports, adding lights and other equipment. There, orchids not in bloom are cared for until they go back into the house again as desired guests.

Materials for orchid houses and rooms are as varied as the needs that create them. Brick, stone, mortar, wood, glass and iron—the usual raw products—have been substantially replaced with finished timber or aluminum frames and wood siding, plastics of all kinds and fiber glass (plain or tinted or corrugated) for lighting control and used as suggested in the planning of sun porches. There are no ground rules governing the applications of these materials. They are too new, though not untried. As a result, most recent constructions reflect personal gardening opinions as well as architectural preferences. And the most absorbingly interesting fact about them is that they work.

Insofar as the management of an orchid house is no different from that of a greenhouse or, for that matter, an orchid window, the same rules and procedures apply for the control of air, light, warmth and humidity. Such modifications as may be made are intended merely to make the orchid house—or room—as comfortable for people as it is for orchids. Detailed instructions are easily secured from any one of several books on the subject, or from the manufacturers of standard greenhouse installations.

By any definition, an orchid house need not be one permanently enclosed with glass or plastic. It also can be a semi-open structure of laths or special screening materials. Usually lathhouses (or screen houses) are thought of as year-round buildings suitable only for the subtropics, or elsewhere if the winter night temperature stays reasonably at 45° to 50°, and in rare cases, no lower than 32°. What has been overlooked is that lathhouses are valuable for summering orchids outdoors, in any of the colder sections of the country. Also overlooked is the fact that—like orchid houses—lathhouses can be exceedingly attractive architecturally, and exceptionally comfortable as outdoor sitting rooms. Even in winter, small sections of lathhouses may be partly or completely enclosed in plastic sheets to extend their usefulness and their pleasures as temporary greenhouses.

There is no reason, cultural or garden, why lathhouses must be boxlike cases stuck into a garden without previous consideration or thought. The Victorians, and before them the Georgians, made full use of their gardens by designing round and curved lathhouses—pergolas and arbors, summer pavilions and gazebos. They added ornamentation, painted them or left the wood stripping to weather naturally. Walks were graveled or paved with slate imbedded in sand.

The architectural designs of commercial orchid houses, available for immediate garden installations, offer an extremely wide variety of choices. Although too large for most home purposes, the solarium arrangement at the top left can be manufactured in smaller ornamental sections as secondary living rooms. The geodesic dome (top right) is a delightful garden-home addition applicable to orchid culture. Ornamental in shape, it can be covered with pliable plastic sheeting, with fixed fiber glass panels, or with aluminum screening. It is variable in height from four to twenty feet, and in diameter, from thirteen to twenty-one feet. The lean-to (bottom) is one of the most acceptable greenhouse variations, with low installation costs and upkeep to recommend it, and considerable charm as well.

Benches and wicker or metal furniture were added for comfort. Potted plants were set in raised beds, arranged in borders, or narrow shelves, or hung from supporting beams. Many of these summer houses were separate, some attached to homes. But no matter where or how they were built, all of these lathhouses were integrated to living as much as they were to plants. And orchids should be no exception to such gracious courtesies, even now. In an age when urban standardization is an economical necessity, small and highly personalized summer orchid houses may be one of the only incentives for personal indulgence.

There are few procedures to be considered in the construction of lathhouses other than their design and location. All wood is preferably redwood in order to withstand weathering. Structural supports should be treated chemically against decay and insect damage, and firmly secured in the ground—if possible—on and in cement. Laths may be spaced horizontally or vertically, and about their own width apart—never more; sometimes a bit less. Crossed laths, in diagonals, as squares or stars, are a pleasant decorative variation from the ground up to two or three feet. Roof lathing, also placed its own width apart, is laid ordinarily in a north-south direction. A more equitable sun-shade proportion is thus maintained. But this requirement is not a rigid one. Circular lathhouses with a center-peaked roof often have their laths laid out like the spokes of a wheel. And where the laths overlap bulkily in the center, some interesting ornamentation is added to conceal the carpentry.

Several plastic manufacturers make pliable screens and cloths which may be stretched lightly over lathhouses for additional protection. Interior sheets of plastic are held in place by thin pipe-iron forms or heavy, galvanized wire, when only a small area needs to be safeguarded. Small ornamental cold frames made from window sashes will occupy less space and offer more protection, especially if soil cables are used to heat them.

Gardening with orchids is not as dependent on the whims of good weather as it once was. There are just as many ways to get around a temperature drop or poor sunlight as one's gardening ingenuity can devise.

The Paphiopedilums

To be perfectly honest, most of the orchid plants long known as cypripediums are not cypripediums; and neither, possibly, are they orchids. The story of this abrupt metamorphosis is part of the long history of botanical confusion that is not yet resolved. The clarification of plant families and names has created almost as much nonsense—and agony—as the original disorderly nomenclature which botanical detectives are now carefully unscrambling. Correct as modern botanists undoubtedly are, it will take more than a generation of orchid gardeners to learn to use the new name for cypripediums, let alone pronounce it—Paphiopedilum.

The first mistake in nomenclature may have been an unconscious error by Linnaeus, the Swedish founder of systematic botany (the procedure by which plants are classified and named). In 1753 he created the generic word cypri-

Paphiopedilum Bit-O-Sunshine Glow, HCC/AOS

In recent years, as paphiopedilums slipped in commercial popularity—there is a cyclic rise and fall in orchid flowers—hobbyists and specialists became more avid collectors. Popular interest in the almost too large flowers was handicapped by their strange and forbidding floral shapes. On the other hand, hobbyists were demanding improved colors in the hybrids and, surprisingly, searching for species currently unknown in the orchid markets. Paphiopedilums, limited to about fifty species, now have hybrids numbering in the thousands —more than any other orchid group except cattleyas. And the slow process of improvement from bizarre species to gently rounded creations with softly luminous colors in yellow and rose and white is clearly demonstrated in Paph. Bit-O-Sunshine Glow. A significant affirmation of the achievements of amateur and professional growers.

pedium, a Greek derivative which is translated literally as Venus' little foot. The original and, of course, romantic name is Ladyslipper, the hardy, lovely yellow-flowering orchid of European woodlands. Linnaeus' pen slipped perhaps, if it did at all, in failing to put an "I" into his coined word—cypripedilum or, colloquially, Venus' Slipper. Be that as it may, Linnaeus' invention persisted; and into the family of cypripediums all slippered or pouched orchids, European and Asiatic, were placed.

This system worked for a hundred and thirty-three years, until Dr. Ernst Phitzer, a German scholar, decided to combine the tropical American and the tropical Asiatic cypripediums into a new family—the paphiopedilums—correctly using, incidentally, the correct Greek suffix for slipper. This did not work very well, since the South American branch was distinct enough from the Asiatics to deserve a name of its own.

During the following years—and through several other indecisive and exploratory steps—the correct terminology for all Ladyslippers has evolved into:

CYPRIPEDIUM—the Ladyslipper of northern Europe, northern Asia, and North America—wild, sensitive, beautiful, and difficult terrestrials, almost impossible to transplant to gardens and rapidly becoming extinct.

SELENIPEDIUM—tall reedlike tropical Americans not usually found in culture.

PHRAGMIPEDIUM—a curious South American cool group (inhabitants of the highlands) whose lateral floral sepals may suddenly and rapidly elongate until they touch the ground, a matter of thirty inches or more. Up these floral ribbons an as yet undiscovered insect is supposed to climb in order to pollinate the flowers. One of the species flowers almost continuously under moderate care.

PAPHIOPEDILUM—the Asiatic cypripediums of Linnaeus, the cordula of Bailey, the cyps of the florist trade, the despair of botanists, the delight of hobbyists and gardeners everywhere—and, as a corsage, either loved or hated by women.

Florists and commercial flower growers bitterly fought the cumbersome new name. There was, they claimed, no way of educating buyers to the brutally tongue-twisting sound of paphiopedilum, even proposing a nickname that did not sound like a breakfast food. By consensus, cyps was retained as a market name for all paphliopedilums and, at least temporarily, as correct garden usage.

But cyps, regardless of what they may be called, indifferent to being non-orchids, are once again as popular among gardeners as cattleyas and cymbidiums. Indeed, at one time they were so fashionable that few European homes were without them; they were rightly considered to be the staunchest of houseplants and responsive to nearly every conceivable home situation. Their vogue lasted for a hundred years and only succumbed—as did many other lovely plants—to the straggliest combination in the history of indoor gardening: asparagus fern, carrot-top foliage and sweet potato vines, all of them casual products of the dislocation which followed World War I.

With their strange shapes and vivid waxy colors, cyps are intemperately admired by those who grow them, perhaps because of their completely artificial appearance. No other flowers look as if they were manufactured out of whimsical dreams, dipped in varnish, weighted with lead and strapped to stems that can barely support them. Though some people do find the varnished look, the heavy pouch, the bizarre stripes and splotches of rich colors inconsistent and even displeasing—these characteristics are nearly perfect environmental adaptations. The flowers, waterproofed against excessive dampness, last for six weeks or

Paphiopedilum Maudiae

Fads in orchids are as unexplainable as fads in clothing. They seem to appear suddenly, disappear promptly, and leave no lingering recollection behind—except rarely, when some floral element is so appreciated that it becomes a permanent fixture. Such has been the case with Paphiopedilum Maudiae, *a success from the time it was introduced as a primary hybrid in 1900. Its vigor made it a European parlor and kitchen plant until World War II. Its flowers (about three inches in diameter), a softly greenish-yellow and white, endeared it to all who liked the cool, luminiscent colors in place of the overly rich plant confections left by the Victorians. Today, commercial growers offer similar shapes and colors in miniature paphiopedilums barely three or four inches in height.*

longer. The colors are attractive to insects and in perfect accord with the surrounding vegetation. The pouches are excellent traps for insuring pollination.

Long, continuous and intensive hybridization has changed the original, sometimes skimpy floral shapes into magnificently full, rounded, classical designs five and six inches across. Colors have been modified to brilliant pastels and deep, rich lusters. White has been intensified and blends through all combinations of the tertiary colors (except blue, although lilac is not unknown), to dark mahogany and a caustic green not found elsewhere. A well-grown, mature specimen plant with many new growths—and a flower from each—may appear to be almost overburdened with blooms. Most cyps, however, bear a solitary flower on a single, short stem. A few may have from three to five; and several species and hybrids may produce up to twenty flowers, one at a time, over a period of months. Unhappily this quality is not commonly bred into the hybrids.

Nonetheless, between the modern complex hybrids and the colorful original species the flowering calendar is wide—a fall-winter peak and a spring-summer interim during which the white vareties tend to bloom. Except for a few weeks scattered through the year, a collection of cyps will always have plants in flower. This delightful capability, the sturdy lasting flowers, and the low well-shaped leaves invariably endear cyps to city gardeners and indoor locations. They do excellently wherever some thought has been given to satisfying their minimal and easily fulfilled requirements.

Cyps originally came from Southeast Asia and the nearby Pacific islands and, unexpectedly, many are not tropical plants. They have been found at sea level and at every elevation up to 7,000 feet, usually growing in limestone soil. In all cases, their source of soil moisture was secure—either rain or natural pools and streams. So two kinds of cultural treatments are immediately indicated: warm for lowland cyps (those with mottled green leaves); cool for the mountain species (plain leaves); continuous moisture and medium shade for both. Although the leaf color is reasonably consistent as a visible cultural indication, it can be confusing. Hybrids are so intermixed that their preferences may be genetically slanted toward either temperature category; or possibly they may split the temperature differential and accept a medium range. The only safe practice is to follow the grower's recommendation, or to assume that a medium temperature is involved and go up or down as plants responsively show a preference.

Actually, there has never been complete agreement about cyp culture. There are, for instance, almost as many ways of germinating cyp seeds as there are growers, even though it is not particularly troublesome anymore. There are also nearly as many ideas about growing cyps—more or less sunlight, greater temperature differentials, higher or lower moisture content within the soils and an astonishing diversity of composts. The best indication of these variable concepts is the recent boost in light intensity from 1,200 to 3,000 footcandles. Or the experiment that a San Francisco grower has continued for five years: Fifteen cyps were left standing in an inch of water, with no damage to the plants or any decrease in flowering. This is nice to know because it implies considerable freedom of choice with cultural techniques.

Nevertheless, while cyps are undergoing such casual changes and experimentation, it is best to begin with some standards. The lowest winter night temperature is 55° for the cool types, with an ideal summer day maximum of 80°. The warm cyps have a useful spread between 60° and 85°. Short variations are not harmful; down to 33° for the cool, up to 95° for the warm. But why ask for

Phragmipedium caudatum

This curious phragmipedium from Ecuador, with its extraordinary yellowish-greenish and dull brown two-inch flowers, is occasionally referred to as the old man (or woman, as the case may be) of orchids. Not so much because of its long ribbon-like petals (sometimes several feet long) which extend to the ground in a few days as, perhaps, an insect ladder, but rather for its slightly exaggerated semblance of infirmity. The name is also a slight reference to the botanical fact that this orchid—as well as all paphiopedilums—may not really be an orchid at all. It may be only the remnant of an intermediate plant form which once existed as a transitional element between orchids and other more worldly plants.

Paphiopedilum Albion 'Wyld Court' *(below)*   *Paphiopedilum* Susan Tucker 'White Caps', AM/AOS—ODC *(opposite)*

When well grown, paphiopedilums are among the most durable orchids, and their flowers are certainly long lasting. And it is not unusual in many collections to try for a preponderance of whites—rare and costly as they sometimes are. Many of the beautiful paphiopedilum hybrids are polypolids, orchids whose chromosomes have somehow been doubled or tripled. As a result some hybrids may be sterile, or produce little viable seed. Sometimes this condition can be overcome by embryo culture, in which un-

ripe seed pods—as soon as fertilization takes place—are opened and the embryonic seeds planted (using special techniques). In this way, seed germination, if it is at all possible, may be significantly increased. More often than not, the complex hybrids may manufacture a lethal factor which kills the seed embryos. So the development of hybrid paphiopedilums is often slow, and vegetative increases are the only answer. Hence the most famous named hybrids are likely to be expensive.

trouble, when it is so easy to operate within the appropriate range? As with other orchids, cyps are now best cooled—protected from the debilitation of excessively high temperatures—with heavier shade, higher humidity and increased air circulation. All this, of course, is based on the expedient of reducing leaf temperature during the critically high periods of heat. In spring, however, the lowest night temperatures are indispensable. Bud initiation seems to be delayed at 65°, rushed to completion at 55° or 60°. This makes cool cyps a poor choice for the southern states, although they are flowered along the banks of Florida canals, which seem to act like localized evaporative coolers.

Light is standardized between 700 and 1,200 footcandles. Within the limitations of cyps' equal day-night preference, this amounts to about 800 footcandles as the daylight exceeds twelve hours (summer). Conversely, in winter, as the hours of sunlight are reduced to less than twelve, the light intensity can profitably be increased to 1,200 footcandles. So medium shade, the sort that is produced by several thicknesses of cheesecloth or light muslin, and even saran, is important in summer, but not so meaningful in winter. In the far South, shade is imperative most of the year.

Some of the assumptions about variable levels of light, for cyps, are only valid if it is believed that the maximum total permissible light for a short period has the same healthy stimulus on cyp growth as the minimum light for a longer time—a mildly complicated way of saying that the full impact of sunlight during the morning in an east window may be just as beneficial as half-light in a southern exposure for the full day. If true, it does seem to explain some of the traditional experiences of window gardening, and it may help to resolve the successful adaption of cyps to just such simple exposures. In any event, cyps are healthfully grown at light levels as low as 300, and pushed as high as 3,000 footcandles. And they are among the most responsive orchids to artificial light, either wholly or as a supplement.

Humidity for cyps, as with most terrestrials, is low, and syringing the foliage is more often a mistake than a necessity. Although continued dryness will shrivel the leaves, atmospheric moisture around 25 percent has not been injurious; 40 percent is normal, and excessive humidity is only very occasionally needed in order to relieve excessively high temperatures. Good, even vigorous, air circulation may be more desirable then, as well as at all times. Air movement tends to produce and maintain a better balance among the other requirements.

Since cyps have no pseudobulbs, their growth is more or less continuous; water is given copiously as it is needed, and the compost is never allowed to dry out completely. This condition has been described as a sort of half-wet, half-dry state, depending on the weather. Nevertheless, some growers and hobbyists withhold water slightly after new growth matures (along with lowered temperatures) in order to stimulate flower buds.

Composts are as varied as the gardener's ideas or the restrictions of the locality (warm climates can utilize mixtures that retain water longer). Soft osmunda is still a good choice, particularly if it is desired to lengthen the periods between each watering. Chopped osmunda and gravel mixtures have much to recommend them, as do humus and gravel. Fine seedling bark, with sufficient coarse sand (6:1) seems to be the best mix so far proposed. With osmunda-based composts, use a balanced fertilizer; with bark, a 30–10–10 until just before flowering. Both can be applied, well-diluted, every second or third watering.

As sympodial terrestrials, cyps are propagated by division—immediately fol-

Paphiopedilum hybrid

Part of the charm of hybridizing paphiopedilums is in remaking some of the early crosses that absorbed the attention of plantsmen before 1920. Crosses then were made wilfully, luckily, even emotionally, but never with scientific accuracy, since genetics was for practical purposes unknown. Also, there was the formidable inability to germinate seeds. Today, seedlings can be obtained in the thousands—and the hundreds of thousands if the need arose. Plantsmen now repeat historic crosses in order to introduce stronger orchid "blood lines," and to reduce the incidence of sterility. The floral diameter of this chocolate brown and yellow hybrid is about four inches.

lowing flowering—leaving at least two healthy older growths attached to each new one. New growths mature without roots, and it is difficult to establish them. However, cyps do not seem to mind repotting at any time, a convenience that makes potting schedules simpler and responses to disease faster. If a fungus appears to be rotting either the base of the plant or the root system, simply take the plant out of its pot, wash off the compost, cut away the infested area, paint the cuts with Bordeaux paste, and repot. For a few days to a few weeks, keep the cyp in a cooler, drier atmosphere and in more shade. Damage as a result of disease is not likely to occur under correct culture. Cyps are free of virus, which cannot be said of many orchids, and are remarkably resistant to harmful systemic organisms. Rot, either bacterial or fungoid, to which cyps are most subjected, looks like translucent wet spots, greasy to the touch. It is most likely to arrive late in the summer or during dull, cloudy, rainy days. And it comes as the consequence of water remaining overnight (or for long intervals) on the foliage; high night temperature; excessive humidity; heavy shade (too little light); cold, damp, stagnant air; lack of air circulation. All of these are easily avoidable conditions. Once securely established, rot is virulent, and only prompt action and absolute cleanliness will prevent further contagion.

It is sometimes disastrous to the enthusiasm and the morale of novices to learn of the hazards—or to become responsive to the difficulties—inherent in growing any plant. Orchids are no exception to this. They have their inborn limitations as well as their virtues. But of all plants—and of all orchids—cyps have fewer objectionable qualities and more desirable ones. They are so sympathetic to personal variations in culture, so willing to grow and flower, that this needs to be stressed. They react quickly—and visibly—to slightly changed situations, and errors are easily remedied. In most cases, it is only a little more or a little less of a single basic need that balances the relationship between the cyps and their environment. Light, temperature, humidity, air, water, food, compost— all of these together make up the environmental formula. And among orchids, the formula for cyps is so effortlessly learned and so leisurely practiced, and the rewards so inevitably magnificent, that gardeners can do no better than to begin with them.

TEMPERATURE: cool, 50° to 75°; warm, 60° to 80°. LIGHT: 600 to 2,000 footcandles. HUMIDITY: 40 percent. AIR: good to vigorous. WATER: continuous moisture. FEEDING: 30–10–10 or 20–20–20 as required. PROPAGATION: division. COMPOST: terrestrial or bark. REPOT: after flowering, 2 to 3 years. HABIT: sympodial terrestrial. REST: none.

The Phalaenopsis

The names of orchids are often perversely, rather than perceptively, conceived. The Latin and Greek derivatives are harsh or meaningless except as references to minute floral distinctions of little charm and no aesthetic value. One of the few exceptions to this botanical caprice, however, is phalaenopsis,

Phalaenopsis Bobby Boy 'Orchidglade'

The large flat flowers (up to four or five inches) of all hybrid phalaenopsis appear simple by comparison with the three-dimensional fullness of other orchids. Their chaste simplicity—including the contemporary hybrids that are departing from the winged forms into star shapes and multiple colors— has been described as "a moment of cool rest in the midst of a hysterical orchid nightmare." Largely because of their once predominantly white color, they seem to give a visual impression of impermanence. But impermanent they are not. They are as lasting and as responsive as the knowledge that a gardener brings to bear on their needs.

which in part, means moth. And in a very exciting way, that is exactly what they look like. Twenty or thirty (a hundred or more is not uncommon) large flowers carried on arching stems, shimmering in softly subdued light, gently rocking in warm air currents—making their resemblance to moths in flight strikingly realistic.

The flowers are simple in shape, rather than complex as most orchids are: flat, with overlapping sepals and petals and a curiously foreshortened cup of a lip. In this simplicity, with their breadth (four to five inches across), lies their complete acceptance by florists. They are without question one of the most adaptable and beautiful orchids for cut flowers.

Of course there are phalaenopsis that could not remotely be compared to moths. Many are strikingly colored and curiously shaped (though small). They are adding hues to the predominantly white spectrum of the major hybrids. There are the singularly beautiful star-shaped forms made famous by Professor Burgeff at Wurzburg, and who fortuitously introduced a variant phalaenopsis hybrid, Wunderfischli (Little-Wonder-Fish!); the red and yellow-gold lip does resemble that small, gaudy fish of the tropics. There is another oddly named phalaenopsis of more recent origin: Cast Iron Monarch—a hybrid developed by Ralph Kiesewetter of New York. The name refers to the extraordinary texture of the flowers: like heavy velvet, long-lasting, remarkably protected against rough handling. Its qualities have been bred into modern phalaenopsis; as have those of a hybrid called Doris—a very large flowered variety produced by the Duke Farm in New Jersey.

Some years ago, Louis Vaughn in West Palm Beach, impelled by the seeming inability of phalaenopsis to respond to further improvement—especially colorwise—began to cross-breed them to less interesting but colorful members of the family and also to interbreed them with related families. His contention, once believed impossible, had been disproved nearly sixty years before by a Belgian horticulturist, Charles Vulysteke. As a result, the color range of phalaenopsis has been extended into spectacular pinks and scarlets, yellows and oranges of incredible softness, as well as barred and striped floral confections—an entirely new world of orchid shapes and colors. No gardener today is without a few plants; many have specialized, insisting that for the time and industry required to grow phalaenopsis no other orchid provides such a long blooming season. The flowers last for months on the plants, beginning in winter and opening sequentially (sometimes all at once) and continue to flower irregularly through spring and part of summer.

Phalaenopsis plants do not live as long as orchids are presumed to, although definitely longer than people may. As monopodials with no storage organs, they have no resistance to inclement conditions. Their yearly growth is slow, each broad, tender leaf closely alternating with the next leaf—a feature which makes them attractive to many gardeners with space problems. Vegetative increases are slow and difficult to make, and can be ordinarily damaging to the parent plants. So they are propagated from seeds. Fortunately, phalaenopsis crosses that are offered commercially have a high standard of competence; parents of known quality seem to provide an assured range of good forms and colors with an expectancy of thrilling combinations. This form of orchid roulette is an exciting game to orchid gardeners. The inexpensive seedlings, their early flowering (three to five years from flasks), and above all the chance of a prize orchid (to perpetuate a gardener's name) provide better odds for the participant than any other form of gambling.

Phalaenopsis Jewel 'Ruby Lip'

There is a Malaysian name for one of the phalaenopsis species, Angrek bulan. Angrek means a type of orchid epiphyte, and Bulan means moon. Hence, Moon orchid, because it is white and lasts from one new moon to the next. In its way as lovely a name as the familiar Moth orchid, perhaps even more so. Only eighty-two years have gone into the breeding of modern phalaenopsis, including two fortunate accidents and the dedicated talents of an amateur grower. John Seden made the first hybrid at James Veitch's nursery in 1886. Not a long time by horticultural standards, especially since phalaenopsis hybridizing was considered to be a dead end until well into the forties of this century, when Louis Vaughn at West Palm Beach, Florida, restructured phalaenopsis with new color.

The formula for growing phalaenopsis is comparatively simple: uniformity of the critical orchid elements, temperature, light, humidity, water, air. They are monopodial epiphytes (with a slight tendency toward terrestrial habits), largely from the Pacific islands off the coast of Southeast Asia—principally the Philippines. The island seasons are uniform, never exceedingly hot and rarely cold, with frequent rain and consistent humidity, ever-present shade. Life in their homelands is easy for phalaenopsis and must be made so in cultivation. A winter night temperature of 65° to a summer day of 80° is a satisfactory range; and never, never lower than a rare 60°. Humidity must be kept high, at least 70 percent during the day and more as the temperature rises above 80°; somewhat less at night and while flowering, but no less important. As a consequence, gentle air circulation is continuously required to avoid stagnant air pockets and condensing moisture. As in cyps, water retained on phalaenopsis leaves is an assured bid for trouble; moisture on flowers spots them. But air unrelieved by humidity (dry air) is fatal. Water is lost from the leaf cells at an amazing rate.

Sunlight can be mellow and should remain at a constant level; a mildly heavy sort of shade in summer, less so in winter. Cheesecloth, translucent plastic, saran, aluminum screening and lath seem to offer a pleasing light, or a pattern of sun and shade in suitable proportions. Care must be taken so that direct sunlight does not touch the leaves; they are sun-sensitive and easily burned. In footcandles, a satisfactory light value begins at 500 footcandles, and it can go to 1,000 or 1,500 footcandles; hence the need for shade throughout the year.

Air from whatever source outside a greenhouse or other enclosed structure should always carry considerable humidity (via automation if possible) so that the level of humidity is not abruptly changed. For this reason, phalaenopsis are not customarily found outside of closed structures unless the humidity of the locality ordinarily remains above 40 percent. Fresh air should not have a fluctuating temperature (hot or cold spurts of air will slow growth as quickly as temperatures below 60°), nor should air be directed on to the plants; gently turbulent, yes—drafts, no.

There is a good deal of disagreement among orchid gardeners about the virtue or the necessity of syringing phalaenopsis foliage to combat heat. This is the kind of altercation that correctly implies more sturdiness in phalaenopsis than is suspected. Some do mist the leaves. Some don't, fearing the crown rot that results from moisture in the leaf crevices, although phalaenopsis are, on the whole, remarkably free from diseases. Some tip the plants in pots or baskets, so that the downward-hanging leaves drain naturally when syringed.

Water that is provided for the roots is constant, constant, constant; never a saturated compost, never a dry one. And composts in the past were so constructed as to put this requirement into practice. This was accomplished by standardizing with osmunda. To this, gardeners added various mixtures of exploded mica, leafmold, humus, coarsely ground, crushed oak leaves, crushed volcanic rock, gravel, sand, chopped tree-fern, and a dozen other related substances. At present, chopped bark is preferred—appropriately graded to the age of the plant—and sometimes laced with coarse sand. As a consequence, feeding regularly accompanies watering, and is withheld every third or fifth time so that the bark may be leached with plain water. When heavier or richer composts are used, a balanced fertilizer or a fish emulsion replaces the 30–10–10 that ordinarily accompanies the use of bark. A high-phosphorous fertilizer is substituted just before flower stems appear.

Renanthopsis Elaine Noa

The renanthopsis—one of the more recently developed multigeneric orchids (renantheras and phalaenopsis)—come as close as any plants can to resembling giant three-inch flying bumblebees with a slightly predatory look. This combination of allied families was unknown before Vacherot in France produced it as an oddity in 1939, and it was not ambitiously pursued until the late 1940's, when color became a phalaenopsis goal (white, as a color, can become pallid after living with it for a while).

Doritaenopsis hybrid

Ordinarily, in crosses between orchid families—related, but with distinctly differ-ent flower shapes and foliage habits—the progeny may combine the worst features of both parents. The doritis-phalaenopsis crosses, however, seem from the begin-ning to have been either very bad or very promising. The sprays of flowers are vertical and often branched. The creamy-yellow flowers of this doritaenopsis was one of the results of back-crossing; a hybrid doritaenopsis (Mem. Clarence Schu-bert) was bred to a species (Phalaenopsis luddemanniana ochracea) with deep ochre-yellow flowers.

Phalaenopsis Golden Sands 'Orchidglade', AM/AOS–SM/SFOS

The abbreviations that follow the name of this pale yellow, gently amber-flecked phalaenopsis are marks of honor. It is customary to have new hybrids judged by officials of the American Orchid Society, whose awards are designed to recognize and to encourage meritorious achievements. Medals are presented to significant individuals, and certificates to orchids of outstanding excellence. The initials, therefore, may be decoded as an Award of Merit from the American Orchid Society, and a Silver Medal given by San Francisco's affiliated orchid society.

Phalaenopsis were among the first orchids to be studied in gravel-culture systems. Kept in large concrete beds of sterile gravel, automatically bottom-fed with nutrient solutions, exposed to increased sunlight—or to an abundance of artificial light—their growth rate and flowering were phenomenal. The technique is still one of the best to induce rapid maturity, early flowering and good substance, vigorous health (leaves were leathery and hard, not soft and flaccid). Plants rarely succumbed to disease, and accommodated themselves to an exceptional light and temperature range. It was an encouraging experiment, although expensive. Yet contemporary methods in bark are remarkably similar and have much the same effective results.

The roots of phalaenopsis are brittle and few and what is called assimilating. Beneath their overall silvery cast, they show considerable green chlorophyll, manufacturing much of their own food requirements as well as, perhaps, some for the plants. Care is needed to preserve them intact; it is not always possible to confine them. They tend to roam freely over the surfaces of composts and overhang the outer edges of pots. Not unlikely, they may have functions to perform other than a merely absorptive one; whatever the reason, preserve them carefully.

How phalaenopsis requirements are met is not quite optional—as it is with so many orchids. A cultural response is more likely to be directed toward modifying a prevailing lack in the climate, whether outdoors or indoors. More often than not it will probably be the humidity, and next pushing the humidity to acceptable levels. If that can be accomplished, there is no more accommodating orchid—indoors in any section of the country; outdoors in Florida and other subtropical regions; or in any kind of orchid house, either large or small.

TEMPERATURE: warm, 65° to 80°. HUMIDITY: 70 percent. LIGHT: 1,000 to 1,500 footcandles. WATER: constant moisture. AIR: continuously gentle. FEEDING: 30–10–10, weekly, or balanced, biweekly. COMPOST: bark or osmunda. REPOT: as required. HABIT: monopodial epiphyte. PROPAGATION: vegetative offshoots, seeds. REST: none.

Vanda Nellie Morley

The long monopodial stems of vandas, elegant as they can be when well grown, and the thick roots (the largest among orchids) occupy more space than most gardeners can afford to give one plant. And beautiful as the flowers are, the urgent plant requirement for almost excessive sunlight to initiate buds makes vandas an unlikely addition to northern collections—except for a special plant or two as a showpiece and, probably, with the assistance of supplementary lighting. They are best grown, and with considerable ease, in the subtropics of the United States, where they can be handled as garden plants the year round.

The Vandas

If ever an orchid may be said to belong, at least away from their homeland, vandas belong to Florida by adoption, to Hawaii by temperament, to Puerto Rico as a matter of convenience. In these places—and a few other small segments of the country—vandas grow prolifically, ecstatically, generously as garden plants the year round. In clumps and hedges, borders and beds the terete (round-leaved) species are at home under the full sun. With some midday protection, the strap-leaf varieties occupy the balance of the subtropical garden spaces:

under trees and on palms, on open porches and in sheltered terraces and other not overly protected areas. So long as there is ample fresh air and moderate to high humidity, vandas have withstood temperatures above 100°. The low temperature is open to argument; it is usually fixed at 58°, but instances of vandas withstanding frosts even below 32° are not unknown.

On such optimistic terms it would be suspected that vandas could get along very well much of the time in any section of the country. Unfortunately, their incredible light requirement limits them. The teretes have taken as much as 8,000 footcandles—and more. This is so much light that, above the Mason-Dixon line, they tend to waste away, and flowering is either limited or, as often happens, nonexistent. Somehow, with all vandas, flowering is tied closely to light intensity rather than temperature or dryness. Fortunately, the strap-leaf species are under no such handicap, and neither are many of the hybrids between the two groups. A good deal of light is necessary, as close to maximum sunlight as can be endured without leaf burn, but it is not out of line with available temperate light.

It seems incredible that vandas, so long ignored except for one species and one hybrid—the wonderful blue vanda and the multicolored Miss Joaquin (an inexpressibly beautiful orchid accidentally created in a Singapore garden)—should blaze into popularity as the result of two activities. The first was their importation and subsequent naturalization in Hawaii as a commercial flower crop, now exported by the millions. And the second, a consequent surging interest in their hybridization. In Europe there is a fifteen-year lapse between seeds and flowers. The Hawaiians drastically shortened that time with their outdoor culture and improved techniques. They also ingeniously crossed vandas with their remoter relatives—the renantheras, rhynchostylis, phalaenopsis and others. In so doing, they widened the vanda color spectrum, adding some new hues to it as well, shortened the rather scraggly growths, and reduced the temperature-light quotient to more manageable factors—an exciting accomplishment by any standards.

Within the continental United States the vandas are culturally separated into the teretes and the semi-teretes (teretes crossed with strap-leafs), which are almost solely garden plants for the subtropics. The semi-teretes crossed back to the strap-leafs and the strap-leafs themselves—as well as the intergeneric hybrids—may be grown in northern greenhouses and some windows, under artificial light and, as often as possible, outdoors in open shade. But which of the many Vanda choices available will do best in a specific set of circumstances is a recommendation that should come from a commercial orchid grower.

Culturally the commonly grown vandas are monopodial epiphytes from the more southerly Asiatic mountain countries. Accordingly they need warmth, moisture, humidity and ample air, especially during their period of rapid growth in the summer months. The temperature requirement generally averages 60° as a minimum and about 80° for a high. This must be understood as an average, for all of them have a capability for short periods of low temperature and longer spells of hot weather.

Watering can be daily outdoors, and much less indoors; in both places the compost should be reasonably dry before rewatering. It is advisable to spray the whole plant, since Vanda roots are few and coarse and many of them are aerial, with the same affinity and need for water as the roots that may be somewhat

Vandopsis hybrid

Strange flowers may result from breeding orchid families. Sometimes the characteristics of one parent are so completely dominant that skeptics assert cross-breeding was not accomplished, merely some form of self-stimulated reproduction. Such a reproductive method, incidentally, is not unknown; it is called parthenocarpy or, more simply, virgin birth. Once in a while the characteristics of two parents blend; and, again, nothing very great has happened. Less frequently, one parent modifies the appearance of another in unusual and exciting ways. The vandopsis—a relatively recent addition from the islands of the China seas, and related to the vandas— seems to have exciting possibilities for hybridizers. Like the vandas, they are robust growers, requiring regular fertilizers, warmth and even more sun. Such new creations can be a preview of tomorrow's orchid spectaculars.

contained by the compost. The tough, extremely leathery leaves of all vandas seem to be inured to moisture as well as to sunlight. Yet watering in winter should be sparing, and omitted during cloudy days; and plants must never remain wet for more than a few hours.

Robust and light-tolerant, vandas accordingly are heavy feeders. A dilute balanced fertilizer weekly during spring, summer and early fall is imperative regardless of the compost. A high-nitrogen fertilizer interferes with flowering, a habit they can indulge—and should be allowed to—several or more times a year. Outdoors the fertilizer can be an organic; indoors the preference is for inorganic chemicals.

Composts are almost anything that may be locally available—a gamut ranging from coarse granite chips and charcoal through several terrestrial combinations to a mixture of bark and tree-fern chunks. The point to remember is to keep the compost firm enough to support a plant, and open enough to keep the roots from smothering. Sometimes a large tree-fern plaque on which all the roots may eventually attach themselves is a pleasantly decorative alternative.

As monopodials, vandas are difficult and slow to propagate. Vigorous plants from time to time send out offshoots—known in Hawaii as keikis—which, after developing roots, can be cut from the plants and potted. Occasionally, if a vanda stem is slightly cut, it will produce keikis; but the normal procedure is to reproduce vandas from seed. There has been a tremendous demand for seedlings, although, in all too many cases, they are inferior to the parent stocks. It is much better to see them in flower before buying them.

Wherever grown and whenever possible, vandas should be grown outdoors; or at least for so long as may be convenient during the summer, when their growth rate is increased. Gradually build up their light tolerance from mild shade to as much sunlight as they can stand without burning. Too much sun is almost instantly noticeable, for it creates water blisters that soon dry up, forming unsightly black spots. Water daily, syringing entire plants, and feed regularly, even somewhat heavily. So treated, vandas overwinter more readily and flowering is stimulated.

Even though the vanda group is limited in number, perhaps a total of fifty species, their hybrids and multigeneric crosses are numbered by the hundreds. Some estimates now suggest more than a thousand. So there is likely to be a variety to meet nearly any home or garden or greenhouse situation. Certainly the floral choice in size—one to four or five inches—and the range in color are extravagant, from the famous blue vanda through deep red and yellow to whites strongly patterned with other colors. The flowers are almost outrageously long-lasting on the plants—often three months—and are carried on short stems of six to twelve flowers. Although vandas do bloom intermittently throughout the year, the peak is in late spring and early summer. The floral shapes are classically simple, round and flat, or imaginatively twisted, and some carry faces reminiscent of indolent teddy bears, or mini-animals on skis. Altogether, vandas are a curious, enjoyable and thoroughly satisfying group of orchids.

TEMPERATURE: warm, 65° to 100°. HUMIDITY: moderate. LIGHT: as much as possible. AIR: vigorous. WATER: copiously as required. FEEDING: balanced, weekly. PROPAGATION: seeds and offshoots. COMPOST: bark and bark mixtures. HABIT: monopodial epiphyte. REPOT: as required. REST: none.

Ascocenda Meda Arnold

When Hawaiian orchid growers discovered that vandas—and all of their associated relatives, both Oriental and African—could be naturalized in the islands, they were overcome with enthusiasm rather than awe. They diligently, intelligently—even wastefully ("stick them in the ground and let them grow")—crossed and intercrossed the best members of the families: vandas, aerides, angraecums, ascocentrums, rhynchostylis, saccolabiums; tall and short, enamel-textured and fleshily plump flowers, fragrant or not, and of any configuration. What happened eventually was a new breed of orchids: the Hawaiian rainbow orchids, dwarf plants with medium-sized flowers of the palest and the brightest hues; dwarfs with minute flowers in solidly packed, cylindrically drooping shapes (now commonly called Fox Tails); vigorous plants for outdoor gardens in the sub-tropics, warm indoor windows and small greenhouses. All of the hybrids are completely charming and utterly incredible.

The Botanicals

All orchids are interesting, and the botanicals (the wild flowers of the orchid world)—so say the collectors, at least—most of all. And they speak with more truth than fantasy. The pleasure in growing commercial orchids is a built-in response. It is the result of a long association with them as corsage flowers; of long-remembered dinner dances, lovely parties, beautifully dressed women. Or the girl-to-end-all-girls. The pleasures of botanicals, however, are acquired, and probably learned. But once enjoyed, they are never given up. In fact, they are the most compulsively habit-forming hobby in orchid gardening.

Almost infinite in their variety, the botanicals have surpassing colors and fragrances. Only black is missing, although dark purples and deeper browns seem to have a blackish cast in subdued light. Few fragrances are unknown, from spicy to sharp, carnation to lime, from vanilla to several of the sweetest perfumes in the plant world.

And shapes! The mimicry of orchids is legendary; shapes reminiscent of animals, insects and birds. Moth, Pansy and Tiger have already been identified; but botanicals exceed these descriptive nouns by the hundreds: Boat, Pigeon, Swan, Nun, Holy Ghost, Flower of the Holy Spirit, Tulip, Bug, Rattlesnake, Candlestick, Punch-and-Judy. If a flower can be appropriately described with an idiomatic name, it is likely to be among the thirty thousand orchid species. That's enough plants to support a dozen lifetimes of collecting, since most botanicals are not cultivated, although many may be available from specialists.

And oddities! There are Palm Polly, a native of Florida, and other similar orchids from Mexico, the West Indies, Formosa and Africa. Their common idiosyncrasy is that they have no leaves. The flowers are borne from the center of a starlike mass of green roots that have taken over the functions of leaves.

And foliage orchids! The most beautiful leaves in the world, confined to two very small families from Java and Sumatra. Temperamental—unless carefully grown—and completely insignificant florally, they were deservedly popular a hundred years ago, until the search for larger and larger flowers pushed them aside. Their bronze-green or emerald leaves glitter with shimmering golden veins. So regal a look that one of them has the Malaysian name Wana Rajah (Forest King).

There are mini-botanicals to four inches, dwarfs to eight; perfect space-savers that are not always miniature in flower. And some plants and flowers that must be examined under a magnifying glass.

In other words, and more simply stated, among botanical orchids there is something for everyone, an orchid to meet nearly any hobby purpose. A collection of fragrances, of a single kind of color, of unique shapes, of miniatures, insect traps and other remarkable adaptations. Of course, there are other sound reasons for growing botanicals. They are vigorous. They are hardy and their culture is within the capabilities of most indoor gardeners. A sunny window and

Angulocaste Olympus

Anguloas and lycastes were intercrossed as early as 1903, discarded, revived and again lost until fresh interest in these two terrestrials arose in the late 1940's. A puzzling cycle, since these hybrids are very simple to grow. Their flowers can be mistaken for excellently shaped crocus or tulips; they are about the same size. In fact, the large yellow flowers of Anguloa ruckerii in Colombia are referred to as Andean tulips. The plicated leaves, like palm fronds, have a classic beauty as background foliage. Winter night temperatures can drop below 50°, but it is the safest low at which to grow angulocastes. Summer growth is protected by cool breezes and semi-shade. The composts are enriched with aged manures and considerable coarse gravel for quick drainage.

Barkeria spectablis

The flowers (somewhat like a garden trowel) are rose or lilac, spotted with a darker, reddish color, each from one to three inches across and blooming in summer when there is a lack of orchid flowers. A native of Guatemala, where it is called Flor de Isabal, it belongs to the epidendrums and is often so listed in botanical catalogs. Hardy and temperate in its requirements, it is nice to have in a collection since its spadelike lip is uncommonly different from other orchids.

Called the Black Orchid only because of the black splotches on its floral lips, the pandurata's flowers are basically emerald green, four inches across and fragrant. It is a warm grower from Borneo, and is handled as a medium temperature terrestrial or semiterrestrial. A hardy, long-lived family under cultivation, coelogynes from the cool Himalayas are particularly commendable house guests. The composts are coarsely terrestrial, enriched with aged manures, kept moist while the plants are active, somewhat drier while resting. Summer shade is a necessity, but winter light can be brightly luminous.

a sort of calculated neglect are well within their tolerable limits. Not always, it must be emphasized, but often enough.

Many botanicals grow easily and quickly to specimen sizes with thousands of flowers, the sort of spectacular that no orchid gardener should be without. Among the epidendrums (remarkably simple to cultivate) a plant grown on a cypress stump had 500 pseudobulbs and leaves and 225 flowers; another (a native of Florida, by the way) has been exhibited with 89 floral stems and 1,000 blooms. An oncidium recently may have set a record with 20,250 yellow and brown flowers.

Such specimens make up the heart—and the drama—of flower shows, and more often than not they are honored with special awards. But largeness in itself does not necessarily mean occupying a large space. A southern gardener once displayed a mass of pleurothallis, on a twelve-by-twenty-six-inch tree-fern slab, whose one-inch-high foliage held 1,800 yellow flowers.

Some botanicals, however, were once indifferent to cultivation, and what it took to make them flower in captivity made their original growers famous. There are still many similar challenges among botanicals although, ordinarily, special treatment is unusual. When a botanical fails to bloom, it may simply be still adjusting to its new growing situation. At times, a year will go by before a botanical may visibly admit a dislike for its position in a window or a greenhouse and require shifting to new quarters. All other conditions being equal, a botanical will generally flower in response to a change in the temperature-water-light ratio, probably to a cooler-dryer (forced resting period) with some increased light.

A case in point is the Floridian Palm Polly. It will bloom during the first year in cultivation, then—with gradually increasing rapidity—sicken and die. Why? No one as yet knows. Change of habitat? A cultural lack? Deprived of some stimulant to growth? The answer waits for some dedicated gardener to supply. On the other hand, calanthes—once notoriously difficult to grow—respond beautifully as the result of experiments made in Maryland by an orchid gardener.

Botanicals, no less than their more familiar and exotic cousins, need a cultural balance of all of the atmospheric and mechanical elements. They will need it in much the same manner and proportions as their closest familial relations in the commercial area do. Either cool, medium, or warm temperatures. Humidity averaging 50 percent, more or less as individually required. Light, air, food and composts, too, remain essentially unchanged. For example, all epidendrums and laelias (even though hardier) are closely related culturally to their cousins, the cattleyas, as are the schomburgkias, broughtonias and others. Equally close to each other in their cultural habits are the deciduous botanical terrestrials: pleiones, calanthes, peristerias and others.

To save confusion and effort, most botanical orchidists simplify their composts, using bark sized to each orchid's root system. Thin roots, fine bark; medium roots, medium or regular bark, and so on. Terrestrials are limited to thin or medium bark mixed with moisture-holding materials such as chopped tree-fern or redwood fiber. Watering, especially for epiphytes, is on the dry side until definite individual wants are indicated. Feeding is regularly and lightly routinized, followed weekly or monthly with a leaching bath of plain water. For plants that, in large part, have been obscured by their more popular and common relatives, and whose flowers have remained relatively unknown—botanical orchids possess unique advantages. They offer inducements which no gardener should overlook

Schomburgkia superbiens

Schomburgkias are fun orchids, with much of the vigor of vandas (to which they are not related) and the floral shapes of sportive cattleyas (to which they are related; they are also similarly grown). Superbiens, which translates as superb or superior, is more familiar to the Mexicans as Saint Joseph's Staff. The many three-inch flowers, largely in hues of yellow, have wavy petals (not unlike, but not so twisted as, the trichopilias, a similar family from Mexico with petals as intricately twisted as corkscrews). The other popular species, S. tibicina, is the most common orchid of the southern Mexico orchid plateaus (its long, hollow pseudobulbs are often occupied by ants). Its name (tibicina) is an Indian derivative meaning pipe—in the musical context—since it can be used as a musical horn or as a signal horn.

—beauty, challenge, and sometimes spectacular and always unusual results. These qualities, together with an enduring stability, a sort of built-in hardiness for those who may grow them with more zeal than consideration, make botanicals an unbeatable combination.

Artificial Light

If orchids are easy to grow—as many experts and most hobbyists insist, and with a good deal of truth—they are most easily grown wholly under artificial light in a carefully climate-controlled room. Under these circumstances most orchids will grow faster, flower more easily and profusely, and remain healthier than those established in greenhouses or gardens. Also, there is an added incentive; less time and labor are involved since the procedures can be automated, and should be with the possible exception of watering and feeding.

Incredible? Not particularly. City gardeners and apartment dwellers practice this kind of gardening, at least in part. Many suburban and country gardeners find it the answer to limited space or limited time. Most orchidists normally use artificial light in order to mature seedlings more quickly than nature permits.

As a result of these gardening experiences and an expanding science research program, few places in a home or apartment cannot be modified to orchid culture and lighting control. The list of acceptable rooms and furniture reads like a home-furnishing catalog. Shelves—especially of glass or translucent material—benches, cabinets, tables, closets, bookshelves, bookcases, dry sinks, altered cold storage freezers, showcases, tea wagons, aquariums, inset wall arrangements, room dividers, the tops of hutches, chests and china closets. Garages, basements and bathrooms have previously been suggested. And there are so many other similar units, including commercially sold plant carts, that only expediency should be a limiting factor.

One way or another, most gardeners have already used artificial light, if only as room light or lamplight near their plants. Common garden plants, even some of the exotics, do not seem to mind this casual arrrangement. But it may even be too much if, as many gardeners believe, the continued light at night is sufficient to inhibit flowering. Cattleya flowering, for example, is delayed if they receive more than fourteen hours of continuous light. So the practical approach to orchids is to flower them in the living room, where they may cozily be admired, and to grow them elsewhere under suitable controlled management.

In the past some combination of household tungsten lamps and fluorescent tubes was used with considerable success. The best seemed to be two 40-watt warm fluorescents and a 25-watt incandescent bulb (in reflectors), or multiple combinations of this unit. Placed directly above orchid foliage, but not close enough to burn it, these two different light sources supplied a reasonable approximation of the sunlight that influences plant growth. Better results are currently being secured with new types of fluorescent tubes designed especially for

Phalaenopsis Mantilla. Courtesy of Rod McLellan Company.

Opposite page, top row: Phalaenopsis Gladys Read 'Snow Queen', FCC/RHS; *Phal.* Estrellita. *Center: Phal.* Cabrillo Star, AM/AOS; *Phal.* Jewel 'Ruby Lip'; *Phal. violacea* 'Borneo Strain'. *Bottom: Phal.* Doris 'Pink Beauty'; *Phal.* Eliza 'Changlon', AM/AOS. *This page, center: Phal.* Allice Gloria (Shaffer's Strain); *Phal. hymen; Phal.* Ghisson 'French Doll'. *Bottom: Phal. amboina; Phal.* Inspiration 'Lemon Drop', AM/RHS–SM/5WOC; *Phal.* Gladys Read 'St. Louis', AM/AOS. *Courtesy of Shaffer's Tropical Gardens.*

plant growing. These tubes are manufactured to reproduce the spectral elements most important to photosynthesis: they are high in red and blue light, low in yellow-green. Both the red and blue radiant energies are utilized by plants to manufacture their foods, the starches and sugars needed for growth. Most of these fluorescents are deficient in far-red rays—the extremely narrow band of light which affects growth-triggering chemicals (bud initiation, for example). This is no obstacle since far-red rays are always present in incandescent lamps, or included in a special fluorescent plant lamp supplied by Sylvania Electric Products.

Very small orchid installations—those primarily ornamental or decorative, such as plant shelves, china closets, aquariums, open valances on hutches—may use several of the 8-watt to 32-watt plant-growing tubes. Install them in pairs, either side by side or end to end. Nearby table lamps generally supply ample far-red radiation. The lilac or lavender glow of the plant fluorescents (excellent as it also is for displaying flowers) is sometimes a little startling in a room where the yellowish orange of the incandescents is customary. Therefore these fluorescents should be considered as drama lights, and used so as not to conflict with room lighting.

No matter how small the growing space, light from plant fluorescents should not fall below 15 lamp-watts per square foot. This is an exact measurement and is easily determined by dividing the square feet of the growing area (length times width) into the rated wattage of the lamps. A two by four foot platform (eight square feet), divided into 40-watts, gives 5 lamp-watts per square foot; into 80-watt plant tubes, the lamp-watts rise to ten per square foot. Photographic meters cannot measure the illumination from plant tubes. They read only the yellow-green rays, not the blue and red portions that plants use.

In the long run it is better to start with larger lighting units built around four 40-watt plant fluorescent tubes that also provide far-red radiation and are mounted in a single overall reflector (or two double reflectors placed side by side). The tubes are placed three or four inches apart on their centers, and the entire assembly hung from chains so that it may be raised or lowered to change the light intensity at the growing (foliage) level. This unit will illuminate a space thirty inches by forty-eight inches. In terms of plants, it can handle an average of fifty, more if the plants are miniatures. In terms of area space lost to other uses, it is small. In terms of cost, labor and time, it is inexpensive and remarkably efficient—a good size for a beginning.

Units of similar size may be added as the orchid collection increases. They can be installed end to end, or, as is done very efficiently, the units may be stacked one above the other, like shelving, with about thirty inches of space between them. Benches and shelves can be any conveniently available table or shelf-framing, or specifically made to fit neatly into a home arrangement. Most of them are sealed with aluminum paint (a good reflecting undersurface) and surfaced with flat all-weather white enamel. The enamel is also applied to all other surfaces in the plant room, walls and ceilings, thus reflecting as much light as possible back on the plants.

LOW-ENERGY ORCHIDS, such as cypripediums and Phalaenopsis, that need considerable shade, should receive 15 lamp-watts per square foot of growing area. Converted to measured averages, the light source is ten to twelve inches from the tops of the orchid leaves. It is almost impossible to burn orchid leaves since fluorescents emit a cool light, so closeness to the tubes is not likely to be hazardous.

Top row: Cattleya dowiana var. *aurea* 'Orchidglade'; *Cycnoches chlorochilon; Ansellia gigantea* var. *Nilotica; Phalaenopsis denevii. Center top: Dendrobium aggregatum* var. *majus* 'Orchidglade'; *Rhyncostylis* Queen Emma 'Loveable', AM/AOS; *Vanda Rothschildiana (above); Angraecum magdalanae (below). Center bottom: Vandenopsis* Emily Yong; *Aeranthes arachnites; Oncidium ampliatum* var. *majus; Epidendrum secundum. Bottom row: Vanda* T.M.A.; *Bepi* Orchidglade; *Catasetum pileatum. Courtesy of Jones and Scully, Inc.*

High-energy orchids, cattleyas and epidendrums, requiring only midday shade, can use 25 lamp-watts, as close to the tubes as possible without touching, to about ten inches below.

Very-high-light-energy orchids (vandas and cymbidiums) do best with plant fluorescents described as High Output and Very High Output. These lamps radiate up to twice the energy of the standards, and orchids may be placed two to four feet below them. They are particularly suitable in windows, where for decorative reasons the light sources are concealed from direct viewing. Unfortunately, these high energy lamps are lacking in far-red radiation. When they are used—and no sunlight is available—from 10 to 20 percent of the total wattage should be provided by incandescent lamps. Except in windows, it is better to install fluorescents that in themselves produce all of the radiant energy necessary for orchid growth.

Most orchids exhibit what plant physiologists describe as a day-neutral photoperiodic response; that is, their growth and flowering are not affected by seasonal changes in day length and night length. For that reason, indoor orchid gardeners keep the lights on fourteen hours a day throughout the year. An inexpensive automatic clock can easily take care of that chore.

All other conditions being equal, orchids under artificial light will flower largely in response to dryer composts and to a day-night temperature differential of 10° to 20°. A cooler night period (about 10°) is also extremely important. After the temperature drop, and in the dark, orchids assimilate their foods. In the morning a temperature rise of at least 10° is necessary to reestablish their daily photosynthetic (food manufacturing) activities.

Much of this information may seem technical, and in a way it is. Some understanding of the principles involved simplifies the task of growing orchids under lights. In all other areas, the culture of orchids is essentially the same as in greenhouses. The minimum night temperature remains unchanged for each of the three categories, although it need not be quite so low. A day temperature is rarely above 20° higher, and never as high as outdoors.

Humidity is moderate—50 to 60 percent during the hours of light, much less during darkness. Watering is somewhat less in quantity, although more frequently given. In the small, enclosed areas associated with artificial light, water evaporation from compost tends to be slow. Conversely, orchids under lights seem to need more water than in other circumstances. Apparently there is an increased rate of transpiration, stimulated by the more active growth processes. The cardinal rule of watering, then, is one of watchful care and never really overwatering orchids. And be doubly positive that the roots of all epiphytes—unless otherwise culturally indicated—are dry before adding more water. Artificial light gardeners will find that there is no common norm for watering; each home installation will set its own requirement and its own pace.

Heating is as simple as a baffled electric radiant heater, or hot-water heat carefully supplied from the home's system. Humidity may be added with a vapor humidifier. An atomizer or mist-sprayer is not suited to indoor complexes. They fog the air, and condensed moisture builds up too rapidly on walls and floors, spreading into other rooms. Large, shallow pans of gravel and water—as in window gardening—do very nicely.

Good ventilation is doubly important, and excellent and continuous air circulation triply so. Major indoor installations are sealed off as much as is possible from both the outside and the remaining inside rooms. Windows and similar

Masdevallia kimballiana

If collectors of botanical orchids were to choose one above all others, it would probably be one of the large-flowered masdevallias (although the actual size of M. kimballiana is barely two inches.) The flowers resemble nothing in the orchid world. The three sepals are joined into one flamboyant unit (brilliant scarlet or orange or tawny yellow, even white) and elongated into tails. Masdevallias are semiterrestrials from the 12,000-foot levels of the Andes. The temperature is never above 65°, snow is always nearby. So they are grown cool, within a 50° to 60° range, in finely chopped osmunda or treefern fiber that is exceptionally well drained, or fine bark and sand. There is not a rest period and soil moisture is constant (they have no pseudobulbs). Humidity is normally present and ventilation must be excellent. Summer heat is damaging and must be cautiously guarded against with both ventilation and shade.

vents are almost nonexistent. So adequate provisions must be made to draw off stale air—gently and automatically. A small electric fan, or two, should operate at all times, gently keeping the air in motion, not only to moderate the atmosphere and to inhibit fungi, but to keep the plants amply supplied with the increased amounts of carbon dioxide they need as the result of artificial-light culture. Indeed, some indoor orchidists (in greenhouses as well) put extra carbon dioxide into the air around their plants, either as a slowly released gas or as the combustion product of flames from nontoxic gas sources. In some cases, merely a lighted candle, whose flame is shielded from the plants, seems to work in small areas.

Insofar as routine feeding is concerned, orchids grown consistently under lights are fertilized more frequently but with greater dilutions. What might be standard in a greenhouse is halved for orchids under artificial lights. Feed them minimal quantities of chemical fertilizers each time they are watered; and every third or fourth watering, flush with plain water. Orchids grown in bark or similarly unbalanced composts will need a 30–10–10 up to the time of flower development. In other, richer organic mixtures, a balanced chemical fertilizer or very dilute fish emulsion is more practicable. Nearly all orchid gardeners can find some application for artificial lighting. It is fully compatible with the space problem in many homes today. A four-by-four-by-four-foot area is not a great loss against the delights that it can contain, or the year-round pleasure that might otherwise be reduced to a summerish sort of activity. Someone once commented that he "became an orchid gardener by simply plugging in an electric light cord." It can happen.

Composts and Potting

Orchid gardening sometimes is a curious inversion of gardening practices— although an unconcious one. Plant introductions are customarily brought to this country with the expectancy that they will easily adapt to new climates and be comfortable. Not so with orchids. Almost insupportable climatic demands are placed on them. They are asked to endure an arrangement of seasons they are not accustomed to as well as long days and short nights, or the reverse (most orchids are equal day-night plants), and a wide diversity of temperature, light and humidity. And this diversity exists even under the most ideal greenhouse cultivation. Yet orchids adjust remarkably well, accommodating their growth and floral seasons to northern summers, rather than flowering in winter, as would seem likely, or not flowering at all.

Part of the conditioning to temperate cultivation that orchids go through is determined by the gardening composts in which they are unaccountably expected to survive, and part by the methods by which the compost is handled. By gradually withholding water from the composts, lowering the humidity and then, if necessary for a brief period, supplying no water at all, the seasonal rejuvena-

Renantanda Seminole

Showy and vigorous, the yellow flowers of Ren. seminole, *spotted violently with red, are the product of a vanda-renanthera cross. They have lost most of the paddle wheel look of the renanthera sepals while keeping most of the renanthera charm. Compact, dwarf and sturdy. A warm grower but kindly inclined toward indoor gardening, it blooms in spring, when color is most needed after drab winter.*

Artificial light has been the most surprisingly successful growing technique adopted by orchidists and is managed with astonishing ease and adaptability. The large installation on the left is merely two wide, free-standing shelves—each limited to two extra-long fluorescent plant tubes—set up in the rumpus room of a Minneapolis home. The orchids are grown on laths set on the rims of deep plastic, gravel-filled trays. Humidity is manufactured by an evaporative cooler hidden behind the shelving. The central heating unit of the house provides ample warmth. In a Connecticut bathroom (bottom left), a small vertical unit serves to speed up seedling orchid growth. The bookshelves, and the aquarium (top right), are the conception of a New York apartment-gardener. The greenhouse installation in Virginia utilizes previously unused space beneath a greenhouse bench.

Epidendrum nemorale

*The small flowers of this epiden-
drum, varying in size from one to
two inches and ten to fifteen to a
stem, are pale mauve and marked
on the lip, sepals and petals with
dark violet purple. A hardy Mexican orchid, it flowers profusely in
summer. There is a wide variation
in the pseudobulbs of epidendrums; small, squat, onion-like to
long and thin—or even elliptical.
Such shapes reflect the climatic
conditions under which epidendrums grow and their cultural
needs. The tough leaves (the reed
types) and the tougher pseudobulbs, carry the plants through
harsh—sometimes intolerable—periods of sunlight and droughts. In
regions of intense sunlight, the leaf
surfaces of orchids become nar-
rower and smaller until the foliage
is pencil-thin, the pseudobulbs
squat. And as sunlight decreases,
the leaves increase in size and softness until the broad, luxuriant
foliage of the shade orchids
evolves.*

tion and flowering of many orchids is insured. This phenomenon could not exist in cultivation without a congruous association between water and the composts in which orchids are grown. Accordingly, the type of compost becomes tremendously important. This fact alone has been constantly reflected in the long and continuing search for successful composts.

The roots of epiphytes will not function in soil, although for a time early Belgian horticulturists seemed to overcome that difficulty. Their orchids—largely cattleyas—grew sturdily in a semidry chopped oak leaf mix, but they could not control the moisture content as the leaf mold decayed. Conversely, terrestrial roots thrive in such a humus and do nearly as well in any compost that is effective for epiphytes. Some epiphytes with thin roots can also exist in either terrestrial or epiphyte composts in the sense of being accommodating to these distinctions.

For many years osmunda was the universally accepted and standard compost. Toxic to no orchid, its physical structure permitted considerable leeway in handling all orchids in spite of its other undesirable limitations—extremely little plant food, slow decay and sometimes an excessive moisture-holding capability.

The root systems of all orchids have an absolute need for air. Without it they would suffocate. Excesses of water, without access to air, literally drown them. After all, in nature epiphytes do grow with their roots freely exposed to light and air. Terrestrial roots roam unhampered through the porous, aerated surface humus. Moisture is always—or often—present as adsorbed water—water retained on the surfaces of the fibrous materials on which orchids naturally live. As a result, these fibers drain quickly without being left a soggy mess. The chemistry of adsorption—as opposed to absorption—permits water retention and releases it easily to orchid roots. Water retained by absorption within fibers, live or dead, is not as a rule accessible to plants.

Living as they do, orchids do not have an unlimited food supply. Neither do they have the apparent metabolic capacity to use it, at least on the present evidence, at a rate comparable to other green plants. Very rich composts may endanger more than they assist them, burning or destroying root systems as chemical salts increase in concentration and the root/soil/osmotic pressure becomes unbalanced. And orchid roots are soft. They do not have the rock-crushing capability of soil-bound plants. They are not devious in seeking out small crevices and exploiting them, or pushing around sharp corners and exploring new channels for food supplies.

So orchid composts do have in common the need to retain some water for limited periods while rejecting most of it. They must be well drained and somewhat easily dried; open, soft, loose; firm enough to support vertical growth, yet not so hard as to hamper root growth; containing nutrient foods such as organic compounds, but usually in limited quantities. In its way, the physical construction is as close to being impossible as a compost formula can be. The best that can be done is to approach it as closely as possible and then adjust or add the other cultural necessities to it.

A practical compost for tree orchids was not discovered until English gardeners began to use the dead roots of a bracken fern found in Devonshire. The Devon fern roots have a grain; tied in small bunches the fern vaguely resembles a whisk broom. Water readily drains, but leaves a film of moisture on all of the fibrous surfaces. Decay is slow and the minute amount of food released is mildly in keeping with the expectedly thrifty orchid capacities. Later, American grow-

ers substituted a local product—osmunda, the dead roots of the Royal fern.

In spite of its virtues, osmunda does require attentive care. It is difficult to handle, hard to pack tightly in pots (useless if it isn't), and deadly when overwatered. When it begins to decompose, it does so rapidly, and the central core, remaining damper and cooler, is avoided by orchid roots. Root development in osmunda is minimal, and not easily induced into the compost. These conditions once led orchidists to believe that orchid roots were necessarily limited in extent. This is not true of orchids in their homelands, where the weight of a root system can be as much as two-thirds of the plant's total weight. Mineral nutrition also was slight, so minute in fact that orchids in osmunda were starved. When balanced fertilizers were finally applied correctly, growth was increased, but osmunda could build up nearly prohibitive concentrations of organic salts. Yet osmunda has been successful—and continues to be—particularly if one abides by the rule of a little sparingly applied.

As a medium in which to grow orchids, gravel culture has not been surpassed where it was applicable. Inconvenient in time and labor, expensive in installation costs, it fantastically improved orchid health and flowering. It proved beyond doubt that root growth can and should be extensive, that orchids can and should be fed—not as much as expected but more than had ever been done before—that the right compost, if it could be found, would radically change several aspects of orchid culture. The search for a suitable compost still goes on, although for the moment it has lost much of its urgency. Two other natural substances have proved substantially better than osmunda: tree-fern fiber (Hapuu), cut up into plaques or chopped for a composted mix; and bark—mostly from fir trees—that has been steamed, processed and chopped or shredded.

Tree-fern, not unlike osmunda in appearance, consists of shreds of closely packed brown fibers. It has a better nutrient content and water-adsorptive capability. Chopped and used with humus, sand or other materials, it is a good additive for terrestrial composts, as well as for orchids requiring considerable water retention in their own composts. Orchids attached to the surface of tree-fern blocks by a nylon thread or a thin copper wire will take root much as they would on tree branches. Incidentally, this is an excellent method of handling miniature botanical orchids, those under three or four inches. It makes a flamboyant and decorative ornamentation for well-lighted windows. The inconvenience of such embellishments is the necessity, often daily, of dipping tree-fern plaques into a bowl of water and mineral nutrients, or holding them beneath a water faucet. But the work is worth the effort since, in all honesty, orchid culture is for show as much as it is for pleasure.

Chopped bark has become a justly popular compost. It is safe, relatively inexpensive and available and requires no dexterity in potting, as does osmunda. It cannot really be overwatered (though frequent watering is harmful), and provides excellent aeration and good surface-water retention. Decay is slower and confined to the bottom of the pots. Although very low in nitrogen, bark does supply some mineral and organic foods. What it may lack can be added as a fertilizer dilution during regular watering session.

Some growers recommend that bark, before being used, be soaked overnight in a solution of ammonium nitrate (one teaspoonful) and water (one gallon). The idea is that the soluble nitrogen remains in the pores and crevices of the bark, and is immediately usable in helping repotted orchids establish themselves. Others go along with the dampening, nothing else; and bark is less dusty when

Lycaste cochleata

There are not many lycaste species, perhaps thirty-five, indifferently distributed along the Sierra Madres of Central America, across the Andes and into the mountains of Brazil and the West Indies. A wide area for so few, it includes naturally both cool and intermediate temperature ranges. They are usually grown as terrestrials, with ample moisture and light while developing new growths, and less water after the leaves fall. The flowers, up to five inches are delicate in appearance, pearlescent with luminous colors of either yellow, pink or white, and rarely brown and green. Carried singly on each stem, but producing a generous number of floral stems. L. Cochleata's flowers have been described as captured sunlight.

moist, more easily firmed into place. Later, a nitrogenous fertilizer is applied more or less weekly. A recent innovation is to alternate a balanced fertilizer and an ammonium nitrate solution. Periodically, perhaps every third or fourth watering, the fertilizer dilution is withheld and only plain water is used—a necessary precaution to leach out retained chemicals.

When bark was first introduced, it was sometimes shredded, as was redwood. The results with orchids were disheartening, since the small fibers held too much water and packed too tightly. Nonetheless, when mixed with bark chips and sand, the combination is suitable for terrestrials and for epiphytes that require continuous moisture. Otherwise, it does not seem to matter what kind of bark is used so long as it is chopped, and is one of the conifers—white fir, red fir, Douglas fir, soft pine—that is steamed and processed. Coarse bark chips work well in wet climates; medium-size particles are preferred if the prevailing climate is dry. Otherwise the bark is graded to match orchid roots.

FINE BARK: 1/8 to 1/4-inch diameter; for seedling and miniature orchids; pot size 1¾ to 2½ inches. MEDIUM BARK: 1/4 to 1/2-inch diameter; most orchids (including cymbidiums and cattleyas); pot size 4 inches or larger. COARSE BARK: 1/2 to 1-inch diameter; fleshy-rooted orchids (vandas and specimen plants); pot size 5 inches and above.

It is rarely advisable to repot orchids more than once every two or three years. A longer interval is desirable if the compost remains sound and the orchids do not spill over the edges of their pots; and the latter condition is a matter of aesthetics only. Orchids suffer no harm no matter how much they have overgrown their pots. Actually, there are only two reasons for repotting: the need to divide a large plant into several smaller pieces, and decomposition of the bark. Some orchid gardeners prefer smaller plants, three or four growths to a pot. Other gardeners specialize in large plants, believing they flower more profusely and spectacularly.

Orchids grown in bark products are repotted only when decomposition is evident. Plants may be tipped gently from the pots and the bark examined. The lowest chips become soft and mushy. At times the bottom of the pots may be solid with a sort of compacted mass from the decaying fragments. Remove the plants, clean away the soft bark, shift to fresh, clean and larger pots; add more bark, tamping it about the roots; firm the top and return the plants to their former positions. The shock of repotting—if any—to orchids in bark is so slight that the old routines (keeping plants in drier, shadier places) may be ignored.

Those orchids that require dividing are carefully removed from their pots without injuring their root systems. All foreign matter—bark or fibrous particles—is gently brushed away or snipped off with shears. Dead roots are cut off. The foliage and pseudobulbs are cleaned by stripping away dead tissues, being careful not to destroy the small incipient growths that will develop into new leads. Gently scrub the foliage and pseudobulbs—unless tender and succulent—with a soft toothbrush or cloth and a mild castile soap solution. Incidentally, this is one of the best methods of finding and removing scale insects.

Divide orchids—never less than three or four old growths to each section—by cutting through the rhizomes or connective tissues with a sharp, clean, single-edge razor blade. At this point orchidists dust the cut surfaces with powdered sulfur or smear them with Bordeaux paste—essentially measures to reduce the chance of spreading virus diseases or other infections. Then repot in bark.

Old-fashioned red clay pots may still be the best containers for holding orchids,

Doritaenopsis Coral Gables

although bark has made plastic pots practical and glazed earthenware no longer objectionable. The only optional factor is the goal of the orchidist: functional or decorative. Plants in plastic pots and glazed earthenware are watered less frequently. And translucent plastic pots seem to improve root growth, possibly by providing some sunlight to roots that possess their own green chlorophyll.

What all types of pots have in common is the need for better than excellent drainage. Plastic pots must have their drain holes enlarged to about twice their normal diameters. So do most red clay and glazed earthenware pieces.

The bottom of each pot, about a third or a quarter of the total depth, is filled with broken crocks, very coarse gravel, or medium-size pebbles (even bark chips). Each orchid is then centered in the pot and the roots spread out. The correct size bark, previously dampened, is poured a little at a time into the pot, around the roots, and tamped into place. As the bark reaches nearly to the rim of the pot it is firmed with the fingers, and the pot lifted and gently tapped against the top of the working table to help settle the particles. The rhizome or the crown sits barely on the surface of the bark and just below the rim, leaving about a half-inch of space into which water can be poured. At this point many orchids will need to be staked. They may be a bit wobbly in the bark, and their foliage—when necessary—should be kept neatly gathered and tied within the boundaries of their pots. Sturdy clip-on wires that attach to the rims of the pots are available for this purpose.

It is customary for sympodial orchids, particularly those with pseudobulbs, to be placed off-center—the backs of the rhizomes against the edges of the pots—leaving room at the front for several years of growth. The length of each division (rhizome) is measured; this would be the minimum basic diameter of the pot—one that does not permit further growth. So the space between the front two pseudobulbs is measured and doubled. That sum added to the length of the division gives the diameter of the pot that would be suitable. In other words, a four-inch division with one inch between its front pseudobulbs would require a six-inch pot to provide space for two years of growth.

To tag or not to tag—labeling plants with their names and meritorious achievements or other needful data—is always a question of aesthetics. The simplest way out of unsightly labels is to cut slivers of white plastic, add identifying numbers and slip the small plastic pieces into the compost at the edges of the pots. They are not seen, and the information can be safely kept on numbered cards or in columned diaries.

In the past, as a rule, repotted orchids were left on the dry side for several weeks, with more shade and higher humidity. They were not fed; or if they were, the fertilizer dilution was half the normal quantities. Once reestablished and showing plumper bulbs and good foliage, orchids were returned to their windows or greenhouse benches.

More often than not, orchid gardeners are now avoiding this safe and older method. Bark definitely seems to stimulate new roots, and there is little need to keep the pot dry or the plants in a temporary asylum. They are being returned immediately to their quarters, remaining there without special treatment. Bark is forgiving, as are the orchids that grow in it. Orchids are more easily shifted in bark than in osmunda, and without shock. The disturbance to their systems is slight since the roots are left intact and relatively undisturbed. Overpotting is not the disaster it once was considered to be. Underpotting has lost its significance as a root deterrent.

Catasetum tenebrosum (top)

Catasetum macrocarpum (bottom)

The virtue of a catasetum is its non-orchid look and its ability to shoot pollen—literally. When an insect touches a flower, the pollen is catapulted toward it with accuracy and considerable power—sufficient force to project the pollen outwards for a foot or more. The flowers vary in size from two to four inches, with green as the most common color. Some flowers resemble ancient helmets or, even, squids; and they can be either male, or female, or both. The pseudobulbs are stout, long, and spindle-shaped, and the villagers of Brazil obtain from them a sort of glue. The C. macrocarpum buds in the lower illustration split open when ripe in a matter of hours to reveal yellow, white, and red oddities that are the most exotic of tropical flowers. Both catasetums are grown as warm terrestrials.

Spots of chocolate brown or mahogany or purple on a background of canary yellow make the numerous three-inch flowers of A. nilotica confusing to the eye. It is the Leopard Orchid of the African island of Fernando Po. The plants are large, about two feet, and can produce twenty to a hundred flowers on a single spray, and do it—frequently—several times a year. Although a warm growing orchid, it is otherwise handled exactly as cymbidiums are. Another of the few ansellia species, A. africana, has maroon spots on a green background.

Aerangis rhodisticta (below)

A delightful miniature and a recent addition to orchid collections, A. rhodisticta was lost for many years. It is a native of the west African cool forests in Uganda (where it was first collected) and Kenya (where it was rediscovered). It is the only aerangis whose flowers have scarlet columns—the others are entirely white. The one-inch flowers, and the three-inch leaves, make it a mini among minis. Although a medium-temperature orchid (many of the aerangis require more warmth), its monopodial habit indicates continuous moisture and its thin roots need the finest of screened bark or sand-humus mixtures.

Most potting, as it must be done, is usually accomplished in the spring or soon thereafter—either as new growth and roots appear or shortly after flowering. Never—unless diseased—during mid-growth or flowering. The actual month, though, may be as variable as the flowering periods. For example, cymbidiums and cyps will ordinarily be repotted from February to March; vandas and Asiatic dendrobiums, sometime during April and May. Phalaenopsis will prefer an August to September period; and the cool odontoglossums and miltonias may wait until October or November.

Whatever the month, the final clue to repotting will be the swelling growths, at the base of recent leads, from which fat, bright green root tips are thrust. All repotting must begin and be complete before new roots are a half-inch in length. Young orchid roots grow with inconceivable rapidity and are tender beyond conception. Casually touched, they break off easily. At this stage they cannot regenerate themselves. If for any reason potting must be delayed, wait until the roots are five or six inches long. Broken accidentally then, they can develop branching root systems. Orchids are only as vigorous as their roots, so special care must be taken to keep the roots healthy and extensive at all times.

Propagations

Vegetative propagation is slow among most orchids, and floral increases are limited in extent and possibilities. Compared with other plants for which stem and leaf cuttings are commonplace, and plant increase is numbered in the thousands, a similar abundance of orchid stock would take several hundred years. This was, in the last century, one of the reasons for stripping virgin forests of their orchid crops. And it has since been the major reason for the huge sums paid for prize orchids and hybrids. There simply wasn't enough stock.

Jungle orchids are protected by law now and exports are strictly controlled. Seed germination, perfected as it is, remains slower than for other commercial flower crops. More poor seedlings are produced than good ones. The ratio is sometimes as much as several thousand to one. But for a single, recent fantastic experiment, orchid propagation might still be a tediously involved and costly practice.

The revolution began in France a few years ago, when Dr. Georges M. Morel, a plant physicist, determined that virus-free orchids could be obtained by aseptically cultivating the apical meristem of a cymbidium. What this means, simply, is that special cells in the actively growing tip of a cymbidium could be surgically excised. When these cells, a small block of plant tissue about an eighth of an inch square, were placed in a viscous nutrient solution and tumbled, they multiplied and grew outward in all directions. Masses of tissue were built up which vaguely resembled tightly packed orchid protocorms, the first embryonic swelling that orchid seeds go through. Cut apart and planted in nutrient agar flasks, clumps of tissue proceeded to grow like protocorms, develop-

Epidendrum hybrid

Hybridizing epidendrums for their own beauty is a very new aspect of orchid culture. The more common crosses made with epidendrums involved cattleyas and laelias and were never actually successful, perhaps because the floral results had no immediate commercial applications. From 1892 to 1930, for example, seventy-nine epidendrum crosses were registered. A very low count by any standards, and not much better since. The most likely new orchids may be found solely among the epidendrums, and not by cross-breeding to cattleyas. This hybrid and other epidendrum crosses are comfortable plant subjects for the most inexpert gardening—and they can stand on their own qualities of beauty.

ing leaves and roots, and becoming, for all practical purposes, small plantlets without having gone through any of the familiar reproductive processes. No flowers, no pollination, no seeds, no seed germination—all were skipped. The plantlets matured normally and at normal growth rates. All were exactly like the parent stock, flower for flower, color for color, size for size, growth for growth. And all bloomed at the same season.

When commercial growers finally realized the tremendous implications of this development—and there was an incredible gap of seven years—the name of the orchid game was meristemming, and its products were called mericlones (plantlets). Imagine $500 orchids going for $5 to $10 each. It happened, and it is being repeated all over the country. Within reason, great orchids can become inexpensively available for the first time in orchid history. For the moment, however, the commercial significance of meristemming is confined to cut-flower nurserymen who can now upgrade their stock. They can select orchids of a desired floral color and shape and know that they will bloom uniformly for a particular holiday. Unfortunately, this technique is not suitable for all orchids. Although practicable for cymbidiums, it is less so for cattleyas; and some orchids, as yet, do not respond at all.

Slow as it may be, at least in terms of quantities, routine propagation does offer flowering-size plants within a year or two. In this respect orchids are like the familiar garden plants. The same methods of division are used, although more carefully. And the only tool is a sharp, very sharp, thin-blade knife and a sterilizing solution (Clorox and water, 1:10) into which the knife is dipped after each cut is made.

The time of the year when orchids may be propagated depends in part on the plants, in part on the convenience of gardeners. Some orchidists wait until after flowering, some until new growths and roots appear, as with repotting. There is merit in making propagations in spring when growth is strong and the weather good. As with more common garden plants, orchids are propagated by divisions of large plants, cuttings, offshoots and layering. Each orchid species will generally indicate the correct method.

Monopodials are vegetatively reproduced almost exclusively by air layering. A cut, about a quarter or a third of the way into the stem, is made three or four leaves from the growing tip and never less than three or four leaves from the bottom. Sometimes, after smearing with a Bordeaux paste, the cut is left open; sometimes a small pad of moist osmunda or sphagnum moss is tied over the cut. The systemic disturbance to the plant forces out a side shoot, which, after it produces two or three leaves and roots, may be cut off and potted.

Not all monopodials are amenable to this treatment—only those that grow tall, such as vandas. The compact forms, phalaenopsis as an example, are difficult to air-layer. It can be done, but the risk of killing the plants is greater. Nonetheless, the flowering stems of phalaenopsis, left on the plants after the blooms are removed, will often produce offshoots. Just what stimulates these offshoots (small plantlets actually) is not accurately known. Most likely it is an increase in warmth and humidity, and reduced light. Another method occasionally used is to cut the flowering stems of phalaenopsis into lengths of three or four inches, immersing the bottom ends into small containers of dilute nutrient solutions. Or to place the stems on a moist bed of vermiculite in plastic cake containers. Plastic lids can be used in order to conserve warmth and humidity; they are opened each morning long enough to dry the plant tissues.

Two of the standard methods of propagating orchids vegetatively are by some form of cutting and rooting (the upper illustration), or by plant offshoots on stems more commonly known as keikis (phalaenopsis in the lower illustration). The dendrobium cutting in the pyrex dish has developed a small plant (its roots are barely visible). The other dendrobium cuttings produced buds and flowers instead, not an unlikely occurrence; and it is a rare gardener who does not choose to leave the flowers. Such a container is also excellent for rooting backbulbs (set gently erect) of deciduous orchids and semi-epiphytes such as oncidiums and miltonias. Backbulbs of most epiphytes will develop more easily in closed plastic bags.

Sympodial orchids are more responsive to propagation. Those with and without pseudobulbs may be divided—three or four growths, as in repotting—and carried on as normal plants. Frequently the back bulbs, as opposed to more recent growths, will have no leaves or roots. Their major job of supporting the growing portions of the plants stops after the third or fourth year. They then function merely as reserves in case the forward sections are damaged. In that event the dormant buds on the back bulbs will quickly produce a lead, and a fresh plant comes into being. Forcing this development is no trick if the back bulbs are placed on moist vermiculite (no excesses of water near the rhizome), with some shade, normal warmth and increased humidity. They are very responsive to the conditions maintained in semi-closed containers such as small aquariums or inside transparent, nontoxic polyethylene bags. Put a small handful of chopped bark into a plastic bag and add water to dampen the bark. Insert the back bulbs and tie the top of the bag with a rubber band. Place it in the light (not shade), light of an intensity normal to the plant from which the back bulbs were taken. When new growths appear and roots are barely visible, pot and gradually harden the propagation over a two- or three-week period to less warmth and humidity.

The number of the pseudobulbs in a propagation will determine the time it takes to reach flowering maturity. Three or four bulbs will do so in a year or two. Without leaves, they will take a year or so longer. Smaller divisions take correspondingly longer, if they succeed at all. Two pseudobulbs are difficult, one almost impossible—except cymbidiums, calanthes and similar terrestrials that are routinely grown from a single pseudobulb; usually these are deciduous orchids.

Sympodials with pseudobulbs can be propagated within their original pots; this is an interesting way of producing large and balanced specimens. Sympodials tend to grow—to move, as it were—in a single direction. One front lead matures and produces another in much the same direction, which is why sympodials move right off the edges of pots. A way to divert this is to cut into the rhizome between the pseudobulbs, leaving at least three pseudobulbs on each side of the cut. The cut does not have to be deeper than one-third of the way through the rhizome. This is enough of a distraction to make the backbulbs believe that they are on their own, and new growth is produced. In another year or so, additional cuts can be made.

A few orchids, notably the reedlike epidendrums and some dendrobiums, can reproduce themselves by means of adventitious plantlets along their growths or floral stems. As would be expected, these plantlets occur when the light intensity is less than normal, warmth and humidity higher—a fact to be remembered if vegetative increases are wanted rather than flowers. Both epidendrums and dendrobiums also can be cut into four-inch sections and placed on moist vermiculite. Shade, warmth and higher humidity will stimulate plantlets that can be potted as soon as roots develop.

Cyps and similar sympodials that have no pseudobulbs are propagated by division. Large plants are separated into smaller clumps of two or three growths, rarely fewer, in order to retain their vigor. One old growth, with a developing new one attached, is not uncommon in nursery practice. But it requires watchful care beyond the capability of most gardeners, who have other jobs to do. After all, orchid gardening at home should not be reduced to a full-time necessity. At the most, it is an avocation with all of the pleasures that such a pursuit implies.

Cycnoches elertonianum

The name cycnoches means swan's neck, a likeness borne out by the orchid's gracefully curving column. They are large epiphytes from South America in the medium-temperature group, with pendulous flower stems and flowers measuring from four to six inches; yellowish and lime green are the basic colors. Cycnoches, like the catasetums, can separately produce small male flowers (the background silhouette), or larger, fewer and lovelier female flowers (foreground), or both male and female flowers at the same time. This reproductive accomplishment caused no end of trouble for botanists who had previously classified male and female flowering plants as separate and distinct species. Not until the related catasetums, many years later, produced male and female flowers on a single plant was the nomenclature mistake corrected.

Seedlings

The care and feeding of orchid seedlings, nurturing them from bottles to maturity, is not unlike that of human infants—a lot of tender loving care, a good deal of wisdom in applying it and a knowledge of when to be lavish and when to be unconcerned. After a year or two any whimsical resemblance ceases, since human infants learn to reason and to talk, inevitably becoming difficult. Orchids don't.

Nonetheless, most orchid gardeners avoid the problems of germinating orchid seeds and carrying on the immature plantlets. Unless, that is, they are completely enamored of the involved techniques and processes which, in a way, are something like a science fantasy. And these techniques are not difficult to learn, only painstaking and time-consuming. From a strictly practical viewpoint, seedlings ready for transplanting from sterile flasks to community pots are much too inexpensive for anyone to bother with the lengthy period—several years—from flower to seed pod to germinating flasks. Orchid gardeners who may want to hybridize their own plants can have professionals carry on after the seed ripens and is ready for planting. For an astonishingly small sum they can advise about the development of orchid seed pods, and suggest collecting them at exactly the right stage for green-pod or ripe-pod processing. They then undertake the complex job of sowing and germinating the seeds and carrying the plantlets through the first critical and dangerous years of their lives.

Sowing orchid seeds is not a simple matter of scattering them on composts, watering them and leaving the rest up to nature. It doesn't work, although orchid seeds have been sown on osmunda at the base of a parent plant and a few seedlings occasionally were grown—if a special fungus was there. Orchid seeds, it must be recalled, have no food reserves. In nature they have an intricate relationship with a fungus which supplies them temporarily with food until they have leaves and roots of their own to take over the work. In modern cultivation the fungus is replaced by sterile nutrient agar—in sterile flasks—which contains the essential foods in an easily assimilable form. The job of maintaining such a sterile environment, from beginning to end, is not an easy one, involving absolute cleanliness. Temperature and light ratios are equally critical; an automatically and rigidly controlled environment is needed for a year or more.

So, while raising orchid seed is interesting, and germinating orchid seed can be exciting—the hazards and the equipment involved are best left to professionals. Even seedlings direct from germinating flasks quite likely should be avoided for the same reasons. Flask seedlings are delicate and sensitive to change. For that matter, so are seedlings established in community pots, although the hazards of handling them are much less. Newcomers to orchid culture are best advised to purchase established seedlings, those that are several years old and already accustomed to normal growing conditions. Then, after the fundamentals of orchid culture are learned, undertake the adventure of growing the youngest seedlings to flowering maturity.

Phaius grandifolius

Few terrestrial orchids are more gratifying to grow than phaius, one of the oldest orchid groups known to cultivation. It goes back as far as 1778, when Phaius grandifolius was brought back from China by a traveler. Ordinarily native to the Asiatic lowlands, it adjusts easily to medium to warm temperatures (especially the hybrids). And although large (it can reach to three feet), the decorative, elliptical leaves are discreetly kept within bounds. The flowers—ten or twenty to a cluster, carried on a stiff stem—are chocolate brown and primrose yellow. Year-round moisture is beneficial, and a sandy, very rich humus soil an absolute necessity. It is a robust plant and, curiously, one of the few orchids whose leaves should not be syringed with water. The four-inch flowers open successively and plants remain in bloom for a long time.

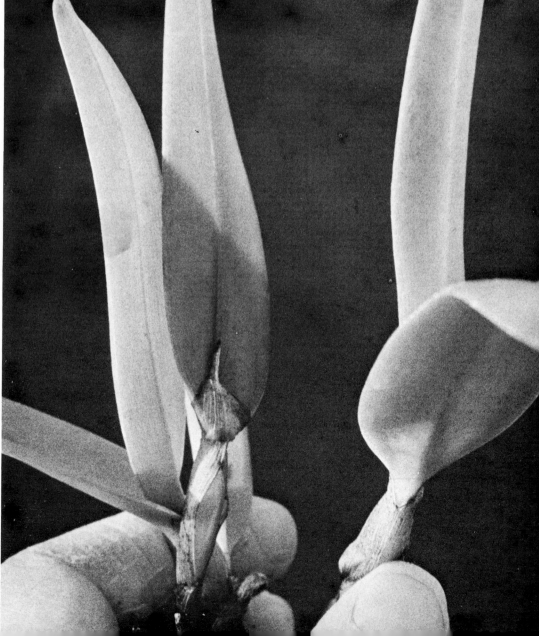

The ripening cattleya seed pod (top left) is often large by comparison with the size of the flower that produced it, and gigantic in relation to the seeds. The original size of the letter "A" is barely three-sixteenths of an inch. Seedlings grow on a sterile nutrient agar gel, and in the illustration (top far right) are almost ready for transplanting to pots. The domed glass (bottom left) with arm holes and cloth sleeves provides a sterile cover while sowing orchid seeds or transplanting them from crowded flasks to roomier ones. The very young plant on the point of the steel fork suggests the care that must be used in handling such tiny objects. The seedling (bottom right), several years from its flask, has several more years to go before it reaches flowering maturity. Such detailed and prolonged work as seed germination and flasking requires special knowledge, special materials and special techniques applied over a period of many months. The procedure can be learned, and often is, by interested gardeners and converted to kitchen and bathroom equipment; but the price paid in time and materials is far, far greater than the costs of dozens and dozens of commercially established seedlings.

However seedlings may be obtained, a few operations are unavoidable after they have arrived. Warm water (75°) may be introduced into the seedling flask several times, to liquify the gel which, with the plants, is carefully poured out into saucers. The plantlets are then extracted and gently cleaned.

It is a sound practice to bathe all plantlets in an anti-damp fungicide for a few moments. The damping-off fungus which accompanies a stagnant wet atmosphere is exceedingly destructive. The condition is later avoided by discreetly airing the seedlings from time to time so the fungus cannot secure a foothold. When it does, it can kill seedlings in twenty-four hours or less.

There was a time when seedlings were handled with a soft wood forceps or cotton-swathed tweezers, even small forked wooden sticks. Wide-spaced fork tines, with blunt points, will do as well; fingers gently and carefully used are better, so long as seedlings are lifted by the tips of their foliage, not by the roots. They are transferred, if small, to community pots (perhaps six to a three-inch pot); the larger ones—an inch or taller—to small plastic one- or two-inch pots.

Fine bark is used as a compost, and into it the smallest plants may be inserted after a tiny hole has been made to receive them. The bark is then prudently pushed around the roots to hold them in place. Roots that cannot be covered—and there will be many—are left exposed. In their own good time they will curve downward between the fine bark chips.

Large seedlings—those from community pots—are freed from the old osmunda (or bark in some cases) and are centered individually in separate thumb pots. Bark is poured around their roots. Firming is done not by tamping the bark with fingers, but by softly tapping the pots against the working table.

After the seedlings are potted, there are several methods of hardening them and carrying them on. Give them their own quarters: a small, portable cold frame, capable of maintaining warmth and humidity; an aquarium (with its own lighting system) in which the seedling pots are set on a layer of damp bark, the top covered with a pane of glass or plastic film for easy removal. Community pots can be placed within polyethylene bags, leaving considerable space above the plants, and sealed with a rubber band. Even large-mouth bottles can be put to use; set the pots inside and seal the bottles with plastic.

The idea behind these cases, bags and bottles is to keep the seedlings out of drafts, to keep the temperature moderately warm and steady, and to be able, within a relatively small area, to build up humidity quickly. Seedlings transpire a lot of water, more in proportion to their size than do adult plants, and use much water as they grow. All containers must be opened from time to time to dry out the plants and change the air. Do this once a day, toward midmorning for an hour, then close the containers; seedling foliage must be dry by sundown.

Moisture is provided not so much by watering the pots and soaking the bark, as by misting the leaves and bark surface once or twice a day with the finest possible spray; perfume atomizers are very suitable. After the seedlings are established (evidenced by increased root activity), the bark can be more heavily watered, but not so haphazardly as to uproot the plants, then permitted to dry out, although not so much as to endanger seedling roots. There is a very close relationship between slight dryness, which encourages root growth, and moisture, which keeps them plump; excesses of either are detrimental.

Seedlings grow well with a minimum night temperature of 60°, and faster if kept at 65°. The immediate danger of too high a temperature is soft growth and susceptibility to disease. The intensity of the sunlight should average 200 foot-

candles, increased (by small weekly amounts) to 500 footcandles at the end of six months. The seedling cases may be kept near windows, and in rooms where there is relatively little temperature change—unless the cases are artificially heated. Bathrooms, with their normally moist air and warmth, are ideal seedling culture rooms. If no southerly windows are available, small supplemental lighting units may be easily installed.

Feeding is extremely important, and the fertilizer solution must be very dilute (about 10 percent of the normally recommended dilution). It can be mixed with water when the seedlings are mist-sprayed, and later, still well diluted, used with each regular application of water to the bark itself. Occasionally withhold the fertilizer so that the bark is leached with plain water. A high-nitrogen fertilizer is customarily used because the seedlings need the extra nitrogen to support rapid development.

After a year the seedlings may be transplanted to larger pots (2½ to 3 inches in diameter); overpotting is somewhat desirable. From this point the seedlings should be progressively treated as mature plants: the temperature gradually dropped to the normal for their particular requirments, the light slowly increased to normal requirements, watering and feeding adjusted to more customary standards.

The growth rate of seedlings—cattleyas, for example—is nearly doubled by subjecting them to supplementary light. Placed under plant fluorescent tubes from just before sundown until a total day length of sixteen hours is achieved, the response is startling. The speedup, accompanied by correct increases of fertilizer, can cut a year and a half from the time needed to mature, more if the seedlings are continuously grown under artificial light for sixteen hours each day. Cattleyas have been known to flower in three years—a long, long way from the century-old norm of eight years.

Pests and Diseases

Epidendrum moyobambae

E. moyobambae has the unlikely merit of resembling a bull moose more than an orchid—at least to some gardeners. Taller than is usually comfortable for window plants, although a medium temperature plant, it needs room—outdoors or in a lathhouse—to look its best. A summer flower, it adds excitement as a floral curiosity.

The best that can be done is never too much where orchids are concerned and the hazards may be pests and diseases. Orchid flowers, as well as tender new growths, can be attacked by insects and destroyed by diseases. In this respect, orchids are no different from other garden plants, although less easily infected. Orchids are tough. Their leaves are leathery, their pseudobulbs hard, their stems sturdy—not a very good diet for marauding pests. When pests do arrive, most often they are the result of inattention. Diseases can strike some orchids with suddenness, killing them within days, as the result of careless culture. So prevention is the only realistic solution—watchful attention and correct culture—for cures can be as drastic to orchids as the infestation.

Indoors, other than a few ants and cockroaches, pests are not likely to be a

Polyrrhiza lindenii (left)

Dendrophylax funalis (far left)

In the evolutionary scale the leafless orchids are judged to be the most recent development of orchid life. The roots alone, containing chlorophyll, are able to manufacture all the food needed in order to produce a flower (at best an inch or so) which does not remotely resemble the popular concept of orchids. The flower of Polyrrhiza lindenii (a native of Florida) has the comic aspect of a dwarf rushing off somewhere with its tail streaming behind. Most Floridians believe it resembles a ghostly white frog. Yet the natives call it Palm Polly. The polyrrhiza is pleasantly fragrant in the evening; the dendrophylax (Jamaica), strongly disagreeable. Grow them on small twigs or pieces of oak bark (where the roots are always exposed and can search out food from the crevices), at medium temperatures in very bright, but indirect light. They like to summer outdoors under semi-shade. Even then, away from their native homelands, they are touchy about growing.

problem. Homes are not conducive to them, and familiarity with the few plants quickly detects any pest. Ants and cockroaches are controlled by ordinary household pesticides, following the manufacturer's directions. Scales and tougher insects succumb to gentle scrubbing with a soft brush or cloth and mild Ivory soap solution. Diseases, since the drier atmosphere is not to their liking, are rare and usually caught in time. The infected area is incised, the diseased material burned, the cuts covered with a Bordeaux paste, and plant and compost dried out for a week or so.

Outdoors, though, or in greenhouses and shelters, closed installations, garages and basements and Wardian cases, there is an ever-present threat. When conditions are correct for pests and diseases—incorrect for orchids—infestations may develop quickly and easily.

Cleanliness is imperative. Many pests and all diseases, especially viruses, must be carried from orchid to orchid: on dirty hands and dirty shears, dirty knives and dirty tools, soiled pots, exhausted composts, infested soil, plant refuse and plant litter. Hands must be clean, before and after working with an infected plant. All tools should be sterilized each time they are handled, and each time they are used on an infection. Dip them often in 70 percent rubbing alcohol, or a 1:10 mix of Clorox and water, or equal parts of a 2 percent solution of sodium hydroxide and 2 percent formaldehyde. The hydroxide-formaldehyde solution is dangerous to mix; let a druggist or chemist prepare it.

Keep clean newspapers on the worktable, each top sheet wrapping up the litter from the orchid that is being cleaned or repotted. Pots can be sterilized. Soak them overnight in a strong Clorox solution and sun-dry them for several days. But it is simpler—and cheaper in the long run—to use new pots.

Routine spraying with a pesticide or fungicide is recommended outdoors: monthly in summer, bimonthly in winter. This is an essential preventive measure in commerical houses, where orchids may be grown by the hundreds of thousands and a personal examination of each plant is impossible. Such a practice indoors, in homes, is of doubtful value to plants. Indeed, it is decidedly dangerous to people and animal pets and should never be necessary. Outdoors and in small greenhouses, spraying when needed comes as the result of vigilance. It is used— if it has to be used at all—at the first sign of an infestation. And, again, it too should never be necessary. If it is possible to avoid spraying, and it nearly always is, don't spray.

This may sound like a garden heresy, but chemical sprays of any kind are as dangerous to human beings as they are to plant life. They must be applied with great care and extreme caution and exactly as the manufacturer indicates. Ordinarily such chemicals as they contain must not be allowed to touch buds and flowers, which are easily injured. Most of the modern sprays, those made with organic phosphates, are also so deadly to human beings and to all animal life that they should not be handled at any time, unless by professionals. The few exceptions are some of the fungicides and the older, formerly standard orchid oil emulsions. Even so, orchid gardeners are well reminded that the need to use them often is the result of cultural carelessness; and using them involves every possible safety precaution.

If chemical sprays are always considered to be the drastic aftermath of poor culture, as they almost always are, then the chances are excellent that gardeners will be able to avoid them. Accurate control of the cultural conditions under

Arachnis moschera

These Malaysian orchids, members of the large tribe of vandas, are given an animal name by the natives; and it is an obviously good one—katunggeg, the Scorpion orchid. The latinized name—Ar-achnis—merely means spider, and once was the name of a legendary Greek woman. The flowers, many with a musky sort of fragrance, are generally large (three and four inches), numerous, and most often a pale yellow-green with purple-brown spots that seem to add to their fearsome appearance. The floral stems are not cut, since the flowers are continuously produced over a long period of time and, frequently, twice a year: the first time in spring, with another season in fall. The vandaceous growth indicates plenty of moisture and light and reasonable, though variable, warmth. They have been known to endure the sun of Florida and the salt air of the nearby ocean.

which orchids are grown is not difficult to manage. Whatever the orchid installation, it must never be too hot or too cold, too wet or too dry, too drafty or too stagnant. In brief, the most desirable balance of temperature, light, humidity, air, water and food for each major orchid group must be maintained. Never more, never less, never unbalanced. Conditions which are favorable to the growth of orchids are not satisfactory to most pests and diseases, and healthy plants are extraordinarily resistant. Thrips, for example, flourish in a hot, dry atmosphere (whereas orchids wilt) and will ordinarily avoid or leave any place where considerable humidity is present. Excessive dampness and cold, continuous moisture on leaves and flowers, a saturated atmosphere, stagnant air, chilling drafts, too little light, too much water in composts, or any combination of these destructive components undermines the health of orchids and encourages disease. In fact, these conditions must be present before diseases can get a start.

Even though a catalog of orchid pests and diseases looks forbidding, only three insects and three diseases are commonly found where orchids are grown in small quantities: ants—whose only danger lies with their close associates, aphids, mealybugs and scales—and cockroaches; both succumb to simple household controls. With no ants, there are no aphids and few, if any, mealybugs and scale.

Scale is the most serious orchid pest, recognizable by its white, cottony masses or by grayish colonies (like miniature oyster shells). Hidden at first beneath leaves, in crevices, on rhizomes or under dry tissues, it can erupt with startling suddenness. Soap and water and a soft brush are the best deterrent and the safest remedy.

Red spider is difficult to see, though its damage is not—yellowish or whitish spots and blotches on top of the leaves, and primarily on orchids with thin leaves. Turn a leaf over and examine it under a magnifying glass. A small greenish or brownish insect sits in the center of a minute reddish web (like flecks of red pepper). Scrubbing with a soap solution is effective, as is a commercial miticide.

Slugs and snails are disasters that should not happen, but will—time and time again. No section of the country is safe from them. Left alone, they devour seedlings, fresh root tips, soft new growths, flowers and buds and succulent leaves. Metaldehyde placed near the plants, as the manufacturer directs, will help to control them, but only searching them out at night with a flashlight and individually destroying them will do much good. Buds and flowers can be protected with a small piece of cotton tied around the base of the flower stem.

Other pests are occasionally found on orchids. But an annual cleansing with soap and water or a mild scrubbing with an oil emulsion will restrain them. Such a job need not be done at one time, merely a few plants at a time. If the orchid collection is large, choose a fundamentally safe aerosol pressure spray that includes rotenone or pyrethrum, and solutions of nicotine sulphate.

All too often, orchid diseases are unsuspected until they happen. Even then they may not be easily identified unless they are specific to a single orchid family. Given poor culture as the initial requirement (damp, wet, cold atmosphere), fungus commonly starts at the tips of leaves and fresh growths, which progressively blacken and die as the fungus moves downward. Fungus can start in the base of leaves and the heart of a plant, where water collects and remains. The damaged tissues feel oily, wet, softer than normal tissue.

The remedy is to lower the humidity, increase the light. Isolate the infected

Epiphronitis Veitchii *(left)*

Although related to the cattleyas, epidendrums and sophronitis are visibly extremely different; so different that botanists once considered them to be unrelated. Then James Veitch, a nineteenth-century horticulturist, crossed Epidendrum radicans (five-foot-tall weeds from Guatemala) with Sophronitis grandiflora (scarcely three inches) from Brazil. The epidendrum had cinnibar red, one-inch flowers and no pseudobulbs. The sophronitis two-inch scarlet flowers and minute pseudobulbs. The result: a reedlike orchid, resembling the epidendrum parent—but only fourteen inches tall—and sterile: the result of combining dissimilar chromosomes. Epiphronitis Veitchii was the first orchid "mule."

Epidendrum ciliare (right)

The whiskers of E. ciliare's lip, which help to give it an appearance vaguely similar to a crouching, defiant tarantula, and its strange greenish-yellow and white flowers make it popular among hobbyists searching for the unusual or the dramatic. It is not a large plant, perhaps ten inches overall, with two-inch flowers. And like most epidendrums from tropical America, it grows well with indifferent treatment and casually medium temperatures.

plant, surgically excising all diseased tissues well below the visible marks of damage. Sterilize the knife after each cut, or use a fresh razor blade each time a cut is made. When the infection is deep it may also be necessary to wash off the compost and cut back the roots. Submerge what remains of the plant in a fungicide solution for the time recommended by the manufacturer; then cover all cuts with a Bordeaux paste as an added insurance against reinfection. Repot and keep the plant in a drier atmosphere, in a fairly dry compost, under shade (a luminous sort of shade) until no further deterioration takes place and new growth begins.

Bacterial rots start as faintly translucent spots (when viewed against light). They spread with incredible rapidity over wet foliage; the leaves become limp and the tissues soft and greasy, somewhat like feeling cotton rags soaked in oil. The diseased spots are roundish and, in color, grayish to brownish. The usual cause is a stagnant, cold atmosphere—not uncommon on cloudy, rainy days—accompanied by excessive humidity. Correct the cultural conditions quickly. If the plant infection is mild, excise the dead tissues, spray with a commercial iron or copper fungicide, isolate the plant and keep it on the dry side.

Serious infections must be deeply and thoroughly cut out, the orchid dipped in a fungicide, and the cut surface covered with Bordeaux paste. Should the infection continue, burn the plant and destroy the pot and the compost. While the cure, at best, is uncertain, leaving infected material around is deliberately inviting further trouble.

Virus diseases, about which little is known, are incurable. Some orchids live with their virus for years; others weaken and die quickly. The virus attacks the entire plant, and once within the tissues it cannot, as yet, be removed. Where virus infections are severe, meristemming (as developed by Dr. Morel in France) may be the only solution. The symptoms of a virus are many and, probably, require an expert to recognize them. Pieces of a suspected orchid may be carefully wrapped in waxed paper, boxed and forwarded by mail to any Agricultural Experiment Station for virus identification. A telephone call to local agricultural advisers listed in telephone directories will secure the address. If confirmed, destroy the plant; otherwise the virus will spread by contact—human and insect—to all other orchids in the collection, particularly through the use of infected knives and shears.

A virus will streak orchid leaves with fine yellow lines that eventually darken. Or it may appear as a sort of corrugated striping with hard dark green ridges and light yellowish-green valleys. Sometimes it occurs as spots that spread in concentric rings. In the last stages of infection new growth is crippled, flowers are either blotched, discolored or distorted.

Unfortunately, many virus symptoms, in the beginning, may be confused with pest or disease damage, nutrient insufficiencies or cultural mistakes. Yellowing leaves are normal on old back bulbs, which no longer need them. Yellowing may occur on leaves exposed to too much light. And leaf yellowing does result from nitrogen deficiencies in bark composts. Blackened tips on cymbidiums, for example, may be the result of overfeeding or overwatering. Rapid wilting of flowers or bud drop is as easily caused by air pollution and ethylene gas as by drastic cultural changes—or virus.

Pests or fungus or disease or virus? Confusoin? Not really. Orchids on the whole are good patients. They do indicate their illnesses and often designate the

Dendrobium linguaeforme

As often as not, expert horticulturists have failed to recognize this photograph of D. linguaeforme—but only because the flowers and leaves are greatly enlarged. Much too frequently magnificent orchid miniatures are bypassed for the lack of a magnifying glass. Not that one is needed to observe the beauty of D. linguaeforme, but it does help. This miniature dendrobium doesn't mind medium temperatures, and is so perfectly at home in terrariums that it is largely used for just that purpose. Blooming so profusely in spring and summer, the half-inch flower clusters can almost conceal the leaves which are unusual in themselves—thickened and tough storage organs.

cause and the cure. One symptom may be misread, two misunderstood, but symptoms most frequently occur in groups. It is almost impossible to mistake the total picture. But by far the best approach to the illness of orchids is to remember that they are accustomed to a healthy life in their homelands, a habit they pass on to their progeny in cultivation. Clean, clear, buoyant air and ample light. Never any temperature or humidity excesses. Orchid gardeners can do no less than to continue those traditions. Meanwhile—just in case—through a program of cleanliness and prevention, never give an insect a break or permit disease to secure a foothold.

Photographic Index

Many of the orchid flowers shown in this book appear larger in size than those ordinarily produced by the corresponding plants. When this occurs, the normal sizes in inches are indicated in the accompanying captions. The macrophotographs were selected because they displayed the complex and fascinating floral designs found in the orchid world, and the distinctly individual orchid responses to their environment and needs. In all cases, incidentally, the owners of the plants are listed. And, for those who like such facts, the photographs made by the author were taken with a Hasselblad and an 80-millimeter planar lens or, predominantly, with a Nikon-F and a 55-millimeter auto Macro-Nikkor. The film was Tri-X developed in D-76.

Book Jacket:
*Blc.** Golden Galleon 'Alpha Nugget', Fred A. Stewart, Inc., San Gabriel, Calif.

Title Page:
Paphiopedilum callosum, John Hanes, San Gabriel, Calif.

* *Brassolaeliocattleya.*

* *Brassolaeliocattleya.*
† *Cymbidium.*

* *Laeliocattleya.*
† *Paphiopedilum*

190

* *Phalaenopsis.*

Index

Index

DATE DUE	